Explorer
Provence

Nick Hanna

 Publishing

Written by Nick Hanna
Revision verified by Nick Hanna
Original photography by Adrian Baker
Reprinted 1999
Revised second edition 1999
First published 1995
Edited, designed, distributed and produced by AA Publishing
Maps © The Automobile Association 1995, 1999.

The contents of this publication are believed correct at the time of printing. Nevertheless, the publishers cannot be held responsible for any errors or omissions or for changes in the details given in this guide or for the consequences of any reliance on the information provided by the same. Assessments of attractions, hotels, restaurants and so forth are based upon the author's own personal experience and, therefore, descriptions given in this guide necessarily contain an element of subjective opinion which may not reflect the publishers' opinion or dictate a reader's own experiences on another occasion. We have tried to ensure accuracy in this guide, but things do change and we would be grateful if readers would advise us of any inaccuracies they may encounter.

A CIP catalogue record for this book is available from the British Library.
ISBN 0 7495 1889 8

Published by AA Publishing (a trading name of Automobile Association Developments Limited, whose registered office is Norfolk House, Priestley Road, Basingstoke, Hampshire RG24 4NY. Registered number 1878835).

Colour separation by Fotographics
Printed and bound in Italy by Printer Trento srl

Titles in the Explorer series:
Australia • Boston & New England • Britain • Brittany California • Caribbean • China • Costa Rica • Crete • Cuba Cyprus • Egypt • Florence & Tuscany • Florida •France Germany • Greek Islands • Hawaii • India • Indonesia Ireland • Israel • Italy • Japan • London • Mallorca • Mexico Moscow & St Petersburg • New York • New Zealand Paris • Portugal • Rome • San Francisco • Scotland Singapore & Malaysia • South Africa • Spain • Thailand Tunisia • Turkey • Turkish Coast • Venice •Vietnam

AA World Travel Guides publish nearly 300 guidebooks to a full range of cities, countries and regions across the world. Find out more about AA Publishing and the wide range of services the AA provides by visiting our Web site at www.theaa.co.uk.

Front cover (a): sunflower field and sunset
Front cover (b): Enjoying a glass of red
Front cover (c): Galloping through a lake
Page 3: Gordes
Page 4: (a) local fragrance; (b) Trophée des Alpes, la Turbie
Page 5: (a) Ste-Baume massif; (b) a Camargue bull
Pages 6–7: (a) Avignon; (b) view of Menton
Page 7: (b) in the Abbaye du Thoronet
Page 8: Rousillon
Page 9: high-prowed boats, Sanary-sur-Mer
Page 27: the Roman theatre, Orange
Page 249: Grasse
Page 271: gate in the old town walls, Aigues-Mortes
Back cover: Èze is the highest perched village in Provence
Spine: woman with geese

How to use this book

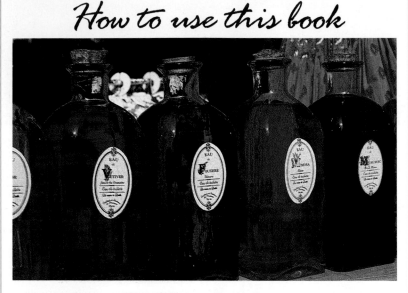

This book is divided into five main sections:

❑ **Section 1: *Provence Is***
discusses aspects of life and living today, from rural architecture to summer festivals

❑ **Section 2: *Provence Was***
places the region in its historical context and explores those past events whose influences are felt to this day

❑ **Section 3: *A to Z Section***
is broken down into five regional chapters, and covers places to visit, including walks and drives. Within this section fall the Focus-on articles, which consider a variety of topics in greater detail

❑ **Section 4: *Travel Facts***
contains the strictly practical information that is vital for a successful trip

❑ **Section 5:
*Hotels and Restaurants***
lists recommended establishments in Provence, giving a brief résumé of what they offer

How to use the star rating
Most places described in this book have been given a separate rating:

▶▶▶   **Do not miss**

▶▶   **Highly recommended**

▶   **Worth seeing**

Not essential viewing

Map references
To make the location of a particular place easier to find, every main entry in this book is given a map reference, such as 176B3. The first number (176) indicates the page on which the map can be found, the letter (B) and the second number (3) pinpoint the square in which the main entry is located. The maps on the inside front cover and inside back cover is referred to as IFC–IBC.

Contents

Quick reference

This quick-reference guide highlights the features of the book you will use most often: the maps; the introductory features; the Focus-on articles; the walks and the drives.

My Provence by Nick Hanna

On my most recent trip back to Provence, I was in the tiny municipal museum of a remote Haut Var village when I came across some fascinating photographs. The record of a local archaeology dig, the pictures revealed some unusual facts about the neolithic peoples who had dwelt in the caves behind the village. Along with clear evidence of human cannibalism, the photographs showed that these people had discovered trepanning. The technique, now medically obsolete, involves removing a portion of the skull. The fact that these cave-dwellers had used it as a form of surgery 300,000 years ago and that the 'patient' had survived is extraordinary.

Obscure though this discovery may be, it is just one example of the richness of Provence's multi-layered history, and its capacity to surprise even the most knowledgeable visitor. Provence is also a dynamic, forward-looking region, and the combination of respect for its heritage and a vision of its future has sparked off numerous innovative projects in recent years, such as the new Musée de Préhistoire des Gorges du Verdon at Quinson, the Musée des Merveilles in Tende, and the 'Sunken Sanctuary' exhibition in Marseille, where the prehistoric paintings of the Cosquer Cave have been re-created in a docklands warehouse – there are also ambitious plans for a full-scale virtual reality experience of this unique cave sanctuary.

Thus Provence is continually reinventing itself, drawing upon the texture of the past to create a heritage for the future. At the same time, I am always reassured whenever I go back by the unchanging patterns of daily life: the quiet 'clonk' of boules being played beneath the plane trees in village squares; the queues of tractors waiting to disgorge their glistening loads at the local co-operative during the grape harvest; the lively village markets, with their eye-catching displays of seasonal produce; and the obligatory lunchtime closure of almost everything except restaurants, during which you might as well forget whatever it was you were trying to achieve and succumb to the temptation of the *plat du jour* and a glass of Côtes-de-Provence rosé in the nearest bistro. *Bon appetit!*

Nick Hanna has travelled in and around Provence by every conceivable means – car, train, bicycle, hitchhiking and on foot – for over 20 years, and although he has written guidebooks to numerous other destinations, Provence remains one of his favourites. He has journeyed across thousands of miles criss-crossing a region that now feels like his second home, and which, despite its familiarity, continues to delight and astonish him, as it has generations of travellers.

PROVENCE IS

■ Despite the picture-postcard images of mellow landscapes, in reality Provence is rugged and mountainous, with arid, wind-blown terrain alternating with the lush river valleys. ■

Mountains, rivers, gorges In the northeast corner of Provence the craggy peaks of the Alpes de Haute-Provence tower above glaciated valleys, such as the Vallée de l'Ubaye, the dramatic mountain passes often cut off by deep snow in winter. To the south, these alpine heights adjoin the Mercantour *massif* on the border with Italy and lead down into the upper valleys of the Var, Tinée, Roya and Vésubie rivers. *En route* to the coast these torrents have created chasms through the pre-Alps which shelter the hinterland and the Riviera resorts.

To the west, the Verdon river has carved out of the limestone of the Plateau de Valensole one of the great natural wonders of the region, the Grand Cañon du Verdon. The Plateau de Valensole and the Plan de Canjuers to the south of the Verdon are amongst the least-populated regions

Spring blossoms on the slopes of the Dentelles de Montmirail

in Provence, desolate, wild areas dominated by *garrigue* (scrubland).

The Durance loops down from the Alps through the heartland of Provence before disgorging into the Rhône. During the summer its stony bed is all but dried out, but in the spring the melting snow transforms it into an impressive, foaming torrent several hundred metres across.

Above the broad curve formed by the Durance are the Petit and Grand Lubéron ranges, reaching their peak at the Mourre Nègre (1,125m). The wide-open, arid plains of the Plateau de Vaucluse beyond the Lubéron are fractured by chasms and fissures which lead down to a vast network of subterranean rivers through which rainwater is carried to spectacular resurgent springs such as the Fontaine-de-Vaucluse.

Rising up to the north of the Plateau de Vaucluse is the imposing bulk of Mont Ventoux, with its barren summit at 1,909m dominating the

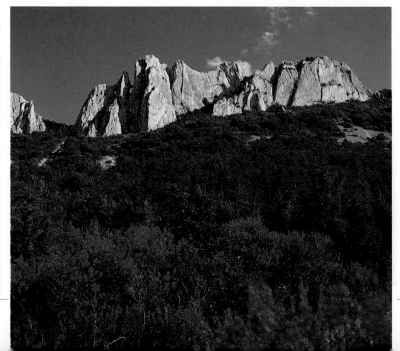

surrounding landscapes. Flanking it to the east is the Montagne de Lure, with the unusual mini-peaks of the Dentelles de Montmirail displaying a jagged profile to the west.

To the south of the Durance's leisurely arc lie the southern Provençal ranges – Ste-Victoire above Aix, Ste-Baume behind Marseille, and Mont Faron over-shadowing Toulon harbour.

The western boundary of Provence closely follows the Rhône, a major artery for communication and transport in Provence since antiquity. Alluvial deposits built up on either side of the river have created the fertile valleys of the Comtat Venaissin and the plains of la Crau and Petite Crau near its delta. Separating the Crau and the Petite Crau is the rugged Alpilles chain.

On either side of the delta, the Grand Rhône and Petit Rhône embrace the marshy wilderness of the Camargue – along with the rest of the Rhône valley, the Camargue is subject to periodic flooding which can have devastating effects.

Three of the most distinctive geographical features of the present-day coastline are the Cap Canaille (which has the highest cliffs in France) and the unusual *massifs* of the Esterel and the Maures.

The 'mud-eater' *mistral* Provence has many winds but the most famous is the *mistral*, whose course is shaped by the mountains and rivers of the region. Originating in the north or northwest, the *mistral* is channelled down the Rhône valley and blasts across mid-Provence and the coast before dissipating itself on the Alpes-Maritimes. The *mistral* (in Provençal: the *mangio fango* – the 'mud-eater') has a profound effect, drying out the soil and clearing up the atmosphere, creating luminous blue skies in its wake. It knocks off roof tiles and sets doors banging, getting on everyone's nerves. Folk wisdom claims that it blows in cycles of three days (a *mistral* blowing for nine days is not unknown) if it starts up by day, although if it begins at night it may last only 'as long as it takes to bake bread'. Generally, it blows for between 100 and 150 days in the year.

Top: view of the Camargue
Below: canoeists work their way through the Ardèche gorges

■ **The people of Provence are mostly Mediterranean in temperament and looks, but they also have their own distinct character based on a strong regional identity and sense of independence. After decades of neglect the Provençal language – a symbol of a shared identity – is undergoing a revival.** ■

The Provençals Who are the real Provençals, and what are they like? Generations of writers and travellers have tried to provide answers and more often than not come up with patronising generalisations. Victor Hugo considered them typically Mediterranean and hot-blooded ('in Paris one quarrels, in Avignon one kills'), whilst almost everyone from Stendhal to Lawrence Durrell thought they embodied the *mañana* attitude – lazy, unhurried, ready to put off work until *demain* or (more likely) *après demain*. This reputation is no doubt partly due to the difficulties newcomers experience getting locals to work on their houses – a story-line which has been mined from the days of Lady Fortescue (who settled near Grasse in the 1930s) through to Peter Mayle in the 1980s.

Dual French–Provençal road signs are now common

Alphonse Daudet was first responsible for portraying the Provençals as whimsical, comic characters through his Tartarin novels, and the enormously popular books and films of Marcel Pagnol have reinforced this stereotype of the light-hearted, playful Provençal who spends all day doing nothing more serious than playing *boules* and drinking *pastis*.

There may be a grain of truth in these caricatures but in reality Provençals are far more serious and hard-working – although they also know how to enjoy themselves. They also have a reputation for surliness and distrust of outsiders (natural enough, one would think, in a region which has seen so many invasions – including invasion by tourism), but once the ice is broken they become welcoming and hospitable.

In rural areas, villages are bound together by a strong sense of community and old-fashioned values (amongst the older generation, at least) combined with a healthy respect and love for the Provençal countryside. Although regular church-going is no longer universally observed, Catholicism is deeply ingrained. Alongside their religious beliefs, the Provençals have retained many customs and rituals, some dating back to antiquity, and a healthy dose of superstitious beliefs.

The Provençal language Although Provençal is no longer widely spoken, the distinctive regional accent is easily recognisable and tells you that you are conversing with a true Provençal – if you can understand what he or she is saying behind the thick nasal twang (where *vin* becomes *ving*, *demain* becomes *demang* and so on) which is often rendered even more incomprehensible by high-speed delivery.

The Provençal language has been in decline since the 16th century, despite the efforts of the poet Mistral who collated his giant Provençal dictionary and published a popular journal, *L'Aïoli*, in an attempt to revive it in the late 19th century. Today, however, there are signs that the sense of regional identity is becoming stronger once more, and Provençal is now an option in many schools. Nearly every rural village now has its name on the road sign in both French and Provençal.

In the post-war years the younger generation deserted many of the old ways, lured away from the traditional lifestyle by the bright lights (and work) in the big cities. But now another generation is taking a far greater interest in their linguistic heritage. Curiously, one of the strangest manifestations of young Provençals seeking out their roots has emerged from Marseille, where learning Provençal has become the latest craze amongst second-generation immigrants.

Drinking pastis *all day long – the whimsical image of the Provençaux*

A disappearing lifestyle: fisherman in Bandol

Local folklore has become a way of asserting their identity and sense of belonging, a trend which has developed hand in hand with the rise of ragamuffin music – a blend of reggae and rap, into which they sometimes weave old Provençal songs. One local raggamuffin band even starts off its performances with the symbolic rallying cry of 'Aïoli!'. Mistral would have been both horrified and delighted.

In contrast to the futuristic ambitions of public buildings in Nice, Marseille or Nîmes, in rural areas of Provence one architectural form remains supreme – the Provençal country house. Although it has some elements in common with an Italian villa or a Spanish hacienda, the Provençal country house is as different from these as it is from a Normandy farmhouse. ■

Perfect adaptation The Provençal house has evolved to cope with the often harsh extremes of the climate in this part of France, the strong sunlight of summer and the bitingly cold winter winds. Its thick walls, sometimes buttressed, merge into the terrain and usually have no windows on the north side and just enough openings on the other three sides to let in light. A perfect example of thermal insulation, the house is well designed to stay cool in summer and warm in winter.

In regions where the *mistral* predominates (most of Provence between the Alps, the sea and the Rhône) the house is usually orientated north–south with a slight turn to the east so that the front of the house is sheltered from the northwesterly *mistral*.

Tiled roofs The characteristic curved roof tiles of the Provençal house are Greek in origin. Their shape (which is tapered at one end) probably comes from being moulded on the thigh of the potter. Traditionally made by hand, they were fired in the kilns at Aubagne, Biot, Moustiers, Vallauris and Apt. The Provençal roof is usually finished off with a *génoise*, a double or triple row of tiles embedded under the eaves.

Definitions First of all there is the *mas*, which could mean anything from a country house to a farm or even a barn. Typically, the Provençal *mas* is a large, low-lying farmhouse which sprawls outwards and encompasses stables, storerooms, dovecots and even sheep pens under one roof. It has evolved and been added to over many generations. In the Camargue and the Crau, it was often built around an enclosed courtyard – again, for protection from the *mistral*.

Then there is the *bastide*, which could also be a farm but was more likely to be a country house, with decorative elements such as balconies, exterior stone staircases and sculpted lintels. It was usually two storeys high, with a third floor adorned by oval 'eyebrow windows' (in Provence known as *oeils de boeuf* – bull's eyes). Unlike the long, low sloping roof of the *mas*, the *bastide* roof had four slopes.

The *bastidon* ('little *bastide*') preserved the same proportions on a smaller scale.

Interiors Inside, the *mas* was often divided in two by a corridor with one side for the owner and the other for the *bayle* (farmer or steward). Terracotta tiles were used on the floors, with roof beams made from whole tree-trunks – left round in *mas*, squared off in the *bastides*.

❏ 'In August, in our region, just before evening, a powerful heat sets the fields ablaze. The whitewashed, beaten soil radiated against the low wall of the abandoned sheepfold. The heart of the house remained cool, however. There remained in this retreat some reserves of shade and freshness that were fed at night and which, during the heat of the day, were a great resource.' Henri Bosco, *Le Mas Théotime*. ❏

❏ 'The village mason understands the compass card, the direction of the rains, the orientation of the light, the cardinal points, the character of the people who will come: with all these insights, the mason then builds the house.' Jean Giono ❏

As well as wall ovens and open hearths, kitchens nearly always had their *pétrins* (wooden trunks which were used for leavening bread dough) and *panatières* (a wooden cage hung on the wall, used for storing bread), both of which might be elaborately carved in the Arlesian style. Another distinctive Provençal feature is the *radassie* in the drawing-room, a three- or four-seater settee with armrests between the seats.

15

A typical example of a mas *(below) and (top) a close-up view of its roof*

■ **Farming and forestry still play an essential role in modern Provence. Fields and forests cover nearly 80 per cent of the region and support 45,000 farms and smallholdings. Together with secondary industries (such as food processing), the land provides employment for 15 per cent of the working population. ■**

A bountiful harvest One of the strengths of agriculture in Provence is the enormous diversity of the produce grown, a cornucopia which includes lavender from the mountains, chestnuts from the forests, flowers from the greenhouses of the Côte d'Azur, rice from the Camargue, *les primeurs* (early crops of fruits and vegetables) such as cherries, strawberries, melons, asparagus and peaches from the fertile plains ... not to mention sunflowers, olives, grapes, apples, tomatoes.

> ❏ Provence produces 52 per cent of all the olives in France, 50 per cent of table grapes, and 30 per cent of its melons, tomatoes and apples. ❏

Changing patterns Despite the buoyant state of agriculture at present, some forecasts predict that by the end of the century the peasant lifestyle will have all but disappeared and that the number of farmers will have halved to just 20,000 or fewer. Pressures from developers, particularly in coastal areas, have forced many farmers off the land – in the Alpes-Maritimes, the number of farmers has declined from 44,000 in 1929 to just 5,200 today. High land costs are another factor, with prices leaping by a third in recent years in some areas (particularly the Var).

Adaptation Agriculture in Provence is having to adapt to competition within the European Union, and to modernise. Greater emphasis is now being placed on food processing (which has a higher added-value),

better marketing, new varieties of fruit and vegetables (there are 12 applied plant-breeding stations in the region), and on other innovations such as biological pest control to reduce crop losses and new irrigation schemes.

Other farmers are moving in different directions, many of which are connected to tourism and the realisation that the rural environment is a valuable attraction in its own right. Some are restoring old olive oil mills, not only so that they can process oil but also to draw visitors. Others are developing 'gourmet routes' through their localities, with farms selling food specialities (*produits de la ferme*). In the Alps, they are even studying the possibility of introducing bison – not only would they be a tourist attraction, but their meat sells at premium prices.

Horticulture The main centres for horticulture in Provence are the Var and the Alpes-Maritimes, which between them grow over 300 varieties of ornamental plants and cut flowers including mimosa, tulips, roses, carnations and 30 different types of palm tree.

> ❏ Provence grows around 172 million roses and 188 million carnations annually, 60 and 90 per cent respectively of the total French production. ❏

Viticulture The patchwork of vineyards that gives the Provençal countryside its characteristic appeal is also undergoing change, notably the upgrading of vine stocks to

❏ The largest area of vineyards in Provence is in the Vaucluse (58,430 hectares), followed by the Var (35,800 hectares) and the Bouches-du-Rhône (13,500 hectares). ❏

produce better quality wines. In the Bouches-du-Rhône, for instance, rough-and-ready *vin de table* accounted for nearly 70 per cent of production 15 years ago; now it is

nearer 20 per cent, with many more vineyards having gained the coveted *Appellation d'Origine Contrôlée* (AOC) status (see also Regional Wines, pages 94–5). Another phenomenon is overseas wine-makers buying vineyards in Provence – in the Var alone, nearly 50 *domaines* have recently been taken over by outside investors, injecting new capital and new ideas into this important sector of the economy.

Lavender is one of many crops which Provence produces in abundance

■ **With something in the region of 500 festivals encompassing around 4,000 separate events, Provence in the summertime is justifiably called 'The Land of Festivals'. The following is but a sample of the cultural riches the region has to offer.** ■

Traditional festivals Many of the traditional village festivals revolve around the natural calendar and the bounty of the earth and the sea. Others have their roots deep in Provençal folklore. Whatever the reason, the day will usually involve a procession of some sort in traditional costumes, accompanied by pipes and drums, culminating in a vast feast with *pastis* and wine flowing freely, when a good time is had by one and all.

> ❑ In the St Eloi processions, horses with their bridles and Saracen-style harnesses ablaze with ribbons and pompons pull chariots piled high with wheat, followed by men and boys on horseback and women and children in horse-drawn carts in Provençal costumes. ❑

On 1 May the cowboys of the Camargue, the *gardians*, put on a rodeo in the arena at Arles for the *Fête des Gardians*, whilst at Whitsun the old sheep migrations between the mountains and the plains are celebrated in the *Fête de la Transhumance* in St-Rémy. St-Tropez has its noisy and ebullient *bravades* on 16 May (in honour of St Tropez himself) and 15 June (to celebrate seeing off the Spanish fleet in 1637), while on 24 and 25 May gypsies from all over Europe arrive for the

pèlerinage (pilgrimage) to les Stes-Maries-de-la-Mer.

In June the atmospheric *procession dai limaca* (in thanksgiving for the olive harvest) takes place in Gorbio, and the highly colourful Tarasque festival (last weekend in June) unrolls in Tarascon. The Feast of St John, 24 June, is celebrated in numerous villages.

St Eloi is one of the most popular saints in Provence, and festivities in his honour (or those fêting St Roch, another popular saint) take place between mid-June and early September in dozens of villages.

August sees the *Fête de la Lavande* in Sault, the *Fête du Muscat* in Beaumes-de-Venise, and the *Fête de la Véraison* with medieval pageantry to celebrate the grapes maturing in Châteauneuf-du-Pape. In September the Camargue rice harvest is celebrated in Arles, the apple harvest in Peyruis, and the *vendange* (wine harvest) in numerous towns and villages.

Cultural festivals Provence has numerous outstanding venues which resonate during summer evenings to the classics, jazz and folk music – or simply act as a superb backdrop to theatre and dance performances. What better stage could there possibly be than the grand arenas of Arles and Nîmes, the forecourt of the Palais des Papes in Avignon, or the exquisite Roman theatre in Orange? And then there are smaller, more intimate locations – the charming medieval tower which gave Simiane-la-Rotonde its name, the cloisters of the various churches or cathedrals, the enchanting *théâtres de verdure* (open-air 'green theatres') set amongst ruins in Draguignan, Villefranche and elsewhere. Another dramatic venue is

CONSEIL GÉNÉRAL Alpes Maritimes

5ème *Festival du* **Conte** *des Alpes-Maritimes*

1994

RAMME

the ruined château in la Tour-d'Aigues, which plays host to the Sud-Lubéron summer festival. Add to this a line-up which includes performers of international calibre and the stage is set for a creative extravaganza which lasts all summer long.

July and August are the busiest months, with jazz festivals in Nice, Toulon and Aix; an international folk-lore festival in Cavaillon; theatre, jazz and classical music in Gordes; music, dance and theatre at Fontaine-de-Vaucluse and l'Isle-sur-la-Sorgue; folklore in Marseille; classical music at the Organa festival in St-Rémy-de-Provence and in Cassis; early music in Entrevaux and Simiane-la-Rotonde.

The gardians *of the Camargue parade on their famous white horses*

In Orange, *Les Nuits d'Été du Théâtre Antique* encompasses everything from pop to jazz, with the renowned *Chorégies* (opera and classics) taking place in the same superb setting.

And then there is the big festival in Avignon (with literally hundreds of theatre performances, films and concerts from mid-July onwards) as well, as dance and photography in Arles.

❏ Over 300 towns and villages have some kind of festival over the summer. Complete listings can be found in the booklet *Provence – Terre de festivals*, available from tourist offices. ❏

Provence - Alpes - C

TERRE DE FEST

La culture au

Pierre AMBROGIANI
"French Can-Can" - 1946 H.S.C. (50 x 65 cm)
Collection du Fonds Régional d'Acquisitions d'Œuvres Proven

Une réalisation de l'Office Régional de la Culture

1994 - 15e année

■ **Tourism plays an essential part in the Provençal economy, as it has done for the last 160 years since foreigners first started holidaying on the Côte d'Azur. Today, around 24 million tourists annually contribute between 36 and 39 billion francs to the region.** ■

Early tourism Tourism on the Riviera started in the 1830s when the English aristocracy started building luxury mansions in which to escape the winter fog of England. In the inter-war years Coco Chanel popularised sunbathing, and the season switched to the summer – a phenomenon that intensified after World War II with the emergence of mass tourism. By the mid-1970s millions of people were holidaying on the coastline, but inland Provence still remained largely unspoiled, discovered only by more adventurous visitors.

Tourism today The Alpes-Maritimes (which includes the Côte d'Azur) is today the most popular destination for foreigners, followed by the Vaucluse, the Bouches-du-Rhône, Var and the Alpes de Haute-Provence. Conversely, the French (who constitute three-quarters of all visitors to Provence) favour the Var and the Alpes de Haute-Provence, followed by the Bouches-du-Rhône, the Vaucluse and the Alpes-Maritimes – which may tell you something if you want to avoid your own neighbours.

❏ On average around 3 million people visit the museums of the coast each year, with a third of that total accounted for by the Musée Océanographique in Monaco alone – making it the eighth most popular attraction in the whole of France. ❏

The number of people who visit the Côte d'Azur (just over 8 million annually) is equivalent to the number of tourists who visit Greece or the entire Caribbean, and the coast accounts for around 25 billion francs out of total tourism revenues for Provence of between 36 and 39 billion francs. Despite these seductive figures, tourism on the coast is in crisis. There is a huge overcapacity of hotel rooms, and the changing patterns of international tourism are also having an effect: due to increased awareness of the dangers of sunbathing, fewer people are taking beach holidays. No longer content simply to fry their brains (*bronzer à idiot* as the French say), holidaymakers want more things to do, they want better value for money, and they want to experience the real Provence.

Harbourside lido, Monte-Carlo

Cultural tourism is now being more heavily marketed, emphasising the extraordinary artistic legacy of the Côte d'Azur, which is blessed with no less than 80 museums, running the gamut from Impressionist paintings to Picasso and Chagall, perfume and honey to wine and wildlife. Many have been upgraded (such as the Matisse museum in Nice) and new ones are being opened (such as the Musée des Merveilles in Tende).

The tourist industry also suffers from a huge seasonal imbalance, with over three million people coming to Provence in August alone. Business tourism is seen as part of the solution – particularly in spreading tourism over a longer period – and it already accounts for around 300,000 people drawn to congresses in state-of-the-art conference

Tourism is now a big money-spinner in coastal resorts

facilities such as the Acropolis in Nice or the massive new Centre de Congrès Auditorium in Monte-Carlo.

The rich natural and cultural heritage has always been the main drawcard in inland Provence, but with increasing numbers of people now wanting to hike, bike or simply do their own thing discovering the mountains and valley byways, the authorities are keen to tap into this market and promote rural tourism. In recent years, they have embarked on a co-ordinated programme that includes supplying management expertise for rural communities who want to diversify into tourism. It also provides grants to upgrade hotels and restaurants and for renovating houses in historic villages.

Initiatives such as these are not only good news for rural communities but also point the way forward for better quality tourism and a sustainable future for this important sector of the Provençal economy.

■ Horror stories of the polluted Côte d'Azur were once commonplace but the seas are once again safe to swim in. The challenge now is managing conflicting demands on the coastline – such as recreation, aquaculture and development – and maintaining the health of marine ecosystems. At the same time, Provence is mobilising its marine industries to place itself at the forefront of global developments in undersea technology. ■

The coast Huge efforts have been made to clean up beaches in recent years and the quality of bathing water has improved enormously, although, given the fact that the Mediterranean is an enclosed sea, Provence is still dependent on neighbouring countries taking similar action. A large proportion of beaches on the coast have been awarded the European Blue Flag. To achieve this, they must not only pass the strictest water quality controls but also meet required standards in 25 other areas (such as having safe access, life guards, first aid posts, and so on). Around Nice an astonishing 22 beaches have been awarded the Blue Flag, as have at

least 24 in the Antibes area – but if the big public beaches are not your cup of tea there are plenty of secluded coves to be discovered where the water quality is also excellent.

❏ The first experimental fish farm was at the Paul Ricard Oceanographic Institute on the Île des Embiez, where they now breed half a million sea bass annually. The Institute was also the first to develop microbacteria which eat crude oil – knowledge which was put to good use in the *Exxon Valdez* disaster in Alaska in 1989. ❏

Mussels are now farmed extensively

Fishing and aquaculture The picture-postcard cliché of the weather-beaten old fisherman mending his nets on the quayside is in danger of becoming just that – a snapshot of the past – given the decline in the coastal fishing in Provence. In the Var, for instance, there are now only 300 fishing boats left. Overfishing, lack of investment, and EU directives to reduce fishing fleets have all had an impact. Faced with declining catches, many fishermen are now turning to fish farming. At present there are just

22

Super! *les moules frites tous les jours.* 45 F

Clean seas have become a major priority for Provençal authorities

over 20 fish farms, but there is enormous potential for aquaculture in Provence, with plenty of suitable coastal sites. The most popular species are sea bass and sea bream (both of which taste no different from their 'wild' cousins) and mussels.

Marine parks Provence has so far only one official marine park, the

☐ COMEX, based in Marseille, is acknowledged as a world leader in offshore engineering and underwater robotics. They have recently developed a hydrogen mixture, called heliox, which allows divers to reach hitherto undreamt of depths of between 300 and 650m underwater. ☐

300ha Côte Bleue reserve offshore from Carry-le-Rouet, west of Marseille. Many more are needed to act as nurseries to replenish declining fish populations. Since 1989, ten marine species in danger of extinction have been protected, and there was a five-year moratorium (until 1997) on catching black groupers, of which very few remain (these big fish have been the victims of overzealous spear fishermen for decades).

Marine research Provence is one of the world's leading research centres for ocean engineering, with 54 companies in this area alone. In total nearly 300 enterprises are involved in marine technology, with projects ranging from the manufacturing of remote-control deep-sea robots, catamarans or passenger submarines to submarine cable maintainance and the development of pollution-control techniques.

■ **The sunny South of France has allied itself with America's sunshine state and, despite the huge cultural differences between these two high-profile regions, it is with some justification that Provence likes to think of itself as 'the California of Europe'.** ■

A far-flung alliance On 6 May 1991 an agreement was signed in Sacramento which twinned Provence-Alpes-Côte d'Azur (PACA) with California, a union based on similarities in climate, technological development, industry, agriculture and tourism. Some of these connections may seem far-fetched to a Provençal peasant tending his vineyards or an Angelino cruising down Sunset Boulevard (although Hollywood was twinned with Cannes long ago), but the twinning has already borne fruit in the form of exchanges in research, training, technology and other areas – including waste management and hydroelectric power. Strategically, PACA sees itself as the southern gateway to the European Union in the same way that California is the gateway to the Pacific basin.

Science parks Launched in the 1970s, Sophia-Antipolis (Greek for 'city of wisdom'–the new Antibes)

❏ If you are flying into Provence on a European airline, there is a good chance your airline reservation will have been routed through one of Sophia-Antipolis' huge computer systems: not only is it the global reservation centre for 15,000 Air France terminals worldwide, but it is also the home of Amadeus, the giant computer network which links together passenger reservations for SAS, Lufthansa, Air France and Iberia. ❏

was France's first science park and is still the largest in the country.

Covering 5,000 hectares in the landscaped hills behind Antibes, it is going to expand by half as much again. Currently there are around 980 enterprises in this futuristic complex, employing 16,000 people: this is expected to reach 1,500 businesses with a total of 30,000 employees by the year 2010. In addition to the multinational companies working in high-technology areas such as telecommunications, biotechnology and robotics, Sophia-Antipolis has training and research centres specialising in solar energy, molecular biology and information sciences.

Although it was Sophia-Antipolis which

Signposts point the way to the future in Sophia-Antipolis

D 98

SOPHIA ANTIPOLIS **GARBEJAIRE**

SOPHIA ANTIPOLIS **HAUT-SARTOUX**

SOPHIA ANTIPOLIS *Collège Eganaude*

24

first sparked the comparisons with California's Silicon Valley, in fact Provence now has five other major science and technology parks. These are on the outskirts of Marseille, Toulon, Aix, Manosque and Avignon. With all this activity, it is perhaps not surprising to discover that Provence is classed as the most important region in the country for high-technology research outside of Paris. It has the fastest growth rate for business creation in France, especially in the high-tech fields, and currently numbers over 8,000 research workers and 18,000 research technicians.

Ultimately, the regional authorities aim to link the six science parks together into a powerful network which will propel the region along the so-called 'high-technology route' to future prosperity. Since the creation in 1987 of the southern European 'high-technology route' which links together eight of the most dynamic regions around the Mediterranean,

Sophia-Antipolis is the largest science park in France

the planners are confident that Provence will fulfil its intention of becoming the technological heart of southern Europe.

❏ The six main science parks and their specialisations are:

Sophia-Antipolis: electronics, telecommunications, information technology.
Toulon-Var-Technopole: mechanical and acoustic engineering.
Marseille-Provence-Technopole: robotics, biotechnology, electronics.
Manosque-Cadarache: industrial robotics, chemical analysis.
Avignon-Montfavet-Agroparc: agro-technologies.
Arbois-Europole: information sciences, electronics. ❏

■ **Dances such as the *farandole* are an important part of the Provençal identity, and not just something staged for tourists' cameras. Similarly, the folk art of making *santons* (little saints) is rooted in ancient traditions. ■**

Dances and costumes Traditional costumes are often worn during village fêtes and festivals. For women, the costume consists of a full skirt and a long-sleeved, black blouse over which a pleated shirt or lace shawl is worn. There are several different types of headgear (usually embellished with lace, velvet or delicate embroidery), always worn on top of a high bun. For men, a white shirt is set off by a lace tie or ribbon and a velvet waistcoat, with canvas

26

trousers supported by a wide woollen belt. They can wear either black felt hats with raised brims or a straw hat.

The best-known Provençal dance is the *farandole*, which is performed by young men and women in traditional costume at village festivals. It is accompanied by a six-beat rhythm on the *tambourin*, a small drum made from calf-skin and decorated with coloured ribbons or cords. The *tambourinaire* hangs the tambourine on his right side and with his left hand he holds a small three-holed flute known as the *gaboulet* with which he plays a piercing tune.

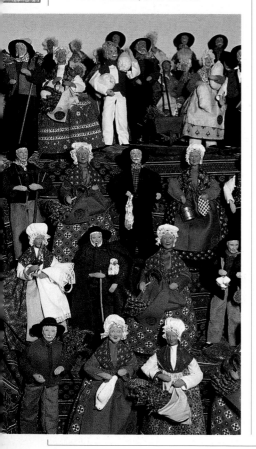

Santons Nativity scenes with small figures known as *santons* (little saints) first appeared in Provence in the 17th century and were originally made from wood, wax or cork. When churches were closed after the Revolution a potter from Marseille, Jean-Louis Lagnel, conceived the idea of mass-producing *santons* in clay, so that every family could have a Christmas crib. Soon the range of figurines produced came to include Provençal characters (the innkeeper, the shepherd, the baker and so on) bringing their gifts to the Christ child, with the nativity setting transposed to a typical Provençal village. Today, *santonniers* still make these traditional figures, usually in clay (sometimes in wood), often with hand-painted finishes or wearing miniature costumes.

Santons are a Provençal tradition

■ **The first traces of human habitation in Provence are found, curiously enough, in some of the Côte d'Azur's most sophisticated coastal area must have appealed as much to Cro-Magnon man as it does to visitors today.** ■

❑ There are no cave paintings in Provence to compare with those at Lascaux in the Dordogne, but in 1991 a local diver discovered a partially submerged cave in one of the *calanques* near Cassis with a number of paintings (depicting horses, bison and deer) thought to be around 27,000 years old – see panel, page 123. Named after their discoverer, Henri Cosquer, the caves now have a special exhibition devoted to them in Marseille – see page 130. ❑

by Cro-Magnon man: these nomadic hunters had found the perfect spot for a camp at the mouth of the Vallée de Paillon, where there was a fresh-water spring next to a small, sheltered beach. Primarily hunters of deer and elephant, the inhabitants built small, circular huts from branches, each with its own central hearth. Palaeolithic remnants have also been found near Menton, notably the skull of 'Menton man' which is believed to date back around 30,000 years. The skeletons were covered in sea shells and necklaces, coinciding with the first use of burial grounds in the late palaeolithic period.

Early hunters The earliest evidence of settlements in Provence dates back 400,000 years and comes from the site known as Terra Amata, just behind the old port in Nice. Unearthed in 1966, Terra Amata revealed several encampments built

From hunters to shepherds During the neolithic era, from around 6000 BC, there was a shift towards growing crops and the domestication of wild

The first Greek settlers landed at Massalia (Marseille) in 600 BC

4th centuries BC the Celtic tribes began descending on Provence, bringing with them iron tools and building the first of their fortified hilltop settlements or *oppidi*. Intermarrying with the local Ligurians, the Celts started to build up powerful alliances and gradually trading links across the Mediterranean region began to blossom, particularly with Asia Minor.

> ❏ Greek traders from the island of Rhodes are attributed with having given Provence's greatest river its current name: *Rhodéenne* is an adjective still in use to describe the plains alongside the Rhône. ❏

Driven by the desire to establish new trading colonies, and by the depletion of their agricultural lands, Phocaeans (they came from Phocis in Asia Minor) set up their first Greek settlements at Massalia (Marseille) around 600 BC, providing a bridgehead for the arrival of Greek civilisation on the European mainland. The Celto-Ligurians welcomed the Greeks as trading partners, exchanging metals (such as copper, gold, tin and silver) and foodstuffs for Greek vases and other artefacts.

The Greeks introduced the cultivation of cherries, olives, figs, walnuts and vines (although vines and olives were both already present in Provence, neither had been cultivated to yield fruit). The Greeks confined themselves to trading up the Rhône and the Durance and along the coast, setting up a series of ports such as Antipolis (Antibes), Athenopolis (St-Tropez), Citharista (la Ciotat), Nikaia (Nice) and Olbia (Hyères).

Ligurian legacy: carving in Vallée des Merveilles and (top) bories

sheep. Those who lived in Provence at this time are known as the Ligurians, although their origins are uncertain. Some say they arrived from the east, others from the Iberian peninsula. Either way, during the neolithic and the Bronze Age, the Ligurians started to build villages, constructing drystone huts known as *bories* and trading with the outside world. Although none of the *bories* which survive today is this old, the Ligurians left huge standing stones (dolmens) and the impressive rock engravings of the Vallée des Merveilles.

Arrival of the Celts and the Greeks

Sometime between the 8th and the

■ **The peaceful arrival of the Greeks was not to be repeated when the Romans descended on Provence with full military force in the second century BC. They stayed for around 600 years and their legacy is a series of monuments which are unparalleled elsewhere in Northern Europe outside Italy.** ■

The cohorts march in

After Rome had conquered Spain in 206 BC, securing the land-route across Provence was the next priority. They were given the perfect excuse in 124 BC when the Greeks of Massalia appealed for help against the Celto-Ligurian Salyens, who were threatening them from their base at Entremont. The Romans came in force, with Sextius Calvinus leading a whole army to pacify the Salyens. Once that had been achieved, the Romans decided to stay permanently, founding their first settlement in Provence at Aquae Sextiae, the present city of Aix-en-Provence.

A Roman bust, Vaison-la-Romaine

Only the Alpes-Maritimes were left more or less under Phocaean control. This new province (or *Provincia*, from where the present-day name of Provence derives) was known as *Gallia Narbonensis.*

The barbarian invasions

Rome's stranglehold on southern Gaul was not yet complete. From 115 BC onwards the region was subject to attacks by several northern tribes, most notably the Teutoni. They were finally defeated by Marius in a battle below Montagne Ste-Victoire near Aix in 102 BC.

The Roman 'Provincia'

In 118 BC Narbonne was founded and became the capital of the Roman territory, which extended from the Pyrenees to the Alps and north as far as Lyon.

Roman remains at St-Rémy-de-Provence

❑ After the defeat of the Teutoni, pockets of local resistance to Roman rule continued through until 14 BC, when the last of the Alpine tribes were subdued. This final subjugation of the *Provincia* was marked by the building of the *Trophée des Alpes* at la Turbie, a monumental symbol of Roman power. ❑

The downfall of Massalia

In the civil wars that followed the conquest of Gaul by Julius Caesar in 51 BC, the inhabitants of Massalia made a huge mistake in not taking the side of Caesar against Pompey. In 49 BC Caesar took his revenge by laying siege to the city and ruining its trade, stripping Massalia of its territory along the coast of the Alpes-Maritimes. Caesar promoted Arelate (Arles) in its place, and before long Massalia was also eclipsed by Aix, Nîmes and Fréjus.

> ❏ The main settlements during this era developed alongside the major Roman roads (the Via Agrippa, which went north through Avignon and Orange from Arles, and the Via Aurelia, which linked Italy with Arles via Cimiez, Fréjus and Aix) and in the Rhône valley. ❏

Pax Romana The next 400 years saw the blossoming of Roman civilisation in Provence, particularly under the Emperor Augustus, Caesar's great-nephew. Augustus established colonies, ruled by veteran legionnaires, at Apt, Arles, Avignon,

Carpentras, Digne, Fréjus, Glanum, Riez and Vaison. These settlements grew into prosperous cities with baths, theatres, arenas, aqueducts, temples and bridges. Arts and culture thrived, and Provence paid its way by supplying the Roman Empire with grain, oil, and even ships.

Early Christianity Legend has it that Christianity arrived on the shores of Provence with the 'boat of Bethany' (see page 141), and St Trophimus is also said to have arrived in Arles at around the same time. Christianity received a major boost under the Emperor Constantine and the first Church council was held in Arles in AD 314. Around a hundred years later, the great monasteries of the Îles de Lérins and St-Victor in Marseille were founded.

Top: Pont du Gard. Below: the theatre at Vaison-la-Romaine

■ After the collapse of the western Roman empire in the 5th century, Provence suffered from numerous invasions and went through a period of anarchy and decline. Once the invaders had been driven out, a period of stability followed, during which troubadours roamed between the powerful courts of the local *seigneurs* and Romanesque architecture flourished. The feudal squabbles continued, however. ■

Wars and bloodshed Since the beginning of the 5th century the Visigoths had been making raids on Arles, and by the time the Roman empire disintegrated they were in control of all the land south of the Durance. At the same time the Burgundians had established their domination to the east and north. Neither of these new overlords lasted long, since they were ousted by the Ostrogoths from Italy. In turn, they were succeeded in AD 536 by the Franks, who carved up the territory into semi-autonomous regions. During

The time of the troubadours was a golden age for Provence

these troubled times life was hard in Provence, with land being appropriated and populations declining through bloodshed, famine and disease.

Saracen invasions The 8th century saw the emergence of the Islamic powers, with Arab armies sweeping up through Spain and over the Pyrenees into France. The Arabs (or Saracens, as they became generally known) got as far north as Poitiers before being defeated by the Frankish General Charles Martel in 732. Martel took advantage of the Saracen retreat to sweep down through Provence between 736 and 740 to reassert Frankish control, mercilessly sacking Avignon, Marseille and Aix. Provence was once more under Frankish rule, and by the end of the century had been integrated into the empire of Charlemagne.

With the demise of Charlemagne's empire in 843, Provence passed through the hands of various rulers before being made in 855 into a kingdom, which also encompassed territory further north in the Rhône basin (such as Lyon). This was of little help to the Provençals, who still had to contend with invasion by the Normans in 859 and the constant threat from the Saracens.

The Counts of Provence A new age of stability and prosperity dawned in Provence when Guillaume le Libérateur (William the Liberator) finally expelled the Saracens in 1032. Provence began to develop its independence during the years which followed, with the local lords

❏ After their rout by Martel, the Saracens switched tactics. They harassed Provence from the coast, successfully establishing several outlaw bases (notably at La Garde-Freinet in the Massif des Maures, from where they terrorised the surrounding countryside for around 200 years) and laid siege to Marseille in 838 and Arles in 842. ❏

(*seigneurs*) controlling their own fiefdoms. The country began to emerge from the Dark Ages, helped along by the Benedictine monasteries which became centres of learning, and agriculture and vineyards thrived. With the Mediterranean no longer controlled by the Saracens, trade links grew (particularly with Spain, Italy and the Orient) and the Rhône became a major artery for commerce with northern Europe, leading to increased wealth for Marseille, Arles, Avignon and Orange. Commerce on the coast benefited enormously from the Crusades, which started in 1095. In the courts of the feudal barons, the troubadours made their first appearance. These roaming entertainers were welcomed in the baronial castles, where they performed popular songs of the day, usually about love.

In 1125 Occitania was divided up between the counts of Toulouse (who ruled west of the Rhône and north of the Durance) and the counts of Barcelona (who controlled most of the land south of the Durance). However, the never-ending game of shifting alliances and squabbles between fiefdoms continued. The counts of Forcalquier fought on, as did the notorious *seigneurs* of Les Baux.

Les Baux was a powerful feudal stronghold in the 12th century

❏ Linguists call the language spoken between the Alps and the Pyrenees at this time the *langue d'oc*, to distinguish it from the *langue d'oïl* which was the dialect in the north of France (*oc* and *oïl* were the words for 'yes' in each region). The *langue d'oc* spread across the whole of southern France, an area dubbed Occitania. Provençal was one of many regional dialects spoken within Occitania. ❏

■ Under the House of Anjou, Provence drew closer to France but was still largely autonomous. During the 14th century the popes settled in Avignon, but by the beginning of the 15th century the popes had gone and in 1481 the last of the Angevins bequeathed his kingdom to France, heralding the end of independent Provence. ■

The House of Anjou Count Raymond-Bérenger V of Barcelona managed to bring some degree of stability to the warring fiefdoms in Provence during the 13th century, and imposed a unified system of law and administration based on Catalan practice. Several of his daughters made illustrious marriages. The most important was the union in 1246 of his youngest daughter, Beatrice, to Charles of Anjou, brother of the French king (later St Louis). Charles became Count of Provence when Beatrice inherited the region from her father, and this ushered in nearly 200 years of Angevin rule.

At the beginning of the 13th century the French had embarked on a crusade against the Cathars (a heretical Christian sect otherwise known as the Albigenses) in Languedoc, sacking Avignon into the bargain as punishment for loyalty to Toulouse (see page 52). The Counts

René of Anjou's castle at Tarascon

❑ Under the Angevins the boundaries of Provence changed. Sault, Gap, Les Baux and Marseille were brought into the fold, whilst Nice, Puget-Théniers and Barcelonnette became part of the Duchy of Savoy (and remained so for nearly 500 years). ❑

of Toulouse were forced to turn over their territories north of Avignon, the Comtat Venaissin, to placate King Louis IX. In 1274 France handed over the Comtat Venaissin to the Holy See in Rome, an event which was to lead to an extraordinary era in Provençal history.

The Avignon popes In 1309 Pope Clement V decided to shift the centre of papal power away from strife-torn Italy closer to his native France. He moved to Carpentras in the Comtat Venaissin, and his successor, Pope John XXII, moved the papal court to Avignon in 1316, beginning more than 100 years of what the Italians called 'the Babylonian Captivity'. It was indeed a time of avarice and debauchery but the city also witnessed a flowering of the arts and culture, the founding of the university, and the construction of dozens of churches and chapels as well as the grandiose Palais des Papes. Started by the third pope, Benedict XII, this was greatly expanded by his successor, Clement VI, who was also responsible for buying Avignon from Queen Joan. Altogether seven popes presided over this glittering court before the papacy reverted to Rome.

The last of the Angevins Whilst the popes at Avignon feuded with Rome, the rest of the country was suffering a succession of disasters, notably the first great plague (1348) and political instability and wars brought about by the death of Queen Joan in 1382. A semblance of normality returned under Louis II of Anjou, and on his death in 1434 sovereignty was transferred to René of Anjou, who passed into popular legend as Good King René.

Top: detail, Palais des Papes, Avignon. Above: Pope Benedict XII

Union with France René's heir, his nephew Charles III, inherited the throne in 1480 but died a year later without an heir, bequeathing Provence to Louis XI of France. In 1482 the *parlement* in Aix approved the union, but the French monarch immediately set about eroding the powers of the Provençal *États-Généraux* (States General), beginning a process of assimilation that signalled the end of an independent Provence.

In the face of Provençal opposition, the French crown was forced to take a more conciliatory line because the region was still a crucial buffer zone with Italy. In 1486 a treaty was signed, designed to ensure the autonomy of Provence and its legal institutions and local customs. This was gradually weakened by successive edicts, however, and Provence surrendered its autonomy to the centralised state. Union swiftly became unification.

❏ One of the greatest blows to Provençal cultural autonomy was the hated Edict of Villers-Cotterêts, passed by François I in 1539: this decreed that French would henceforth be the official language in schools, churches and the administration. It dealt a deathblow to the Provençal language and is still cited today by Provençal nationalists. ❏

■ **During the 16th century the reformist ideas of Calvin took a firm hold in Provence, where Protestantism became a symbol of rebellion against royal control as much as it was a protest against the old Catholic order. Repression was followed by a further loss of autonomy for Provence – and the third and deadliest outbreak of the plague.** ■

The Vaud heresy The Vaudois were the first sect to suffer the wrath of the established church against Protestantism. The Vaudois lived quietly in the villages of the Petit Lubéron until the 1540s, when the *parlement* at Aix ordered a crackdown. During five days in April 1545, blood ran through the village streets as 3,000 people were massacred and 600 were sent to the gallows.

This was the beginning of half a century or more of bloodshed and mayhem as the Catholic church resisted the 'heretical' ideas of the Reformation.

The spread of Protestantism Calvin's doctrines appealed to the Provençals not only as a reaction to the bloated Church hierarchy but also as an expression of opposition to the French state. Reformers sacked the cathedral in Orange, destroyed the abbey at St-Gilles, and pillaged churches throughout Haute Provence. The backlash brought more violence (with massacres at Barjols, Sisteron and Orange) and atrocities continued until the arrival of the plague in 1580 put a temporary stop to hostilities.

Trouble continued to ferment when the Huguenot Henri de Navarre became heir to the

French crown in 1584. The traditionalist Catholic League was formed to counter Protestant influence, seizing Paris and eventually murdering Henri III. After Henri de Navarre's conversion and

Fort St-Nicolas, a symbol of Louis XIV's power over Marseille

❏ Outside the cities and ports, Provence stagnated. In the countryside the peasantry eked out a living based on cereals, sheep, vines and the recently introduced art of raising silkworms, which provided the raw material for a nascent textile industry. ❏

accession to the throne (as Henri IV) he issued the Edict of Nantes, in 1598, which guaranteed the right of worship to Protestants.

Louis XIII and Louis XIV With the assassination of Henri IV in 1610, Louis XIII came to the throne and the influence of the French state increased under the statesmanship of Cardinal Richelieu, who further whittled away the powers of the regions. Richelieu overrode the *parlement* in Aix by imposing his own agents, the *intendants*, who collected taxes and had control over military and fiscal affairs. The *États-Généraux* (States General), having resisted contributing to the royal purse, were

❏ The Vaudois' beliefs originated with Pierre Valdo, who had founded a sect in Lyon as a reaction against the excesses of the avaricious papacy. Drawing on elements of Manichaeism (which had also been central to the Cathar heresy), they preached poverty and a rejection of the ecclesiastical hierarchy. ❏

simply banned from holding parliamentary assemblies.

Dissension continued, notably in Marseille, which rebelled in 1659: Louis XIV quickly repressed the uprising, and built the Fort St-Nicolas so he could monitor what he called '*ce peuple violent et libertin*'. In 1685 Louis XIV revoked the Edict of Nantes, and thousands of Protestants fled fearing reprisals.

Above: victims of the 1720 plague
Top: members of Louis XIV's family

Early 18th century Despite his hostility towards Marseille, Louis XIV made it a free port, and at the beginning of the 18th century it prospered on trade with the Near East. Unfortunately this also led to the third and worst outbreak of the plague in 1720, carried by a ship from the East, during which 100,000 died in Provence – 50,000 from Marseille alone, half the population of the city.

Maritime commerce also led to the creation of great wealth and the construction of some of the magnificent *hôtels particuliers* (private mansions) in Avignon, Aix and Marseille. A boom in shipbuilding (principally in Marseille, Toulon and la Ciotat) led to massive deforestation of areas such as Mont Ventoux.

■ **The upheavals of the Revolution and its aftermath were as keenly felt in Provence as they were elsewhere in France. Despite hopes to the contrary, under the First Republic ancient 'Provence' disappeared as an entity in its own right as new *départements* were created.** ■

Discontent and Revolution The decadence of the Sun King's court, followed by corruption and the abuse of privileges under Louis XV and Louis XVI, led to widespread discontent throughout France where the economic gap between rich and poor was creating hardship, unemployment and famine. Provence was no exception, particularly since the loss of the silk harvest and a steep drop in the price of wine in 1787. The following year, a heavy frost wiped out a large percentage of the olive groves in the region, and in 1789 there was widespread rioting over the price of bread. As the Bastille was being stormed in July 1789, the people of Provence followed

❏ In 1792 the *Féderés* (National Guard) from outlying regions were summoned to Paris to defend it from counter-revolutionaries. Five hundred Marseillaise marched to the capital singing Rouget de Lisle's *Hymn to the Army of the Rhine* (composed for the war against Germany several months earlier). This stirring song instantly became known as the *Marseillaise*, now France's national anthem. ❏

suit and looted and pillaged châteaux and churches. Guillotines were set up in the streets of Marseille, and aristocrats were lynched in Aix.

The aftermath The enthusiastic reception for the Revolution in Provence was partly because the Provençals hoped to regain privileges lost during the preceding centuries. Unfortunately the Jacobin-dominated National Assembly proved to be even more centralist than the *ancien régime*. In 1790, local government was dissolved and the region was divided into three *départements*: the Bouches-du-Rhône (capital, Aix and after 1800 Marseille); the Var (capital, Toulon) and the Basses-Alpes (capital, Digne). A year later the Vaucluse was created, and in 1793 the annexation of Nice led to the addition of the Alpes-Maritimes.

In the White Terror, unleashed in 1795 following the execution of Robespierre, thousands died in Provence, as elsewhere. After

Napoléon (left) brought defeat to the English fleet in Toulon (top) when it came to the aid of the Royalists

Napoléon's surprise *coup d'état* in 1799 order was restored, but Provençals showed little enthusiasm for the Napoleonic wars that followed. With the defeat of Napoléon in his Russian campaign, Provence also lost much of the Alpes-Maritimes *département* which was handed over to Sardinia at the Congress of Vienna in 1814.

A year later, Napoléon escaped from exile on Elba and marched up through Provence, before being conclusively defeated at Waterloo and sent further afield, to remote St Helena. The restoration of the Bourbons after Waterloo led to further bloodshed between royalists and republicans in Provence, but their eventual replacement on the French throne in 1830 by the 'Citizen King',

Thousands died in Provence after Robespierre's execution

Louis-Philippe, created little interest in the south, which had endured its share of civil unrest and tumult.

The 1848 Revolution Continuing discontent over harsh economic conditions led to the overthrow of Louis-Philippe and the creation of the Second Republic in 1848. This was supported in Provence, but the election of Louis-Napoléon in 1850 and his subsequent coronation as emperor was bitterly contested. Many areas, particularly in the Provençal Alps, turned once more to armed revolt. In the reprisals that followed thousands were shot or deported.

France's national flag, originally from Martigues

❏ As well as the national anthem, France also acquired its national flag from Provence during the Revolution. The red, white and blue tricolour adopted by the revolutionaries had previously been the flag of the small town of Martigues, west of Marseille. ❏

■ **Improved communications and economic growth began to transform Provence as it emerged from isolation in the 19th century. The discovery of the Riviera coastline, first by aristocratic tourists, then by writers and artists, placed it firmly on the international map. Although development was brought to a halt by two world wars, the pattern had been set for the 20th century.** ■

Rural depopulation In the second half of the 19th century the foundations were laid for profound changes in the pattern of life in Provence. Marseille rose to become France's premier port, largely due to a booming trade with the newly acquired colonies (such as Algeria) and the Far East after the opening of the Suez Canal in 1869. Traditional industries, such as sugar refining and the manufacture of 'Marseille soap', expanded alongside new activities such as shipbuilding.

Although Provence remained essentially rural in nature, increased economic activity was already starting to affect village life. Migrations to the cities began, and land was turned over, for example, to horticulture in the Var and orchards in the Rhône

❏ The arrival of the railway along the coastline in the 1860s, connecting Paris with Marseille and Italy, marked the real beginning of the winter tourist season on the Côte d'Azur. ❏

valley. Extensive vineyards were planted, although the devastating onslaught of phylloxera in the 1870s destroyed vast areas. The development of light industries signalled the end of many traditional rural activities such as silk production, tanning and dyeing.

Writers and artists Provence also witnessed a linguistic and literary revival under the auspices of the Félibrige, founded by Frédéric Mistral and a group of like-minded poets and writers in 1854. Harking back to the 'golden age' of the troubadours, the Félibrige mounted a spirited defence of Provençal culture in the face of constant erosion by the French state.

Early 20th century This saw an acceleration of demographic changes, such as rural depopulation and the arrival of immigrants from around the Mediterranean to work in the coastal cities. The economic gap between the booming coastal region and deprived inland areas increased.

A second generation of artists (amongst them Matisse, Dufy, Bonnard, Derain and Vlaminck) descended on the coast, exchanging grey northern skies for the dazzling Mediterranean light. The *belle époque* mansions of the Côte d'Azur

W Somerset Maugham, one of the post-war crowd

marked a new era in architecture, financed by the thriving tourism industry. The effects of World War I were largely felt in the north of France but conscription drained Provençal villages of their already dwindling manpower. After the war, tourism was quickly re-established and a new wave of talent (in the form of writers and *literati* such as Gertrude Stein, Anaïs Nin, Somerset Maugham, Katherine Mansfield and others) discovered the joys of the Riviera high life. Picasso and Jean Cocteau also spent time on the coast.

World War II During World War II, Provence was part of the 'free' zone controlled by the Vichy government in the south, but once the Allied counter-offensive began in 1942, the Germans marched on Marseille and Toulon. Resistance groups were particularly active in the Vaucluse and the Provençal Alps, where reprisals and deportations followed their courageous harassment of enemy forces.

Two months after the D-Day land-ings on the beaches of Normandy, the Allied forces landed on the beaches between St-Raphaël and St-Tropez. Within a month they had swept the Germans back and by 15 September most of Provence had been liberated.

Cézanne's house and studio, Aix

❑ At this time Provence's greatest artist, Paul Cézanne, was painting the landscapes around his home town of Aix or on the coast at l'Estaque near Marseille. Van Gogh came south to capture the brilliance of the southern light on canvas – and eventually to go mad and be hospitalised, first in Arles and then in St-Rémy. ❑

■ **Provence was slow to recover from World War II. With the arrival of mass tourism on the Riviera and the establishment of heavy industries near Marseille, the economy picked up, but growth was still largely confined to the coast. Mass immigrations led to the emergence of unsavoury right-wing political groups. ■**

Post-war years World War II had taken a heavy toll on the infrastructure of Provence, particularly in cities such as Toulon, Marseille and Avignon. In the Alpes-Maritimes, where there was heavy fighting, particularly along the Italian border, whole communities were devastated. Towns such as Breil, Sospel and Lantosque lost almost half their populations; Castillon lost all but 47 of its 300 inhabitants.

Recovery after the war was slow, and the task of rebuilding cities such as Marseille was jeopardised by a decline in international trade. Nice airport opened in 1946 (with flights to Paris, Brussels and Stockholm), but tourism did not pick up again until two years later, partly because the beaches had to be cleared of mines and concrete blocks put there by the Germans as obstacles to the Allied landings.

❏ The delineation of the boundaries of Provence-Alpes-Côte d'Azur (PACA) in the 1950s created one of the largest regions in France, covering over 31,000sq km, nearly 6 per cent of the country's total land mass. ❏

Expansion and growth In the 1950s work began on the *autoroute* Esterel–Côte d'Azur, and the right-wing Médecin dynasty rose to power in Nice, heralding the end of socialist politics in the south. When Algeria regained its independence in 1962, hundreds of thousands of colonists returned to France. Derisorily known as the *pieds noirs*, they brought with them racist attitudes that were fuelled by the French government's policy of encouraging immigration from North Africa.

The 1960s saw massive expansion of the petro-chemical industries around the Étang de Berre and Fos-sur-Mer, west of Marseille. Oil refineries sprang up thanks to the South European oil pipeline and huge tanker terminals were built. Coincidentally, the first marina opened in Cannes in 1964.

In inland Provence massive irrigation schemes such as the Canal de Provence and the development of hydroelectric power helped to slow the decline in the agricultural and industrial economy, although rural depopulation continued to accelerate. This trend was slowed to some extent by an influx of newcomers, artists, potters and hippies, who rebuilt old village houses in their quest for the rural idyll.

The first purpose-built ski resort, Isola 2000, opened in the 1970s in the Alpes-Maritime. Tourism on the coast, meanwhile, went into overdrive, and the fragile Mediterranean seaside became overrun with concrete. Hideous tower blocks, such as the controversial Marina Baie-des-Anges, disfigured the coast and rapidly became a byword for insensitive development on the Riviera.

❏ The population of Provence escalated dramatically in the post-war years: from 1.5 million inhabitants in 1870 it had grown to 2 million by 1950, 3 million by 1960 and nearly 4 million by 1982. Today it stands at just over 4.4 million. ❏

Originally established in 1956, the regional administration of Provence-Alpes-Côte d'Azur (PACA, which includes the Hautes-Alpes) was put on a new footing in the 1970s with the creation of the *Conseil Régional* (Regional Council), which had its first assembly in 1974. In 1982, power was decentralised to the *Conseil Général* (General Council) of each *département*, with responsibilities covering education, transport, economic development, the environment and social and cultural affairs.

In the 1980s Jean-Marie Le Pen's fascist *Front National* party started to gain a foothold in the south, swept along by a tide of anti-immigrant sen-

Top: the autoroute at Marseille
Above: a townscape (Bollène) that
reflects the changes of recent years

timents and economic recession. Its particular stronghold has been around Marseille, where roughly half of the 200,000 North African immigrant population now lives. During the 1990s, the *Front National* consolidated its hold on the region's town halls, gaining control of Orange, Toulon and Marignane in 1995 and Vitrolles (near Marseille) in 1997. The Far Right has struck a popular chord with its platform of 'immigrants out', lower taxation, and cleansing corruption on the Riviera (see page 235).

A view over Bonnieux and the Lubéron region

Vaucluse Despite being one of the smallest *départements* in France, Vaucluse can boast attractions that range from grand Roman monuments to sleepy wine villages, from the red ochre cliffs of Roussillon and Rustrel to mighty Mont Ventoux.

Mont Ventoux and the north Rising like a sentinel at the northern gateway to the Vaucluse, Mount Ventoux is the highest peak between the Alps and the Pyrenees. The ascent to the top is one of the most awesome in Provence and the views will take your breath away – sometimes almost literally, since the winds come from all directions of the compass. The *mistral*, howling down from the north, has reached record levels of 230kph at the summit. Legend has it that this is the origin of the mountain's name (from *ventour*, the Provençal for windy) but it

Lavender, sage, rosemary and thyme – the constituents of herbes de Provence – are on sale in a variety of packages and containers throughout the Vaucluse

Vaucluse truffles
'Proust conjures up Combray, its panorama and its good people. From a teacake dipped in a cup of herb tea', says the famous chef Curnonsky, 'an exiled citizen of Carpentras could call into being his native town, with its monuments and all the resources of its countryside, as in a dream, from a truffle stew'. The Vaucluse is the country's top truffle region, accounting for 74 per cent of all truffle sales in France. This highly prized fungus (known in Provence as *rabasse*) grows around the root of the downy oak, a small tree that is planted in rows in fields known as *truffières*. They are harvested from November to March and sold in the markets (usually on a Saturday morning) in Carpentras, Valréas, and, to the west, Richerenches and Grillon.

may also be that the barren limestone summit, often covered in snow, gave rise to *ven top*, meaning 'white mountain' in Celtic.

To the west of Mont Ventoux lies the jagged curtain of peaks known as the Dentelles de Montmirail, with enchanting wine villages such as Gigondas, Rasteau and Beaumes-de-Venise nestling under the flanks of the Dentelles. On the other side of the Dentelles, the town of Vaison-la-Romaine straddles the Ouvèze river. On the right bank of the Ouvèze are the remains of a prosperous Roman settlement, partly built over by the 18th-century town, which is now the heart of Vaison. On the left bank of the river, the medieval village encircles a dramatic ruined castle which further enhances the appeal of this popular spot.

Roman ruins are much in evidence in the historic town of Orange, sprawling beneath the St-Eutrope hill whose northern slopes accommodate the multiple tiers of the ancient theatre. Its magnificent backstage wall, one of the best preserved in Europe, provides a dramatic setting for summer choral performances. Orange, too, has its *arc de triomphe*, another imposing legacy from the time when the town was an important staging post on the Roman highway up through the Rhône valley to northern Gaul.

From Orange it is but a short hop to Châteauneuf-du-Pape, rising amidst a sea of vineyards which produce the full-bodied Rhône wines that have earned this small village an international reputation.

Avignon and the plateau de Vaucluse Heading south again, Avignon presents an unpromising façade, girded by industrial suburbs – unless you arrive by river steamer (as did Dickens and Robert Browning) and witness the ramparts, with the Palais des Papes rising behind them like a medieval tableau. Within the ramparts is a different city, a feisty, lively place infused with cultural riches during the summer season and always full of fascination. Even if some are disappointed by the famous bridge, no one can fail to be awed by the Palais des Papes, part-church, part-fortress, and undoubtedly one of the most extensive feudal castles in the world.

Across the river Villeneuve-lès-Avignon has considerable charm, as does the attractive town of l'Isle-sur-la-Sorgue further to the east of Avignon. The river which runs through it rises at Fontaine-de-Vaucluse on the edge of the Vaucluse plateau. The funnel-shaped cavern out of which the spring rises lies at the foot of towering cliffs over 200m high, with the river running down a beautiful valley through the village and on down to the Rhône. The site was originally known as *Vallis Clausa* ('the closed valley'), which later became Vaucluse and eventually gave its name to the entire *département*.

This enchanted valley cast a spell on the great humanist poet Petrarch, but to experience it as he did you would be wise to avoid the peak summer months, especially as the source itself is at its most dramatic out of the main tourist season, during the winter and spring.

Fluorescent traces added to rivers far away have shown the source has a huge catchment area, covering over 120sq km from Mont Ventoux to the eastern extremes of the Vaucluse plateau.

On the southern escarpment of the plateau, to the east of the *fontaine*, the village of Gordes is perched some 300m above the Coulon valley in a spectacular setting that also attracts considerable crowds. Hidden away behind the village in a lavender-scented valley is the 12th-century Abbaye de Sénanque, whose pure silhouette, stripped down to the essentials, echoes the spirituality of the Cistercian monks who built it.

Another way of life, another bewitching testament to the past, is reflected in the remarkable Village des Bories behind Gordes. In Provence there are at least 5,000–6,000 *bories* (drystone huts), the majority of which are in the Vaucluse.

The Lubéron And so to the Lubéron, where the conversion of old houses has turned this corner of Provence into one of the most fashionable addresses for foreigners and Parisians. No matter, since there are still many wild and unspoilt corners, secret valleys and lovely villages to be explored. Most of the region is part of the Parc Naturel Régional du Lubéron.

On the southern flanks of the Lubéron the vegetation becomes more Mediterranean in character, hinting at the coastal hinterlands which start below the Durance, the natural boundary that marks the southernmost extent of the Vaucluse.

Some of the drystone huts in the extraordinary Village des Bories near Gordes. The reason for their construction is still debated

47

The Sabran family home, commanding the hilltop above Ansouis village

▶▶ **Ansouis** 45C1

Ansouis is built on a rocky spur dominated by the castle keep of the **Château de Sabran**▶▶ (*Open* afternoons except Tue in winter. *Admission charge*), home of the Sabran family for the last 800 years. From the north the château displays an impregnable exterior – part of the original fortress – but, as you circle it, it changes to reveal an 18th-century mansion façade with gardens and terraces shaded by chestnut trees. The interior of the château is furnished in a way that reflects this dual identity: the ground floor displays a collection of arms and armour, whilst upstairs Flemish tapestries and Italian Renaissance furniture predominate. From the first floor balcony you get a good overview of the elegant garden (no visits). The 18th-century Provençal kitchen (still in use today) features several very fine handcrafted pieces.

Adjoining the château, the church of St Martin contains busts of St Delphine and St Elzéar (see panel).

Down at the end of the village, veteran diver Georges Mazoyer has assembled his **Musée Extraordinaire**▶ (*Open* afternoons. *Admission charge*) featuring minerals, fossils, shells and paintings of underwater life, and a little 'Blue Grotto' built into the vaults.

▶ **Apt** 45C2

A busy market town proclaiming itself not only capital of the Lubéron but also world capital of crystallised fruits, Apt has been a prosperous urban centre since Roman times.

Its principal monument is the old **Cathédrale Ste-Anne**▶ (*Closed* Mon. Guided tours Jul–Sep, Mon–Sat 11am and 5pm, Sun 11am), famous for its ancient crypt, on two levels, which is said to house the bones of Ste Anne. The saint is depicted in a fine set of 14th-century stained-glass windows at the end of the apse; her shroud is displayed amongst the reliquaries in the *trésor*.

Next door to the church is the 16th-century **Tour de l'Horloge**, which straddles the rue des Marchands: on Saturday mornings this old shopping street and all the neighbouring thoroughfares overflow with the stalls of Apt's lively **market**. Other sights include the **Musée Archéologique** (*Open* daily except Tue and Sun) and the **Maison du Pays du Lubéron**▶ (*Closed* Sun all year, Sat afternoon in winter), which houses an information centre, a palaeontology museum (*Admission charge*) geared towards children, and a bookshop.

A celebrated celibate couple

In 1298 Charles II of Naples hatched a plan to unite two grand families loyal to his cause by arranging the marriage of Elzéar de Sabran to Delphine de Signes. Unfortunately Delphine, brought up in a convent, had already taken a vow of chastity and would go ahead only on the basis that Elzéar took a similar pledge – which he duly did. They maintained this virtuous relationship until Elzéar died. Delphine survived another 37 years, living a life of poverty and devoting herself to good works, with many visions and miraculous healings attributed to her. Both were later made saints.

Protecting the Lubéron

■ **Created in 1977, the Parc Naturel Régional du Lubéron now covers around 140,000ha in the Vaucluse and the Alpes de Haute Provence. The greater part of it lies in the Vaucluse.** ■

The natural setting Between Manosque and Cavaillon the Durance river, flowing westwards towards the Rhône, takes a mighty loop within which the Lubéron range lies. Stretching 65km from east to west, the mountains are divided in two by a wooded valley, the *combe de Lourmarin*. To the west is the Petit Lubéron, whilst to the east the Grand Lubéron reaches its summit of over 1,000m at the Mourre Nègre.

One of the most striking features of the Lubéron *massif* is the contrast: to the south, the rich agricultural land sloping gently down to the Durance is characteristically Mediterranean; to the north the steep ravines and abrupt cliff faces are cooler and forested with downy oaks.

Wildlife The variety of natural features in the Lubéron has created a species-rich environment where plants such as the fragrant Etruscan honeysuckle, aspic lavender and downy rockroses thrive. Predators that have all but disappeared in the rest of Europe – such as Bonelli's eagle, the white Egyptian vulture, the eagle owl and the migratory eagle Circàete Jean Le Blanc – retain a precarious foothold here.

The human impact The most startling evidence of early habitation are the curious *bories*, or drystone huts, which can be seen dotted about the countryside. Although some were built as recently as the 18th century, many date back to the Iron Age.

The Middle Ages left the Lubéron with numerous *villages perchés* (perched villages), strategically positioned high above the valley floors. Surrounded by an intricate network of cultivated land, many of these villages (particularly those on the northern slopes) went into a decline with the changing agricultural patterns of the last century.

Revitalised in the 1950s by a large influx of Bohemians and artists who rebuilt many ruined houses, the enchanting Lubéron villages now face a new threat to their identity, that of being totally swamped by tourism.

On the mule train
Walking tours off the beaten track, through some of the most evocative scenery in the Parc Naturel Régional du Lubéron, are organised in conjunction with the *Maison du Parc* in the *Voyages au Naturel* programme. Your luggage is transported by mule on these seven-day tours, which take place from April through to October. Contact the Lubéron Regional Park, tel: 04 90 74 08 55.

49

Living projects
As well as conducting scientific studies on the natural environment and publishing information for visitors, the *Maison du Parc* (which administers the park from Apt) carries out restoration projects in rural areas and has created nature trails and other attractions. In particular, you can visit the Sentier du Conservatoire des Terrasses en Culture (Open Air Terrace Museum) at Goult (see page 75), the botanic trail through the Forêt des Cèdres (near Bonnieux), and the Sentier des Ocres (Ochre Trail) at Roussillon (see page 83).

Top: rockroses
Left: unmistakable but rarely seen, the white Egyptian vulture

Drive Grand Lubéron

This drive encompasses one of the most beautiful valleys in the Lubéron as well as the principal châteaux of the Sud-Lubéron, before traversing the *massif* to return to Apt. Around 80km, but allow all day if you plan to visit the châteaux or walk up to the Fort de Buoux.

From Apt, take the D113 to the tiny hamlet of Buoux, which is surrounded by fields of lavender. Continue past here and the road descends further into the wild and beautiful **Vallon de l'Aigue Brun▶▶**. The **Fort de Buoux▶▶**, reached via a steep footpath, commands a magnificent view of the Vallon de l'Aigue Brun – hence its strategic importance, since this was once the main pass across the Lubéron. First occupied by the Ligurians, then the Romans, the site was fortified in the 13th century.

Back on the D113, the elegant belltower of the 12th-century **Prieuré de St-Symphorien** (not open to visitors) rises above the tree-tops on your left.

Follow the D943 through the *combe de Lourmarin* until you come to **Lourmarin▶** itself at the mouth of the valley. This lively town was once the home of Albert Camus, who moved here after winning the Nobel Prize for Literature in 1957 and is buried in the cemetery. On the edge of the town is the imposing **Château de Lourmarin▶▶** (*Open* daily. *Admission charge*). The older part of the château was built between 1495 and 1525, whilst the 'new' part was begun in 1540.

Abandoned in the 19th century, the château was salvaged in the 1920s by a wealthy Lyonnais industrialist, Robert Laurent-Vibert, who hired a team of 40 artisans for the four years which it took to complete the restoration. At his untimely death in 1925 the château was bequeathed to the Academy of Arts, Agriculture, Science and Belles Lettres at Aix, and a foundation set up to encourage talented young French people. The older part now houses an arts library and accommodation. The Renaissance wing contains a collection of old Provençal and Spanish furniture as well as souvenirs from Laurent-Vibert's travels in Egypt, Indonesia, Morocco and Russia.

Leaving Lourmarin behind, take the D27 and then the D135 to Ansouis (see page 48), passing through the Côtes du Lubéron vineyards flanking the foothills of the Lubéron *massif*. From Ansouis, take the D56 and then follow signs to la Tour-d'Aigues. In the middle of this large market town is one of the most astonishing Renaissance ruins in Provence: the remains of the **Château de la Tour-d'Aigues►►**, built in the latter half of the 16th century. Early engravings show it to have been a hugely ambitious palace.

The southern slopes of the Lubéron massif, *overlooking the Durance valley*

In 1780 it was badly damaged by fire, and then finally torched during the Revolution in 1792. Now, the ruins accentuate the dimensions and make a spectacular backdrop for the performances held here as part of the Sud-Lubéron Summer Festival. The cellars of the château contain several exhibitions (*Open* daily; closed Tue afternoons and Sat and Sun mornings. *Admission charge*) including the **Musée du Pays d'Aigues** and the **Musée des Faïences.**

From la Tour-d'Aigues follow the D956 towards la Bastide-des-Jourdans and turn left on the D216 for the sleepy hamlet of Vitrolles. The road then becomes the D33 as it winds up over a pass in the Grand Lubéron and then down to the old Roman village of Céreste. In contrast to the valley of the Aigue Brun, the mountain here is cloaked in *garrigue* scrub and oak forests. Return along the N100 to Apt.

VAUCLUSE

The Avignon Festival
Founded as a drama festival in 1947 by Jean Villar, in 1967 the festival brief was widened to include cinema, music and dance, and at the same time fringe events (*le festival off*) became increasingly popular. Today, around 120,000 people descend on Avignon for this sell-out arts extravaganza, which takes place from mid-July onwards for one month. For details contact the Bureau de Festival d'Avignon, 8 bis rue de Mons, 84000 Avignon (tel: 04 90 82 67 08).

Standing forlornly on the last remaining arches of Avignon's famous bridge, the Chapelle St-Nicolas is part-Romanesque, part-Gothic

►►► Avignon   44A2

Introduction Avignon has always evoked extreme reactions from visitors. On the one hand it is a major centre for art and culture, a lively, innovative city, which over the centuries served as a channel for the influence of the Italian Renaissance on the rest of France, nurtured the Provençal literary group the Félibrige, and gave birth to one of the country's most celebrated cultural events, the annual Festival of Dramatic Arts. It is an inevitable 'must see' on every tourist itinerary.

On the other hand Avignon has never been a likeable city, provoking detestation from many a traveller since medieval times. Petrarch called it a living hell, 'the sewers of the earth'; Henry James loathed it at first sight, and Lawrence Durrell railed against it in his novel *Monsieur*. In the summer months the place is full of outsiders who flock here to mine the gold dust of tourism with no care for the city and its rich heritage.

And yet, unlovable though it may be, Avignon has a magnetism that was recognised long ago in the Provençal proverb, '*Quau se lèvo d'Avignoun, se lèvo de la resoun*' ('He who takes leave of Avignon takes leave of his senses').

The Rocher des Doms, overlooking the confluence of the rivers Rhône and the Durance, was occupied in neolithic times but, despite flourishing as a river port, the settlement was eclipsed by Arles and Nîmes in the Roman period and sank into relative obscurity. By the 12th century it had grown into a large town and, surrounded as it was by feuding baronies, Avignon declared itself a sovereign state and ruled its own affairs. The first ramparts were erected and trade prospered largely thanks to the rebuilding of the bridge over the Rhône, which was then the only route between Italy and Spain up-river from the sea.

Avignon made a strategic mistake in allying itself with the Albigensians (followers of the heretical Cathar sect) in the 13th century, as a consequence of which Louis VIII razed the city in 1226 and pulled down its defences. However, it was also as a result of the Albigensian Crusade that the papacy acquired a large slice of Provençal territory which became known as the Comtat Venaissin.

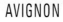

Trompe-l'oeil
*paintings on the east
side of the place de
l'Horloge depict
scenes from the
city's past*

53

The papal court decamped *en masse* to Avignon in 1309 and stayed for the next 100 years or so.

Avignon in this period was a thriving city of between 30,000 and 40,000 people, a large proportion of whom were under holy orders in the numerous convents, churches and chapels that had been built. The university, founded in 1303, housed thousands of students, and the best Sienese artists were summoned to embellish the pontifical palaces. The city became a refuge for exiles – including a sizeable Jewish community – but its open doors also attracted criminal outcasts and adventurers, and the city's name became a byword for filth, debauchery, overcrowding and vice. The Italians, envious of the loss of the wealthy papal court, declared it the 'second Babylonian Captivity'.

In 1377 St Catherine of Siena persuaded the seventh pope, Gregory XI, to return to Rome, where he fell sick and died. The Italian cardinals seized the chance and forcibly elected an Italian pope, but when the French cardinals returned to Avignon they elected another pope, Clement VII, thus setting off the Great Schism, which saw pope and anti-pope struggle for supremacy and control of the Church's income for the next 40 years.

After this issue was finally resolved with the election of Martin V in 1417, Avignon remained papal property and was ruled by the cardinal legates until 1791, when the Comtat Venaissin became part of France during the Revolution.

Before the Revolution, Avignon had been an important publishing centre, thanks to freedom from French censorship laws, and the printing presses continued to roll through the 1800s, helping to foster the growth of the nascent Félibrige movement (see pages 60–1). Its cultural influence was firmly re-established in recent times with the creation in 1947 of the annual Avignon Festival.

*The many steeples
defining Avignon's
skyline led Rabelais
to call it* la ville
sonnante – *the
ringing city*

Walk Avignon

Around the periphery of the town centre there are numerous interesting back streets with fine old mansions, churches and other sights. Allow 2–3 hours for this circular walk from place de l'Horloge.

From place de l'Horloge, head west towards rue St-Étienne. At the beginning of this street are some of the few Roman relics from early Avignon, stone blocks dug up from what was the place du Forum (now place de l'Horloge) and part of a Roman arcade. At No 18, the ironwork balconies of the house are discreetly embellished with balloons to mark the spot where Joseph de Montgolfier invented the hot-air balloon.

Follow the street down to place Crillon, where the lovely façade of the old **La Théâtre Comédie**►► (built in 1734, restored in 1979) faces the Porte de l'Oulle. Take a small passageway (rue Mazan, beside the theatre) to reach rue Joseph Vernet. Along the street there are several impressive 18th-century façades, as well as the **Chapelle de l'Oratoire** (now an exhibition centre), the **Musée Calvet** (see page 58) and the **Musée Requien** (see page 58).

Cross over the cours Jean-Jaurès into rue Henri Fabre. Continue down the rue des Lices, where, on your left, is the immense, unusual **Almône Générale**► (General Almshouse), built between 1546 and 1557. Only the central portion remains, a three-storey arcade with a fine sundial (1789) on the top floor. The building is now part of the neighbouring École des Beaux Arts.

Turn right into the **rue des Teinturiers**►►, one of Avignon's oldest and most picturesque streets. Immediately on your right is the remains of the Chapelle des Cordeliers. Just past here is the **Chapelle des Pénitents Gris**►. Towards the end of the street are several derelict water-wheels which powered the textile factories after

Carved panel, Église St-Pierre doors

which it is named. Retrace your steps and turn left into rue de la Masse, then into rue du Roi René. On the left is the **Chapelle Ste-Claire**, supposedly the location of the first meeting between Petrarch and Laura (see panel on page 58). Towards the end of rue du Roi René there is a cluster of lovely old mansions, including the **Hôtel d'Honorati de Jonquerettes** (No 12), the **Hôtel Fortia de Montreal** (Nos 8 and 10) and the elegant Italianate **Hôtel Berton de Crillon** (No 7).

Backtrack briefly and turn down rue Collège de la Croix; cross two pedestrianised shopping streets through the arches of rue Bernheim-Lyon, to arrive at place Jerusalem. This was the heart of the old Jewish ghetto, once encircled by walls, although now only the synagogue remains. Just beyond here, place Carnot is dominated by the Gothic façade of the **Église St-Pierre►**; the magnificent carved walnut doors date from 1551.

Hidden away behind the church (take the alleyway leading off from the beginning of rue des Sciseaux d'Or) is the **Musée Théodore Aubanel►** (*Open* by appointment), which celebrates the life and times of one of the leading lights in the Félibrige: the museum houses a collection of old printing equipment and a number of rare documents and first editions.

Continue down rue Banastèrie until you reach the **Chapelle des Pénitents Noir ►►**. Nestling incongruously alongside the walls of Avignon's present-day prison, the delightful baroque façade is ornamented with a relief showing cherubs holding the head of John the Baptist, encircled by rays of sunshine piercing through the clouds.

Take rue Migrenier and then a series of steps which lead up to the **Rocher des Doms►►**, one of the most peaceful parks in the city, scattered about with fountains and statues – and a sundial that tells the time by your shadow. From the belvedere, there are views across the Rhône to Villeneuve-lès-Avignon.

Steps lead back down the other side of the park past the Palais des Papes to place de l'Horloge.

Fountain, Rocher des Doms

55

VAUCLUSE

The shepherd boy's bridge
In 1177 a shepherd boy called Bénézet was told by a voice from the sky to leave his sheep and go and build a bridge over the Rhône. Initially hesitant, Bénézet set off for Avignon with an angel disguised as a pilgrim. The bishop laughed at him, and sent him to the provost who, equally derisory, told him that if he could lift a huge stone he could build the bridge. This Bénézet did, hefting it down to the river bank. The awestruck crowd started donating money for the bridge. It was completed in 1185.

56

Decorative panelling brightens up the antique carousel in place de l'Horloge

What to see The central core of Avignon lies within its 14th-century walls, although this represents just a small part of the city which sprawls several kilometres eastwards towards the *autoroute de soleil*. The walls are over 4km long but unfortunately only one small section of the rampart (adjacent to the Porte du Rhône) is accessible.

Projecting from the city wall by the Porte du Rhône is one of Avignon's most photographed landmarks, the **Pont St-Bénézet**►► (*Open* daily. *Admission charge*). On the second pier, the Chapelle St-Nicolas is part Romanesque, part Gothic. Since it was first built, the bridge has been swept away several times by the Rhône; in the 17th century the Avignonais finally abandoned it to fate.

At the heart of the city is the **place de l'Horloge**►, a huge square shaded by plane trees and overrun with cafés. Towards late afternoon it comes alive with a pageant of buskers, jugglers and portrait painters. An antique carousel spins round in front of the **Hôtel de Ville** whose clock tower gave the square its name.

To the south of place de l'Horloge is the **Église St-Agricol**► (not open for visits), the oldest church in Avignon after the cathedral.

North of place de l'Horloge is the **place du Palais**►, once a densely populated area which was cleared on the orders of Benedict XII who feared that his enemies would be able to sneak up to the palace walls through the houses.

Looming above the square is the gigantic **Palais des Papes**►►► (*Open* daily; guided tours in English available. *Admission charge*). Inside this veritable fortress there is a maze of rooms, galleries, passageways and chapels; pillaged of all its furnishings during the Revolution, you have to use a great deal of imagination to envisage the decadent, luxurious lifestyle that went on inside. In 1810 it was converted into a barracks and the soldiers hacked off many of the murals to sell to collectors. Turned over to the Historic Monuments Board in 1906, it has been under restoration ever since.

Passing through the reception area in the old guardroom, you emerge into the Courtyard of Honour. On the left is Benedict XII's austere, military-style Vieux Palais and, on the right, Clement VI's Gothic-style Palais Neuf.

The usual route through the building goes first to the Consistory Hall in the Vieux Palais, where ambassadors and dignitaries were received. The original frescoes were destroyed by a fire in 1413 and replaced with fragments of Simone Martini's frescoes (dated c.1340) from the Cathedral porch. Portraits of the nine popes line one of the walls. Leading off this room is the Chapelle St-Jean, with frescoes by Matteo Giovanetti (painted 1346–8). On the floor above is the Grand Tinel, or banqueting hall, a huge, 45m-long room with beautifully restored panelling in the shape of an inverted ship's keel on the ceiling.

Past here is the papal Antechamber, hung with Gobelin tapestries, and then the papal Bedchamber, decorated with murals. Through here you come to one of the loveliest rooms in the palace, the Chambre du Cerf, which was the pope's private study. The delightful frescoes depict scenes of hunting and fishing against a panorama of the forest that encircles the room: most likely painted by Giovanetti, the frescoes were commissioned by Clement VI. From here the route leads through to the Grand Chapelle (or Chapelle Clementine), bigger even than the banqueting hall.

At the top end of the place du Palais is the **Musée du Petit Palais**▶▶▶ (*Closed* Tue. *Admission charge*). Once a cardinal's residence, it was converted in 1958 to house two important collections – medieval works formerly in the Calvet Museum and those from the Campana collection in the Louvre. The former consist of 600 sculptures and around 60 paintings, including important works by the 15th-century Avignon school, particularly the Requien Altarpiece by Enguerrand Quarton. The most important works, however, are the 13th–16th-century Italian paintings from the Campana collection.

Busy outdoor cafés overflow into the place de l'Horloge

Beneath the bridge
Only four of the 22 original arches remain of the bridge that is immortalised in a popular song as the Pont d'Avignon. The bridge once spanned two branches of the Rhône (and the île de la Barthelasse between them) to connect with Villeneuve-lès-Avignon. Although the song as it has come down to us celebrates dancing '*sur le pont*', in reality it was '*sous*' (beneath) the bridge on the island, where there were once dance halls.

Dragons and eagles on the façade of the Hôtel des Monnaies come from the coat of arms of Cardinal Borghèse, who built it in 1619

The myth of Laura
Petrarch was born in Arezzo but his family was exiled in 1302 and eventually came to Avignon in 1314. It was outside the Chapelle Ste-Claire in 1327 that he first caught sight of Laura, who was to become his muse for the next 15 years: he continued to pour his heart out long after she died in 1348. Laura was Laure de Noves, who was already married to Hugo de Sade at the time Petrarch met her.

Next to the palace is the **Cathédrale Notre-Dame-des-Doms►**, built between 1140 and 1160 but added to many times since. Worth noting in the interior is the Romanesque dome and the splendid Tomb of John XXII attributed to the English sculptor Hugh Wilfred. Opposite the Palais des Papes is the **Hôtel des Monnaies►** (the old mint, now the music conservatory), which boasts a flamboyant 17th-century façade.

Avignon has a number of other museums, displaying some engrossing exhibits. Housed in one of the grandest mansions of the city at 65 rue Joseph Vernet is the **Musée Calvet►►** (*Closed* Tue. *Admission charge*) – its remarkably wide-ranging collection encompasses everything from Egyptian mummies to tapestries, wrought-iron work, Greek and Roman vases, and Dutch, French, Italian and Flemish paintings spanning the 16th to the 19th centuries.

In comparison, there is a strong Provençal theme to the exhibits in the **Palais du Roure►►** (*Open* Mon–Fri. *Admission free*). Built in 1469 on the site of an old tavern, the mansion belonged to the Baroncelli family and from 1891 to 1899 Baron Folco de Baroncelli-Javon worked here with Mistral, editing their Provençal journal, *L' Aïoli* (see page 61).

It now houses a centre for Provençal studies and a large collection of Provençal costumes, *santons* and antique furnishings.

Some superb examples of Provençal *faïence* and 18th-century furniture are on display in the **Musée Louis Vouland►** (*Open* Tue–Sat. *Admission charge*). Finally, there is the **Musée Requien** (*Open* Tue–Sat), which houses a small natural history collection, and the **Musée Lapidaire** (*Closed* Tue. *Admission charge*), with sculptures and stone carvings across the centuries housed inside the 17th-century chapel of a former Jesuit College.

Just over the river from Avignon is the town of **Villeneuve-lès-Avignon►►**. In the 14th century the cardinals at the papal court built themselves houses here to escape the noise and bustle of Avignon; it still maintains a peaceful, village-like atmosphere and has several interesting and worthwhile places to visit. Foremost amongst these is the **Chartreuse du Val-de-Benediction▶▶▶** (*Open* daily. *Admission charge*), which was the largest and most important Carthusian monastery in France until the Revolution, when art treasures were sold off and the outlying properties taken over by homeless families.

Since the beginning of this century the buildings have been gradually repurchased and restored. Of its former treasures, all that remains are the 14th-century frescoes by Matteo Giovanetti in the refectory chapel. Also worth noting is the ornate tomb of Innocent VI in the church. In 1973 parts of the monastery were taken over by the *Centre International de Recherche de Création et Animation* (CIRCA), which promotes a wide range of contemporary artistic and cultural activities, with workshops and exhibitions all year round (*Open* daily).

On the hill above the Chartreuse is the **Fort St-André▶**, a massive citadel flanked by watch towers. Inside the twin-turreted gateway there are a series of vaulted barrack rooms, including one with a bread oven so that the soldiers could withstand a long siege without missing their *baguettes*.

On the right of the gateway are the ruins of the **abbey of St-André**, destroyed during the Revolution and now a private residence with lovely Italianate gardens. Apart from the small Romanesque chapel of **Notre-Dame-de-Belvezet** on the west side, most of the rest of the fort's interior is a jumble of ruined houses (the old village of St-André), but from several vantage points there are fine views of Avignon, Mont Ventoux and the Rhône Valley.

A similar panorama unfolds from the top of the 39m-high **Tour Philippe le Bel▶** (*Closed* Tue and Feb. *Admission charge*), also built to keep watch on Avignon and to protect the French end of the Pont-St-Bénézet.

In the town centre, the **Église Notre Dame▶** has a well-conserved cloister (now used as a summer festival venue) and once housed a superb 14th-century *Madonna and Child* carved out of ivory: this rare work – and many others – now resides in the nearby **Musée Municipal▶▶** (*Open* daily. *Admission charge*).

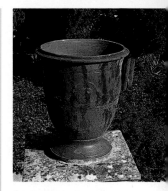

An ancient vase provides a focal point in the lovely gardens of the abbey of St-André

The cowboy baron
The eccentric Marquis Folco Baroncelli-Javon left his native city of Avignon in 1890 to lead the life of a *gardian* in the Camargue. In 1905 he went to Paris to see Buffalo Bill Cody's Wild West Show, and invited Cody and his American Indian companions down to the Camargue. The Indians pitched their wigwams around Baroncelli's home and a lassoing competition took place between Buffalo Bill's cowboys and the *gardians*. Some of the gifts that the Indians gave Baroncelli can be seen in the Musée Baroncelli in les Stes-Maries-de-la-Mer.

Cypresses and pines protect the elegant rose parterre in the St-André gardens

■ **You can't go far in Provence without coming across the name of Frédéric Mistral, the region's most famous poet. Plaques inscribed with his verses are found everywhere from remote beauty spots to bustling town centres, and many a street or park is named in his honour. But Mistral was more than just a poet; he helped spark off what was to become a major revival of Provençal language and literature in the 18th century. ■**

The patrician figure of Frédéric Mistral at the age of 76, pictured with his family

Close to home
'Frédéric Mistral neither sought nor wished for metropolitan success, and was content to spend his long life quietly and happily in Provence, in the very village community in which he had been born. Occasionally he would visit Paris but Mistral was not happy away from Provence, and there he lived out his dedicated life...there are few lives of great writers, perhaps few recorded lives of human beings, as fortunate and enviable as that of Frédéric Mistral, voluntarily circumscribed within the limits of the halcyon landscape into which he had the superlative good fortune to be born.' James Pope-Hennessy, *Aspects of Provence*

Mistral was the only poet in a minority language ever to be awarded the Nobel Prize

Early talent Frédéric Mistral was born on 8 September 1830 in the Mas de la Juge, his parents' farm just outside the village of Maillane near St-Rémy-de-Provence. He went to school at the abbey of St-Michel-de-Frigolet and then in Avignon, where his interest in his native language (his mother was a Provençal speaker) was awakened by Joseph Roumanille.

After finishing law studies in Aix, Mistral moved back to Maillane to help his father with the farm and devote himself to poetry. At the age of 21 he had already embarked on what was to become his most famous work, the epic poem *Miréio*.

The founding of the Félibrige Soon afterwards he joined together with a group of like-minded poets to form the Félibrige, an association dedicated to the rebirth of Provençal (the name itself comes from *félibre*, meaning doctor, although why they chose this name remains a mystery). The seven (Roumanille, Mistral, Brunet, Giera, Aubanel, Mathieu and Tavan) had their first meeting in the Château Fort-Segugne on 21 May 1854. A year later Roumanille and Mistral launched the annual *Armanan*

CALENDAU (CANT SETÈN)

AQUELO NESCO S'ENCAFOURNO
DINS UNE COUMBO AREBRO E SOURNO
E VEN PIÈI UN MOUMEN QUE LA ROCO SUBRA
S'ENARCO AMOUNT QU'ES PAS DE DIRE
VOUS PARLE DOU ROUCAS DOU CIRE:
NI CAT NI CABRO NI SATIRE
N'EN RESPONDE SEGUR JAMAI L'ESCALARAN

F. MISTRAL

CENTENARI DE CALENDAU
1866 · 1966
LOU'S I LOU MUNICIPE DE SAUT
E LI FELIBRE

Provençau, the first journal to be written in Provençal.

Mistral's cause was helped enormously by the publication in 1859 of *Miréio*, which made him instantly famous. This tragic poem tells the story of a beautiful young girl who falls in love with a man whom her parents consider unsuitable; she runs away to seek help from the Holy Marys at les Stes-Maries-de-la-Mer in the Camargue but dies on the beach from a broken heart.

By now established as the region's greatest writer, Mistral began work on a monumental encyclopedia, *Le Trésor de la Félibrige*, which was to become the most important reference work on Provençal culture ever published. He also published the second of his major epics, *Calendau*, which tells the story of a young fisherman from la Ciotat who falls in love with a water-nymph. In 1876 Mistral married and moved into a house opposite his mother's in Maillane (where he lived until his death in 1914).

In the 1890s Mistral and the Félibrige founded a museum in Arles devoted to Provençal arts and culture (the Museon Arletan) and started a new, more popular journal called *L'Aïoli*. In 1904 he became one of the first recipients of the Nobel Prize for Literature.

Provençal revival The romanticism and nostalgia of the Félibrige for the chivalrous days of the troubadours was embodied in their poetry and their impassioned defence of a lifestyle which they saw being gradually eroded by progress and the imposition of the French language by the central state in Paris.

The greatest achievement of the Félibrige was to create a huge revival of interest in Provençal traditions, legends and folklore, which has ensured their continuance today. Their greatest failing was never to engage on the political level (unlike their cousins the Basques) and thus to allow 'Occitania' to be eventually eclipsed by French culture.

Mistral has been almost deified by his admirers since his death; when he was alive he attended the unveiling of a bronze statue of himself in the Forum at Arles. Showing that his feet were still firmly planted on the ground despite the veneration bestowed on him, Mistral commented that the statue looked like a passenger waiting for a train to come into the station. 'All he needs is a suitcase!' said the man who will always be remembered with honour and gratitude in Provence.

The countryside
'There are gardens of beans, orchards with apples, pears and peaches, cherry trees that catch your eye, fig trees that offer you their ripe figs, round-bellied melons that beg to be eaten, and beautiful vines with bunches of golden grapes – ah, I can almost see them!' *The Memoirs of Frédéric Mistral*

Mistral, aged 62, soon after he began his Provençal journal, L'Aïoli

VAUCLUSE

Muscat Festival
The best time to visit
Beaumes is during the
annual Wine Festival
(July/August), when all the
local vineyards set up
stalls at various points
around the village and
everybody wanders, glass
in hand, happily trying out
one after the other. To
soak it all up, other stalls
sell goats' cheeses, *foie
gras* pâté, and local
specialities such as melon
with Muscat or melon
sorbet with Muscat.

Built on the site of an ancient priory, St-Martin dates from the 11th century

▶▶ **Barry** 44A4

This extraordinary cave-village is one of the best pre-served in Provence. From the parking area, a track leads past a series of houses that look as though someone has slapped the front half of a stone cottage onto a cave dwelling: which is exactly what did happen, since the inhabitants didn't need to build a whole house, or even a roof, and simply adapted the caves to their needs by carving most of the internal rooms out of the rock-face.

Nevertheless, they were at constant risk from rock-slides. After several villagers had been killed in the 19th century, the entire population abandoned Barry and moved down the hill to St-Pierre on the plain.

▶ **Beaumes-de-Venise** 44B3

Best known for the subtly flavoured Muscat wines that bear its name, Beaumes has been producing this nectar since the Middle Ages – the Popes at Avignon owned a 70ha vineyard here in the 14th century and Anne of Austria, visiting in 1660, presented the church with a set of liturgical vestments in recognition of the villagers' wine-making skills.

Built around a rocky cliff at the southern flank of the Dentelles range, Beaumes-de-Venise is named after the grottos that dot the hillside where the first inhabitants lived (the Provençal word for grotto is '*baume*'). The suffix 'de-Venise' refers to the fact that the village was part of the ancient territory of the Comtat Venaissin.

Above the village, the ruins of the 12th-century **château** loom over the ancient streets. These are now private property, but follow the Grand Rue up through the village to come across some of the old grottos which riddle the rocks beneath the castle walls.

Bollène 44A3

This unassuming town has grown rapidly from a mere market garden centre to a major conurbation with the development of the nuclear facilities on the nearby Donzére-Mondragon canal. Climb up to the viewpoint next to the parish church of St-Martin and this huge industrial conglomeration is all too easily visible to the north of town. Beyond the church is a park dedicated to Louis

Pasteur, who discovered an inoculation against swine fever whilst staying here (in a house on avenue Pasteur) in 1882.

Hidden away down the back streets in the rue de St Sacrament is the excellent **Centre de Documentation Provençale** (*Open* Sat afternoons or by appointment; tel: 04 90 30 41 39), which has over 1,800 works on every aspect of Provençal life as well as tapes, records and books for sale.

The River Lez, which runs through the town, has not been kind to Bollène. In 1413 the river broke its banks and destroyed the town's main bridge, the Chapel Notre-Dame du Pont alongside, and drowned quite a few people. The chapel and bridge were rebuilt, only to be swept away again in 1745. Bollène was again seriously flooded in 1951, and in 1993 water levels reached a record 2.5m in the streets.

▶▶   Bonnieux   45C1

Hugging the northern flank of the Lubéron, Bonnieux is a large and lively terraced village which rises up steeply towards the 12th-century church and cemetery at its summit. From the terrace surrounding the church there are sweeping views across the valley and neighbouring *villages perchés*.

Half-way up Bonnieux's main street, rue de la République, an ancient bakery has been converted into the unusual **Musée de la Boulangerie▶** (*Open* daily except Tue; closed Jan–Mar. *Admission charge*). The museum covers just about everything there is to know about bread-making from harvesting the wheat onwards.

Just near Bonnieux on the D149 heading northwards is the **Pont Julien▶▶**, one of the best-preserved Roman bridges in Provence. The triple-arched bridge was probably built around 300 BC and named after the nearby town of *Apta Julia* (now Apt).

▓▓▓▓   Buoux   45C1

See page 50

The inhabitants of this troglodyte village at Barry made their living smuggling salt and matches into neighbouring Dauphiné during the 18th century

An ancient bread oven in the Musée de la Boulangerie at Bonnieux

Characteristic blue-and-white faïences, *which contained herbal remedies, in the old pharmacy of Carpentras's Hôtel-Dieu*

Carpentras's patron saint

The patron saint of Carpentras is St Siffrein (after whom the cathedral is named), who was thought to be a monk from the Ile des Lerins, sent by the abbot to evangelise in Venasque (12km to the south of Carpentras) in the 6th century BC. He died in Venasque but since no one is sure of the date, his saint's day was set on 12 July, which was the anniversary of his remains being moved to Carpentras in AD 980. This was later changed to 27 November to coincide with a major pilgrimage and fair, inaugurated in 1525 (and still celebrated today). St Siffrein was famed for healing possessed souls, and legend has it that his mystical powers reached out from beyond the grave. His tomb was robbed and his robes stolen, but as the thieves set out on the road to Carpentras they were suddenly struck blind and forced to abandon their spoils.

► ► **Carpentras** *44B2*

Carpentras has been famous as a market centre since the 5th century BC, when a Celtic tribe known as the Meminiens set up their stalls on a busy crossroads just outside of the present town. Later, Greeks and Phoenicians came upriver from Marseille to buy wheat, honey, goats, sheep and skins. Under the Romans the town prospered, although little remains from this period except a small triumphal arch. In the 14th century, Clement V, having been proclaimed Pope by King Phillip, chose Carpentras as his second main residence outside Avignon.

From the 14th century onwards Carpentras was one of the four main refugee centres in the Comtat Venaissin (the others were Cavaillon, Avignon and L'Isle-sur-la-Sorgue) for Jews fleeing persecution under Philippe le Bel in France. Despite the best efforts of a succession of bishops in later centuries, (notably Mgr d'Inguimbert, who commissioned the Hôtel-Dieu), Carpentras went into economic decline. Its fortunes were only revived with the building of a canal from the Durance in the 19th century. The desert-like *garrigue* around the town blossomed into fruit and vegetable gardens which today supply early season produce (principally grapes, cherries and strawberries) for the tables of France.

Every Friday there is a huge market that spreads throughout the town; from November to April, truffles change hands at enormous prices in the **place Aristide Briand**; and the town is well known for *berlingots* (mint-flavoured caramels).

Walk Carpentras

Allow around two hours for this walk, which delves into some of the town's hidden corners. *See map opposite.*

Start at the tourist office and follow the rue Vieux Juiverie into rue de la Fornaque. Directly opposite you will find a magnificent, carved doorway, typical of the Provençal style of the period. The two Atlas-type figures supporting the portico are from the school of Pierre Puget.

Turn back up the rue des Marins, at the top of which in the place des Pénitents Noirs is the disused old chapel of the Pénitents Noirs. Turning down rue Moricelly there are many fine old mansions, in particular those at Nos 71–83 and at No 57.

The rue Moricelly leads you into the place Ste-Marthe, with a pretty fountain in the middle; to one side of the square is an even more ancient fountain embedded in a stone post.

Continue down rue du Collège, with the college itself on your left. The mid-17th-century chapel is now used for art exhibitions.

Weave your way left into rue

Stallholder in the market

Eysseric et Pascal, right into rue Joseph Fornery and into rue Piquepeyre. On your right, the immensely tall, misshapen wall forms part of an old Carmelite monastery. The Franchini family have spent the last 30 years restoring it. Make your way through the back streets to the Porte d'Orange (see page 67).

From the gateway, walk up rue Porte d'Orange and turn left into rue Place de l' Horloge. Almost immediately on your right is a small passageway leading into a courtyard: the attractive ceiling here was discovered as recently as 1990. It dates from the 14th century and traces of a fire that took place in the 18th century can still be seen. Inside the courtyard, look up to admire the intricate ironwork of the 16th-century Bell Tower.

Continue down rue Place de l'Horloge and then turn right; at the end take rue Gaudibert-Barret and then left down rue Serpentine (one of the city's oldest and smallest streets) to return to the tourist office.

The vivid colouration of the stained glass in Carpentras cathedral shows it to have been heavily restored since the 15th century

Rebuilt many times over the centuries, the cathedral lacks a unifying style

What to see In the middle of the pedestrian zone of the city centre the **Cathédrale St-Siffrein** is no great beauty to behold, mixing together as it does architectural styles from many different periods. The interior contains work by Mignard, Parrocel and Duplessis, and, most notably, gilded wooden sculptures by Jacques Bernus.

Next to the cathedral is the **Palais de Justice** (ask at the tourist office for details of guided tours), formerly the Archbishop's Palace, commissioned by Cardinal Bichi in 1640. Tucked away behind the cathedral and the Palais de Justice is a **Roman arc de triomphe**▶ that was built under Augustus in the 1st century AD to commemorate victory over the Francs. Built at the same time as the triumphal arch in Orange, it is not nearly as tall and only one arch of the original three remains. However, the smaller scale allows you to get a much closer look at the bas-relief sculptures of the enslaved captives on the east and west faces. It is a pity that this arch, the only Roman relic in Carpentras, is so hemmed in and concealed by the buildings around it.

Another monument that is remarkable for being so inconspicuous is the **Synagogue**▶ (*Open* Mon–Fri) on the place de l'Hôtel de Ville. The original synagogue was built in the 14th century but eventually became too small to serve the population of over 2,000 Jews who lived in the surrounding ghetto. When the synagogue was rebuilt in 1741 Bishop d'Inguimbert gave permission only on the condition that it was no higher than the cathedral – hence its position today, almost dwarfed by the surrounding houses. The oldest synagogue in France, the richly decorated interior of the *salle de culte* (restored in 1954) testifies to the wealth of the Jewish community.

Carpentras has a handful of museums (*Open* daily except Tue) of no great distinction, but on a rainy day you can take your choice between the municipal collections which are displayed in the **Musée Comtadin** (folkloric mementoes) , with the **Musée Duplessis** (local 16th- and 17th-century paintings) on the floor above. Near by is the **Musée Lapidaire** (prehistoric and Gallo-Roman finds), housed in the former Convent of the Visitation, and the **Musée Sobirats** (a furnished period mansion).

On the south side of the tree-lined boulevard which encircles the city centre is the imposing **Hôtel-Dieu►**, built in the 18th century by Monseigneur d'Inguimbert and still in use as a hospital. Once inside, the most delightful part of the Hôtel-Dieu is the ancient **pharmacy►►** (*Open* Mon, Tue and Thu 9–11.30. *Admission charge*). Almost unchanged since the 18th century, this is one of the best-preserved antique pharmacies in the whole of France. It contains an excellent collection of *faïences* as well as pestles and mortars, brass scales and all the other paraphernalia of the apothecary's trade. The room is decorated with landscape panels painted by Duplessis.

On the other side of town is the impressive **Porte d'Orange►►**, the last remaining tower of the ramparts, which were built between 1357 and 1395 on the orders of Pope Innocent IV. They originally consisted of 32 towers and four gates but sadly they were nearly all demolished from 1840 onwards in the name of 'urban expansion'. This huge, 27m-high tower is unusual in that it is *ouverte à la gorge* ('open-throated'), which means that it was open at the back so that troops could be easily replenished from the town. From the top (accessible only on guided tours; tel: 04 90 63 00 78), there are views across Mont Ventoux and the Plateau de Vaucluse.

The *boule aux rats*
On the southern side of the cathedral is a flamboyant Gothic doorway that was known as the Porte Juive, through which Jews entered in order to be baptised. Above the doorway is one of the cathedral's most famous curiosities, the *boule aux rats*. The symbolism of this globe covered with rats has never been satisfactorily explained: it may be a play on the town's name in Latin, *carpere ras* (the nibbling rat); it may represent the Christian world being overrun with sin and hereticism; or it may be connected with the dreaded plague that swept the country in the 14th century.

67

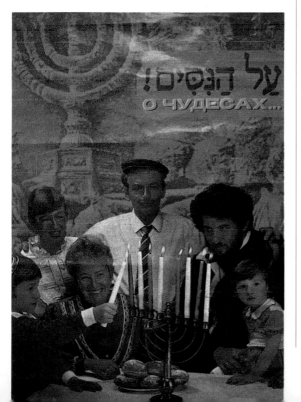

Family values, as portrayed on a poster in the synagogue

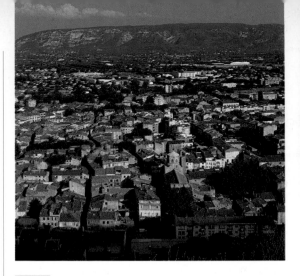

The view from Colline St-Jacques, where Cavaillon was founded by the Celto-Ligurians before it moved down to the plains in the Roman era

Cavaillon melons
In 1864 the writer Alexandre Dumas, who was very fond of melons, heard that the library at Cavaillon couldn't afford to stock his books, so he agreed to supply them with copies in exchange for an annual rent of twelve melons, which were sent to him in Paris. The melons he so enjoyed were the heavy, oval-shaped Cantaloupe melons. Since then many new varieties have been introduced, the most popular being the small Charentais melon, which *aficionados* consider to be absolute nectar.

▶ **Cavaillon** 44B1

Surrounded by market gardens irrigated by the Durance and the Coulon, Cavaillon is one of the biggest agricultural towns in France. By the end of your stay, you will be left in no doubt that this is the melon capital of France – there is even a Brotherhood of the Knights of the Order of the Melon. This prosperous town also grows an enormous quantity of prime fruit and vegetables – something for which it has been known since Roman times.

The only relic of the Roman era is a small **triumphal arch**▶, built in the 1st century AD. It was moved stone-by-stone to its present position at the foot of the Colline St-Jacques in 1880. The town's other main monument is the **Cathédrale St-Véran**▶, an elegant Romanesque structure dating from the 12th century with a charming cloister on the south side. Near by in the rue Hébraïque is the old **Synagogue**▶, sole remnant of the large Jewish population that lived in the surrounding ghetto prior to the Revolution. The ornate interior is masterly; beneath the Worship Room the ancient bakery has been converted into a small museum.

Cavaillon also has an **archaeological museum** (*Closed* Tue. *Admission charge*) inside the chapel of the old Hôtel Dieu on Grand Rue.

▶ **Châteauneuf-du-Pape** 44A2

The fame of this small town revolves around the wines which bear its name. The first vineyards were planted here in the 14th century by the Avignon popes, one of whom, Jean XVII, also built a castle at the summit of the village as a summer residence. The **Château des Papes**▶ was set on fire in 1562 during the Wars of Religion and then finally blown up by the retreating Germans in 1944. The two remaining walls give a good idea of the scale of the original château, and from its hilltop vantage point there are fabulous views down the Rhône valley.

At the bottom of the village, in the **Musée du Père Anselme**▶ (*Open* daily), there is an interesting display on wine-making through the centuries.

ENTRÉE

Musées de Cavaillon

Synagogue · Musée Juif Comtadin · Hôtel-Dieu

Châteauneuf vineyards

■ The relatively small area of just over 3,000 hectares of vineyards which surround Châteauneuf-du-Pape on the left bank of the Rhône produces one of the world's most prestigious and well-known wines. ■

Hot rocks As you approach the vineyards you will notice something curious – there is no soil visible at all, only a sea of smooth pebbles between the vines. This alluvial shingle has a beneficial effect, magnifying the heat of the sun on the grapes by day and keeping them warm long into the night. This super-heated micro-climate and the wide spacing between the vines produce a wine with the highest minimum strength (12.5 per cent alcohol) of any French wine.

The first *appellation contrôlée* Châteauneuf's most distinguished grower was the late Baron Le Roy de Boiseaumarie, who initiated a series of quality controls in 1923 that later became the standard for the national system of *appellations contrôlées*.

Unlike most Côtes du Rhône winegrowers, whose product uses just one variety of grape, growers here can choose from up to 13 different types. The result may differ slightly from grower to grower but is a characteristically deep red, full-bodied wine with a strong bouquet. There are plenty of opportunities for visiting vineyards in the region, among the best-known of which are the Château Le Nerthe, the Château de Beaucastel, the Château Rayas, the Château de la Gardine and the Domaine des Fines Roches.

The annual production of Châteauneuf is over 13 million bottles of wine, of which only 700,000 are white – this elegant, pale wine with a subtle bouquet is something of a rarity and well worth trying while you are here.

Festive tastings The annual *Fête de la Véraison* (which is held to celebrate the grapes achieving maturity) takes place at the beginning of August, when all the producers set up their stalls in the streets of the village. The business of wine-tasting is much easier and more fun during the festival – accompanied as it is by dancing, processions and a medieval pageant.

Opportunities for tasting the famous wines are never far away in Châteauneuf-du-Pape

► **Crestet** 44B3

This charming little village, which derives its name from the rocky crest on which it is built, is one of the most unspoiled perched villages in the region. With no shops or cafés, there is little to do except enjoy a leisurely stroll through the cobbled alleyways and admire the ancient wooden doorways of the old houses. There is a minuscule square with a bubbling fountain and a 12th-century church, behind which a path leads up between rocks and wild fig trees to an old **château** (no visits).

► **Cucuron** 45C1

The village of Cucuron lies on the southern flank of the Grand Lubéron and is the starting point for the 10km-long trail to the Sommet du Mourre Nègre.

A short distance from the church in the rue de l'Église is the **Musée Marc Deydier**►► (*Open* daily, afternoons only in low season). Aside from the usual displays of Gallo-Roman finds and old agricultural tools, the prize exhibits are photographs of the village taken around the turn of the century by Marc Deydier, the town clerk after whom the museum is named. The graphic quality and extraordinary clarity of these superb photographs (reprinted from some of the 2,618 negatives in store) is matched only by their value as a vivid ethnographic record of everyday life in Cucuron, depicting charcoal-making, harvesting with steam tractors, and street scenes.

►► **Dentelles de Montmirail** 44B3

See pages 72–3

►►► **Fontaine-de-Vaucluse** 44B2

In the summer months this little village is swamped with thousands of visitors drawn to the fabled fissure where the River Sorgue rises from the depths and disgorges at a rate that makes it one of the most powerful resurgent springs in the world. People used to come to pay homage to Petrarch, who lived here between 1337 and 1353, but now it is the source itself which exerts such a strong fascination, pouring forth in the peak months at a rate of between 100 and 200 cubic metres per second.

The source is around 2km from the centre of the village,

Probing the depths
The first attempt to explore the Fontaine de Vaucluse was made in 1878, when a potholer reached 23m. Jacques Cousteau sent the remote control *Télenaute* down to 106m in 1967, and in 1983 a second probe, the *Sorgonaute*, reached 245m but exploded on another attempt a year later. The bottom was finally reached in August 1985, when the mini-sub *Modexa* settled on the sandy bed at 308m. A high-performance probe, the *Spélénaute*, went down in 1994 to venture into the passageways that disappear back into the mountain.

There is little to disturb the peace in Crestet apart from the sound of running water

A riverside view of Fontaine-de-Vaucluse

reached by a path along the river bank, which in former days must have been a blissful walk: now it is a circus of buskers, T-shirt and souvenir sellers, with numerous restaurants and bars built out over the water (even in the 1950s the writer James Pope-Hennessy complained that 'all has been commercialised and made vulgar ... I confess to feeling beside Petrarch's fountain, as I have felt in Venice, that here was one place to which I had come a hundred and fifty years too late').

A handful of museums and exhibitions have sprung up along this path, amongst which is **Le Monde Souterrain de Norbert Casteret**▶ (*Open* May–Aug, Wed–Sun 10–12, 2–6 (Jul–Aug 6.30); Feb–Apr and Sep–Nov, Wed–Sun 10–12, 2–5. *Admission charge*). Guided tours focus on the history of caving and the specimens collected over the years by France's most celebrated speleologist.

At the exit you will find yourself in a vast underground concrete souvenir centre, at the other end of which is the **Moulin à Papier Vallis Clausa**▶, which displays the ancient paper-making equipment which was once powered by water-wheels on the banks of the Sorgue. On the other side of the path the excellent **Musée de la Resistance**▶▶ (*Closed* Tue. *Admission charge*) is an evocative tribute to the men and women of the Resistance and to the hardships of life in wartime France. The most recent exhibit to open is the **Musée Historique de la Justice et des Châtiments**▶ (*Open* daily. *Admission charge*), which houses a macabre collection of instruments of torture, death and imprisonment (including a genuine guillotine) personally assembled by one of the country's last executioners, M. Meyssonnier. A more gentle evocation of the past can be found back down in the village at the **Musée Pétrarque**▶ (*Closed* Tue. *Admission charge*).

Petrarch and the source
'Here I have the Fountain of the Sorgue, a stream that must be numbered among the fairest and coolest, remarkable for its crystal waters and its emerald channels. No other stream is like it; none other is so noted for its varying moods, now raging like a torrent, now quiet as a pool... I would speak of this more at length, were it not that the rare beauties of this secluded dale have already become familiar far and wide through my verses.' Petrarch, 1347

𝒟𝓇𝒾𝓋ℯ Dentelles

This round tour from Vaison-la-Romaine skirts the jagged limestone pinnacles of the Dentelles and encompasses many charming hill villages, several of which are famous for their wines. Allow 5–6 hours.

Leave Vaison-la-Romaine by the D938 towards Malaucène. After about 4km turn right to **Crestet** (see page 70), then follow the signs for the **Centre International d'Art et de Sculpture►►**. Surrounded by dense woods, the Centre is housed in the former studio of sculptor François Stahly, where artists explore the theme of art and nature. The *Chemin de Sculptures* is a magical mystery tour through the pine and oak trees, where sculptures in stone, wood and iron appear as if growing from the ground on either side

of the marked trail.

Return to the main road and continue on to **Malaucène** (see page 76). Follow the boulevard back in the direction of Vaison but take a left turn on the D90 signposted Suzette and the Dentelles.

After passing through vineyards and fields of sunflowers the road begins to wind up through the forest, and shortly the Dentelles can be seen on your left.

Turn left at the tiny hamlet of Suzette and cross the valley to reach le **Barroux**. The 12th-century **château►** (*Open* daily Jul, Aug, Sep, afternoons in Jun and Oct. *Admission charge*) was sacked during the Revolution and abandoned until restoration work began in 1929. Set alight by the Germans in 1944, it

burned for 10 days and the long struggle to restore it again began in the
1960s. The château is well worth
visiting, particularly the curious dog-
leg chapel – impenetrable rock forced
a change of building direction.

Follow the D938 towards
Carpentras, turning right after 3km to
Beaumes-de-Venise (see page 62).
From Beaumes take the Vacqueyras
road and turn right just outside
Beaumes to **Notre-Dame
d'Aubune►**. This small Romanesque
chapel lies on the southern slopes of
the Dentelles beneath a series of
terraces cultivated for centuries.

Continue on to **Vacqueyras**. Its
only claim to fame (apart from its
wines) used to be a statue of
Rambaud de Vacqueyras, a famous
Provençal troubadour. His statue was
stolen, alas, a few years ago and has
never been replaced. From
here you can detour to the
sulphur springs at
Montmirail, fashionable
enough to warrant a casi-
no next to the *station
thermal* in the 19th cen-
tury, when over 1,000
guests a year (including
Mistral) took the
waters here.

Serrated pinnacles of the Dentelles

Take the D7 on to **Gigondas** (see
page 74). Turning right out of the
village, follow signs for the **Dentelles
de Montmirail**. The road soon
becomes an unmetalled track, at the
top of which is a car park with signs
for the footpath to the pass, the **Col
de Queyron►**, at the centre of the
Dentelles' peaks.

Return to Gigondas and continue,
via Sablet, to **Séguret►►**. Almost in
ruins by the 1950s, Les Amis de
Séguret set about breathing life back
into it by restoring many of the monuments and reinvigorating local crafts
and culture. There is a Provençal folklore festival in August.

Return to Vaison via the D88 and
the D977.

*Vineyards shelter in the
shadow of the Dentelles*

An old château dominates Gigondas

APARE
The Sentier du Conservatoire des Terrasses en Culture (Open Air Terrace Museum) is the result of several years' research and on-site work by an organisation known as APARE (*Association pour la Participation et Action Regionale*). Formed in 1979, APARE's first project was to restore a small shepherd's hut in the Montagne de Lure. Since then they have organised hundreds of summer camps with volunteers working on projects relating to the heritage and environment of Provence.

The thick drystone walls of the bories *near Gordes*

▶ **Gigondas** *44B3*

A small village with a reputation for strong, full-bodied red wines, Gigondas has little in the way of sightseeing but plenty of opportunities for the serious imbiber to try what many consider to be one of the best wines in Provence. Around the main square there are at least half a dozen *caves* within weaving distance of each other, including the Caveau de Gigondas, which stocks bottles from 40 different Gigondas *domaines*.

▶▶▶ **Gordes** *45C2*

Seen from afar, houses seem to cling precariously to the hillside terraces which lead up steeply to the centre of Gordes. In the heart of the village is a 15th-century château whose profile is visible from miles away.

Gordes was set to become yet another victim of rural depopulation and decline until 1938 when the Cubist painter André Lhote fell for its charms and gave it a new lease of life. The village's future as a centre for art and tourism was sealed in 1970 when the Hungarian artist Victor Vasarély bought the château and installed a permanent exhibition of his famous geometric works on the top floors. (The collection was transferred to Fondation Vasarély in Aix, which was closed in 1997; the year in which Vasarély himself died.) Be sure to visit the first floor of the château, where the Grande Salle (which is part of the Mairie) has a magnificently decorated Renaissance fireplace. Built in 1541, its pediments and pilasters are ornamented with flowers and shells.

In an area as rich in historical relics as Provence, perhaps none is as curious and compelling as the fascinating **Village des Bories**▶▶▶ (*Open* daily. *Admission charge*), 4km outside Gordes. Reached down a narrow, winding lane enclosed on either side by stone walls and *garrigue* scrub, the *bories* seem to grow out of the landscape around them, with the thick walls of the enclosures merging into the dwelling houses, which are joined by yet more walls to other, smaller huts that housed livestock and were used for storage.

The *bories* were built using an ingenious technique whereby each layer of flat stone slightly overlaps the next to create a corbelled vault, which is then topped off with flagstones. No mortar was used in the construction of these sturdy dwellings. Similar drystone huts exist elsewhere in Europe, some of them dating back to neolithic times. In Provence there are probably between 5,000 and 6,000, with the majority found in this part of Vaucluse. Often seen in fields (where they are used as shepherds' huts) some have been converted into modern homes.

The integration of architecture and the environment is complete, but what is astonishing is that this particular group of *bories* is thought to have been built in the 18th or even the 19th century – making them contemporary with the Renaissance château in the village. The question as to why they were built here at this time (to escape the plague?) remains unanswered.

Also in the vicinity of Gordes is the **Abbaye de Sénanque**►►► (*Open* Mar–Oct, Mon–Sat and Sun afternoons; Nov–Feb, afternoons only. *Admission charge*). One of three Cistercian monasteries in Provence, the 12th-century abbey makes an extraordinary impression rising from the lavender fields in a lonely valley 4km north of the village. As well as an exhibition on the monks' way of life (several of whom have now reoccupied the monastery after a period when it was used as a cultural centre) there is a lovely cloister and, if you're lucky enough, your guide will sing a Gregorian chant in the church, where the purity and clarity of the acoustics are extraordinary.

► ▓▓ Goult 45C2

Just off the N100, which runs parallel to the Lubéron range, Goult is the site of the unusual **Sentier du Conservatoire des Terrasses en Culture**► (Open Air Terrace Museum), where you can ramble around a sign-posted trail explaining the nature and function of ancient hill terraces and the intricate techniques of drystone walling.

Alongside the traditional shelters and cabins many old (and increasingly rare) varieties of olives and almonds have been planted at the Open Air Terrace Museum.

Hillside terracing
Many of the hillside terraces which once covered large areas of the Provençal hills, and are very labour-intensive to maintain, have fallen into disuse, largely due to the mechanisation of farming. However, terracing has unique qualities as a growing environment: resistance to erosion and fire, and the micro-climate is of great benefit to plants. Now, attempts are being made to grow specialised crops (such as kiwi fruits, raspberries and Japanese artichokes) on terraces, and traditional plantations of apricot, almond, olive, peach and fig trees are being irrigated to increase yields.

The serene Abbaye de Sénanque, set among oak trees and lavender

Antiques to go

L'Isle-sur-la-Sorgue has a reputation as the antiques capital of Provence. This is partly because of its large antiques market, which has been held every Sunday since 1967 on the avenue des Quatre Otages alongside one of the canals. There are now nearly 200 permanent bric-à-brac and antiques dealers spread throughout five 'villages' (often in converted warehouses and the like) around the town centre. There are two annual antiques fairs, lasting four days: at Easter and in mid-August.

Eyes down for antique bargains in l'Isle-sur-la-Sorgue

▶▶▶ l'Isle-sur-la-Sorgue 44B2

Soon after the start of its journey from Fontaine-de-Vaucluse down to the Rhône at Avignon, the River Sorgue briefly divides around an island on which sits l'Isle-sur-la-Sorgue, a charming town that has built its fortunes on the river that runs through it.

No one is sure when the inhabitants of the village decided to dig three canals through their island estate, but in the Wars of Religion they put their mastery of the river to good use by flooding the surrounding plains so that they were out of reach of cannon fire. Later they built a whole series of water-wheels across the canals, their paddles powering what was to become a hive of industry including grain, oil and paper mills, tanneries and textile and silk works.

The wealth these enterprises brought to the town is evident in the riches displayed in the baroque **Notre-Dame-des-Anges▶▶** in the town centre. The magnificent interior is mostly the work of 17th-century artists of the Avignon school. Also worth seeing is the 18th-century **Hôtel-Dieu▶** with its intricate wrought-iron gates and ancient pharmacy (ask for the concierge at the main gate to be allowed inside), and the **Hôtel Donadú de Campredon▶** (*Open* May–mid-Jul, daily; closed Mon. *Admission charge*). It hosts temporary art exhibitions – in the past these have included works by Miró, Matisse, Dufy and Poliakoff.

Unless you are hunting for antiques (see panel), the main pleasure in visiting l'Isle-sur-la-Sorgue lies in strolling through the streets, watching the soothing waters running beneath small ironwork bridges and past terraces and balconies replete with flowering plants. Of the 64 water-wheels that once existed, only a handful remain: on the **Quai des Lices** and **Quai Berthelet** three of these magnificent wheels have been restored, and alongside **rue Jean-Theophile** and **rue Jean Roux** some of the remaining moss-encrusted paddle-wheels still revolve slowly and steadily to the rhythm of the waters.

▶ Lacoste 45C1

This hilltop village on the northern flank of the Lubéron is still a fashionable address for Parisian *residences secondaires* despite (or perhaps because of) its heritage as the home for many years of the notorious Marquis de Sade (see panel). Dating back to the 11th century, the **château▶** used to be one of the grandest in the region. Pillaged in the Revolution, it fell into ruins and stayed that way until the current owner, a retired teacher called André Bouër, began his lifelong and quixotic task of restoring it; 40 years on, it is clear he still has a long way to go (the interior cannot be visited).

▶ Lourmarin 45C1

See pages 50–1

▶ Malaucène 44B3

An attractive town encircled by a boulevard of plane trees, Malaucène is the major base for hiking, riding and cycling expeditions up nearby Mont Ventoux. Four **fortified gates** mark the entrances into the old town: follow rue St-Étienne and rue du Château up past the crumbling old

Still slowly turning under their mossy burdens, the paddle-wheels of l'Isle-sur-la-Sorgue are nearly 200 years old

clock tower (which was used as a look-out point during the Wars of Religion) to reach the belvedere created from the ruins of the ancient château.

► ► **Mazan** *44B2*

Seven kilometres east of Carpentras, Mazan is the sort of town you could easily pass by without giving it a second glance. However, behind its solid gateways, the centre of the town (which mostly dates from the 16th and 17th centuries) is a delight to explore and there are many architectural details – statues in niches, fountains and ancient doorways – to savour as you wander around the streets

Opposite the church, a bell-tower marks the Chapelle des Pénitents Blancs which now houses the **Musée Mazan►** (*Open* Jun–Sep, daily; closed Tue). Although there is little that is dramatic here (apart from a chilling skeleton from the 4th century of a young woman who was killed by a stone from a catapult, which left a gaping hole in the front of her skull), it is clear that the people of Mazan have raided their attics – their treasures seem to speak to us from across history in a way which a grand museum could never do.

The miscreant marquis
The Marquis de Sade, author of *120 Days of Sodom* and *Justine*, was born in Paris in 1740. His debaucheries forced him to leave the city when he was 31 for Lacoste, where he spent much of his wife's money embellishing the château. His sexual preferences have come to be called sadistic after his name and earned him the death sentence in 1772, when he fled to Italy in the company of his wife's sister. He lived at Lacoste between his numerous prison sentences until his death, in 1814, in a lunatic asylum at Charenton.

Media village
With many celebrities using it as their Provençal *pied-à-terre*, Ménerbes probably has the highest profile of all the Lubéron villages; past residents have included the actress Jane Birkin, Dora Maar (Picasso's mistress during the 1930s), and the late President Mitterand. The village shot to prominence in the 1980s with the publication of Peter Mayle's best-selling books *A Year in Provence* and *Toujours Provence*, and although his whimsical portrayal of local characters earned him few friends it brought tourists by the coachload. Mayle himself decamped to California in the early 1990s, but the appeal of Provence was sufficient to draw him back again by 1996 – his new home, however, is well hidden from the road.

Stonework merges into the natural surroundings in Oppède-le-Vieux

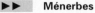

▶▶ Ménerbes   45C1

The layout of this village on the northern flank of the Lubéron is inevitably compared with the shape of a ship, with its narrow promontory projecting like a prow out over the valley. Walking up through the village towards the promontory you pass the Mairie and a 17th-century **bell-tower** on your right, with the archway between them framing a picture-postcard view of the Lubéron. Past here there is a 14th-century **church** (with more lovely views from the old cemetery) and the ruins of an ancient **citadel**.

Just outside Ménerbes (signposted along the D3) is the **Musée du Tire-Bouchon▶▶** (*Open* daily except Sun in winter. *Admission charge*). This new museum has a fascinating collection of over a thousand corkscrews from all over the world, displaying every conceivable variation and elaboration on this humble utensil. The museum is part of the Domaine de le Citadelle, and admission includes a tour of the winery and cellars. The winery is well worth a visit; it has a high-tech control panel with so many lights it looks like it could launch the space shuttle.

▶▶ Oppède-le-Vieux   44B1

Built on a limestone pinnacle set against the dramatic backdrop of the steep north-facing slopes of the Petit Lubéron, this evocative village is still partly in ruins and not (as yet) overrun by the trinket trade.

Oppède-le-Vieux was once a thriving community clustered around the base of the castle, but this was pillaged during the Revolution and the village itself went into a decline after the Comtat Venaissin was handed back to France, finally being abandoned altogether in 1910 when the remaining inhabitants moved down the hill to Oppède-les-Poulivets.

Recolonised by artists during the 1940s, some houses have been restored, but in the upper half of the village it is sometimes difficult to tell where houses end and ruins begin. Overgrown pathways wind up between ancient archways to the summit, where there is an old **church** with massive flying buttresses and, further on, the ruins of the **château** itself (take great care because there are many dangerous unprotected drops).

▶▶▶ Orange   44A3

Once an important Roman city, Orange has always been
considered the gateway to Provence – initially as a major
settlement on the Via Agrippa, which followed the Rhône
valley and, later, the first stop on the railway lines and
roads that led south into the sunshine.

Despite the construction of the *autoroute du soleil* just
to the west, traffic on the N7 still thunders past one of
Orange's most famous monuments, the Arc de Triomphe,
before engulfing the city and making navigation around
the outer boulevards somewhat hazardous. Thankfully
almost the entire city centre is pedestrianised, creating a
pleasant environment with many squares linked together
where you can wander from café to café under the shade
of the plane trees.

After the Roman era the town passed through the hands
of various feudal lords, including the House of Baux from
1173 to 1530. It was then inherited by René de Nassau,
whose strongly Protestant family turned Orange into a
refuge for dissenters amidst the surrounding sea of
Catholicism. Maurice de Nassau fortified the town in the
early 1600s but to no avail, since it was then razed by
Louis XIV after war had broken out between the king and
Maurice's nephew, William of Orange, who led The
Netherlands to victory against Spain and secured Dutch
independence in 1648. In 1678 the House of Orange
regained the town, but it was ceded back to France under
the treaty of Utrecht in 1713.

Whether the town of Orange gave its name to the Dutch
royal family or vice versa is by no means clear, but what is
certain is that the Dutch connection was bad news for the
town's heritage, since Maurice de Nassau pulled down
the Roman monuments to use the stone for his fortifications: only by chance did the theatre survive, because its
massive rear wall was needed as part of the defences.

*The top-heavy Arc de
Triomphe in Orange
celebrates Rome's
victory over the Celtic
tribes*

Resisting Rome
Once a Celtic settlement,
Orange's downfall came
when the inhabitants
defeated the Roman
legions in a huge battle in
105 BC. Three years later
the legions returned under
General Marius to exact
their revenge, almost
entirely wiping out the
town. It was not inhabited
again until 35 BC, and this
time it was by veterans of
the Second Gallic Legion,
who were given the
territory in return for their
part in Caesar's conquest
of Gaul. They set about
building a prosperous,
well-ordered town,
complete with theatre,
gymnasium, temples – and
of course the Arc de
Triomphe, which
personified their victory
over the barbarians.

The fully restored tiers of seating in Orange's Théâtre Antique can hold up to 10,000 spectators

Closed for 300 years
The last recorded performance in the theatre during the Middle Ages was the *Farce de Clin Bérnard*, performed by travelling players in 1514. Less than 50 years later, the Wars of Religion were causing devastation across the region, and Orange was sacked in 1562. The population took refuge in a series of caves in the Colline St-Eutrope behind the theatre, and constructed small houses and cabins in the theatre itself, some of them on the tiers of seating. Fortifications and watchtowers were also built, and the princes of Orange installed a prison in the western wings that was later put to infamous use during the French Revolution. Work began on clearing the theatre in 1834, and the reconstruction was completed by 1856.

Today Orange is an industrial and market garden centre and a strategic base for the French Air Force, who have been established at Caritat, east of the town, since 1936. Tourism has formed part of the economy since amateur historians started coming here in the last century to see two of the finest Roman monuments in Provence.

The first of these is the superb **Théâtre Antique▶▶▶** (*Open* daily; guided tours in English several times daily in summer. *Admission charge* includes entry to the museum). Considered to be one of the best-preserved theatres in the Roman world, the main focus of interest is the enormously impressive stage wall.

Standing 36m high and measuring 103m from end to end, the grandeur of the wall testifies to the important role that the theatre must have played in the lives of the citizens of the colony. Decorated with columns, marbles, statues and mosaics, it is said to have been described by Louis XIV as 'the finest wall in my kingdom'. Hidden passageways within the wall allowed the stagehands and actors to move about unseen, and the huge wooden stage was fitted out with traps so that actors and props could disappear and reappear at will. Above the central 'Royal door' stands a statue of Augustus; dating from the 1st century, it has been reconstructed from fragments.

The semi-circular auditorium (or *cavea*) is built into the slope of the St-Eutrope hill and could hold up to 10,000 spectators – graded according to rank, as shown by the inscription found on one of the lower tiers 'EQ. G III', i.e., *Equus Gradus III*, 'third row for knights'.

Outside the main theatre, excavations have uncovered a number of other structures that may have been part of a forum or a temple complex.

The second important monument is the magnificent **Arc de Triomphe▶▶**. Like its counterpart in Paris, it has also

From orgies to operas
Roman theatres were used for a wide variety of enter-tainments, which could include anything from circus performances to lottery competitions. Drama, however, was the main focus, with Roman comedies proving more popular than heavyweight Greek tragedies. In the Middle Ages mystery plays were performed, but it was not until the end of the 19th century that the theatre at Orange entered its heyday again with the staging of a festival of choral music and opera that became known as the *Chorégies*. This (principally popular opera) festival continues today, with the addition of a repertoire of pop, jazz and classical music throughout the summer months.

been left stranded in the middle of a roundabout – in this case, on the N7 (which follows the route of the Via Agrippa from Arles to Lyons) just to the west of town.

Built about 20 BC to commemorate the Second Gallic Legion's victories, the triple archway is one of the oldest of its kind in existence and – despite the erosion of some features – one of the best preserved. The three arches are flanked by columns and echoed by the three horizontal planes, including the unusual double attic. On the north face of the arch the reliefs depicting captured trophies and Roman naval supremacy (prows of galleys, oars, anchors and tridents) are easily visible, although you will need either binoculars or exceptional eyesight to interpret details of the battle scenes on the topmost attic, which is about 20m from ground level. Originally topped off with a bronze chariot drawn by four horses, the archway was dedicated to Tiberius some time after it was built.

In the first-rate **Musée Municipal**▶▶ (*Open* daily. *Admission charge*), the light and airy rooms on the ground floor trace the history of Orange and display fragments and friezes recovered from the theatre. Old engravings and prints show the theatre before it was restored – neglected, overgrown and sprouting houses inside and around the periphery, many of them built from the stones of the theatre itself.

Outside the museum, the rue du Pontillac passes beneath an archway set in a large chunk of Roman wall that may have once encircled the *forum*. In the middle of town is the Romanesque **Cathédrale Notre-Dame**, with the grand **Hôtel de Ville** just next to it.

The best views of Orange are from the **Colline St-Eutrope**, reached either by car or on foot. In front of the ruined foundations of a fortress there is an orientation table with views of the city and the Rhône valley beyond.

Roman legionnaires battle it out against the Celts in a detailed frieze on the Arc de Triomphe

▶▶ Pernes-les-Fontaines *44B2*

Like its neighbour l'Isle-sur-la-Sorgue 11km to the south, Pernes-les-Fontaines has achieved prominence thanks to the harnessing of water. In Pernes' case, the languid stream of the Nesque was channelled from the 15th century onwards into a series of fountains which today give the town its own particular appeal. There are now 36 in all, ranging from the ancient (**la fontaine Reboul,** over 400 years old) to the sublime (**la fontaine de Cormoran,** dating from 1761) to the ridiculous (**la fontaine Villeneuve,** built in 1952 and reputedly so hideous that moss has been allowed to grow all over it; only the old villagers can remember what's underneath).

Apart from the fountains, Pernes ('les Fontaines' was added only in 1936) has one or two outstanding sights worthy of a stop. The first is the lovely 16th-century **Porte Notre-Dame▶▶** which has a small chapel, **Notre-Dame-des-Graces,** built on to one of the piles of the bridge. Stepping down to the walkway beside the Nesque, you will discover a photogenic cameo of the bridge, the chapel and the keep framing the town's clock tower.

A visit to the interior of the **Tour Ferrande▶▶** (accessible only on guided tours; tel: 04 90 61 31 04. *Admission charge*) is a must. Inside the tower is a series of frescoes thought to date from around 1285, (possibly the oldest in France), although their origins are a mystery. Some are being restored, but the tower should remain open.

A blood-red legend
The soft rock of Roussillon is red either because of the combination of oxides in the quartz, or because, many years ago, a young troubadour, Guillem de Cabestaing, came to sing at the court of Raymond of Avignon, the lord of Castel-Roussillon, and fell in love with his pretty young wife Seremonde. The old man went out hunting but returned to ambush the lovers, killing the handsome Guillem and, unbeknown to his wife, serving up his heart at a banquet. Discovering this, Seremonde threw herself from the cliffs in Roussillon, forever staining the ground red with her blood.

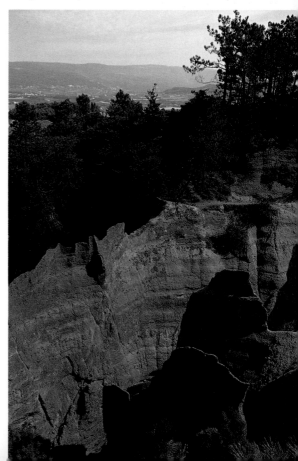

The eroded cliffs of the Chausée des Géants (Giants' Causeway) display the many hues of the ochre upon which Roussillon was built

The Sentier des Ocres (Ochre Trail) at Roussillon passes through old mine workings and quarries

► **Rasteau**   *44B3*

The vineyards that slope gently downwards from the village of Rasteau produce a naturally sweet wine (similar to the Beaumes-de-Venise), but Rasteau is also one of the leading villages in the *Côtes du Rhône* appellation, with a famous wine route, the Route Orange, passing its doorstep. There is a ruined 12th-century château, but it is wine which attracts visitors, particularly the **Musée du Vigneron** (*Open* daily in summer; afternoons and weekends in winter; closed Tue) on the road out towards Roaix.

►►► **Roussillon**   *45C2*

It is hard to walk around this photogenic hill village without obscuring someone's video lens or tripping over art students sketching in the streets and alleyways.

Roussillon owes its unusual aesthetic appeal to the many different shades of ochre (17 in all, we are told) that have been used as if from an artist's palette to tint the village houses in intense colours ranging from golden yellow to blood red. Of course the villagers didn't plan it that way; they simply used the nearest available materials – the ochre rocks that for many centuries formed the basis of an important mining industry here.

Ochre has been used for colouring since prehistoric times, and when the Romans occupied nearby *Apta Julia* they were quick to spot the potential of the extensive deposits around Roussillon. Commercial exploitation began in earnest in 1780, with ochre powders shipped all over the world from Marseille. At the beginning of the 20th century over a thousand people were employed here and nearly everyone in the village was an *ocrier*. The decline set in with the discovery of synthetic dyes and by 1930 the industry had all but collapsed.

Ochre was mined either in tall, underground galleries or in the open air. The former are closed for safety reasons but you can visit the disused quarries at the end of the village, where there is a **Sentier des Ocres**►► (*Open* daily. *Admission charge*) with information signboards.

► **Rustrel**   *45C2*

Although it shares a common heritage founded on ochre mining with nearby Roussillon, Rustrel is not in itself particularly compelling. However, the old quarries on the southern side of the Doua valley near by, known as the Provençal **Colorado**►, are popular with walkers.

The Colorado walk
To reach the ochre quarries, head back from Rustrel towards Apt and take the D22 to Gignac: shortly you will see a signpost on the left for Colorado. From the main car park there is a slightly confusing network of footpaths leading off through the woods, but just head away from the road and within a few minutes you will arrive at the quarries, a fantastic landscape of richly toned colours. Bear eastwards in order to reach the towering red pillars known as the *cheminées des fées* (chimney-stacks of the fairies).

Lavender honey, scented sachets, essential oils and dried lavender are among the many products from this aromatic plant on sale at a roadside stall near Sault

▶ Saignon 45C2

Way above the Calavon valley, Saignon is slung like a hammock between two rocks – on one of which are the remains of an old castle and, on the other, the parish church. Approaching Saignon from the direction of Apt, it is easy to see why it has been a natural fortress since Celto-Ligurian times: the towering rocks on which the village is built would be enough to dissuade any attacker. Today it is a typically peaceful Provençal village with nothing more demanding of your attention than an old clock tower, a pretty square with a fountain in the middle and washing-troughs off to one side, and an unusually broad-beamed, 12th-century church.

St-Didier 44B2

Lined with plane trees, the main street in St-Didier ends up at a medieval gateway and church behind which a small square leads into the **Château de Thézan▶**. This 15th-century building was converted in 1863 into a hydrotherapy centre, which today is renowned for the treatment of nervous diseases; it isn't open to the public but you can peek into the courtyard to see the Renaissance doorways and windows of the main façade.

The power of healing is also at the centre of the nearby **Hermitage of St-Gens▶**, past the neighbouring village of le Beaucet on the D39 (see panel).

St-Gens
On the right-hand side of the nave in the Hermitage of St-Gens is the rock in which St Gens was apparently buried after his death, with numerous crutches and walking-sticks propped up near by as testimony to the efficacy of his miracles. Behind the hermitage a path leads up to a spring which St Gens caused to gush out of the rock. A procession in his honour (he is the patron saint of farmers) is held here every May.

▶ St-Saturnin-les-Apt 45C2

Set on the southern slopes of the Vaucluse plateau, the village today is mostly known for its cherries, olive oil, asparagus, honey and truffles. Its violent past, however, is all too evident in the ruins of the 11th-century **château** that sprawls across the rocks above the village; at the top of these atmospheric ruins is a small Romanesque **chapel,** from where there are magnificent views across the surrounding countryside (the chapel itself is closed). Back down in the village, the remnants of past fortifications are evident in the **Portail Ayguier** (1420) and later additions such as the **Tour du Portalet**, the **Porte de Rome** and **Porte de Roque**.

▶▶ **Sault**   45C3

Set on a rock spur on the edge of the Vaucluse plateau, Sault makes a good base for excursions to Mont Ventoux or the wilder corners of the Baronnies and Lure Mountains to the north and northeast. The ancient capital of the Comté de Sault, only vestiges remain of its château, but the *vieille ville* features several medieval and Renaissance houses. The parish church, dating from the 12th to 14th centuries, is remarkable for its barrel-vaulted nave supported by unusually slender columns.

The municipal museum, **Musée de Sault** (*Open* Jul–Aug, Mon–Sat 3–6pm, otherwise by appointment) contains prehistoric and Gallo-Roman artefacts as well as an Egyptian mummy. The new **Maison Départmentale de la Chasse et de l'Environment** (*Closed* Mon–Wed. *Admission charge*) has exhibitions covering the flora and fauna of the Vaucluse and the role of hunting.

Nearby To the south of Sault is the Plateau d'Albion, which houses a massive French Air Force base together with underground bunkers concealing the country's strategic nuclear missiles. From Sault to Carpentras the D942 runs westwards through the Gorges de la Nesque, a deep canyon which cuts through the calcerous rock of the Vaucluse plateau. Perhaps the most dramatic point is the 300m-high **Rocher du Cire** (the Wax Rock) 11km from Sault – the inspiration for Mistral's poem *Calendau*.

Country treats
The products of the surrounding countryside play a prominent role in the economy of Sault. First, there are the rare mushrooms and truffles from the oak woods (*saltus*) that gave the village its name. Then there is nougat, a Provençal speciality made here by the Boyer family for generations. Add to this lavender honey (a lavender festival is held here in August) and a highly regarded local *saucisson*, and you will realise why the Wednesday markets are patronised by people from far and wide.

The squat profile of Saignon's 12th-century parish church

*Harvest time
in the vineyards
surrounding
Suze-la-Rousse*

▶▶ **Séguret** *44B3*

See page 73

▶ **Sérignan-du-Comtat** *44A3*

The principal attraction of this small village 8km from
Orange is the **Harmas de J-H Fabre**▶▶ (*Open* daily
except Tue. *Admission charge*). Jean-Henri Fabre was the
son of a Languedoc peasant who rose to become one of
the most eminent entomologists of the 19th century.
Fabre's prodigious output of published works (which
encompassed algebra, chemistry, astronomy and geology
as well as entomology) includes the famous *Souvenirs
Entomologiques,* which earned him the nickname of the
'Virgil of Insects'.

When he bought a house on the outskirts of Sérignan-
du-Comtat, he built a high wall around the garden and
planted thousands of species of herbs and flowers, creating a botanical wilderness where he could study insects
and plants to his heart's content. He christened it the
Harmas, from the old Provençal word *herme* meaning a
plot of untended land. He lived here until his death in 1915
at the age of 92.

Although Fabre was primarily an entomologist, a visit to
the Harmas is about much more than just bugs and butterflies: on the ground floor, for instance, there is a selection of his wonderfully delicate water-colours of the fungi
of the Vaucluse, of which he painted 700 in all. Alongside
editions of his 95 published works are letters from Mistral
and Darwin and his collection of coins. Upstairs in his
study the glass cabinets that line the wall contain shells,
fossils and minerals, whilst on top, his colossal herbarium
of France and Corsica contains some 325,000 specimens.
Fabre's minute desk, with his collecting satchel nearby,
gives the impression he just stepped out yesterday.

The gardens, which are still much the same as Fabre

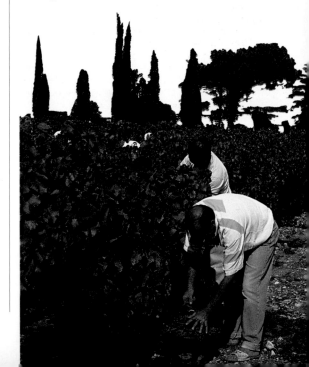

left them (complete with home-made insect traps), are best appreciated in April or May.

Suze-la-Rousse *44A3*
This village near Bollène has become the vinological capital of Provence thanks to the con-version of its 12th-century castle into the **Université de Vin** (*Open* daily, conferences permit-ting). The lavishly equipped château runs courses on all aspects of wine, from marketing to wine-tasting, mostly aimed at professionals but also open to the serious amateur. There is a huge library with a comprehensive collection of books on every subject relat-ed to wine.

House walls and quarry walls merge in the upper village of les Taillades

► **les Taillades** *44B1*
It is worth a quick detour off the Apt–Cavaillon road to see the upper half of this village, a rather bizarre assemblage of rocks and houses that has arisen because the old village was built on top of a quarry. Park in the square next to the post office and walk up to the old church at the top, passing by the Théâtre des Carrières (summer perfor-mances) and a number of dwellings where it is difficult to distinguish between house and rock.

On the D31 in the modern village, the lovely paddle-wheel on the Canal de Carpentras once powered a flour mill.

► **le Thor** *44B2*
Apples and the white dessert grape Chasselas were once the traditional mainstays of this modest market town in the Sorgue valley. On the banks of the Sorgue is one of the most impressive Romanesque churches in the Comtat, **Notre-Dame-du-Lac►►**.

Completed at the end of the 12th century, it marks the transition between the Romanesque and the Gothic, with the Gothic influence evident in the vaulting of the nave (one of the earliest examples of its kind in Provence). The west portal is finely detailed and shelters a wooden statue of the Virgin with what it is described as a 'Provençal haircut'.

Surrounded by vineyards, the Université de Vin is housed in a 12th-century château

Nearby Three kilometres north of le Thor, the **Grotte de Thouzon►►** (*Guided tours* daily in summer; Sun after-noons in winter. *Admission charge*) is one of the prettiest cave systems in Provence. Discovered in 1902 whilst a quarry was being excavated in the side of the Thouzon hill, its 230m-long gallery was almost immediately opened up to visitors. Unlike many grottos, the gallery is almost horizontal (so it is an easy walk) and has some near-perfect examples of fistulous stalactites (known as 'macaronis'), thin and transparent 'draperies', and small internal pools called 'gours'.

la Tour-d'Aigues *45D1*
See page 51

87

■ The intensity of the Mediterranean sun beating down on the hillsides of Provence forces wild, aromatic herbs to increase their yield of essential oils – thus making them more pungent and more efficacious in the many herbal remedies or recipes for which the region is celebrated. ■

Herbs in all their various forms provide an aromatic souvenir of Provence

Shepherd sorcerers The Provençal shepherd has long been considered a kind of sorcerer, a plant magician who is thoroughly conversant with the wild herbs of the hills and their healing properties. He knew that the sap from marsh mallow was good for healing cuts, that the juice of snails could strengthen rotten nails. He would cure the wounded foot of a sheep by transferring the illness to a patch of turf – at sunset. His knowledge of plants, of where they were to be found and when they should be picked, was legendary.

Many country people in Provence still cure themselves with age-old remedies such as 'red oil', which is made from the flowers of St John's wort (hypericum) mixed with olive oil and used in the treatment of wounds and burns. Sage is a popular cure-all and is used for everything from hangover cures (in sage soup) to steam baths for acne.

Garlic is a well-known antiseptic (cut a clove in half and rub it on the skin as an antidote to bee stings) and useful for 'cleansing the blood'. It is also used as a remedy for corns, worms and warts. Thyme can be used to protect against respiratory infections and coughs – it is also supposedly an aphrodisiac.

Many of these cures are now being revived thanks to the current fashion for treatments such as herbalism, aromatherapy and other forms of natural healing.

The Plant Magic Man In the early 1970s the writer Lawrence Durrell was passing through Arles market when he came across a stall selling fresh herbs and herbal cures run by a local man called Ludo Chardenon. Driven to desperation by eczema, Durrell bought a herbal tea and was astonished when his painful condition cleared up in ten days: the infusion had succeeded where the top doctors of London and Paris had failed.

Durrell befriended Ludo Chardenon, and wrote a feature on his life story for the *International Herald Tribune* in 1972, christening him 'the Plant Magic Man'. A decade later Durrell persuaded the 'Plant Magic Man' to write a book of his recipes, which is still in print today: *In Praise of Wild Herbs – Remedies and Recipes from Old Provence* (Century Publishing) is a fascinating compendium containing cures for everything from acne to worms, covering

The dying fields
Although it has not yet struck the Vaucluse, a deadly fungus is killing off the fields of fine lavender in the neighbouring *département* of the Drôme. Since 1985, plants have been withering and turning grey due to a tiny fungus, *Fusarium*, which it is thought might be flourishing because of climactic changes. Lavender prefers arid conditions, and too much spring rain in recent years has upset the balance. Recently scientists met at Nyons in the Drôme to try and solve the problem; if they don't come up with a solution soon, a whole way of life will be lost.

ageing, baldness, cellulite, obesity, rheumatism, stress and much more in between.

Lavender and lavandin The scent of lavender is one of the most characteristic aromas of Provence; rare is the souvenir shop that does not have bundles of scent bags stuffed with its fragrant flowers. The Romans treasured it for its soothing qualities, and added it to their baths (hence the name, from *lavare*, 'to wash' in Latin). Today it is used in everything from soaps to expensive perfumes.

The main growing area for lavender in Provence is the so-called 'mauve triangle' between Sault, Banon and Séderon, which accounts for 70 per cent of national production (the other main growing area is on the other side of Mont Ventoux, north of Nyons in the *département* of the Drôme).

The first lavender distillery started up in the 1880s to supply lavender essence for the apothecaries of Apt and Carpentras. After World War I, systematic cultivation began in response to demands from the *parfumeurs* of Grasse and by 1929 there were 47 stills around Sault, producing 10,000 kilos of essential lavender oil. Only a handful of distilleries now remain.

Most bouquets and other products which you buy in the shops are made using lavandin, a hybrid lavender which grows prolifically at low altitudes. The most highly scented and highly prized lavender is *lavande fine*, which grows at higher altitudes and carries its own Appellation d'Origine Contrôlée (AOC) like wine; at around 400 francs to the kilo, it is ten times more expensive than lavandin.

►►► Vaison-la-Romaine 44B3

Over the centuries, the inhabitants of Vaison have moved backwards and forwards between the two banks of the River Ouvèze. The first settlement was the Celtic stronghold on top of the hill when Vaison was the regional capital of the Voconces people. Conquered by the Romans in the 2nd century BC, the inhabitants moved down to the more fertile plains on the other side of the river and lived alongside the Romans in what then became *Vasio Vocontiorum*. Accorded the status of a federated city, the town prospered and its population grew to 10,000 inhabitants: luxurious villas, a theatre, baths, an aqueduct and a bridge were constructed.

Vaison became a bishopric in the 4th century and the building of the cathedral began in the 6th century; the latter was one of the casualties of the Frankish invasions that devastated much of the town. In the 12th century Count Raymond of Toulouse built a castle on the site of the old Celtic fortress and gradually people moved away from the Roman town to the greater safety of the *Haute Ville*.

Vaison became part of the Comtat Venaissin in the 1300s, remaining papal property until the Revolution. In the 19th century the inhabitants were on the move again, drifting back down to the left bank and leaving the *Haute Ville* to fall into ruins.

As they started to rebuild the town they uncovered parts of the Roman town, although it was not until 1907 that excavations began in earnest. Spread over an area of 13 hectares, the **Roman ruins►►** (*Open* daily. *Admission charge* also includes cathedral cloister – see below) lie in two halves on either side of the place Abbé Sautel and the tourist office in the centre of town.

To the east is the *Quartier de Puymin*, built around the base of a hill. On entering, you immediately find yourself in the middle of a huge villa, the Maison des Messii; next door is the *Portique du Pompée*, a public courtyard with gardens and a pool. Built into the north slope of the hill, the **theatre►** held around 6,000 people and was probably constructed about the 1st century AD. Restored in the last century, it yielded several fine statues which are now in the **Museum►►** alongside most of the other important finds from the excavations.

On the other side of the road excavations are still going on in the *Quartier de la Villasse*. A Roman street leads down to the city baths and another huge villa. This has become known as the *Maison au Buste d'Argent*, after the silver bust of the owner which was found here, and included mosaic floors and two gardens with pools. Next door is the *Maison au Dauphin*, also with private gardens and baths.

Leaving the Quartier de la Villasse at the exit next to the baths, a pathway alongside the excavations will take you to the former cathedral of **Notre-Dame-de-Nazareth►►**,

The Roman legacy is highly visible in Vaison-la-Romaine

Vaison's colourful market spreads over the lower town every Tuesday

which many consider to be one of the finest Romanesque monuments in Provence. On the north side, the lovely 12th-century **cloister▶** has several finely carved pillars supporting the arcades.

The two halves of Vaison are connected by a 17m Roman bridge, from where a road leads up through the fortified gateway into the narrow streets of the **Haute Ville▶▶**. Deserted at the beginning of the century, many of its houses have been carefully restored and a handful of discreet craft shops and art galleries can be found amongst the cobbled streets and fountains. There are views back down to the town and across to Mont Ventoux from the ruins of the 12th-century château.

Gourmet days
Every November, Vaison hosts *Les Journées Gourmandes* – 'five days in the Provençal autumn dedicated to the most subtle of pleasures' – which brings together wine-makers, restaurateurs, bakers, cheese-makers and growers in an extravaganza of eating and drinking. The best of local food and wines are displayed, tasted, discussed – and simply enjoyed. Full details from the Maison du Tourisme et du Vin, place du Chanoine Sautel, 84110 Vaison-la-Romaine (tel: 04 90 36 02 11).

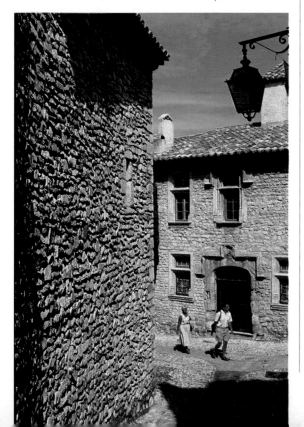

The cobbled streets of the **Haute Ville** *lead up to the ruins of an old château*

Memorial to British
cyclist Tommy
Simpson, Mont
Ventoux

Petit-St-Jean

Valréas is the setting for a spectacular and colourful festival on 23 June each year, when the town celebrates *La Nuit du Petit-St-Jean*. Over 300 participants in full costume march through the streets by torchlight up to the Château de Simiane for the enthroning of 'petit St-Jean', represented by a four-year-old child who becomes the protector of Valréas for the following year. The spectacle dates back many centuries and was originally a pagan ceremony in honour of the Sun, Water and Fire, later to be transformed by the church into a summer solstice celebration.

► **Valréas** *44B4*

Valréas sometimes appears with '*l'Enclave des Papes*' tacked on after its name, a description that harks back to when Pope Jean XXII acquired this territory with the aim of expanding the Comtat Venaissin northwards. Unfortunately, King Charles VII heard of this plan and forbade the sale of further land, leaving Valréas and the surrounding villages isolated.

When the *départements* of France were created in the 18th century, Valréas opted to remain part of the Vaucluse (and hence part of Provence) even though it was then, as it is now, encircled by the *département* of the Drôme.

Valréas today is a pleasant town ringed by a boulevard of plane trees, its economy mostly dependent on the cardboard industry and – somewhat more enticing – the production of Côtes du Rhône wine, asparagus and lavender.

Within the medieval town centre, the most imposing monument is the mainly 18th-century **Château de Simiane**►, housing the town hall and contemporary art shows in the summer.

There are several fine old mansions to be seen in Valréas, as well as the Romanesque church of **Notre-Dame-de-Nazareth**►, which has a particularly interesting doorway on its south side.

► **Venasque** *44B2*

Overlooking the Carpentras plain, Venasque is another village whose commanding position makes its value as a

An old fountain in
the quiet streets of
Venasque

strategic site immediately obvious – in this case, dominating the only route through the mountains between Carpentras and Apt. Occupied since Celtic times, it later became a refuge for the bishops of Carpentras against barbarian invasions. For reasons unknown, this small village gave its name to the entire territory of the Comtat Venaissin.

Alongside this honour, it also possesses one of the oldest religious buildings in France, the **Baptistry▶▶** (*Open daily; closed Sun mornings and Wed. Admission charge*) next to the church. Dating from around the 6th century AD, it may originally have been a pagan temple dedicated to Diana, Venus or Mercury. There are many curiosities inside: fragments of a sarcophagus dating from AD 420; the elegant columns that bear evidence of usage in Roman times; an octagonal font set in the floor; and a strange arrangement of holes bashed in the walls of the north apse, designed to improve the acoustics.

At the opposite end of the village is a huge medieval curtain wall with three turrets, which barred the entrance to this once formidable stronghold.

▶▶▶ Ventoux, Mont 45C3

The highest peak between the Pyrenees and the Alps, Mont Ventoux (literally the 'windy mountain') dominates the Vaucluse plateau and the Rhône valley, marking the northern entrance to Provence, with its summit often in the clouds at 1,909m.

From Malaucène the D974 winds up past **Notre-Dame du Groseau** (an octagonal chapel which is the only surviving part of a 12th-century monastery) and the **Source du Groseau**, a spring that the Romans channelled in an aqueduct to Vaison. From here on up the views become increasingly spectacular, and nearer the summit, the vegetation thins out until only rocks remain. Once at the top, turn your back on the radar towers and radio masts and soak up one of the most astounding views in Provence, extending from the Alps down to the Mediterranean.

Mont Ventoux was once covered in dense forests of oak, cedar and pine. By the beginning of the 19th century the forest had all but disappeared (cut down to build warships in Toulon), but in the late 1900s a massive reforestation programme began, with extensive plantings of Austrian pine and cedar of Lebanon; these now provide a habitat for wild boar, deer, and over 100 bird species including owls and rare eagles. Mont Ventoux is also home to 950 species of plants, both Alpine and Mediterranean.

In 1990 a large part of the mountain was designated a UNESCO Biosphere Reserve and research into its unique flora and fauna continues at the forest ecology laboratory in Malaucène.

The summit of Mont Ventoux

Conquering Mont Ventoux
The first recorded ascent of 'the Provençal Giant' was by the poet Petrarch, who climbed it in 1336 with his brother. From the 18th century onwards there were many scientific expeditions, which led to the building of an observatory in 1882. Later, when a road was built, the steep climb became a proving ground for cars (a de Dion-Bouton made it in 2hrs 15 minutes in 1909) and bicycles (it is one of the most demanding stages of the Tour de France; British cyclist Tommy Simpson died on the way up in 1967).

93

Mountain sports
Many sporting activities take place on, and above, the slopes of Mont Ventoux, such as skiing, paragliding and mountain biking; plus daytime and night-time walks (you reach the summit at dawn) in the summer from Malaucène tourist office (tel: 04 90 65 22 59).

■ **With the exception of a few notable vine-yards, wines from Provence used to be sniffed at by connoisseurs but in recent years the quality has improved enormously, adding to the pleasures of the sunny south. ■**

Wine to go

Walk into almost any *cave cooperative* and you can sample local wines and buy them direct by the bottle or case – usually much better value than other outlets. You can also buy your wine *en vrac* (in bulk), which is what most locals do. Simply turn up at the *cave*, pay at the cash desk, and your container is filled from a petrol-pump type nozzle from the vats below. You can buy old-fashioned *bonbons* (wicker-covered glass jars) in hardware stores or inexpensive plastic containers, which hold up to 33 litres in the *cave* itself.

Although said to have been enjoyed by the kings of France in the 17th and 18th centuries, Provençal wines have not had such a glowing reputation in this century and many have only recently acquired the coveted AOC (*Appellation d'Origine Contrôlée*) status. Hugh Johnson's definitive *World Atlas of Wine*, published at the beginning of the 1970s, is typically dismissive: 'An optimistic description of Provence wines always mentions the sun-baked pines, thyme, and lavender and claims that the wine takes its character from them. This is true of some of the best of them…others get by on a pretty colour and a good deal of alcohol. "Tarpaulin edged with lace" is a realistic summing up of one of the better ones.'

However, in the last couple of decades the quality of Provençal wines has improved significantly and this is reflected in Johnson's more recent comments ('rock hills of limestone and shale, and in some cases a cool breeze off the sea, can give considerable distinction to certain eras'). You will certainly find plenty of reasonably priced, highly drinkable bottles on your travels through the region.

In addition to the main *appellations* listed below there are numerous wines designated VDQS (*Vin Delimité de Qualité Supérieur*) which, whilst unlikely to be memorable, are at least good value.

Côtes du Rhône Although not generally considered a Provençal wine, there are several Côtes du Rhône vineyards in the Vaucluse. Most Côtes du Rhône wines are made from a blend of grape varieties, resulting in a robust, full-bodied flavour that develops considerably in depth and subtlety if left to mature (preferably for at least five or six years).

The *appellation* Côtes du Rhône Villages is much more restricted and produces a superior wine, more complex and firmer than the normal AOC. Within the area covered by this guide, the Côtes du Rhône Villages *appellations* come from Beaumes-de-Venise, Cairanne, Rasteau, Roaix, Sablet, Séguret, Valréas and Visan. In addition, vintage wines (Grand Crus) are produced by Gigondas (rosé and red), Vacqueyras (red, white and rosé), Rasteau (Grenache sweet apéritif wine) and Beaumes-de-Venise (Muscat sweet apéritif wine).

The best-known wine from this area, right in the heart of the Côtes du Rhône district, is that of Châteauneuf-du-Pape (see page 69).

Bandol Covering around 813ha, the territory of the AOC Bandol (one of the earliest in the region, it was designated in 1941) also covers neighbouring vineyards in Sanary, la Cadière, le Castellet and (to a lesser extent) le Beausset, Evenos and Ollioules.

These fine wines owe their unusual characteristics to a high percentage of Mourvèdre grapes (up to 80 per cent in the reds) blended with Grenache and Cinsault varieties. The reds are soft and dark, with undertones of spice, vanilla and blackberry. They keep exceptionally well – 10 to 15 years for the reds.

Cassis The small area of the AOC Cassis wines (covering just 200ha) means that they can be pricey since output is limited. The calcareous soil around this little seaside port produces a light, dry white with a freshness that seems to come from the sea.

Côtes-de-Provence One of the most recent AOC areas (classified in 1977), Côtes-de-Provence specialises in those dry, fruity rosés which seem to slip down all too easily on a hot summer's day when served well chilled. Seventy-five per cent of production is rosé, with just 20 per cent red and five per cent white. With over 100 million bottles produced annually, the *appellation* ranks sixth by volume in the whole of France.

95

Vineyards in Provence are now producing some highly palatable wines

BOUCHES-DU-RHÔNE

The Espace Van Gogh in Arles, a town that has played a significant role in the story of Provence since the 6th century BC

Introduction The Bouches-du-Rhône is one of the oldest inhabited regions in Provence, its roots reaching deep into history and tapping the sources of early civilisation. It has some of the best monuments from Roman and medieval times and it was later the cradle of Provençal culture, the home of the troubadours, and the inspiration for great artists such as Cézanne and Van Gogh and writers such as Mistral and Marcel Pagnol.

Bordered by the Durance to the north and the Rhône to the west, the Bouches-du-Rhône is mostly low-lying (below 300m) although at Cap Canaille it has the highest cliffs in France. It is the most densely populated and heavily industrialised *département* in Provence and yet has more protected areas (covering over 200,000 hectares) than any *département* in the whole of France.

Marseille and the east The 'capital' of the Bouches-du-Rhône is Marseille, the oldest city in Provence and nowadays almost as well known for organised crime as for its famous fish soup, the *bouillabaisse*.

Marseille's one million inhabitants live at the heart of an industrialised coastline which expands westwards around the nearby Étang de Berre, and yet within a short distance in the other direction there is a sublime coast-

VINCENT
VAN-GOGH
1853 · 1890

Sheep on the Grand Crau
Irrigated by canals, the plains of the Petite Crau yield crops in abundance. The Grand Crau, by contrast, is relatively barren, mostly comprising a vast sea of stones which was deposited by the Durance before it changed course to disgorge itself into the Rhône further north. Between the stones, tufts of grass (known as *coussous*) support a large sheep population, which grazes here between mid-October and early June. In the summer, the sheep are taken to their Alpine pastures: this *transhumance*, as it is known, is now done by lorry, but the ancient procession is still celebrated in the *Fête de la Transhumance* in St-Rémy-de-Provence.

line of pine-covered cliffs gashed by deep inlets, the famous *calanques*. Nestling beneath the cliffs is the port of Cassis, its streets crowded with gastronomic pilgrims in search of its renowned seafood and delicate white wines.

East of Marseille are the hilliest parts of the Bouches-du-Rhône, with the crest of the Massif de la Ste-Baume marking the boundary with neighbouring Var. Beneath the wooded slopes of Ste-Baume, the town of Aubagne is a major ceramics centre that produces (amongst other things) small clay figures known as *santons*, used in Christmas cribs.

Running parallel to the Ste-Baume massif are the limestone ridges of the Montagne Ste-Victoire, which dominate the landscapes around Aix-en-Provence.

La Crau At the centre of the Bouches-du-Rhône is the vast plain known as la Grande Crau, or just la Crau, divided in two by the jagged peaks of the Chaîne des Alpilles, which culminates in a modest summit at la Caume (387m). To the north of the Alpilles are the fertile plains of the Petite Crau, where the abundant harvests of soft fruit and vegetables are well protected from the dreaded *mistral* by long rows of cypress and poplar. The man after whom the wind was named was born here in the small village of Maillane, and the legends and customs of the Petite Crau were some of the

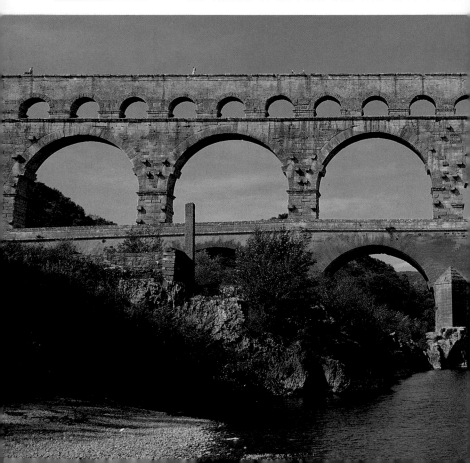

primary sources of inspiration for Frédéric Mistral.

Sheltering beneath the northern flank of the Alpilles is the delightful town of St-Rémy-de-Provence, with the ancient ruined city of Glanum on the slopes above it. West of St-Rémy, the Renaissance castle at Tarascon stands guard on the banks of the Rhône, symbol of the centuries-old mistrust between Provence and the Kingdom of France.

On the south face of the Alpilles the windswept heights of les Baux dominate the Grand Crau, stretching away down to the Rhône delta. Now drained, the Grand Crau was once swampland with settlements on isolated outcrops: one of these was the former Abbaye-de-Montmajour, whose ruins still dominate the countryside.

Bordering the Grand Crau, the lively town of Arles has more than its share of historic monuments, testimony to its role as the Roman capital of Provence. Its neighbour to the west, Nîmes, shares much of the same heritage and is part of a 'tourist triangle' (which also includes Arles and Avignon) around Provence, even though it is in Languedoc-Roussillon.

The Camargue Finally, there is the domain of flamingos, white horses, cowboys and bulls – not to mention mosquitos – down in the Camargue, that marshy triangle which has been created by the joint efforts of man and the mighty River Rhône.

Mighty Bouches-du-Rhône
Of all the *départements* in Provence, the Bouches-du-Rhône has the highest population (1.8 million), with the greater proportion of this accounted for by the two major cities, Marseilles and Aix (1.2 million between them). It also has the highest proportion of farmland (75,000ha), sells the most fish (10,500 tonnes landed annually), has the greatest number of industrial enterprises (8,900) and the largest number of hotels and restaurants (6,838). However, it is in fact smaller in size (covering just over 5,000sq km) than either the Var or the Alpes de Haute-Provence.

99

One of the wonders of the Roman world, the Pont du Gard

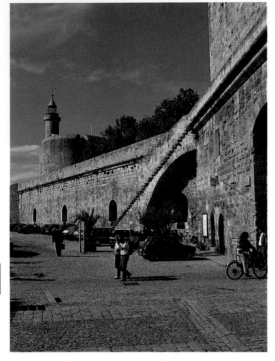

*The Tour de
Constance rises
above the impressive
fortifications of
Aigues-Mortes*

**The Tour des
Bourguignons**
Alongside the canal at the
southwest corner of
Aigues-Mortes' fortifica-
tions is the Tour des
Bourguignons, which
gained its name after a
gruesome incident during
the Hundred Years War.
Thanks to the treachery of
the town governor, the
Bourguignons captured
Aigues-Mortes in 1421 but
the Royalist troops swiftly
recaptured it, massacring
hundreds in the process.
There were so many
corpses that they were all
thrown into this tower and,
in order to avoid an
outbreak of the plague,
covered in salt until they
could be buried.

►►► Aigues-Mortes
96A2

The western half of the
Camargue is dominated
by the imposing fortified
walls of Aigues-Mortes.
Although it is in the
département of the
Languedoc and not the
Bouches-du-Rhône, it is an
essential part of the tourist
circuit around the delta.

In the 13th century the
land around Aigues-Mortes
was owned by the monks
of the powerful Abbaye de
Psalmody nearby, but
when Louis IX (St Louis)
began building a port here
in 1241 they agreed to
exchange their territories
for the Château de
Villevieille near Sommières.
Louis IX was desperate for
a French port on the
Mediterranean, since the
coast on either side was
controlled by the Counts of
Provence and the Kings of
Aragon, and without this
base he would have been unable to launch his long-
dreamt-of crusades.

The unappealing name of Aigues-Mortes ('dead
waters') was given to the port to distinguish it from the
nearby town of Aigues-Vives ('living waters') 20km further to the north.

By 1248, the port was complete and Louis IX and his
30,000 knights set off in an armada of 1,500 ships to liberate Jersualem. This Seventh Crusade was a disaster for
the king, but he survived and came home to prepare for
the Eighth Crusade against North Africa. This time,

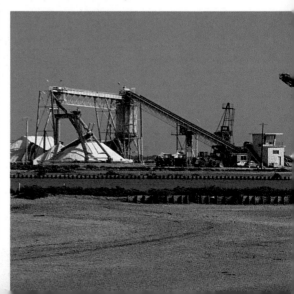

Aigues-Mortes was to be his last glimpse of French soil, for he died of typhoid at the gates of Tunis in 1270.

Two years after his death his successor Philip III began construction of the town's remarkable ramparts, which took nearly 30 years to complete. The fortifications, which extend for over 1.5km around the town, contain no less than 15 towers and 10 gates and have been preserved almost entirely intact to this day. The reason for this is that Aigues-Mortes soon went into decline, left high and dry by the retreating waters in the middle of the 14th century.

The most impressive of the towers is the massive **Tour de Constance▶▶▶** (*Open* daily. *Admission charge*) which, due to its impregnability, was soon put to use as a prison: Philippe le Bel imprisoned 45 Templars here in 1307, but its most notorious period was in the 17th century when hundreds of women, all of them Protestants rounded up in the Cévennes, were incarcerated in the tower in appalling conditions. One of these women, Marie Durand, was kept here for 38 years because she refused to renounce her faith (you can still see where she carved the one word *register* – 'resist' in her local dialect – into the stone wall).

From the top of the 52m-high tower there is a terrific view across the town and the Camargue, and beneath it you can walk around parts of the ramparts.

Unlike most medieval towns, Aigues-Mortes is laid out in a neat grid pattern with the streets converging on the tidy central square, **place St-Louis**, where there is a statue to Louis IX by Pradier, commissioned in the 19th century to commemorate the Seventh and Eighth Crusades. On the corner of rue Jean-Jaurès is the attractive church of **Notre-Dame-des-Sablons▶** (Our Lady of the Sands) where sunlight streaming through the stained glass windows colours the simple, airy interior. On the opposite side of the square the former **Cloître des Capucins** now houses the tourist office.

The town has a handful of decent hotels and restaurants, and in the latter you might like to try the local speciality, *taureau à la gardienne*, which is a beef and olive stew.

Salt and wine tours
Aigues-Mortes is an important salt-production centre (rivalling the Salin de Giraud at the other extremity of the Camargue) and is famous for its local wine grown entirely in sandy vineyards, the *Vin du Listel*. Tours of both the wine cellars and salt pans are organised every Wednesday and Friday afternoon in July and August by the tourist office (reservations required, tel: 04 66 53 73 00).

101

Over half of French salt production comes from the Salins de Midi outside Aigues-Mortes

▶▶▶ Aix-en-Provence   97D2

Aix owes its origins and even its name to the thermal springs discovered here in pre-Roman times. A Celto-Ligurian tribe, the Salyens, built a fortified camp at Entremont (3km north) around the 2nd or 3rd century BC, but their harassment of the local population led the Greeks of *Massalia* (Marseille) to plead for help from their allies in Rome. In 124 BC Sextius Calvinus duly razed Entremont, and later set up his own camp. Twenty years later 200,000 Teutoni barbarians arrived – to be defeated by the Roman general Marius. Montagne Ste-Victoire was so named after this great victory.

Under the Romans monuments and aqueducts were built – later destroyed in the Dark Ages. In the 12th century Aix became the capital of the Counts of Provence; the university was founded in 1409; and its golden age came under the reign of Good King René (1434–80).

After René's death in 1480 Aix endured many centuries of plagues, wars and religious disputes before blossoming in the 17th century into a wealthy, bourgeois city with political and cultural influence.

Above and right: just two of Aix's many fountains

The town declined somewhat from 1880 onwards, when regional power was transferred to Marseille.

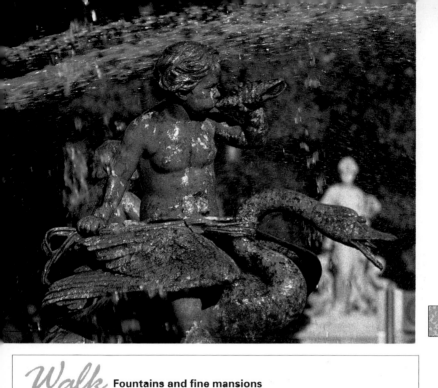

Walk Fountains and fine mansions

This walk covers the best of Aix's fountains and fine mansions, as well as the contrasting areas of the Quartier Mazarin and the old quarter. Allow 2–3 hours. *See map opposite.*

From place Général de Gaulle walk up the right-hand side of the cours Mirabeau.

Turn down rue Joseph Cabassol opposite the Fontaine des 9 canons. On your left further down is the **Hôtel de Caumont**, designed by the architect of Versailles, now the Conservatoire de Musique et Danse. At the end of the road is the **Lycée Mignet**, once the Collège Bourbon.

Go left down the rue Cardinale to the **place des Quatres Dauphins▶**, which has a 17th-century dolphin fountain. Continue on (with a possible detour to the Musée Paul Arbaud in rue du 4-Septembre) to the place St-Jean de Malte for the **Église St-Jean-de-Malte** and the **Musée Granet** (see page 105).

Turn left and left again back to the cours Mirabeau, briefly acknowledging King René before crossing the boulevard to see the old advertisement for the *Chapellerie du Cours Mirabeau* at No 55, where Cézanne grew up in his father's hat shop.

Follow the small passageway beside the shop through to the place de Verdun, which is dominated by the 18th-century **Palais de Justice**. There is a regular flea market (*marché aux puces*) here and the neighbouring **place des Prêcheurs** has a food market on Tuesday, Thursday and Saturday mornings. Above the square is the **Église Ste-Marie-Madeleine▶** with works by Rubens and Van Loo.

Continue up rue Mignet, which has several fine 18th-century buildings and the crumbling façade of the ancient Monastère de la Visitation. Turn left down rue Boulegon, continuing on to the **place de l'Hôtel de Ville** (see page 105). From here, either detour northwards up rue Gaston de Saporta towards the **Musée du Vieil Aix**, the **Musée des Tapisseries** and the **Cathédrale St-Sauveur** (see pages 105–6), or return through the **Vieil Aix** backstreets to the cours Mirabeau.

Architectural details such as this wood carving enliven Aix's many belle époque mansions

Dried flowers make a colourful display in one of Vieil Aix's street markets

What to see To feel the pulse of Aix take a preliminary stroll down the **cours Mirabeau►►**, a wide boulevard with a canopy of huge plane trees which shield the passers-by from the sun as they flit from café to café, socialising and checking out everybody else's outfits and partners in what is essentially centre stage for smart Aixois society. Locals call it simply *le cours*, as if there were no other of importance. Apart from one or two book-shops the north side is almost entirely cafés and *patis-series*, with tempting ice-creams, cakes and cocktails on offer, inviting you to sit and watch the parade. One of the most elegant cafés (with prices to match) is the *fin-de-siè-cle* **Les Deux Garçons**, with its interior a riot of gilded mir-rors and antique lights. The south side of the boulevard is characterised by splendid 17th- and 18th-century man-sions with façades of honey-coloured stone ornamented with fine wrought-iron balconies and carved doorways.

Running down the middle of the cours Mirabeau is a series of fountains, including the mossy-covered **Fontaine Chaude** with bubbling hot spring water, and the **Fontaine du Roi René**. At the other end, the roads from Avignon and Marseille meet at the roundabout in place Général de Gaulle, with its spouting jets from the fountain of **La Rotonde**.

To the south of cours Mirabeau are the orderly streets of the **Quartier Mazarin►►**, created in 1646 by Michel Mazarin, archbishop of Aix, specifically for the lawyers and nobles attending parliament. At 2a rue du 4-Septembre is the **Musée Paul Arbaud** (*Open* daily except Sun. *Admission charge*), which houses a fine collection of *faïences* from Moustiers-Ste-Marie and Marseille, works by Puget and Fragonard, sculptures, and an enormous collection of manuscripts, rare editions and books on Provence. Once the home of collector and bibliophile

Paul Arbaud, the house itself is fairly remarkable, with handcrafted ceilings and fireplaces, silk wallpaper and carved wooden doorways.

Also in the *quartier* is the **Musée Granet**►► (*Open* daily except Tue in winter. *Admission charge*) devoted to art and archaeology. Upstairs is a disappointing, unimaginatively displayed collection of 18th- and 19th-century paintings. Cézanne is represented by a miserly eight paintings, donated in 1984 by the French government to remedy the total absence of his works in his native city. More interesting are the finds, in the basement, from the ancient oppidum of Entremont. The Celto-Ligurian sculptures (unearthed in the 1940s) rank amongst the oldest known pre-Roman works in France and include some fascinating ritual masks, statues and torsos.

Next door to the museum is the 13th-century **church of St-Jean-de-Malte,** with its elegant fortified Gothic façade.

The harmonious urban planning of the Quartier Mazarin seems a world away once you cross into the chaotic, busy streets of **Vieil Aix**►►, on the other side of the cours Mirabeau. This is an area to wander in at a leisurely pace, stopping to admire the many handsome old buildings or fountain-splashed *places* and soaking up the lively atmosphere of people milling around the markets, shops and restaurants.

At the centre of the old town is the **place de l'Hôtel de Ville**, which is at its best when filled with the colours and heady scents of the flower market on Thursday and Saturday mornings. The square was built in 1741 to create space in front of the classical Italianate **Hôtel de Ville**►, which was rebuilt in the late 17th century by Pierre Pavillon. Tacked onto a corner of the town hall is the 16th-century **Tour de l'Horloge**►, which has an astronomical clock as well as one defining the seasons.

On the south side of the square, the old **Corn Exchange** (now the central Post Office) boasts a massive pediment statue by Chastel. Around the back of the Post Office, the **place Richelme** has a daily fruit and vegetable market and is one of the city's main hang-outs for buskers and students.

Old Aix has a variety of museums, including the **Musée des Tapisseries**► (*Closed* Tue. *Admission charge*) inside the grand old Archbishop's Palace. Most of the whimsical Beauvais tapestries were collected by archbishops in the 17th and 18th centuries; contemporary textiles are also featured.

Another fine old mansion, the Hôtel Boyer d'Eguilles, now contains the **Muséum d'Histoire Naturelle** (*Closed* Sun morning) which has all the usual fossils and bones as well as an astronomy section and a clutch of rare dinosaur eggs.

Tasty Aixois treats
Aix is one of France's biggest exporters of prepared almonds, with which they also make a delectable local speciality, the *calisson*. The almonds are ground into a paste and then mixed with fruit syrup and glazed melons before being trimmed with icing sugar. *Calissons* were first created in Aix in 1473 and they are still made by hand, with around a dozen shops specialising in them. One of the oldest is the Confiserie Bremond at 16 rue d'Italie where you can watch them being made on Friday mornings (by appointment, tel: 04 42 27 36 25).

The whimsical Tour de l'Horloge, a landmark of Vieil Aix

The Good King René
René d'Anjou (1408–80) inherited the titles of Duke of Anjou, Duke of Lorraine, Count of Provence, and King of Sicily, Naples and Jerusalem in 1434. During the first half of his reign he flitted between his various kingdoms, unsuccessfully playing at diplomacy and politics, until he settled in Aix in 1471 and devoted himself to patronage of the arts instead. He was himself a poet, musician, painter and linguist (he spoke six languages fluently). He introduced Muscat grapes and silkworms to Provence, but it was probably not the general populace who coined the term 'Good King René' since he taxed them heavily to pay for his indulgences.

Mirabeau's misfortunes
Later to achieve fame as a political leader during the Revolution, at the age of 23 the penniless Count Mirabeau decided to marry the aristocratic Émilie de Covet Marignane. Although his suit had already been rejected, he sneaked into her house, leaving his carriage outside the door for all to see in the morning. Her virtue compromised, the marriage had to take place but his father-in-law cut off the young couple's allowance. Mirabeau promptly ran up debts all over Aix and was imprisoned in the Château d'If. Once released, he eloped to Amsterdam with another married woman but was summoned back to Aix for the divorce case – which he lost.

An elegant door-knocker is just one detail on Pierre Puget's classic Hôtel de Ville

Just north of the Tour de l'Horloge in rue Gaston de Saporta you'll find the **Musée du Vieil Aix** (*Closed* Mon. *Admission charge*) with an assortment of curiosities, that includes a set of masks and mechanised marionettes portraying characters in the ancient *Fête-Dieu* ceremonies. This religious festival, once celebrated throughout Provence, was originally initiated in the 13th century by Pope Urban IV; King René revived it in the 15th century and turned it into a massive, popular procession with costumed groups and festivities lasting up to five days. The celebrations were abandoned after the Revolution, but several attempts were made to revive them from the early 19th century onwards.

At the top of the same street is the **Cathédrale-St-Sauveur►►**, whose charm largely derives from its curious hotchpotch of styles from different periods. The west face, for example, combines a Romanesque doorway from the 12th century, a flamboyant Gothic façade from the early 16th century, and a belfry from the 15th century. Inside, the 5th-century octagonal **baptistry►** is one of the oldest in France; the Roman columns supporting a Renaissance cupola above the pool were originally part of a temple to Apollo which stood on this site.

The cathedral is full of art treasures, including a series of 16th-century tapestries originally woven for Canterbury cathedral, and Nicolas Froment's *Triptyque du Buisson*.

Just outside the old city centre on rue Tava is the **Pavillon de Vendome►** (*Open* 10–noon, 2–5; closed Tue. *Admission charge*). Built in 1665 as a summer house, it was the last work of Pierre Pavillon and now houses a small museum of period furniture.

Cézanne in Aix

■ **Paul Cézanne was a lonely genius, struggling for most of his life against the incomprehension, and often ridicule, of the public. Driven by an inner conviction, he remained aloof and unsociable, painting feverishly until the very end, intolerant of the bourgeois Aix society into which he was born.** ■

Early years Born on 10 January 1839, Paul Cézanne received a classical schooling in Aix. His father, first a hatter and then a successful banker, made him study law, but it soon became clear that the young Cézanne preferred painting.

Parisian sojourn Cézanne went to live in Paris in 1862 at the urging of his friend Zola, and there he fell in with Monet, Sisley, Renoir, Manet and other young painters. He exhibited with the early Impressionists but their work met with derision and sarcasm.

Return to Aix Rebuffed, Cézanne took no further part in Impressionist exhibitions. He retreated to Aix, painting in solitude in his attic studio in the rue Boulegon or in the Provençal countryside, where his work took on a new richness that went beyond the analytical vision of Impressionism. His mastery of the underlying geometric structure of landscapes grew, and he returned repeatedly to the hilltop village of Gardanne, near Aix, as well as to the Jas de Bouffan and the banks of the Arc river.

Fame at last In the final decade of his life, from 1895 onwards, Cézanne completed over 300 paintings – many of which are amongst his masterpieces. It was only then that he began to achieve some recognition, although it was in Paris, Berlin and Vienna rather than Aix itself.

Final days When his mother died in 1897 Cézanne built himself a Provençal-style house, Les Lauves, on a hill above the cathedral: he painted in this studio from early morning onwards, stopping only for lunch before setting off to work on landscapes in the afternoon. In 1906, aged 67, he was still painting in the open countryside every day despite ill health and fatigue. On 15 October that year he was caught in a rainstorm, collapsed walking home, and died peacefully from pneumonia on 22 October.

In the footsteps of Cézanne
The Office du Tourisme in Aix (2 place Général de Gaulle; tel: 04 42 16 11 61) produces an excellent leaflet called the *Circuit Cézanne*. The first part guides you step by step around locations within Aix where Cézanne lived, studied and worked, whilst the second part describes a round tour of some 40km in the environs of Aix to see the locations which he immortalised in his paintings, including the Arc valley, the Pont des Trois Sautets and the views of Montagne Ste-Victoire from the D17 (now the *route Cézanne*).

107

Still life with apples, bottle and chairback, *1900–6 (pencil and gouache)*

Reliquaries in the Église St-Trophime, Arles

▶▶▶ **Arles**   *96B3*

Introduction Once the Roman capital of Provence, then an important religious centre in the Middle Ages, Arles later became a focal point for the Provençal renaissance of the 19th century. Today it is the unofficial capital of the Camargue.

First a Celto-Ligurian settlement on the banks of the Rhône, just where the river divides into its Petit and Grand branches, Arles became a major centre for trade between the Greeks of *Massalia* (Marseille) and the inland tribes in the 6th century BC. Its future was assured when the town built a fleet of 12 boats to help Julius Caesar conquer Marseille in 49 BC.

For five centuries Arles thrived at the crossroads of trade routes between Italy and Spain (the Domitian Way) and between the Mediterranean and Northern Gaul, and was a significant centre for the early Christian church, hosting several major synods. Arles went into decline from the 13th century onwards – when it was overtaken in political and economic importance by Aix and Marseille.

In the 19th century Arles re-emerged as a major focus for Provençal folk traditions, furniture and crafts. Its women, who still wore the distinctive Provençal costume, inspired Daudet's famous play *L'Arlésienne* (1866), later turned into an opera by Bizet. Mistral thought Arles the embodiment of old Provence and founded his Museon Arlaten here in 1896.

Walk   Roman remains and ramparts

This walk will allow you to see most of Arles' major monuments in one circular route, as well as the remains of the Roman and medieval ramparts. Allow 3–4 hours. *See map opposite.*

From the boulevard des Lices head down rue Jean Jaurès to the place de la République. In the far corner, turn right up the rue de la Calade, past the *sous-préfecture* housed in a 17th-century mansion, to reach the **Théâtre Antique** and, just past here, the **Arènes**.

After visiting the arena, climb the steps on the east side to the place de la Major, where there is a viewpoint next to the **Église Notre-Dame de la Major**. Built on the foundations of a palaeo-Christian sanctuary (itself built on top of a pagan temple dedicated to Cybele), the church has elements from several different epochs and contains, inside, a wooden statue of St Georges, patron saint of the *gardians* of the Camargue.

Head down rue Madeleine to place de la Redouté, where two round towers mark the old **Porte de la Redouté** (or Porte d'Auguste) in the Roman ramparts where the Aurelian Way once led into the city.

Follow around the outside of the ramparts, turning in again down rue Portagnel, across place Voltaire and down rue de la Cavalerie to the Porte de la Cavalerie. Walk through the gardens next to the remains of the medieval ramparts to reach the banks of the Rhône. Turn left and walk down the riverbank until you come to the **Musée Réattu** and the **Thermes de Constantin**.

Head up the sinuous rue du Sauvage, at the end of which is the **Hôtel d'Arlaten** and then the **place du Forum**. Continue up to rue de la Calade, turning right past the old lapidary museum, left around the corner to the **Museon Arlaten**, and then right down rue President Wilson back to the boulevard des Lices.

St-Trophime cloister and tower

Cooling water flows from a streetside fountain

What to see Most of the sights in Arles are within a square kilometre of the city centre, bordered on one side by the Rhône and on the other by the **boulevard des Lices**. Here are the main tourist office and numerous cafés in which to sit and watch the world go by (most enjoyable on a Saturday, when there is a huge market here).

At the heart of the town is the **place de la République▶** with its unmistakable obelisk (dug up in 1675, it was once part of the Roman forum). Facing the square is the **Église St-Trophime▶▶▶**, one of the most glorious monuments to the Provençal–Romanesque style. Built on the site of a 5th-century church during the 11th and 12th centuries, the most striking aspect of St-Trophime is the great portal, a masterpiece of classical decoration possibly inspired by the triumphal arches of Glanum and Orange. Behind St-Trophime are the equally famous **cloisters▶▶▶** (*Open* daily. *Admission charge*), which were probably the work of the same master craftsmen who created the façade of the Abbey of St-Gilles.

At the end of the square is the baroque **Hôtel de Ville▶**, whose lobby boasts an unusual flat-vaulted ceiling.

The **Museon Arlaten▶▶** (*Closed* Mon in winter. *Admission charge*) focuses on traditional Provençal life, ranging from costumes to furniture to the *gardians* in the

Contemporary festivals
Throughout the summer there are contemporary events and exhibitions in Arles, the most important of which are *Rencontres du Sud* in July (with a busy programme of dance, drama, music and opera) and the renowned *Rencontres Internationales de la Photographie,* which has numerous photographic shows and workshops with top international photographers. Art exhibitions are held in the Espace Van Gogh, a multimedia centre installed in the former Hôtel-Dieu where Van Gogh was treated after he cut off part of his own ear.

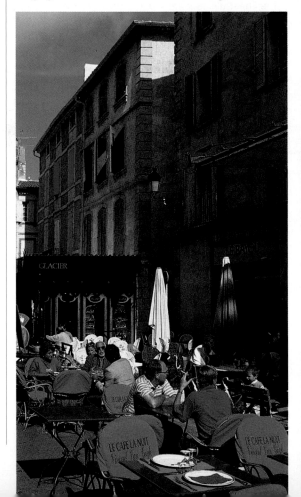

Al fresco eating is de rigueur in the lively place du Forum

Camargue. It was founded by Mistral in 1896 and, as the great man requested, it is still staffed by attendants wearing traditional Arlesian costumes. Provençal *santons* are on display in the **Chapelle de la Charité** (*Open* daily. *Admission charge*) next to the tourist office.

Arles' social hub is the attractive **place du Forum▶**, with busy cafés and restaurants presided over by a statue of Mistral. Down towards the river past the place du Forum is the 14th-century priory of the Knights of Malta, which now shelters the **Musée Réattu▶** (*Open* daily. *Admission charge*). The museum houses a collection of 57 ink and crayon drawings by Picasso, which the artist donated in 1972 as a gift to the people of Arles because he had so much enjoyed the bullfights here.

Arles' star attraction is undoubtedly the amphitheatre, the **Arènes▶▶▶** (*Open* daily. *Admission charge*), which was probably built around the end of the 1st century AD. It is only just bigger (by 3m) than the amphitheatre at Nîmes, although slightly less well preserved – the latter retains its third-storey attic. Turned into a fortress during the Saracen invasions, a village was later built inside the arena (which also happened at Nîmes). You can climb up one of the three remaining towers for a view over the arena and the city, with the Rhône behind it.

The **Théâtre Antique▶** (*Open* daily. *Admission charge*) just to the south, was built during the reign of Augustus, but was pillaged for stone in the 5th century by Christians eager to build churches. Although a mere shadow of its former self, the theatre is still a suitably impressive venue for the annual *Fête du Costume* (dance and drama), which takes place in July.

Between the théâtre and the boulevard des Lices is the Jardin d'Été (*Open* daily) with its lovely cedars and a bust of Van Gogh.

Another Roman monument which merely hints at past glories is the **Thermes de la Trouille▶** (or Thermes de Constantin. *Open* daily. *Admission charge*), near the riverfront. This huge bath house is the largest in Provence and once formed part of Constantine's palace on the waterfront.

The Roman cemetery in Arles was at the **Alyscamps▶** (*Open* daily. *Admission charge*) to the southeast of the town centre; many of the hundreds of elaborately carved sarcophagi were given away to visiting nobles in the 16th century, and the huge necropolis was carved up by railway lines and workshop buildings in the 19th century. The 12th-century **Église St-Honorat▶** is the only one left of 19 chapels that once studded the Alyscamps.

The old Pagan and Christian art museums have now been combined into the excellent **Musée de l'Arles Antique** (*Open* daily except Tue. *Admission charge*) on the Presqu' île de Cirque Romain. Housed in a superb modern building, it offers an evocative insight into the prehistory of the region and Roman Arles, with scale models of all the town's major monuments as they once were.

Traditional festivals
Arles has a lively calendar of traditional festivals including the *Feria Pascale* in April that marks the beginning of the bullfight season, the *Fête des Gardians* in May with the Camargue 'cowboys' parading on horseback through the streets, and the *Fête d'Arles* in late June, with torchlight processions where everybody wears local costumes. Another festival, revived at the beginning of the 1980s, is the *Fêtes des Prêmices du Riz,* which takes place in September to celebrate the rice harvest from the Camargue.

111

The Hôtel de Ville overlooks Arles' place de la République

Global tickets
If you are planning to visit most of the monuments and museums in Arles, buy a global ticket from the tourist office or any participating site. The tourist office organises various themed walking tours throughout the summer.

■ **Alongside Cézanne (see page 107), Van Gogh is another towering genius whose work will for ever be linked with the light-filled landscapes of Provence and the brilliance of the southern skies.** ■

Self-Portrait with Bandaged Ear, one of two self-portraits painted by Van Gogh early in 1889 while convalescing in Arles after cutting off a piece of his right ear

Arrival in Arles Van Gogh took up painting at the age of 27, having previously been an art dealer, a teacher and an evangelical preacher. He moved to Paris in 1886, where he fell under the spell of the Impressionists. He moved to Arles in 1888 and, although he wrote that the town had 'a worn and sickly look' about it, he nonetheless stayed, captivated by the vivid colours around him. He mostly lived on place Lamartine, where he rented a cheap room opposite the Café de l'Alcazar, which he painted as the *Café de Nuit*. He also painted *La Maison Jaune* and the famous drawbridge of the *Pont de Langlois* (few of the locations he painted remain today).

Confrontation with Gauguin Van Gogh dreamed of setting up an artists' colony in Arles, and implored Gauguin to come down and join him. This Gauguin eventually did, but he hated Arles. Van Gogh's dreams were shattered: he threatened Gauguin with an open razor. Later, in a fit of remorse, Van Gogh went home and cut off part of his left ear, which he gave to a prostitute. Gauguin took the first train back to Paris.

Move to St-Rémy Van Gogh was hospitalised in the Hôtel-Dieu but the townspeople petitioned the mayor to get rid of him. He finally left of his own accord in May 1889, checking in as a voluntary patient at the sanatorium of St-Paul-de-Mausole in St-Rémy. While there he worked feverishly, producing over 100 drawings and 150 canvasses, including some of his most famous paintings such as *Les Blès Jaunes* and *Les Oliviers*.

Final days A year later Van Gogh left the sanatorium (supposedly 'completely cured') and went to stay in Auvers near Paris – he had convinced himself that the southern sunshine was contributing to the agony of his mental illness. Two months later, in July 1890, he shot himself, and died two days later.

► **Aubagne**   97D1

Once a small market town for fruit and vegetables grown in the surrounding Huveaune valley, Aubagne is now effectively a suburb of Marseille, surrounded by *autoroutes* and three industrial zones. Home of the French Foreign Legion, find out what they're about at the **Musée de la Légion Étrangère** (*Open* Tue–Sun in summer; Wed, Sat and Sun in winter).

Aubagne is also the birthplace of Marcel Pagnol, who set many of his works in the town and surrounding countryside. Characters from his books have been made into *santons* which are displayed in **Le Petit Monde de Marcel Pagnol** (*Open* daily) inside the tourist office.

► **Barbentane**   96B3

Barbentane's main attraction is the classic **Château de Barbentane**►► (*Open* daily, Sun only in winter; closed Wed in spring and autumn. *Admission charge*). Started by the Marquis of Barbentane in 1674, finished over a hundred years later, its style owes much to the great châteaux of the Île de France. The house is still occupied by the Barbentane family and its rich furnishings are the result of over 400 years of antique collecting. The interior, which is often used for magazine shoots, is dripping with 18th-century tapestries, Aubusson carpets, porcelain, statues, chandeliers and priceless furniture. On the outskirts of Barbentane is **Provence Orchidées** (*Open* daily 10–12, 2–5. *Admission charge*), which has an 'exotic garden' with tropical plants, orchids and butterflies.

Nearby On the D35E, 5km south of Barbentane, is the ancient **Abbaye St-Michel-de-Frigolet**►► (*Open* daily for guided tours, hours vary. *Admission charge*), founded by the monks from Montmajour. Surrounded by hillsides of fragrant herbs, the abbey got its name from the Provençal word for thyme, *ferigoulo*. This is one of the ingredients in the monks' liqueur, *Le Frigolet*, which you can buy in the abbey shop. In the 11th-century **chapel of Notre-Dame-du-Bon-Remède** the sumptuous gilt panels were donated by Anne of Austria, who came here in 1632 to pray for a son; in 1638 she gave birth to Louis XIV.

Potted history
Aubagne is a major production centre for traditional Provençal ceramics, which have been made here since the 16th century. Local potters specialise in *santons* and beautiful decorative pots, vases, plates and so on, which can be bought from artisans' shops in the old town or during the annual fairs. Every two years in May Aubagne hosts the Journées Nationales de la Faience, and during August France's largest ceramics fair, the *Argilla* (from the Latin for clay, *argile*) – also biennial. Every other December over 50 artisans specialising in *santons* gather for the *Biennale de l'Art Santonnier*.

113

Untouched during the Revolution, the Château de Barbentane has been lived in by the Barbentane family for over 300 years

Troubadours
Despite their warring habits, some of the *seigneurs* of Baux were fond of more refined pastimes. In the 13th century their citadel became famous for its court, with troubadours visiting from far and wide to compose passionate odes to the daughters of Baux.

Red 'Bauxite' rocks
In 1821, geologists discovered that the red rock from the hills surrounding les Baux could be smelted to create aluminium. They christened it bauxite in honour of the village.

Citadelle des Baux

Plein Tarif :
28 F

N° 062154

▶▶▶ **les Baux-de-Provence**   96B3

Les Baux is one of the classic sights of Provence, a powerful evocation of the feudal dynasties that once ruled the country. It is also a classic case of tourist overcrowding, with over 1.5 million annual visitors – visit out of season if you can.

Perched on a barren rock plateau jutting out southwards from the Alpilles chain, les Baux had been a stronghold since Ligurian times but it first achieved notoriety in the 10th century when it became the power base for the ambitious *seigneurs* of Baux, who claimed to be descended from Balthazar of Bethlehem, one of the three kings who attended Christ's Nativity. They pinched the Star of Bethlehem for their coat of arms and waged war incessantly. They gained control over 79 surrounding towns and villages – secure in the knowledge that their eagles' eyrie at les Baux was impregnable.

The last of this troubled family was the princess Alix of Baux, and on her death in 1426 les Baux became the property of the Count of Provence, Louis III d'Anjou. Later, King René gave it to his second wife, Jeanne de Laval, and a temporary peace reigned, until les Baux became a Protestant stronghold under the Manville family, and more troubles beset the fiefdom during the Wars of Religion. They then made the fatal mistake of siding with the Duke d'Orleans in a rebellion in 1632 against Louis XIII, who retaliated by besieging the citadel.

Tired of their bothersome overlords (and partly prompted by Cardinal Richelieu), the inhabitants of les Baux asked Louis XIII to demolish the citadel and the castle and ramparts were pulled down in 1633.

For nearly two centuries les Baux became a ghost town, until the 1940s when Raymond Thuilier opened his famous hostelry, L'Oustaù de Baumanière, which attracted celebrities and politicians. Gradually the forgotten village was restored and the tourist trickle turned into a torrent, engulfing les Baux in souvenir shops, *crêperies*, art galleries, ice-cream parlours and boutiques.

If you can stand this overload there are some interesting places to visit within the village, such as the 16th-century **Hôtel de Manville**▶ which now houses the town hall and a small **musée**▶ (*Open* daily in summer; Mon–Fri in winter. *Admission free*) tracing the history of les Baux.

On the other side of the village, on place l'Église, is the

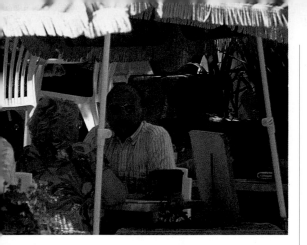

The cafés and souvenir shops in this once-deserted village are, in the high season, packed with tourists

Église St-Vincent▶, which was partly hewn out of the rock in the 12th century. On Christmas Eve the famous pastoral festival (see panel) takes place here. Across the square is the old **Chapelle des Penitents Blancs**, decorated by Yves Brayer in 1974.

Rue du Château leads up through the middle of the village to the entrance to the **Citadel▶▶▶** (*Open* daily. *Admission charge*) where there is a small **musée▶** inside the Maison de la Tour du Brau. Strewn across the arid plateau there are about a dozen buildings still standing.

Explanatory signboards here are poor, if not non-existent, but this may change as the whole site is being redeveloped, with excavations planned to last through until 2010. In 1993, the discovery of ceramics proved that les Baux was occupied as long ago as the Bronze Age.

To the north of les Baux is a valley, leading into the Alpilles, known as the **Val d'Enfer** (the Valley of Hell), whose tortured-looking rock formations, eroded gullies and caves were supposedly the inspiration for Dante's *Inferno*. Jean Cocteau shot scenes from *Orphée* in the deserted quarries here in 1950 and one of these huge underground caverns has now been converted into the extraordinary **Cathédrale d'Images▶▶**. Thirty-five projectors beam powerful, enveloping images across the ceilings, walls and even the floor of the vast space within the enclosed quarry. Projection is continuous, with the show lasting 30 minutes (*Open* daily; closed mid-Nov–mid-Mar. *Admission charge*).

Christmas festivities
In a chapel on the right-hand side of the Église St-Vincent is the *charette de l'agneau* (lamb's cart), which plays a key role in the *fête du pastrage* on Christmas Eve, in a tradition dating back to the 16th century. During midnight mass, an angel hidden behind the altar announces the Nativity to shepherds at the back of the church. The shepherds come forward, dancing and singing traditional Christmas songs, accompanied by shepherdesses with flowers and fruits strung about them. They are followed by the chariot bearing a new-born lamb.

115

Les Baux is perched romantically on a rocky outcrop

A duck trap
Duck hunting is big business in the Camargue, and many of the large estates have flooded huge areas to create freshwater marshes. The ducks are shot as they move every morning and evening between the saltwater marshes in the reserve (where they rest in the daytime) and the private freshwater marshes (where they feed at night). The reserve is therefore unwittingly acting as a gigantic duck trap. This is causing problems not only because of excessive hunting (between 100,000 to 150,000 are shot annually), but also because the shot used is killing other aquatic birds through lead poisoning.

▶▶▶ The Camargue   96B2

Approaching the Camargue from Marseille, the road skirts the Étang de Berre and passes through the industrial nightmare of the Port de Fos complex, a wasteland of oil terminals, cranes and chimneys, criss-crossed by a web of roads, railway lines and electricity pylons.

Then all of a sudden, once you have crossed the Rhône on the Bac de Barcarin ferry, a transformation takes place: here are groups of pink flamingos elegantly picking their way through the shallow lagoons in search of food, whilst birds of prey stand sentinel on the fence posts by the roadside. The space around you seems infinite as the horizons of the marshes, lagoons and the sea stretch away into the distance. The silence is almost total apart from the honking of geese as they migrate in ever-changing, fluttering ribbons across the open sky.

All the more extraordinary for its proximity to industrial civilisation, the Camargue is a rich tapestry of many different ecosystems, a haven for wildlife and a joy for anyone seeking tranquillity or long, wild walks amidst its watery landscapes.

The Camargue is a vast delta formed by the two branches of the Rhône (the Grand Rhône to the east and the Petit Rhône to the west) where they meet the sea. In the Middle Ages communities of monks settled on the edge of this swamp to collect valuable salt and reclaim the land, but by the 17th century they had been replaced by ranchers whose primary purpose was the raising of

The neat little cabanes *that dot the Camargue were the traditional homes of the* gardians

the famous white horses and the black, longhorn bulls which thrive on the saline pastures. Sheep were also grazed here in the winter, before being moved up to Alpine pastures during the annual *transhumance*. It may appear to be a wilderness but in fact it is an environment

*An avenue of plane
trees shades a quiet
Camargue back road*

Flooded
The vulnerability of the
Camargue was highlighted
in 1993 when the Rhône
burst its banks and flooded
over 12,000 hectares of the
delta; over 5,000 bulls,
horses and sheep were
evacuated by helicopter
and lorry whilst frantic
efforts were made to fill
the breaches in the dyke.
Over 130 million cubic
metres of fresh water
flooded into the system,
altering the salinity of the
lagoons and marshes dra-
matically. Undoubtedly
many mammals died, and
although floods have
occurred previously (principally in 1960 and 1978)
they have never caused
such a sudden change in
salinity, which may have a
brutal effect on the entire
ecosystem.

shaped by human activities with several overlapping
zones. The conflict between different users of the
Camargue is graphically illustrated by the problem of duck
hunting (see panel).

The whole of the delta is part of the *Parc Naturel
Régional la Camargue*, created in 1970, which covers
85,000ha and aims to achieve a balance between
traditional activities, the interests of local inhabitants, and
nature conservation. At the core of the regional park the
most sensitive areas have been classified as nature
reserves; the most important is the *Réserve Nationale
Zoologique et Botanique de Camargue* (first protected in
1928) covering 13,500ha around the Étang de Vaccarès.

On average, visitors spend less than half a day in the
Camargue and in this time you can only see the 'postcard
Camargue' – the bulls, horses and flamingos. To
appreciate it fully, you have to put in some effort – walk,
hire a bike, ride a horse, or go on safari to get the most
from this wonderful region.

*The hardy horses of
the Camargue are
well adapted to the
salty marshlands*

Rosy pink flamingos

The most spectacular and photogenic of the delta's residents are the flamingos, one of the three 'icons' of the Camargue (bulls and horses are the other two). These beautiful birds are easily seen at any time of year, although the greatest numbers (up to 50,000) are present during the spring and summer. Most migrate to Africa or Spain for the winter, but around 5,000–6,000 stay on. During March and April their pink plumage is shown off to best effect in spectacular courtship displays. Flamingos feed mostly on small invertebrates, and have been known to live for up to 34 years.

Do's and Don'ts

Not all wildlife in the Camargue is as charming as the flamingos: the mosquitos, for instance, are voracious and ever-present – they breed prolifically in the marshes. Never venture out without adequate protection, except perhaps on windy days in winter when you should be all right. The wind (specifically the all-powerful *mistral*) can also be a hazard if you are cycling or walking long distances. Lastly, don't go marching off down the beaches or the *Digue-à-la-Mer* without adequate supplies of water.

What to see Apart from Arles (see page 108), which is within easy reach of the Camargue, the main accommodation and tourist centres are at les Saintes-Maries-de-la-Mer (see page 141) and Aigues-Mortes (see page 100). From les Saintes-Maries you can hike part or all of the way along the *Digue-à-la-Mer*, a sea wall that divides the unspoiled beaches and lagoons around the southern perimeter of the Étang de Vaccarès. The reserve of the Étang de Vaccarès itself is open only to visitors with a special permit, but you can still find many vantage points on the surrounding roads (principally the D37) from where you can watch birdlife.

The headquarters for the reserve is on the eastern side of the Étang de Vaccarès, where the Centre d'Information Nature▶▶ (*Closed* Sun. *Admission* donation) at la Capellière has one of the best and most up-to-date displays on the Camargue. There are two observatories (*Open* sunrise to sunset) within a minute or two of the Centre and a 1.5km walking trail.

Continuing on past la Capellière, you will arrive at Salin de Giraud, a quaint town that was created at the turn of the century by a Belgian company to house factory workers: hence the neat streets, shaded by plane trees and acacias, which are laid out in a strict grid pattern. Most of the employment now is with the *Salins du Midi*, who manufacture salt in the massive lagoons south of town: after the 'harvest' in late summer the huge salt mounds are a startling sight, gleaming in the sun and lining the edge of the lagoons in long, serried ranks. There is a viewpoint just off the D36D south of Salin de Giraud for an overview of this rather unusual production process.

Further down the same road is la Palissade▶ (*Open* daily; closed Sat and Sun from Sep–mid-Jun. *Admission charge*). This former private hunting estate was bought by a private conservation group in 1976 and is unusual in that it is one of the few areas in the Camargue not controlled by dykes, with the waters of the Rhône mixing with sea water in the lagoons, giving rise to fauna and flora typical of the lower Camargue before it was altered. Inside la Palissade there are audio-visual displays, a herbarium and an aquarium. Several walking trails criss-cross the 702ha estate, with guided tours available on request.

Back on the west side of the Étang de Vaccarès there are two more observation points on the edge of the reserve. The Maison du Parc Naturel Régional du Camargue▶▶ (*Open* daily in summer; Sat–Thu in winter), 4km north of les Saintes-Maries-de-la-Mer, has displays, including a 15-minute video (*Admission charge*), and huge plate glass viewing windows. To get in close to the birdlife, go to the Parc Ornithologique du Pont de Gau▶▶ (*Open* daily. *Admission charge*), a few metres away, which has signposted trails around the Étang de Pont de Gau (a half-hour walk), or the more extensive Étang de Ginès sanctuary, where bulls graze in the summer. Large aviaries near the entrance to the park house predators such as buzzards, black kites, Egyptian vultures and eagle owls (the bird park looks after injured predators sent here from all over Europe).

If you've overdosed on avian antics, you could visit the Château d'Avignon▶ (*Open* daily Apr–Oct. *Admission charge*) 13km north of les Saintes-Maries, an 18th-century mansion converted into a luxurious hunting lodge by the Marseille industrialist Louis Prat-Noilly in the 19th century. The interior has some fine Gobelins and Aubusson tapestries as well as paintings and carved woodwork.

Dotted about the countryside you will see many vast farmhouses (or *mas*), often surrounded by trees and nearly always built with their backs to the biting north-westerly *mistral*. Many of the *mas* were originally owned by wealthy Arlesians and managed on their behalf by the *bayle* (steward), whilst the *gardians* had their own traditional homes, little *cabanes* with thatched roofs that you can also see by the roadsides.

The *gardians* were at the heart of the romantic image of the Camargue conjured up by Mistral and the Félibrige, and they still play a major part in the Provençal tradition of the *cocardes* – (see page 132), travelling from village to village throughout the summer with their bulls and horses.

A good introduction to the traditions of the Camargue is the inspirational **Musée Camarguais▶▶** (*Open* daily; closed Tue, Oct–Mar. *Admission charge*), in an old barn at the Mas du Pont de Rousty, which was until recently a working sheep and cattle ranch. As well as exhibits on the geology and history of the Camargue there are sections on the *gardians* and farmhouse life in the last century. The 3.5km walking trail crosses pastures and the swamps of the Marais de la Grand Mar.

To see the *gardians* in action you can head down to the **Domaine de Méjanes▶** (*Open* Sun and public holidays Easter–mid-Jul), which is owned by the *pastis* magnate Paul Ricard. In typical Ricard style he has turned this huge estate into a popular entertainment centre with bullfights and *ferrades* in the stadium, horse-rides, and even a *petit train* (*Open* daily; Dec, Jan and Feb, Sun and Sat afternoons only. *Admission charge*) that does a 20-minute circuit of the marshes.

Jeep safaris of the Camargue and boat tours of the canals operate from les Saintes-Maries-de-la-Mer, or you can hire mountain bikes or go horse-riding.

119

Looking towards the Camargue from the bell-tower of the church in the centre of les Saintes-Maries-de-la-Mer

■ **The mass of marshes, canals and lagoons that make up the Camargue delta provide a wide diversity of habitats for an enormous number of wildlife species, including the greatest variety of aquatic birds – some 400 different species – found in one place in the Mediterranean.** ■

Threatened dunes
The beaches and sand dunes are one of the most threatened areas in the Camargue, partly due to rising sea levels and partly because the Rhône has too many dams on it and no longer carries enough silt downstream to replenish the delta. Dykes and sea groynes have had to be built to protect the beach, and wooden fencing erected to stop the dunes disappearing.

Salty zones Starting at the coast, the first and most obvious ecosystem encompasses the beaches and sand dunes. In the winter months, rainwater accumulates beneath the surface of the dunes and nourishes spring plants such as perfumed *Helichrysum* and sea wormwood, elegant sand lilies, and delicate sea rocket and sea stock. Once the supply of water is exhausted other species appear that are better adapted to survive the summer heat, such as sea holly and sea spurge.

Also on the coast are the salt pans, centre of a vast salt-production industry since the 19th century. Sea water is pumped across a series of lagoons between April and September, gradually increasing in density until it finally reaches the settling beds completely saturated with salt. Between August and October the salt starts to crystallise and it is then raked up into giant mounds (known as *camelles*) over 20m high before being washed, dried and crushed.

The constant water levels of the salt pans throughout the summer months, as well as the wealth of

Eagle owl nestlings – rarely seen but part of the prolific birdlife here

invertebrates living there, make them very attractive to colonies of flamingos, terns and black-headed gulls, as well as solitary species such as the oystercatcher, shelduck or redshank.

The third type of habitat in the lower half of the Camargue is the *sansouire*, huge, flat expanses of salt-marsh between the sea and the lagoons covered in scrubby vegetation: flooded in winter, they become mudflats in the spring and autumn and a salty desert in the summer. These wide open spaces are typical of the Camargue, their role changing with the seasons. On the higher ground of the *sansouire*, where only sea lavender and glasswort can survive the changing water levels, skylarks thrive all year round. When it is flooded in winter, tens of thousands of duck use the *sansouire* as a daytime resting place. From February onwards the water level drops and thousands of waders stop here on their long journey from northern Europe down to Africa.

In the summer months, herds of cattle and horses, no longer free to roam, graze behind the endless barbed wire fences.

Freshwater zones The freshwater marshes with their extensive reed beds provide ideal conditions for many species of bird that you can easily see from the roadside, such as herons, moorhens, coot, mallards and egrets.

Another inhabitant of the freshwater marshes that you are likely to see is the enchanting coypu, which makes a curious burbling noise as it swims across the surface in search of aquatic plants (it is particularly fond of bulrushes) to nibble on. The coypu is often mistaken for a beaver, but it is an entirely different family (it was introduced from South America); there are beavers, mostly along the banks of the Rhône, but they are nocturnal and rarely spotted.

On slightly higher ground are the remains of the grasslands, which provide a vital habitat for the colourful bee-eater as well as rollers and hoopoes; the grasslands are a particularly beautiful sight in the spring, when they are covered in white daisies, and again in the autumn, when they are a mass of purple sea lavender.

Agriculture has also taken its toll on the woodlands, remnants of the riverine forest which used to cover most of the north part of the delta. The predominant species are white poplar, willow, ash and elm, and there are still narrow belts along the banks of the Rhône that provide nesting sites for owls, woodpeckers, tits and starlings. Herons and egrets also nest here, feeding in the daytime in the freshwater marshes.

Rice paddies
Cattle and horses once used to graze on the richer pastures of the grasslands, along with sheep, but huge areas of this productive ground were converted to rice paddies in the 1950s. In the 1960s the Camargue was growing nearly a third of France's rice requirements, but since 1970 production has dropped dramatically and only a third of the former paddies are now in use for growing rice. Instead, other crops such as fruit and vegetables have taken over, thanks to the fact that the paddies cleaned the soil of salt.

Wading birds such as storks find rich feeding grounds in the Camargue marshes

The attractive port of Cassis was a favourite of the turn-of-the-century Fauve artists

The Route des Crêtes

One of the wildest coastal roads in Provence is the 17km-long Route des Crêtes between la Ciotat and Cassis. Take avenue Camusso out of la Ciotat and follow the twisting road as it dips and plunges along the clifftops, with spectacular views from the many stopping places en route. From the heights of Cap Soubeyran and Cap Canaille you can peer over the edge of the highest cliffs in France, with the sea pounding the rocks nearly 400m below. The hillsides behind the cliffs, devastated by fire several years ago, now sprout neatly curving rows of replanted pines.

▶▶▶ Cassis   97D1

Squeezed into a little bay between the cliffs of the Gardiole (which conceal the famous *calanques*) to the west and Cap Canaille to the east, this photogenic fishing port has long been popular with visitors. It is also a great favourite with the Marseillais, who flock here throughout the year to eat a huge seafood meal, washed down with copious quantities of the excellent local *vin blanc*, in one of the many restaurants that line the dockside.

Presiding over the port is a rambling château built by the *seigneurs des Baux* at the beginning of the 13th century, now privately owned by the Michelin tyre family. In the centre of town is the small **Musée d'Arts et Traditions Populaires** (*Open* Wed, Thu and Sat, afternoons only. *Admission free*), with local paintings, amphoras, coins and other relics.

Apart from seafood restaurants, the main attraction of Cassis is its proximity to the magnificent **calanques**▶▶▶, which are long, narrow inlets (like small fjords) eroded from the limestone cliffs of the Gardiole. There are several ways to see them: by passenger boat (regular departures from the quayside, with tour lengths that vary according to how many *calanques* you want to visit); you can also hire kayaks, small motorboats and windsurfing equipment; or, you can set out on foot (see Calanques walk, page 124).

Hemmed in as it is on all sides by high hills, there isn't much space around Cassis for vineyards, so the annual production from its 200ha of vines is highly prized: the light, fruity whites go admirably with local seafoods and *bouillabaisse*. If you want to take some home, some of the best *caves* are the Clos Ste-Magdeleine (tel: 04 42 01 70 28), the Domaine Caillol (tel: 04 42 01 05 35), the Domaine de Paternel (tel: 04 42 01 76 50) and the Clos Val Bruyère (tel: 04 42 01 73 36).

▶   la Ciotat   97D1

Entering la Ciotat from any direction, you can't miss the industrial architecture that symbolises its maritime past – the massive, gaunt gantries, now immobilised, which dominate the small harbour at the centre of the town. La

Ciotat has been a port since the 4th century, when the Greeks from Marseille set up an anchorage here, and in the 17th century the local mariners invented a system (called *la caravanne*) to get the most from their ships by never sailing empty from one port to the next – today, every modern shipping line operates a similar back-to-back cargo system.

The first boats were built here in 1836 and the first dry dock opened in 1936, but the dockyards were finally shut down in April 1990. Exhibitions on the town's maritime history are housed in the **Musée Ciotaden** (*Open* Mon, Wed and Sat afternoon and Sun morning), opposite the tourist office.

With the derricks now standing idle above the fishing boats and pleasure craft in the harbour, la Ciotat has turned to tourism for its survival, with glossy brochures extolling the virtues of the beaches of the '*Golfe d'Amour*' and the '*Ville des Lumières*': the appropriately named Lumière brothers gave the first ever public showing of motion pictures here (see panel). Capitalising on this connection, there has been an annual film festival since 1981 and, more recently, an annual jazz festival as well.

Behind the dockyards to the west of town, in the shadow of the Bec de l'Aigle (eagle's beak) promontory, rearing 70m high, is a small wilderness area now protected as the **Parc Naturel du Mugel**►► (*Open* daily). Pathways lead through typically Mediterranean vegetation to a viewpoint beneath the Cap. In the park, the Atelier Bleu du Cap de l'Aigle (tel: 04 42 08 07 67) runs courses on the ecology of the reserve. There is an underwater nature trail in the Calanque du Petit Muguel.

The Cosquer cave

In 1991 a local diver, Henri Cosquer, discovered an underwater fissure in one of the calanques that led to a cave containing hundreds of wall paintings, similar to the famous Lascaux paintings, depicting bison, horses and over 50 human hands in charcoal. Declared a historic monument in 1992, the cave has since been walled up to prevent public access – several divers have lost their lives attempting to see it. There is now a permanent exhibition devoted to the caves in Marseille (see page 130).

Lumière Brothers

By inventing the simple technique of piercing the edge of a roll of film with holes and running it through a toothed mechanism attached to a projector, Auguste and Louis Lumière gave birth to modern cinema. In 1895, they showed the first ever moving picture images to a private audience in la Ciotat. Three months later these same films were shown to a public audience in Paris, where spectators almost jumped out of their seats as a train approached them on the screen in *L'Entrée du train à la Ciotat*. The film festival (now encompassing photography and art exhibitions) takes place in the second half of July.

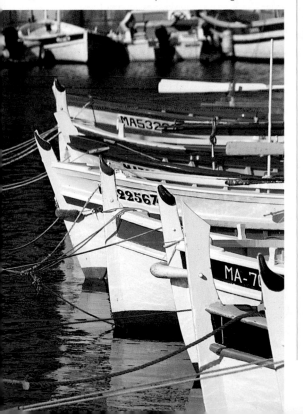

Fishing boats tied up at the Cassis quayside, their catches by now being prepared in the waterfront restaurants

Walk The Calanques

From the Calanque de Port-Miou just outside Cassis harbour to the Calanque de Callelongue at les Goudes, south of Marseille, the 20km-long coastline is criss-crossed with walking trails. This walk, from Cassis, is one of the easiest and takes around three hours return.

From Cassis, follow the signs for les Calanques and park at the end of the road. Walk along the length of the Calanque de Port-Miou through the old quarry. Untypically, Port-Miou's entire length is taken up with yacht berths.

Climb up the terraces over a low ridge to reach the **Calanque de Port-Pin►**, named after the *pins d'Alep* that once covered the Domaine de la Fontasse behind the inlet but which were mostly burnt down in 1990. The small shingle beach gets very crowded, since this *calanque* is the easiest to reach from Cassis, whether on foot or by water.

Continue up a narrow gully and climb up to the Plateau de Cadeiron. From here, there are wonderful views back to the magnificent cliffs of the Montagne de la Canaille rearing up above Cassis bay. In front of you, the ground starts to fall away until you reach a viewpoint over the **Calanque d'En-Vau►►**, one of the most spectacular of all the *calanques*. Beneath the dramatic, chalk-white cliffs and needle-like rocks, there is a small sandy beach, with rocky steps leading down – if you've warmed up enough for a swim.

Beyond En-Vau you can see the Riou archipelago (comprising the islands of Jarre, Jarron, Calseraigne and Riou itself).

The cliffs continue down into the limpid depths, sheltering a rich profusion of marine life that makes their steep underwater slopes as much a favourite with local scuba divers.

From here, you can either continue along the GR98 all the way to les Goudes (at least a full day's walk), or turn back along En-Vau out towards the pinnacle known as *Doigt de Dieu* ('God's finger'), and thence around the headland back to Port-au-Pin and Cassis. Note that in the summer months (15 June to 15 September) it is forbidden to stray off the GR98 because of the fire risk.

Walkers in the Calanques

▶ Gémenos 97D2

This village outside Aubagne is worth a detour for the nearby **Abbaye de St-Pons** (see page 166), or, if you are passing through on the way to Ste-Baume, stop in the main square and look inside the courtyard of the unusual **Granges du Marquis d'Albertas**, a huge building designed to house agricultural workers which was built in the second half of the 18th century. Bacchus astride a barrel over one of the four doorways (three are now closed off) attests to the function of what was essentially a huge barn with accommodation above. Most of the hundreds of rooms are now empty, the cobbles in the courtyard long gone, but the original circular fountain in the middle still remains.

Graveson 96B3

Once surrounded by swamps, Graveson is part of the fertile Petite Crau. Just outside Graveson is the **Musée des Aromes et du Parfum**▶▶ (*Open* daily. *Admission charge*), founded by aromatherapist Nelly Grosjean. Fragrant aromas permeate the whole of this converted farmhouse and barn, which houses a number of huge copper alembics (stills) as well as other traditional distilling equipment – some still in use. Essential oils, soaps and perfumes made from the local herbs are on sale; Nelly Grosjean also holds one-day aromatherapy courses (tel: 04 90 95 81 72 for details).

▶ Maillane 96B3

In the 14th century the village of Maillane was almost wiped out by the plague. Amongst those who repopulated it was a man from Tarascon called Mermet Mistral: several centuries later, Maillane was the birthplace of Frédéric Mistral (see pages 60–1), Provence's most famous literary figure. Mistral was brought up in the *Mas du Juge* (no visits) just outside Maillane, but on the death of his father in 1855 he moved with his mother into *Au Lezard*, a house in the middle of the village (opposite the *tabac*). In an alleyway alongside is the house Mistral moved into 20 years later when he married, and where he lived until his death in 1914. The latter is now the recently refurbished **Museon Mistral**▶▶ (*Closed* Mon. *Admission charge*).

Gleaming copper stills at the Musée des Aromes et du Parfum in Graveson

Speedboats, yachts and fishing boats rub shoulders in Marseille harbour

Laid out in the 17th century, La Canebière is Marseille's main thoroughfare

▶▶ Marseille 97D2

Introduction Compared to the glittering resorts of the Côte d'Azur or the historically rich inland cities of Provence, Marseille has never been a prime tourist destination and its image is one of work not play. However, as France's second biggest city (after Paris) and the Mediterranean's largest port, it has tremendous vitality and a cosmopolitan atmosphere that you cannot help but admire, even if you are unlikely to fall in love with the place.

Opening out to the sea from its niche between mountains and towering cliffs, Marseille's reputation precedes it, attracting all the worst labels – 'the gangster capital of France', a 'fascist hotbed', 'a dirty, vulgar and noisy city' – and yet to the casual visitor none of this is necessarily apparent. Like any major city, there are areas to be avoided at night – but then both Nice and Avignon have much higher crime rates per head of population than Marseille.

Marseille boasts over a dozen theatres, four times that many galleries and art exhibition centres, numerous music venues with everything from world music to chamber music, and of course the renowned Marseille opera. It also has a carnival every March, which celebrates the story of Protis and Gyptis and the founding of the city by the Greeks (see panel on page 130).

The settlement – which they named *Massalia* – prospered rapidly. As a maritime people, the Massalians established a series of trading posts along the coast (notably at Nice, Hyères and Antibes) and their explorers ventured as far afield as Senegal, in Africa, and the Baltic.

For protection from the Celto-Ligurian tribes it allied itself with Rome, but *Massalia*'s standing as a free city was irrevocably damaged when Caesar sacked the city in 49 BC for remaining neutral (ie not taking his side in his war against Pompey). Despite this, *Massalia* remained a stronghold of Hellenic civilisation. Its port declined in importance until the crusades, when it profited hugely by providing transport to the wars.

In 1720 a single ship, the *Grand Saint-Antoine*, slipped through the quarantine net around the port and unleashed the plague that was to devastate much of Provence; in Marseille alone, half the population died. But the town bounced back, benefiting particularly from the opening of the Suez Canal in 1869.

Walk Marseille

This walk takes in many of the best museums of Marseille, as well as the interesting old quarter of Le Panier. Allow 3–4 hours.

Start at the tourist office on the quai des Belges. Take rue Beauvau down to place Reyer for the **Opéra▶▶** – the wonderful art deco interior dates from 1924. From here, head northeast for the pedestrianised rue Paradis. Turn south, and in rue Grignan on your left is the **Musée Cantini**. Continue to the rue de Rome and turn left: keep going until you reach La Canebière.
   Go through the Bourse shopping centre (entrance to the **Musée d'Histoire**). Exit through the **Jardin des Vestiges** and follow the Grand Rue across rue de la République to

the place Daviel. Take the steps past **Clocher des Accoules** (all that remains of one of the city's older churches; parts date back to the 7th century) and follow the signs for the route through the old quarter of Le Panier to la Vieille Charité. Continue down rue du Petits Puits, take the steps in the place des Treize Cantons to reach the **Cathédrale de la Major**. Esplanade de la Tourette leads you to a belvedere, with a superb view over the old port. Go down the steps to the quay, and follow it along until place Jules Verne, for the Musée des Docks Romains and the remarkable Maison Diamantée, which houses the **Musée du Vieux Marseille**. Rejoin the quai du Port and walk back round to the quai des Belges.

Puget's birthplace
Just near the Centre de la Vieille Charité in the Le Panier quarter, a small plaque on the wall of an unremarkable house (3 rue du Petits Puits) celebrates the birthplace of one of the 17th century's most remarkable sculptors, Pierre Puget.

Towering above the city, Notre-Dame de la Garde was used as a Nazi headquarters during World War II – bullet marks are still visible on the walls

The big blue
First it was Richard Rogers in Nîmes and now another British architect, Will Alsop, has joined the ranks of those who have designed controversial and prestigious buildings in Provence. Alsop's daring new departmental headquarters (L'Hôtel du Département) in Marseille is unmistakable, a sculpted statement in bright blue that expresses the essence of post-high-tech architecture. Partially raised on stilts, it echoes one of the most famous architectural experiments in social housing – Le Corbusier's Unite d'Habitation, which still stands on the outskirts of Marseille.

With the loss of France's colonies in the 1950s the importance of trade again declined, but Marseille was left with the legacy of thousands of immigrants who had flocked here from North Africa in the 1960s (the population grew from 660,000 in 1955 to 960,000 in 1975); none of this was new to Marseille, which had welcomed refugees over the centuries. But, combined with unemployment, racial tensions have now been fuelled by the rise of Jean-Marie Le Pen's *Front National*, whose supporters still command a third of the vote in the city.

What to see At the heart of the city is the **Vieux Port▶▶**, where a bronze plaque on the quai des Belges marks the spot where Protis first stepped ashore. Fishing boats still pull in here every morning to unload their catches, which are sold straight to waiting customers. Alongside are the tourist boats for trips out to the **Frioul Archipelago** and the **Île d'If** (see page 131).

Leading up from the Vieux Port is the broad boulevard of La Canebière, Marseille's most famous street – though now full of dreary banks and airline offices. To the north is an area of steep streets and narrow alleyways known as **Le Panier▶**, Marseille's oldest district. Before World War II it housed fisherfolk and many Italian and Corsican refugees, and later gave shelter to hundreds of Jews hoping to escape the Nazis by catching a ship to America. In January 1943 the Nazis gave all 20,000 inhabitants one day's notice to quit and blew the whole lot up, rounding up 3,500 victims for the concentration camps in the process. The only buildings not destroyed were the Maison Diamantée and the 17th-century Hôtel de Ville on the quayside.

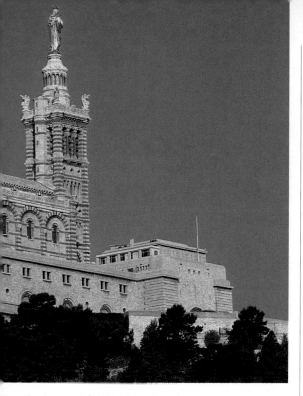

The first playing cards reached Europe from China via Venetian merchants in the 13th century, and this new-found pastime soon found its way to Marseille. The first recorded mention of cards in France occurs here, in the minutes of a public notary who, in 1381, was moved to ban a merchant of the city from playing a game known as *naipi* or *nahipi* (the forerunner of the Tarot). By the 17th century it had become a popular pastime, and the first card makers started up in 1631. Marseille Tarot cards became classics of the art.

The Tricolore *flies over the entrance to the 17th-century Hôtel de Ville*

On the south of the Vieux Port the quai de Rive Neuve houses ship-chandlers' shops and the new Théâtre National de Marseille de la Criée, with the **Basilique St-Victor** (see page 131) behind. From here, the road continues around the walls of the Fort St-Nicolas to the **Château de Pharo**, built by Napoléon III as a gift for the Empress Éugenie.

Past the headland, the Corniche President John Kennedy (with views over the offshore islands) leads to several artifical beaches, a small yachting basin, and the new **Marseille Aquaform▶▶** (*Open* daily. *Admission charge*). This enlightening aquarium and research centre houses many rare and fascinating species from tropical and Mediterranean waters.

Museums Marseille has numerous museums and it pays to be selective – or you will get exhibition fatigue. Starting on the north side of La Canebière, just across from the tourist office is the **Musée de la Marine et de l'Economie de Marseille** (*Closed* Tue. *Admission free*) housed inside the Palais de la Bourse – France's first stock exchange. Displays trace the maritime history of Marseille from the 16th century onwards, with models of old trading ships, paintings and engravings.

Just behind is the Bourse shopping centre, with the **Musée d'Histoire de Marseille▶▶** (*Open* Mon–Sat 12–7. *Admission charge*) on the ground floor. Here is the wreck of an ancient Roman merchant vessel, discovered in 1974, which sank in one corner of the Roman port (now unearthed in the **Jardin des Vestiges▶**, outside· the museum). Audio-visual displays explore the Greek heritage of *Massalia*.

Protis and Gyptis
In 600 BC a shipload of Greek colonists from Ionia landed in what seemed like an ideal spot, the Lacydon inlet, and went to seek permission from Nann, the local king, to start a settlement. The king was throwing a banquet that day, during which, according to custom, his daughter Gyptis would choose her future husband. She went for Protis, the good-looking leader of the Ionian delegation, and as their wedding gift the king bequeathed them Lacydon (now the *vieux port*) where they founded a colony.

The flooded sanctuary
A new exhibition devoted to the Cosquer caves (see page 123) is one of the latest attractions in the heart of Marseille's docklands. *La Grotte Henri Cosquer – Le Sanctuaire Englouti* (the flooded sanctuary) at 10, place de la Joliette (tel: 04 91 56 53 05) re-creates the history, vegetation, climate and the way of life in the Upper Paleolithic era when the caves were in use. The exhibition (*Open* daily. *Admission charge*) explores the context of the remarkable paintings found in the caves, which were believed to have been used as a sanctuary for communicating with animal spirits.

The gilded Madonna atop Notre-Dame de la Garde is the largest in France

Inside the unusual **Maison Diamantée►** on rue de la Prison is the **Musée du Vieux Marseille►►** (*Closed* Mon. *Admission charge*) with an eclectic selection of curiosities ranging from traditional Provençal *santons* and Arlesian furniture to gory paintings of the 1720 plague and a fine display on the manufacture of playing cards (once an important local industry), which includes the famous Marseille tarot cards (see panel, page 129).

Across the place Jules Verne is the **Musée des Docks Romains►** (*Closed* Mon. *Admission charge*), built over the site where all the artefacts were recovered. Huge storage jars for oil, grains and wine sit on the 1st-century Roman quay.

Further north in the Le Panier quarter is the **Centre de la Vieille Charité►►**, a wonderful building which was designed by Pierre Puget. Built out of rose-coloured stone, the courtyard is surrounded by three floors with arcades of different heights, with a curious elliptical baroque chapel as the central focus. The hospice became a barracks earlier this century, fell into disrepair, then was thoroughly renovated in the 1980s as a multimedia art and culture centre. It also houses the excellent **Musée d'Archéologie Méditerranéenne►►** (*Closed* Mon. *Admission charge*) which features a number of revolving exhibits from around the Mediterranean basin.

Marseille's oldest art museum is the **Musée des Beaux-Arts►** (*Closed* Mon. *Admission charge*) in a wing of the Palais Longchamp in the eastern quarter of the city. Much more centrally located is the **Musée Cantini►►►** (*Closed* Mon. *Admission charge*), the main focus for 20th-century art, with a collection of over 400 contemporary works of which only a small fraction are ever on display. Artists represented include Dufy, Bacon, Balthus, César, Max Ernst and Miró.

Churches and cathedrals
The most prominent church in Marseille is **Notre-Dame de la Garde►►**, which stands sentinel on an outcrop 162m above

the city. This Romano-Byzantine monster is surmounted by a 10m-high gilded Madonna and was built in the latter part of the 19th century. It is worth making the trek up here (or taking bus No 60) for the fabulous view of Marseille spread out beneath you.

Built in a similar neo-Byzantine style, the **Cathédrale de la Major** ►► (*Closed* Mon) overlooks the modern docks on the north side of the *vieille ville*. With its 70m-

high basilica and 444 marble columns supporting the roof, it is the largest church built in France since the Middle Ages. Despite its grandeur, it is not as interesting as the **Ancienne Cathédrale de la Major**►►► (*Closed* Mon) that it replaced and which sits alongside in its shadow. Although the older building was partially destroyed to make way for the new cathedral in the 19th century, what remains is a superb example of 11th-century Provençal Romanesque.

Across on the other side of the harbour is the **Basilique St-Victor**►►, originally part of a powerful abbey which spawned over 300 monasteries and priories throughout Provence and overseas. Founded in the 5th century, the abbey was damaged by the Saracens and later rebuilt with added fortifications – its walls are 3m thick. Inside, you can descend into the **crypt**► (*Closed* Sun morning. *Admission charge*), which has a series of sarcophagi hidden away in its ancient passageways. In the Chapelle Notre-Dame de Confession there is a black wooden statue of the Virgin which is venerated in an ancient Candlemas ceremony (see panel).

The Islands No visit to Marseille is complete without a visit to the infamous **Château d'If**►► (Boats from quai des Belges; journey 15 minutes, throughout the day, except in bad weather. *Admission charge*), perched on the rocky islet of the Île d'If. François I decided to build a fort here after visiting the island in 1516, and it was completed in 1531. However, it was soon turned into a prison and in the 17th century hundreds of Protestant prisoners perished inside its gloomy walls. Novelist Alexandre Dumas used it as the setting for his book *The Count of Monte Cristo*.

The other islands in the Frioul archipelago are Île **Pomègues** and Île **Ratonneau**, where Julius Caesar anchored his fleet in preparation for the siege of Marseille in 49 BC. In the 17th century, the Île Ratonneau became a quarantine centre for plague victims, with the ruins of the old **Hospital Caroline** on a hilltop attesting to the belief that the sea winds would sweep the germs away. These barren-looking islands, alive with wild plants and flowers, can be visited on a round trip that also encompasses the Île d'If.

The massive Cathédrale de la Major

Candlemas at St-Victor
On Candlemas Day (2 February) a large procession gathers at the Basilique St-Victor, where the Archbishop blesses green candles in front of the black statue of the Virgin. The faithful then take their candles back home, where they are lit to celebrate regeneration and rebirth. On the same day, small loaves are baked in the shape of boats, called *navettes*, to commemorate the arrival on Provençal shores of St Lazarus and Saints Mary Magdalene and Martha in les Saintes-Maries-de-la-Mer.

On the Roman quay

■ **Summer is the season of bullfights in the Bouches-du-Rhône, with posters plastered on trees and billboards everywhere advertising Cours de Taureau in the nearest town with an *arène* worthy of the name. Unlike Spanish bullfights, the bulls are not put to death.** ■

Rami
One well-known bull, Rami, who belonged to *manadier* Marcel Mailhan, died a natural death at 24 years old – a record longevity that is celebrated by a monument over his tomb in the Camargue!

Young tourneurs *in the making?*

The bulls All the animals used in Provençal bullfights come from the Camargue, most of which probably would not exist were it not for the bulls, which provide the economic *raison d'être* for maintaining the pasture lands. The Camargue horses are also bred largely in order to manage the *manades* (herds) of bulls.

The Camarguais bull, lighter than its Spanish counterpart (some of which are also reared here), is a vigorous, agile and intelligent breed. It is not suited to agricultural work and were it not for the *cours* it would probably exist only in zoos. The animals suffer no great hardship: each bull spends a maximum of 15 minutes in the ring, appearing perhaps a dozen times in a year. At the end of its career, it retires to graze in the Camargue.

The game The *Cours Camarguais* (also known as the *Cours à la Cocarde*) is more of a game than a fight, a contest of agility, courage and skill between the bulls and the participants. Dressed in white, the *razeteur* has a long hook (the *razet*) with which he has to snatch a *cocarde* (rosette) from between the horns of the bull. He is helped by a *tourneur*, whose role it is to distract the bull. He has to accomplish this within a 15-minute time limit, and if he does, gains a prize. He risks being chased out of the ring by the bull, or forced to leap over the barricades –

The Roman arena at Arles, packed to capacity

and he hopes he doesn't fall back on to the bull's horns beneath him.

The round-up A tradition with more practical origins is that of the *ferrade*. At one year old, the young bulls are separated from the herd, chased on horseback and then grappled to the ground by the *manadier* (herdsman) in order to be branded. This too has evolved into a spectator sport, as has the *abrivado*, during which the bulls are driven through the streets on their way to the arena, chasing or being chased by the crowds.

Anyone can try Although nowadays the *Cours Camarguais* is organised on a professional basis (it became an official French sport in 1975) and the *razeteurs* train rigorously, most of the fun for the hundreds of people who flock down to their local ring on a Friday or Saturday night is in the *Cours à la Vachette*. The local youth – and sometimes even children – leap into the ring to be chased by the *vachette* (which has capped horns) and to try and tempt it to jump after them into a shallow pool in the middle. Cash prizes are the reward for this risky-looking game!

In the arena The most spectacular settings for local bull-fights are in the old Roman arenas such as at Arles, where at least 30 *cours* are held each year. However, if you find Spanish-style *corridas* (where the bulls are put to the death) distasteful, avoid the arena at Nîmes, which still clings to old traditions, dating back to Roman times when the Nîmes arena had a reputation for bloodthirsty games.

Origins
The first recorded bullfights were held in honour of King Louis and Queen Yolands in Arles in 1405. The birth of the *Cours Camarguais* as it is today dates back to 1793, when a Commissaire called Fréron was welcomed into Arles with a spectacle which involved the now characteristic *cocarde* in which the winner was awarded a prize. It was the Marquis de Baroncelli who stimulated the revival of this colourful tradition in the last century.

Comic capers
The *vachette* often vaults over the inner barrier around the ring, and as it chases round the outside everybody leaps to safety *inside* the ring – just like a comedy cartoon, the bull's progress can be measured by the escaping bodies popping one by one back over the barrier. When it gets half-way round, the *vachette* is sent back in the ring again.

The serene cloisters of the Abbaye-de-Montmajour

The much-photographed and painted Miroir des Oiseaux, Martigues

► **Martigues** 97C2

Martigues is a pleasant base for exploring the Étang de Berre or for stopping over *en route* for the Camargue, not least because of the picturesque canals that run through its centre between its three separate 'villages'.

On the southern side of the main canal is Jonquières, the busiest village if you are looking for a meal or a drink. In the middle is L'Isle, which has several restored 17th- and 18th-century houses as well as the splendid **Église de la Madeleine►**, which recently had a much-needed facelift. From the bridge next to the church is a celebrated view known as the **Miroir des Oiseaux►** (the birds' mirror). This little cameo of fishing boats moored in a curve of the canal at the *quai Brescon* was painted by Corot, Ziem and several other turn-of-the-century artists. Works by Ziem and others are on display in the **Musée Ziem** (*Closed* Tue. *Admission charge*) on the boulevard du 14 Juillet in the third village of Martigues, Ferrières.

► **Maussane-les-Alpilles** 96B3

Situated at the foot of the Alpilles with the fertile Plaine de la Crau stretching away to the south, Maussane-les-Alpilles is a prosperous village that made its fortunes from olive oil: at the beginning of the century it had over a dozen olive mills, but today only one survives, which still presses olives in the traditional way (*Open* daily except Sun: follow the signs for the Cooperative des Baux down rue Charlour Rien on the north side of the main road).

► **Miramas-le-Vieux** 97C2

Miramas-le-Vieux has recently been restored (and the streets recobbled) to create the kind of medieval *village perché* which you are more likely to expect in the Vaucluse. The manicured ruins of the old château are the setting for music concerts on summer evenings.

Keep going on the D10 and you will reach **St-Chamas**, a former fishing village currently reorienting itself towards yachting and tourism. In the town centre, the **Église►►** has an impressive baroque façade attributed to the 17th-century Aixois architect Pierre Pavillon. Just outside is a well-preserved Roman bridge, the **Pont-Flavien▶**. Built in the 1st century AD, it is framed by two triumphal arches.

▶▶▶ Montmajour, Abbaye-de-   *96B3*

Set on a hillock 5km north of Arles, Montmajour was one of the most powerful monasteries of medieval Provence, and even in ruins is still an impressive sight.

Montmajour owes its origins to one of the early Christian saints, St Trophimus, who fled here from Arles to hide in a cave in the hillside. Later, a group of hermits took up residence to safeguard the site, which led to the founding of the monastery in the 10th century. Under Benedictine rule the abbey went from strength to strength, establishing numerous priories and starting on the Herculean task of reclaiming the surrounding marshlands. Thanks to these land-holdings, the abbey became very wealthy – and decadent. In 1639 a group of reformed monks was sent in to sort it out, but those already in residence, reluctant to leave a fat sinecure, sacked the abbey in revenge.

In the 18th century Montmajour was partly rebuilt, but Louis XVI disbanded the abbey in 1786. Restoration began in 1907.

The 12th-century **upper church▶**, never completed, is an impressive, austere structure. On the right of the nave is an interesting crypt, part-built into the side of the hill, with fine Romanesque vaulting. The **cloister▶▶▶** ranks among the most important in Provence, with finely detailed carvings of demons and beasts on the bases and capitals of the cloister's colonnades.

From the 26m-high **keep**, an impressive fortified structure constructed in 1369, there are wonderful panoramic views across to the Alpilles, Arles, Tarascon and the Plaine de la Crau. From the keep, go down the side of the hill to the wonderful little **Chapelle St-Pierre▶▶**, which is half carved out of the hillside in the caves where St Trophimus sought refuge. The chapel is sometimes closed, but the abbey is open daily (*Admission charge*).

Fresh fish
Until big industry moved into the nearby Fos complex, the village of Martigues relied almost entirely on fishing, and there are still plenty of working boats moored up on the canal sides. In July and August the abundant sardine catch is distributed free every evening, freshly grilled, in an old custom known as the *sardinades*.

Montmajour was one of the most important medieval monasteries in Provence

Olive festival
The annual harvest of green olives from Mouriès' 80,000 trees is around 1,200 tonnes. If you want to try out their famous olives (as well as a multitude of other olive products), the best time to come is in the middle of September, when there is an annual, two-day festival, which also features bullfights and Provençal dances.

► **Mouriès** *96B3*

Mouriès is well known for its peppery oils – so if you are an olive oil aficionado this is the place to come. Mouriès is around 6km southeast of Maussane-les-Alpilles. Olive oil mills have been part of the landscape here for over 100 years. There were 18 mills in 1882; now there are only two (the *moulin cooperatif* and the *moulin moderne*), but they still produce 200,000 litres of olive oil between them each year.

►►► **Nîmes** *96A3*

Although situated 25km west of the Rhône and well outside the borders of present-day Provence, Nîmes shares much of the Provençal heritage – in particular, a glorious past as a Gallo-Roman city.

Nîmes first rose to prominence as the capital of the Celtic tribe of the Volcae-Arecomici, when it was known as *Nemansus* after a sacred and prolific spring that the Celts revered. The settlement was also strategically positioned on the main Spanish–Italian trade routes, and when the Romans forged through in the 1st century AD the inhabitants were quick to embrace their new overlords. *Nemansus* became *Colonia Nemausensis*.

Augustus reciprocated the Celtic welcome by heaping privileges on the town and encircling it with a monumental, 8km-long wall; soon after, a large amphitheatre was added, as well as the celebrated Maison Carrée and the aqueduct of the Pont du Gard, which brought water to the city's baths and fountains.

After the decline of Rome, Nîmes fell into the hands of the Visigoths, followed by the Franks. In the 16th century the town sided with the Protestant Huguenots, which led to considerable bloodshed, but peace was restored with the Edict of Nantes in 1598. The 17th century saw further conflict,

One of the best-preserved Roman temples in Europe, the Maison Carrée in Nîmes was built in the 1st century BC

but after the troubles Nîmes concentrated on building up its textile industry, and by the 18th century over 10,000 people and 300 looms were churning out silk fabric and serge for export. One of its best-selling lines was a hard-wearing blue serge that became known simply as de Nîmes ('from Nîmes'), and when some of this fabric found its way to California in 1848, Levi Strauss adopted it to create his famous denim jeans.

Nîmes has had little success since; to quote an early guidebook: '20th century Nîmes has stagnated...and it has been supplanted by Montpellier'. Enter, in 1983, the dynamic Jean Bousquet, former head of the locally based fashion empire of Cacharel, elected mayor on a ticket of turning Nîmes' fortunes around.

By pouring money into arts and culture, and in particular by commissioning world-class architects to embellish the city with buildings and monuments, Bousquet has sought to regain the crown from rival Montpellier and rejuvenate the city. Some resent his high-handed approach, but his ambitions have put Nîmes firmly back on the map.

What to see Most of the sites are within easy walking distance of each other within the city centre. First stop – the spectacular Arènes▶▶▶ (*Open* daily. *Admission charge*), one of the best-preserved Roman amphitheatres in existence. Dating from the turn of the 1st century AD, its mellow, honey-coloured sandstone exterior is now completely black from exhaust fumes and pollution.

A lapidary Cupid in the Jardin de la Fontaine

The Arena Village
After gladiator fights were banned in the 6th century under the influence of Christianity, the Nîmes arena was turned into a fortress by the Visigoths. Later, people started to move in and build houses inside it (a fate that also befell the arena at Arles and the theatre at Orange); by the 18th century this had grown into an entire village, with 2,000 people, 200 houses and even a couple of churches. It took over 30 years to clear the whole lot away in the early 19th century.

The place aux Herbes is the focal point of Nîmes's old quarter

Detail of one of the many statues in Nîmes's delightful Jardin de la Fontaine

Despite this the arena is in remarkable condition, and on the upper storeys you can still see the sockets for the posts that held the *velum*, an adjustable awning which sheltered spectators. Now the arena has the 20th-century equivalent, a massive inflatable canopy weighing over nine tonnes that is put up in the winter months: it takes a team of engineers over three weeks to erect (the canopy goes up in October and comes down in April; during these months visits to the arena are by guided tour only for safety reasons).

The other 'must' in Nîmes is the **Maison Carrée▶▶▶**, a delightful temple also in exceptional condition. Built in the 1st century AD and modelled on the Temple of Apollo in Rome, it was dedicated to Augustus' grandsons, Caius and Lucius. Surrounded by elegant Corinthian columns, it remains almost perfectly intact, despite having been used as (amongst other things) a stable in the Middle Ages.

Facing the Maison Carrée on the place du Forum is a high-profile reminder of Bousquet's commitment to modern architecture, the **Carrée d'Art▶▶**, which opened in 1993. Its name – 'art square' – echoing the 'square house' opposite, this beautifully designed Norman Foster building takes up the purity of line of the ancient temple and translates it into 20th-century idiom. Inside, light pours down a huge central well to the library on the basement floors; the upper levels house the **Centre d'Art Contemporain▶▶** (*Closed* Mon. *Admission charge*). There is a café beneath the roof canopy with great views of Nîmes and the Maison Carrée beneath.

Just north of the Carre d'Art is another Bousquet-inspired project, the **place d'Assas▶**. Designed in 1989 by Martial Raysse, water flows across the square between two figures representing Nemausa – deity of the original spring – and Nemausus.

Water also plays a central role in the wonderful **Jardin de la Fontaine▶▶** near by. Created in the late 18th century, the gardens channel the waters of the Nemausus spring through a series of Roman-style pools beneath a maze of balustrades and statuary. On the left of the lower promenade are the remains of the **Temple of Diana**.

Follow the gardens uphill for the **Tour Magne▶** (*Open* daily. *Admission charge*) at the top of Mont Cavalier. This 30m-high tower was once part of the city walls built by Augustus; steps lead to a viewing platform at the top.

The heart of the city, old Nîmes, is almost entirely pedestrianised and is a pleasure to wander around. In the middle of the old quarter is the place aux Herbes, dominated by the **Cathédral Notre-Dame-et-St-Castor►**, which has been rebuilt many times over the centuries. Its west front (facing the square) is ornamented with a classical frieze illustrating Old Testament stories. In a corner by the cathedral is the **Musée de Vieux Nîmes►►** (*Open* daily. *Admission charge*), which has a well-presented collection of Renaissance furniture, and historical documents.

On the eastern side of the old quarter, the **Musée d'Histoire Naturelle et de Préhistoire►** (*Open* daily. *Admission charge*) is worth a look for its extensive collection of sculpted *menhirs* (dolmens) and Gallo-Roman bits and pieces such as jewellery, pots, oil lamps and household items. A model shows the full extent of Augustus' amazing wall that once encircled the city.

South of the Arènes, the **Musée des Beaux Arts►** (*Open* daily. *Admission charge*) has some significant Roman mosaics as well as paintings and other works spanning the 15th to the 20th centuries.

Nearby Nîmes is inevitably associated with the nearby **Pont du Gard►►►**, and it is well worth a detour to see what has always been considered 'one of the wonders of the Ancient World'.

The Pont du Gard owes its existence to the almost insatiable thirst for water of the average Roman city – not just for domestic use but for the many fountains and public baths – and their desire for totally pure water. When the spring of Nemansus was deemed no longer sufficient, the city engineers did not hesitate to carve out an aqueduct from the Source d'Eure near Uzès, nearly 50km away. Faced with the impetuous River Gard in their path, the Romans – or rather their slaves – erected this stunning masterpiece built of masonry blocks weighing up to six tonnes each. Its three tiers of arches span the valley for 275m and reach a height of 48m above the river.

Despite the huge numbers of people who come to visit the aqueduct, the area immediately surrounding it has thankfully been kept free of intrusive buildings (shops, cafés and so on are located well away from the bridge), so you are left to gaze in awe at this grand gesture to Roman public hygiene.

The fountains of Nîmes are a constant reminder that the town owes its origins to the waters of the spring of Nemansus

Glanum's Mausoleum: inside there are statues of Caesar and Augustus

▶▶▶   **St-Rémy-de-Provence**   *96B3*

Despite nowadays being heavily dependent on tourism, St-Rémy is still undoubtedly one of the most delightful towns in all Provence. Encircled by a boulevard of plane trees, the centre of the town is a warren of fine old buildings, pretty squares, plant-filled alleyways and cooling fountains. Its charms inspired Provençal poets such as Joseph Roumanille, Marie Mauron and Marcel Bonnet, as well as novelist Gertrude Stein.

On the edge of the circular boulevard is the **place de la République**, with outdoor cafés and a lively market on Wednesday mornings. Facing the square is the neoclassical **Collegiale St-Martin**▶ with its famous organ: built in 1983, it is said to be one of the finest contemporary organs in Europe. Regular recitals take place on Saturday evenings between July and September.

Behind St-Martin in the shady place Favier, the 16th-century **Hôtel Mistral de Mondragon**▶ houses the **Musée des Alpilles**▶ (*Open* daily. *Admission charge*), with well-presented exhibits on local folklore, geology, ethnography, and Nostrodamus (see panel, page 145). Next door in another fine Renaissance palace, the **Hôtel de Sade**▶, is the **Musée Archéologique**▶▶ (*Open* daily. *Admission charge*), devoted to finds from Glanum excavations, including some well-preserved temple decorations, statues of the gods, and everyday Roman items such as jewellery and jars. Another old mansion, the **Hôtel Estrine**, contains the **Centre d'Art Presence Van Gogh**▶ (*Closed* Mon. *Admission charge*), with audio-visual displays and documentaion on Van Gogh, and exhibitions of contemporary works.

Nearby Within walking distance down the D5 (1km outside St-Rémy) are the ruins of **Glanum**▶▶▶ and the remarkable Roman monuments known as **les Antiques**▶▶▶, consisting of a well-preserved mausoleum and a triumphal arch by the side of the road. The 18m-high mausoleum, with elaborate bas-reliefs on the podium, was erected in around AD 30. The triumphal arch, dating from around the same time, was one of the first of its kind in Provence.

Opposite the Antiques is the entrance to the site of **Glanum** itself (*Open* daily. *Admission charge*), where excavations since 1921 have uncovered many different layers of habitation from the Celto-Ligurian period through to its sacking in AD 270. There is an enormous amount to see, including the Forum, the *thermae* (baths), a sacred well from the Gallo-Greek period, several large private houses, and the remains of various temples. One of these has recently been partially reconstructed, with the mouldings, columns and elaborate capitals faithfully copied (using ancient tools and techniques) from the originals kept in the Musée Archéologique.

Just below the site is the former monastery of **St-Paul-de-Mausole▶**, where Van Gogh was hospitalised (see page 112). It is still a private sanitorium, but you can walk down the main driveway and visit the church and the 12th-century cloisters.

The entrance to the Musée des Alpilles, housed in a 16th-century building

▶▶   les Saintes-Maries-de-la-Mer   96A2

This seaside resort is a popular base for visiting the Camargue and has plenty of things to do, including horse-riding, cycling, sailing, windsurfing and the beach.

The resort is at its busiest during the annual *Pèlerinage des Gitanes*, a gypsy pilgrimage that takes place on the last weekend in May each year to honour Sarah, the black Egyptian slave who was washed ashore along with the three Marys (see panel). Sarah's remains are interred in a reliquary in the crypt of the **Église▶▶** in the centre of the old town. This stately Romanesque church, strengthened during the 12th century after a series of Saracen raids on the town, is one of the best examples of fortified churches in Provence; from its bell-tower (*Open* daily Apr–mid-Nov) there is a panorama of the vast, open spaces of the Camargue.

Just near the church is the **Musée Baroncelli** (*Closed* Tue. *Admission charge*), with displays on local wildlife, Arlesian costumes and furniture, and a few mementos of Baroncelli's life, including signed photographs from his American Indian friends (see panel, page 59).

Baroncelli's **tomb** is down on the waterfront next to the *arènes*, and although (strangely) unmarked, it is unmistakable because it incorporates carvings of his two main passions, a horse and a bull.

The legend of Sarah
According to legend, Sarah arrived here with Mary Magdalene, Mary Salome, Mary Jacobe, and several disciples after they had been cast adrift from the Holy Land. Once they reached the Camargue in the 'boat of Bethany', the disciples dispersed; the elderly Mary Salome, Mary Jacobe and Sarah stayed and were eventually buried in the oratory that they had built here. Their tombs soon attracted pilgrims, particularly gypsies from all over Europe who had adopted Sarah as their patron saint. At the end of May, effigies of the saints are carried down to the sea to be blessed during the annual *Pèlerinage des Gitanes*.

Drive The Alpilles

An extension of the Lubéron range, the Alpilles are one of the prime landmarks in the middle of the Crau plain. This tour goes through the heart of the range and encompasses interesting places around the base of the Alpilles (about half a day); you could also extend it to include les Baux (allow a full day).

From St-Rémy take the D99 eastwards, turning right down the D74A across the Canal des Alpilles towards **Eygalières**▶▶, a charming little town with a long history. In the streets are many fine old houses; there are the remains of the 12th-century castle keep of the old château; below the ruins on the north side of

The remains of a Roman aqueduct at Barbegal

the hill, the 17th-century **Chapelle des Penitents Blancs** has been converted into the small **Musée**▶ (*Open* Sun afternoon or by calling the caretaker, M. Pezet, tel: 04 90 95 92 51), which has a wonderfully haphazard collection of local ethnography.

Follow the D24B east towards Orgon, to see the charmingly simple, 12th-century **Chapelle de St-Sixte**▶▶ on a hillock to the right of the road. There is an annual pilgrimage from Eygalières at Easter (it is not otherwise open). Return via Eygalières and turn left down the D24, a lovely scenic road that winds through the heart of the Alpilles, surrounded on either side by pine forests and vineyards. Turn right at the hamlet of le Destet towards Maussane on the D78, which snakes around the south face of the Alpilles along an ancient route once used for the annual *transhumance*.

At **Maussane** (see page 134) you can either detour back up to **les Baux** (see pages 114–15) or continue on the D17 towards Paradou, where outside the village a huge hangar houses **La Petite Provence du Paradou▶** (*Open* daily. *Admission charge*). This 'Provence-in-miniature' features over 300 figures – shepherds, gypsies, farmers, fishermen and so on – integrated into a vast, three-dimensional tableaux with working windmills

one of the few surviving examples of a Roman flour mill. This interesting structure – the only one of its kind powered by hydraulics – consisted of no less than 16 mills, linked up with two parallel series of paddle-wheels in the middle. Turn right down the D33 towards **Fontvieille▶**. This attractive town largely owes its reputation to the link with novelist Alphonse Daudet. An avenue lined with pines to the south of town leads to the **Moulin de Daudet▶▶** (Daudet's windmill. *Open* daily; closed Jan. *Admission charge*), set on a hillock with views across to the Alpilles and the Tarascon plain. Just outside the windmill there is a small museum containing first editions of his writings, portraits, manuscripts and other memorabilia.

From Daudet's windmill a path leads back to Fontvieille, past two other windmills, to the **Château de Montauban▶** (*Open* daily. *Admission charge*), where Daudet actually stayed whilst in Fontvieille; it now houses an exhibition – 'Bonjour Monsieur Daudet' – which focuses on Daudet's personal life. Take the D33 out of Fontvieille until you come to the lovely **Chapelle St-Gabriel▶▶** just before the N570. This is nearly all that remains of a once-thriving Gallo-Roman settlement, *Ernaginum*, which was a port for rafts that plied the surrounding marshes. The drying-up of the marshes signalled the death knell for the town. From here, return to St-Rémy on the D32 and the D99.

The impressive 12th-century Chapelle St-Gabriel and (top) the Italianate rose window on its façade

and other careful touches. Turn off down the D78E until you see the **Aqueduct de Barbegal▶▶**. Park near the remains of the aqueduct and follow it between a cutting in the rocks to the edge of a small escarpment: beneath you, the slope of the hill is covered with a series of ruins –

A decorative time-
piece on the clock
tower, Salon

The Tarasque monster
After arriving in the 'boat
of Bethany', in les Saintes-
Maries-de-la-Mer, Ste
Marthe came to Tarascon
only to find the town terrorised by an amphibious
monster which devoured
local children and cattle
alike. Ste Marthe tamed
the beast by showing it her
crucifix, after which it was
captured and led away on
a lead. To celebrate this
miracle, in 1474 the Good
King René organised an
annual carnival – which
still takes place on the last
Sunday in June – with a
ferocious, dragon-like
Tarasque led through the
streets snapping his
mighty jaws at onlookers;
bonfires, fireworks, bullfights and dances precede
the parade of the captive
monster.

▶ **Salon-de-Provence** 97C2

Salon's fortunes were founded on soap-making and
olive oil, but its present-day prosperity is largely
due to the French Air Force flying school just
outside of town.

The medieval seer Nostradamus moved
here during the last years of his life (from
1547 to 1566), and his house in the old
quarter is now a modern museum,
La Maison de Nostradamus (*Open*
daily. *Admission charge*). A series of
tableaux depict scenes from his life, as
well as key moments in the development of Renaissance philosophy.

Just near Nostradamus' house, the
lovely old **Porte de l'Horloge**▶ was built
of honey-coloured stone between 1626 and
1664. Opposite the gateway in place Crousillat
is the beautiful 18th-century **Grand Fontaine**▶,
which has become so encrusted in moss that it looks
like a huge green mushroom cloud.

The nearby **Musée Grevin de la Provence**▶ (*Open*
daily. *Admission charge*), has waxwork displays depicting
key events in the history of Provence. Salon also now
has the **Musée de Coca-Cola** (*Open* daily. *Admission
charge*), Europe's only museum devoted to the ubiquitous fizzy drink.

Within the 'old' town centre, the 13th-century **Église St-
Michel**▶ has a noteworthy part-Gothic and part-
Romanesque façade. At the top of the hideous new square
in the old town is the imposing **Château de l'Emperi**▶▶
(*Closed* Tue. *Admission charge*), a massive fortress dating
back to the 10th century; it now houses the **Musée d'Art
et d'Histoire Militaire**▶. The collection of over 10,000
items includes arms, uniforms, waxwork figures and flags,
spanning the period from Louis XIV to World War I.

Just to the north of the town centre is the **Église St-
Laurent,** which houses the tomb of Nostradamus.

▶▶ **Silvacane, Abbaye de** 97C3

Set amidst fertile fields on the south banks of the Durance,
the Abbaye de Silvacane (*Open* daily except Tue.
Admission charge) was the last to be built of the three
great Cistercian abbeys in Provence (the other two being
Sénanque and le Thoronet). Its name comes from *silva
cana* ('forest of rushes'), which was all that was here
before the monks set about draining the marshes to
create farmland. Founded in the 12th century, the abbey
prospered until pillaging and disastrous crops in the
14th century ruined it. It was turned into farm
buildings before restoration began in the 19th
century. As with its sister abbeys, the
uncompromising austerity of Silvacane's architecture reflects the chaste lives of the
Cistercians. The stark beauty of the clean-
lined, pale stone church is echoed in a
charming cloister with an old fountain.

▶▶ **Tarascon** 96B3

A former port on the banks of the
Rhône, Tarascon is famous for its

145

The Provençal seer
Born in 1503 in St-Rémy, Michel de Nostradamus astonished his teachers at an early age with his knowledge of the stars and became known as 'the young astrologer'. His studies at medical school were frequently interrupted by the plague, so he wandered the country studying plants and trying to find a remedy for this dreaded disease. He began to have notable successes in curing people, and was called upon from far and wide. He moved to Salon in 1547, and published the first of his astrological predictions in 1555. They were an immediate sell-out, and he was summoned to Paris to predict the futures of Henri II's four sons. Nostradamus died peacefully in 1566, but his *Centuries* (predictions) are still widely read today.

fabulous castle and the equally fantastic legends woven into its history – principally the story of Ste Marthe and the Tarasque (see panel).

King René spent the last ten years of his life surrounded by troubadours and artists in the fairy-tale **Château►►►** (*Guided tours* daily. *Admission charge*) overlooking the Rhône. The building of the castle was initiated by Louis II of Anjou in 1400 and finished off by his son, the 'Good King René', in 1449. It was used as a prison from 1800 right up until 1926.

Considered to be one of the finest fortified medieval châteaux in the whole of France, its massive walls and crenellated towers contrast markedly with the graceful and elegant interior architecture, particularly the flamboyant *cour d'honneur* where the royal apartments are linked by a spiral staircase.

Ste Marthe's remains, conveniently discovered in 1187, lie in the **Collegial Ste-Marthe►►** just opposite the château. The church has suffered many indignities over the centuries, having lost its best sculptures during the Revolution and been bombed in World War II.

Tarascon has another claim to fame in the contemporary legend of Tartarin, a comic figure invented by the novelist Alphonse Daudet in 1872, who bumbles through life bragging about his improbable adventures. After shunning Daudet for many years because the ridiculous Tartarin made them into a laughing-stock, the people of Tarascon eventually forgave him to cash in on the fat man's fictional life in the **Maison de Tartarin** (*Closed* Sun. *Admission charge*) on the boulevard Itam.

■ **Despite modernisation and the presence of missile sites, country life in Provence continues according to the cycle of the seasons, a calendar which alternates periods of intense work with equally intense festivities to celebrate the fruits of the earth.** ■

Spring blossom (top) and autumn vines

Van Gogh on summer
'I keep remembering what I have seen of Cézanne, because he has exactly caught the harsh side of Provence. It has become very different from what it was in spring, and yet I certainly have no less love for this countryside burnt up as it begins to be from now on. Everywhere is old gold, bronze – copper, one might say – and this with the green azure of the sky blanched with heat: a delicious colour, extraordinarily harmonious, with the blended tones of Delacroix.' Van Gogh, in a letter to his brother, Theo.

Spring Spring unfolds quickly in Provence, and by February or March, almonds and mimosa are starting to bloom, soon followed by carpets of wild flowers. Olives and vines (if they have not been seen to in November) must be pruned, and cereal crops sown.

By April, plums, peaches, apples, apricots, pears and quinces are in blossom, and fires are lit in the orchards to stop frost killing the delicate buds. The sheep are sheared, and Easter celebrated with the first spring lamb. The first nightingales and swallows appear. In Arles, Pain de St George is baked to celebrate the feast day of the patron saint of the Camargue on 23 April.

Summer 1 May is considered the beginning of summer in Provence. *Primeurs* (early fruit and vegetables) brighten up market stalls, with asparagus, cherries, peas, apricots, melons, and strawberries from the market gardens heralding a taste of sunshine. The flocks are shepherded back to the hill pastures, following the ancient traditions of the *transhumance*.

The autumn sowing of wheat is ready for harvesting in June, with migrant workers in their thousands descending from the mountains to cut the ripe sheaths. On the summer solstice, St John' Day (24 June), bonfires are lit on hilltops to celebrate the end of the harvest. Other harvest festivals celebrate St Eloi or St Roch, and nearly all involve a great deal of wine and merriment, music and dancing, and huge banquets in village squares with grand *aïolis*.

As the summer progresses Spanish broom scents the *garrigue*, the lavender fields are resplendent with colour, and thyme, rosemary, marjoram and sage can be culled from the wild. Melons, peaches and almonds are in abundance, and August is the perfect time for *ratatouille*, with courgettes, tomatoes, aubergines, garlic, onions and peppers overflowing in the markets. Honeysuckle, clematis and myrtle blossom on trellises and sunny walls.

Autumn September is dominated by the grape harvest, the *vendange*, a time when friends, neighbours and families get together to pick grapes and spend long evenings quaffing jugs of wine and laughing after the day's arduous labour. The countryside is a patchwork of red, gold and rust-coloured tones as the leaves turn in the vineyards and forests. Mushrooms, particularly the much sought after *cèpes*, begin to spring up in woodlands and everybody is out at weekends with collecting bags and sticks for turning over leaves to seek them out. Figs are in season, and the rice harvest is in full swing in the Camargue.

The *vendange* continues through into October (depending on the region), and chestnuts are collected in the woods. A less peaceful harvest also gets under way as the hunting season opens, and shotguns obliterate the sound of birdsong on every hillside. Wild boar and walnuts appear in the markets.

Winter The last major harvest of the year, picking olives, starts in November (in his twilight years Mistral named his last work *les Olivades* since he knew, too, that his season was over). The first bottles of heady young wines go on sale. The encroaching cold weather signals the *transhumance* of sheep back down from the mountains and hunting begins in earnest for the black diamonds known in Provençal as *rabasse* (truffles). Whilst hardy souls are out hunting or truffling in the forests, the countryside seems to hibernate and many people only venture forth to warm themselves with hearty, nourishing soups and stews in the local tavern. Christmas is a major celebration in the depths of winter.

Pope-Hennessy on spring
'An April landscape, discovered at dawn from a moving train: Then, as I watched, the sun rose, and with it the whole panorama ceased looking like an underexposed photograph and came literally to light – the cabin roofs shone orange, the fields turned out to be scattered with poppies the colour of new blood, the long green grass was streaked with yellow flowers and cobalt flowers and round scabious flowers that were a hard, firm mauve. Over the distant crimson hills the sky was already blue, and the few people in the fields were a very dark walnut brown. Nothing I had expected of Provence equalled the harsh and yet mysterious quality of this flying landscape.' James Pope-Hennessy, *Aspects of Provence*

147

A summer harvest

Right: the gardens of the Villa Ste-Claire in Hyères
Top right: a fountain in Cotignac

Provençal pines

The Var's long coastline has numerous unspoiled beaches shaded – and scented – by the characteristic maritime pine (*pinus pinaster*), with its dark blue-green foliage and reddish-coloured bark. Another species common along the coast is the Aleppo pine (*pinus halepensis*), which has a lighter foliage and grey bark. Less common, and usually found growing in isolation, is the splendid Umbrella pine (*pinus pinea*), which owes its name to its easily recognisable shape.

Introduction Bordered by the hinterland of Marseille to the west and the Riviera to the east, the Var coastline stretches for 430km along the shores of the Mediterranean. It is, quite simply, the most affordable and accessible coastline in Provence. Affordable because you are not paying the over-inflated hotel and restaurant prices of the Riviera, and because it has more than twice as many campsites than any other *département* (nearly 300 in total). Accessible because it has over 150km of beaches, most of which are free, and because 177km of the coastline is open to the public thanks to the *Sentier du Littoral* (coastal path). The Var is also blessed with two unusual wilderness areas, the Massif des Maures and the Massif de l'Esterel.

The coast Tourism in the Var is oriented towards the sea, with plenty of opportunities for scuba-diving, windsurfing (notably L'Almanarre beach at Hyères and 'Brutal' beach at Six-Fours) or just messing about in boats. The Var has 65 ports and marinas (twice as many as the Côte d'Azur), and although some of the new marinas tend to be huge and characterless there are other, smaller ports which are perfectly charming.

And then there are the resorts: laid-back and friendly ports such as Sanary-sur-Mer or Bandol; simple beach resorts such as les Lecques or Cavalière; smarter spots such as le Lavandou or St-Raphaël; and, of course, not forgetting flashy St-Tropez (usually considered part of the Côte d'Azur, although in fact part of the Var).

Inland With three-quarters of the population living in coastal areas (and 80 per cent of tourists spending their time there too), the inland expanses of the Var are sparsely populated and well worth exploring. From the coastal *massifs* the plains roll northwards, covered in a patchwork of vineyards (producing the renowned Côtes-de-Provence wines) and a smattering of villages and larger towns such as Draguignan and Brignoles. North of Draguignan, in the Haut Var, olives, truffles and honey still provide the mainstay of many small communities.

The historic sites The Var is not without its share of historic monuments, from the brooding mass of the Chartreuse de la Verne high up in the Massif des Maures to the Romanesque purity of the Abbaye du Thoronet in the valley of the Argens; other outstanding sights include the Collégiale Ste-Pierre at Six-Fours and the Cité Episcopal of Fréjus. One of the oldest pilgrimage sites is the cave where Mary Magdalene reputedly spent the last years of her life, in the mountains of Ste-Baume on the western edges of the Var.

With all this, as well as plenty of appealing villages with welcoming bistros beside sun-dappled squares, it is perhaps not surprising that the tourism statistics show that on average people spend longer on holiday in the Var than they do in any other *département* of Provence.

VAR

REGION HIGHLIGHTS ◄◄◄◄◄

149

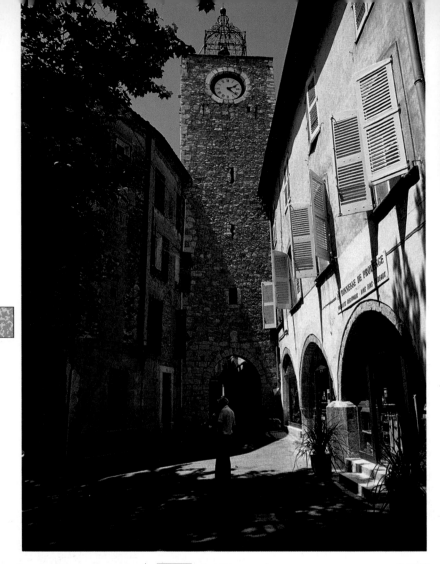

Originally a watch-tower, Aups' Tour de l'Horloge now has a fine belfry

► ▬▬ **les Arcs** *148B2*

Les Arcs is an attractive medieval village in the Argens valley between Draguignan and Fréjus. The old quarter, known as le Parage, culminates in the ruins of a 13th-century castle from where there is a view over the Massif des Maures and the surrounding vineyards that today provide les Arcs with its main source of income. Inside the **Église St-Jean-Baptiste** there is a large Provençal pastoral tableau (*crèche*) depicting le Parage as it once was, and a 15th-century polyptych by Jean de Troyes.

In the opposite direction (4km northeast on the D91), the **Chapelle Ste-Roseline►** (*Open* 3.30–6 and all day Sat in summer; Wed and Sun 2.30–5 in winter; closed Jan and Feb) is worth a small detour. Originally part of the 11th-century Abbaye de la Celle-Roubaud, this Romanesque chapel was restored in 1970 and contains a bronze relief by Giacometti, stained-glass windows by Ubac and a mosaic by Chagall .

► **Aups** *148B3*

This small town in the middle of the woodlands of the Haut Var, dominated to the northeast by the Montagne des Espiguières, is famous for its honey and truffles (the truffle market is held every Thursday morning from November to mid-March). Although still mainly an agricultural town, it is becoming an increasingly popular base from which to tour the Haut Var or visit the Grand Cañon du Verdon (23km to the north; see page 190).

As well as the remains of its medieval ramparts, several fountains and a 16th-century tower with a fine wrought-iron belfry, Aups has an attractive Gothic church, the **Église St-Pancrace►**, which has a recently restored Renaissance doorway.

►► **Bandol** *148A1*

Bandol is one of the busiest resorts west of the Côte d'Azur, with a pleasant, tree-lined promenade running the length of the port. It has all the trappings of the Riviera – discos, nightclubs, watersports and a casino – without the usual sky-high prices, which makes it a popular family resort.

Bandol has three beaches, the best of which is the Anse de Renecros sheltered behind the headland on the west side of town. There is a lively Provençal market every morning in the place de la Liberté in the centre of town. The hills behind Bandol have been completely disfigured by a series of ugly, low-rise apartment blocks, but down in the town you can ignore them and concentrate instead on the yachts bobbing in the harbour and the palm trees along the port.

A hundred years ago Bandol was better known for the cultivation of immortelle flower bulbs (which were exported as far afield as Russia and America) and for its tuna fisheries. As the flower trade gradually died off at the beginning of the century, literature flourished in its place; Katherine Mansfield, Aldous Huxley and D H Lawrence were amongst the illustrious literati who descended on Bandol at the time.

The tuna fisheries are also long gone, and today the quayside is lined with boats offering deep-sea fishing, scuba-diving or simply *promenades en mer*. A frequent ferry service links the port with the offshore island of Île de Bendor►, which has three hotels, diving and wind-surfing schools, an exhibition centre, an 'artisans village', and the *Exposition des Vins et Spiritueux►* (*Open* daily in summer except Wed). Housed in a huge hall decorated with art students' frescoes, the museum contains over 8,000 bottles of wine and liqueurs culled from over 50 countries worldwide.

Just near Bandol on the D559B towards le Beausset is the **Jardin Exotique et Zoo►** (*Open* daily except Sun morning. *Admission charge*). The greenhouses and rock gardens display thousands of rare varieties of succulents, cacti and other tropical plants; in the small zoo there are parrots, toucans, flamingos, gibbon and gazelles.

Further up the same turning off the main road is the newly opened **Musée de l'Automobile Sportif►** (*Closed* Mon. *Admission charge*). Over 60 pristine racing cars and roadsters from France, America, England, Germany and Italy are displayed in a purpose-built hall.

Wine-tasting
In the Argens valley the local wines can be sampled at the *Maison des Vins des Côtes-de-Provence* (*Open* daily in summer), around 3km south of les Arcs, where there is an exhibition on the history of Provençal wines and a restaurant specialising in regional food.

Bandol is one of Provence's best-known areas for wine, particularly the reds. Head inland and you will pass several vineyards where you can stop for tastings, or else check out the selection available at the *Maison des Vins du Bandol* on the allées Vivien in Bandol.

151

Boats in the resort of Bandol, tied up alongside the promenade

A statue adorns the old palace which now houses Brignoles's Musée du Pays Brignolais

Flight-seeing
In the middle of the Circuit Paul Ricard at le Camp du Castellet is the Aerodrome du Castellet, from where you can take a flight in a plane over the coast for a bird's-eye view of the *calanques* at Cassis or other areas: with the cost shared between three people, these spectacular flights are relatively inexpensive. Contact the Aero-Club du Soleil (tel: 04 94 90 70 50).

▶   **le Beausset**   *148A1*

Although the suburbs of le Beausset have expanded considerably in recent years, the old town centre retains much of the atmosphere of a typical Provençal town. Napoléon stayed in a house on the rue Pasteur for a month in 1793, but le Beausset's most recent claim to fame is being the home town of a gang that carried out one of the most successful bank robberies in French history, in Toulon in the late 1980s. Of the 20 or so gang members, only one has so far been caught.

In the town square there is a lovely old fountain dating from 1832 with three sculpted dolphins in the middle (although the dolphins are entirely hidden beneath a mass of mossy vegetation). On the outskirts of the village, the Cave des Maîtres Vignerons du Beausset (tel: 04 94 98 70 17) sells *vin du pays*, Côtes-de-Provence AOC and Bandol wines. On a hillside 400m above le Beausset is the Romanesque **Chapelle Notre-Dame du Beausset-Vieux**▶▶ (*Open* Sat all day; every day 2–6 in summer).

Built on the site of a Celto-Ligurian settlement in 1164, the chapel was at the centre of the original settlement of le Beausset before the inhabitants moved down the hillside to the present location in 1506. Inside the chapel there is a gilded statue of the Virgin from the workshops of Pierre Puget and, on the right-hand side of the nave, an 18th-century wooden statue of Christ that once stood outside the chapel, where it was miraculously untouched by a fire in 1936 – apart from the right hand, which is missing.

Alongside the chapel there is a gallery with an interesting collection of around 80 *ex-votos,* including an unusual olive-wood group dating from the 15th century. An outbuilding houses a typical Provençal crib scene, or *crèche.*

From the tower atop the chapel there are sweeping views across to the Bay of Ciotat (Baie de la Ciotat), Toulon and Ste-Baume.

▶▶   **Bormes-les-Mimosas**   *148B1*

Bormes would probably be just another *village perché* were it not for the bright yellow, vanilla-scented mimosas that it has adopted for its own and which flower throughout the village during the springtime; in summer the streets are filled with bougainvillea, huge pots of geraniums and colourful windowboxes. As the most celebrated 'floral village' in Provence, there are no less than three flower festivals (February, April and June).

Bormes-les-Mimosas has been 'carefully' restored by artists and second-home owners and there is the usual plethora of potteries and galleries as well as the **Musée Arts et Histoire** (*Open* Jul–Aug, Tue–Sat and Sun mornings; Sep–Jun, Sun mornings and Tue), which traces the history of Bormes. The museum also holds regular exhibitions of contemporary works.

There are lovely views of the coast from the courtyard of the medieval château.

▶ **Brignoles**   *148B2*

A large and lively town midway between the Haut Var and the Côte d'Azur, Brignoles has an extensive and very attractive medieval quarter and is a good stopping point for a night or two if you are touring in the area. The heart of old Brignoles is best explored on foot (the tourist office provide a comprehensive leaflet, *Visite de la Vieille Ville*). The star attraction, not to be missed, is the fascinating **Musée du Pays Brignolais**▶▶ (*Open* daily. *Admission charge*), housed in the 13th-century summer palace of the Counts of Provence.

The museum was started by a local doctor in 1947 and since then has expanded to include two floors' worth of curiosities, an enormous 13th-century wine press, the world's first reinforced concrete boat, designed by local inventor Joseph Louis Lambot in 1849, and the Gayole sarcophagus, dating from the 1st century AD. Discovered some 9km west of Brignoles, its incredibly well-preserved bas-reliefs depict both pagan and Christian figures.

The second floor is less compelling, but amongst some dire local paintings there is an outstanding collection of 18th- and 19th-century *ex-votos* and an automated Provençal *crèche*, or tableau.

Ex-votos
Provence has some splendid collections of *ex-votos* – offerings (usually paintings) giving thanks for having been saved from some personal tragedy. Originating in Italy, they first appeared in Provence in the 17th century and reached their peak of popularity in the mid-1800s. *Ex-votos* display an intriguing compendium of the hazards of pre-industrial life, with people shooting themselves accidentally, being squashed under carts, falling out of windows, sawing their hands off and so on. The paintings are usually crude and naive and always combine images of the terrestrial (the sick-bed, the accident, etc.) with the divine (the saints intervening from heaven).

153

Bormes's château is surrounded by pantiled houses

The old church and adjoining château overlook the cobbled streets of le Castellet

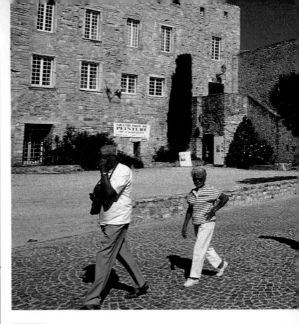

Sweet chestnuts
Collobrières was once an important centre for cork-making, but now it is sweet chestnuts from the surrounding forests that provide the economic mainstay: if you have a sweet tooth then you should visit the *Confiserie Azurienne*, where there is a shop selling everything imaginable made from chestnuts, from ice-cream to nougat to *marrons glacés*.

► **la Cadière d'Azur**   *148A1*

Not as picturesque as neighbouring le Castellet across the valley, Cadière has far fewer tourists and is a much quieter, more genuine *village perché*. Three portals lead up into the old part of the village, where the 12th-century **Église St-André** has a fine marble altarpiece. At the top of the village is the old **Chapelle Ste-Madeleine** built by the Pénitents Gris (now a private house) and, further down, the Chapelle Notre-Dame-de-la-Misericorde, which was built by the Pénitents Noirs and is now used for jazz concerts and other events in summer. On the D266 just outside the village, olive oil and other regional specialities can be bought at the excellent *Moulin de St-Come* (tel: 04 94 90 11 51).

►► **le Castellet**   *148A1*

Surrounded by the terraced vineyards of Côte-de-Provence wines, le Castellet was one of the first *village perchés* to be rejuvenated by artisans who were encouraged to settle here in the 1950s. It now has a well-established mix of craft shops, art galleries, potteries, cafés and restaurants.

The delightful flower-filled streets lead up to the parish church (parts of which date from the 12th century) and the old château (rebuilt in the 15th century), which now houses the *mairie* (town hall) next door. To the left of the *mairie* is the so-called *Trou de Madame*, a gateway that leads onto a small balcony with magnificent views northwards across the vineyards in the valley and the foothills leading up to Ste-Baume.

The place de la Mairie in the peaceful Haut Var village of Cotignac

► **Cogolin**   *148C2*

On the edge of the Massif des Maures 6km inland from Port Grimaud, Cogolin does have the odd ruin, but most people come here for shopping rather than sightseeing since it has a lively crafts-based tradition.

First and foremost are Cogolin's famous pipes, which are made at two workshops in the main street (*Fabrique de Pipes Courrieu* and *Pipes Roux*). Even if you are not a pipe-smoker it is worth glancing in their windows just to

Film set
Le Castellet's photogenic medieval streets have been used more than once for film sets, most notably by Marcel Pagnol who shot *La Femme du Boulanger* here in the 1930s and returned more than 50 years later to film scenes from *Manon des Sources*. But the village's cinematic associations go back further, since it was here that the Lumière Brothers bought a house (now the Castel Lumière hotel) to use as a pre-production studio in 1895 for the production of France's first moving picture (see panel, page 123).

see the amazing variety of pipes made here: pipes with lids, pipes with faces, pipes with frills, inlaid, carved, long-stemmed, short-stemmed, even some with two bowls.

Cogolin is also famous for its carpets, an industry that started up in the 1920s with the arrival of Armenian immigrants who brought with them a tradition of hand-knotted ancestral rugs; you can see them being made in the workshops of *Le Manufacture de Tapis* in boulevard Louis Blanc (open weekdays). Other craftsmen in the village specialise in pottery, ironwork, corks for the wine trade, cane furniture and top-quality reeds for wind instruments.

► Collobrières   148B1

Time seems to have passed by this large village in the heart of the Massif des Maures where there are few concessions to modernity apart from a factory on the outskirts that turns out chestnut products by the lorry-load.

Otherwise, Collobrières is a rest-stop on the long and winding road up to the **Chartreuse de la Verne**►► (*Open* daily except Tue; closed Nov), isolated amongst the forests of the Maures. Founded in 1170, this Carthusian monastery has been ransacked and rebuilt many times and is still undergoing restoration. The rambling complex of cloisters, chapels and monks' cells (each of which has its own garden) is built from a combination of dark red schist and green-coloured serpentine, a local Maures stone.

The high walls that surround the monastery give it a dark, brooding presence, but it has uninterrupted views of the forested hills and the Gulf of St-Tropez beyond.

►► Cotignac   148B2

This dreamy Haut Var village is dominated by two ruined towers on top of an 80m-high cliff that is riddled with caves and grottos. Behind the Romanesque parish church (with a façade rebuilt in the 19th century) is an enchanting *Théâtre de Verdure* where concerts are held in the summer. Wine, honey and olive oil are the village's main products.

Twin bells atop the medieval parish church in le Castellet

■ **Provençal cuisine is at its best when bursting with the aromatic, sun-drenched flavours of the Mediterranean. The essential ingredients – peppery olive oil, piquant garlic, the ubiquitous tomato and herbs such as thyme, rosemary and basil – are combined in many colourful dishes usually described as à la Provençale. An added bonus is that the Provençal style of cooking is good for your health!** ■

Apéritifs

The locals like their *pastis* before a meal. Pastis is an amber-coloured spirit distilled with anis and other herbs, which goes cloudy when water is added. It is an acquired taste but hugely popular in Provence – perhaps due to its potency (at 45 per cent proof, its effects are quickly felt in the southern sun!). Pastis is usually accompanied by a dish of black or green olives, or canapés spread with a savoury paste called *tapènade*, an appetising purée of capers, olives and anchovies.

Created in Provence, pastis was once illegal – if you have one too many, you'll probably find out why!

Soups *Soupe au pistou* (essentially a thick minestrone, heavily flavoured with basil and garlic) is usually made in summer, but Provence's famous fish soups can be enjoyed year round: the most substantial of these is *bouillabaisse*, which is more of a stew than a soup and usually served as a meal in its own right. Originating in Marseille, *bouillabaisse* can include a myriad number of fish such as the hideous-looking *rascasse* (spiny hog fish), *loup* (sea bass), *rouget* (red mullet), eels, crabs, and anything else that the fishermen have pulled out of the sea that morning. The fish are cooked together very quickly in a *bouillon* (stock) containing saffron, garlic, herbs and fennel and served up separately from the liquid at the table, accompanied by a spicy red paste called *rouille*: you spread the *rouille* on croûtons, sprinkle them with cheese and dunk them in your soup, accompanied by bits of fish.

You will also find *rouille* being served with the less expensive (although no less tasty) *soupe de poissons*, whilst another classic fish soup, *bourride*, is more properly accompanied by *aïoli*.

Aïoli Aïoli is a thick mayonnaise made with plenty of garlic and rich olive oil, served alongside raw vegetables (*crudités*) as an hors d'oeuvres, or as an *aïoli garni*, with freshly cooked cod, potatoes and hard-boiled eggs that are dipped into it.

Salads and vegetables The wonderfully full-flavoured, sun-ripened local tomatoes appear in many dishes: sliced with onions, sprinkled with olive oil and basil, in a simple, appetising *salade de tomates*, or stuffed with rice, aubergines, breadcrumbs, parsley and garlic, and baked as *tomates farcies*. They are an essential ingredient in *salade niçoise* alongside salad leaves, black olives, tuna, hard-boiled eggs and green beans. No two *salades niçoises* are ever the same and the ingredients vary, as they do in the classic *ratatouille*, a vegetable stew of tomatoes, aubergines, onions, peppers and courgettes braised with olive oil, garlic and herbs.

Meat The most common dish is lamb, usually grilled with savoury herbs or served stuffed with sausage, garlic and herbs and cooked in a sauce *à la Provençale*. The best and tastiest lamb is the lean, spicy *agneau de Sisteron*, which has grazed on mountain pastures. Beef often comes braised in red wine and vegetables as a succulent *daube de boeuf*, or in the Camarguais version as *boeuf à la gardianne*. Rabbit and hare are also simmered in wine and herbs.

Fish Naturally enough, fish features heavily on menus in coastal restaurants, with some of the best choices being *loup de mer* (sea bass) grilled with fennel or vine shoots, *rouget* (red mullet) served whole, *pageot* (sea bream), sardines or *merlan* (hake). Up in the hills, *truite* (trout) often has a very short journey from a mountain stream to your table. The shellfish is usually excellent, and includes everything from *moules* (mussels) to *gambas* (giant prawns), *palourdes* (clams), *oursins* (sea urchins), and crabs and lobsters.

Cheeses Local cheeses are usually made from the milk of goats (*chèvres*) or ewes (*brebis*). In any market you can find an enormous selection of goat's cheese, which is usually either very creamy and fresh (with a fairly mild flavour) or has been left to dry out, in which case it has a much stronger, sharper taste. *Petits chèvres* are small roundels of goat's cheese, often flavoured with bay, thyme and other herbs. *Poivre d'âne* is a goat's cheese with a particularly peppery flavour, whilst *Banon* is a creamy sheep's cheese.

Desserts and fruit Desserts are always served after the cheese in France and the range of tempting flans, pastries and fruit tarts is enough to melt your resolutions about a light meal. However, you can always salve your conscience with some fresh fruit – and there is plenty to choose from in the appropriate season, including strawberries, cherries, figs, peaches, nectarines, apricots, pears and dessert grapes.

Snacks
Apart from *baguette* sandwiches, pizza slices and the ubiquitous *frites* (french fries), a popular option is the *pan bagnat*, a monster bread bap spread with olive oil and filled with *a salade niçoise*-type mix. *Croque monsieurs* (toasted cheese and ham sandwiches) are not particularly Provençal, but *pissaladière* (a delicious onion, olive and anchovy flan, best eaten cold or just warm) is very much local. In Nice the speciality is a slice of the extremely filling *socca*, a highly palatable pancake made from chick pea flour. Another Provençal speciality is the *fougasse*, a baked slice containing olives, sausage, cheese and other ingredients.

A salade niçoise – *no two versions are the same*

Market day in Draguignan, the Var's biggest inland town

► **Draguignan** *148B2*

Descending from the isolated villages and sparsely populated countryside of the Haut Var, Draguignan comes as something of a shock. Spreading over the entire valley, the outskirts of the town are an unattractive conglomeration of commercial centres, hypermarkets and second-hand car lots. And yet, hidden away like a pearl inside this ugly outer shell, Draguignan has an extremely well-preserved *vieille ville* and, as an extra bonus, one of the best ethnographic museums in the whole of Provence. The absorbing **Musée des Arts et Traditions Populaires**►►► (*Closed* Sun mornings and Mon. *Admission charge*) displays the culture and heritage of the Var through a series of imaginative reconstructions, full of detail and authentic props, of country life. Olive-oil pressing, silk culture, wine-making, agriculture, cork manufacturing, bee-keeping, hide-tanning and tile-making are all faithfully covered. There are also Provençal costumes, musical instruments, religious art, and temporary exhibitions on a variety of topics.

Above the old town stands the **Tour de l'Horloge**►, on the site of the first settlement here. Built in 1663, it replaced an earlier keep that was part of the medieval

The solid silhouette of the Tour de l'Horloge rises above Draguignan's spires and rooftops

fortifications. Between the tower and the crumbling 13th-century **Chapelle de St-Sauveur▶**, just below it on the hillside, is the recently built, absolutely charming **Théâtre de Verdure▶**, an open-air theatre artfully created with rocks, lawns and olive trees in perfect proportion. Contact the tourist office for details of concert performances in this lovely setting (tel: 04 94 68 63 30).

▶ Embiez, Île des   148A1

Like Bendor, the Île des Embiez is owned by Paul Ricard. Apart from a couple of small beaches, the main attraction for visitors is the **Institut Océanographique Paul Ricard** (*Open* daily; closed Wed mornings in winter. *Admission charge*), where there are several small aquarium tanks with around 100 species of Mediterranean fish and displays on marine ecology and local shipwrecks.

Ferries cross from le Brusc at regular intervals. The islands also have their own underwater seabus, the *Aquascope*, which tours the marine world around the coast (tel: 04 94 34 01 48).

▶ Entrecasteaux   148B2

This small village is dominated by the 17th-century **Château▶** (*Closed* Wed. *Admission charge*), which was restored in the 1970s by an eccentric Scots painter, Ian McGarvie-Munn. The interior is rather bizarre, since parts are furnished in contemporary style (and decorated with McGarvie-Munn's own paintings), whilst others display period furnishings. Photographic and art exhibitions are also held inside the château, and there is a charming semi-formal garden, designed by le Notre.

▶▶▶ Esterel, Massif de l'   148C2

Romantic travel posters in the past used to depict SNCF trains emerging from the tunnels in the Esterel *massif* to landscapes of brilliant red cliffs and bright blue seas: it is still so, but if you restrict yourself to the train or even the *Corniche d'Or* (the N98) alongside the railway line you will be missing one of the great splendours of Provence, an evocative wilderness hidden away behind the coast.

The Esterel (see page 171) is one of the Var's best-kept secrets. Most of the range (over 4,500 hectares out of a total of 6,000 hectares) is only accessible on foot or by mountain bike. There are numerous tracks throughout the Esterel (some of which may be closed off in summer due to the fire risk), for which the best source of information is a map produced by the Office National des Forêts (National Forests Office), available from the tourist offices in St-Raphaël or Fréjus. There are also 42km of maintained roads, offering fabulous drives through parts of the *massif*.

▶ Evenos   148A1

High above the Gorges d'Ollioules, the sombre walls of Evenos' 12th-century castle create a spooky atmosphere. It is worth the drive up the twisting road to walk around the outside of the walls (the interior is closed off). Huddled around the castle and a 13th-century church, the tiny village itself is actually quite cheerful, with plenty of the crumbling houses having been restored. There is just one *auberge*, called, simply enough *On Mange, On Boit* ('One Eats, One Drinks').

Strange sights
A square at the entrance to Evenos is dedicated to the Provençal writer Marie Mauron, who graphically describes the castle as 'black and torn apart, standing tragically against the open sky', adding that 'the approaching silhouette, the ruins of dark basalt, wring your heart'. It is indeed a strange place, as is the Grès de Ste-Anne outside the village of Ste-Anne d'Evenos below the château. This weird moonscape of sandstone formations (reached via a path on the right of the road just to the south of Ste-Anne) has many hidden grottos and startling formations and is at the base of the nearby Gros Cervau (the 'big brain') range.

The 1960s meet the 16th century in Entrecasteaux's château

The Saracens
Apart from generally pillaging the surrounding countryside (until finally expelled by Count William in AD 973), the Saracens also introduced the tambourine, flat roof tiles, and the art of cork-making to Provence; the latter was to become the economic mainstay of la Garde-Freinet until the 19th century.

A palatial quayside residence in Port Grimaud

► ▓▓▓▓ **Fréjus**   *148C2*

Fréjus and its neighbour, St-Raphaël, lie at the mouth of the Argens river between the Massif des Maures and Massif de l'Esterel. Now merged together into a somewhat characterless holiday conglomeration, Fréjus does have several relics that are worth investigating.

Founded by the Romans, Fréjus never recovered from Saracen attacks in the 10th century, nor the silting up of its harbour, leaving the port 3km inland. The sandy delta created by the Argens river is now Fréjus-Plage – crowded, but handy for nearby children's attractions such as the water theme park Aquatica off the RN98 or the Zoo-Safari Park next to the A8 autoroute. Compared with others in Provence, the **arènes** (*Open* daily. *Admission charge*) is not particularly impressive, although some of the upper tiers have recently been rebuilt. Most of the other **Roman remains** – the theatre and remnants of the aqueduct and harbour wall – are somewhat scattered, so hopping on the town's *petit train* is a good idea on a hot day.

Fréjus's real treasure is the **Groupe Épiscopal**►►► at the centre of the old town. Begun in the 10th century, the **cathedral**►► (*Guided tour* also includes the baptistery, museum and cloister; closed Tue. *Admission charge*) boasts a magnificent set of carved walnut doors from the Renaissance. Protected by a set of shutters for the last 200 years, they are only opened on a guided tours. The octagonal **baptistery**►►► dates from the 4th or 5th cen-

tury and is one of the best preserved of its era in France.

The final part of the cathedral complex is the charming **cloister**►►►, with its slender columns and fantastic panoply of wood carvings on the ceiling – only 400 remain of the 1200 panels. The remarkable **archaeological museum**► contains finds from *Forum Julii* (see panel), including the famous double-headed bust of Hermes, discovered in 1970. This is in fact a copy; the priceless Hellenistic original never emerges from secure storage.

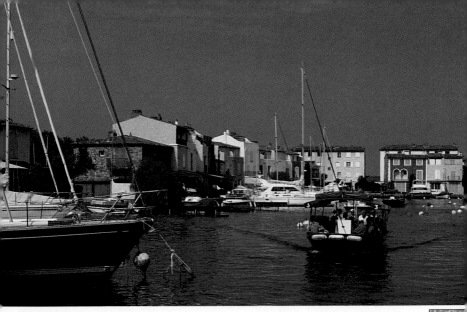

> **la Garde-Freinet**   *148B2*

Straddling a pass across the rolling hills of the Massif des Maures, this now peaceful village was one of the last Saracen strongholds in Provence during the 10th century, and France's main cork-producing town in the 19th century. You can take a 20-minute hike up to the **Fort Freinet**► to the west, from where there are extensive views back across to the le Luc plain and the foothills beyond. The new **Musée International de la Colombophilie** (*Open daily except Tue and Sun. Admission charge*), which claims to be the first museum in the world devoted to racing pigeons, is worth a visit.

> ►►   **Grimaud**   *148C2*

A picture-perfect *village perché* on the eastern flanks of the Massif des Maures, Grimaud is named after the Grimaldi family who owned it from the 10th century onwards. The rue des Templiers, with its arcades and Gothic doorways, leads up to the Hospice of the Knights Templars and the Romanesque **Église St-Michel**►. Overlooking the village are the ruins of the Grimaldi **château**►, with views down to the Gulf of St-Tropez and inland across the Maures.

Down on the coast is **Port Grimaud**►►. With its hundreds of pastel-shaded villas lining over 8km of quayside along the canals, it was designed by architect François Spoerry in the 1960s as a community of seafarers where everyone could have their boats parked outside their own front doors. Inevitably this pastiche of a fishing village has become a tourist attraction in its own right, with most yacht-owning residents simply jetting in for their summer holidays.

It is worth a look just once, if you are passing by, just to experience this 'Provençal Venice', although restaurants and cafés are absurdly overpriced and the compulsory parking outside the gates is expensive. View the whole *ensemble* from the top of the church tower – and boats leave regularly from beside the main square for trips around the canals.

Boats are the only way to get around in Port Grimaud

The Roman port
The port of Fréjus, or *Forum Julii*, was founded in 49 BC by Julius Caesar as a staging post on the coastal road which later became known as the Aurelian Way. It was the first Roman town in Gaul, and was soon turned into a major naval base by Octavian (later to become the Emperor Augustus), who used it to build a fleet of fast, light galleys with which he defeated Antony and Cleopatra in the Battle of Actium.

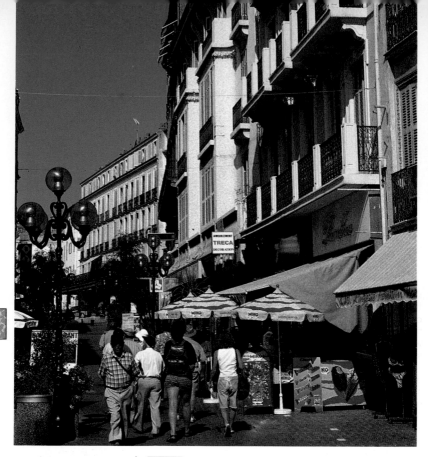

Once a fashionable resort, Hyères thrives on local horticulture

Mad about palm trees
Palm trees were originally introduced to France from the Canary Islands in 1864 by an amateur horticulturalist, the Comte Vigier. He planted the first three trees in Nice in 1865, and in 1867 the first seeds found their way to Hyères. Hyères very quickly became the 'palm tree capital' of the Riviera, sending 300,000 trees a year all over Europe. Some 12,000 majestic palms currently grace the streets of Hyères les Palmiers and there is even an association, the *Fous des Palmiers* ('mad about palms'), for enthusiasts to swap seeds, knowledge and growing tips.

▶▶ **Hyères** *148B1*

The cultivation of fruit, flowers and vegetables has long been an economic mainstay in Hyères, and today the sale of flowers alone (principally roses, marigolds, irises, tulips and gladioli) brings in around 400 million francs annually and accounts for around 20 per cent of France's total production.

Hyères is also well known for its palm tree nurseries (see panel), hence the recent change of name to the more exotic Hyères les Palmiers. This embraces Vieux Hyères, the modern town, and the Port d'Hyères down on the sea front.

From the place Clemenceau in the centre of town, the 14th-century **Porte Massillon** leads through into the old town, where all streets eventually converge on the spacious place Massillon, site of the daily market. At the top of the square is the half-rounded **Tour St-Blaise▶**, built by the Knights Templar in the 12th century. Behind the square is the **Collégiale St-Paul▶**, which houses over four hundred *ex-votos* (dating from 1613 right up to 1985) and a huge Provençal *crèche* (tableau) re-creating the Hyères of yesteryear.

To the right of the church a huge archway leads beneath a Renaissance house up to the **Parc St-Bernard▶** (*Open* daily), which culminates in the **Villa de Noialles** (no visits) at the top of the hill. Now a private arts centre, the Cubist-inspired villa was designed by the architect Robert Mallet-

Stevens for the arts patron Charles de Noialles in 1924. The park itself displays a wide variety of Mediterranean flowers and shrubs, with the pathways opening up into delightful vistas where you least expect them. Follow the old walls westwards from the park to an insignificant-looking gateway that leads into the **Villa Ste-Claire▶** (*Open* daily), where the gardens of similar style, although far more extensive, have a glorious profusion of Mediterranean flowering plants under the management of the Botanic Conservatory of Porquerolles.

Back down in the main town, the **Musée Municipal** (*Closed* Tue) contains antiquities from the ancient port of Hyères, as well as two engraved menhirs found near by. More flowers, plants and exotic trees (as well as a small zoo and a tropical greenhouse) can be found in the 7ha **Jardin Olbius Riquier▶** (*Open* daily) on avenue Gambetta.

▶▶▶ Hyères, Îles d' 148B1

The three islands off the coast of Hyères have been known since the 17th century as the *Îles d'Or* thanks to the golden glint of the mica shale in their southernmost cliffs. They are scattered about with forts and the French military still maintains bases on two of them, but their wild natural landscapes have been partially protected since the 1960s.

The islands are covered in dense vegetation – pine, eucalyptus, lavender, heather and rosemary scent the sea-swept air; spring is the best time to come, when migrating birds pass through. The underwater flora is also protected, and spear-fishing prohibited. The entire archipelago is currently being upgraded to the Parc National des Îles d'Hyères.

The islands can be reached by ferry from most nearby ports, including Toulon, la Tour-Fondue, Hyères-Plage and le Lavandou.

Porquerolles▶▶▶ is the most easily accessible, the largest of the three and the only one that is permanently inhabited. The village (also called Porquerolles) has cafés, restaurants and one or two hotels, as well as bike hire shops. You can cycle or walk as far as the lighthouse on the south coast, or visit the gentle sandy beach of Notre-Dame at the northeastern tip of the island.

Port-Cros▶▶ is the most hilly of the three, and its wealth of flora and fauna has been protected since 1963. France's smallest national park, it has marked walking trails (which you are forbidden to wander off) around the island or across the middle to the Vallon de la Solitude or the Vallon de la Fausse-Monnaie.

The third island, the **Île du Levant**, is mostly occupied by the military. What hasn't been claimed by them has been taken over by a nudist colony set up in the 1930s in the village of Heliopolis.

The Tour St-Blaise is all that remains of a Knights Templar lodge

Forests and fires

■ **Hot, dry summers mean that fire is an ever-present menace in Provence and yet, contrary to popular belief, fires cause much less damage than they used to. In addition, tree-planting programmes mean that there is now a far greater area of woodland than there was a century ago. ■**

Re-afforestation
The Foundation for the Protection of Mediterranean Forests replants an average of 60,000 trees every year. Just as you may see many burned-out areas in Provence, you will also see many others where signs proclaim 'this area has been replanted by the schoolchildren of the village – please respect their work'. In fact, through schemes such as these and natural regeneration, the forests of Provence have crept back up from 600,00ha just over a century ago to almost 1,107,000ha today. All is not yet lost for the woodland heritage of Provence.

The aftermath of a forest fire, an all too common sight

The forests The forests in Provence are dominated by conifers such as the maritime, umbrella and Aleppo pines, as well as cedars. Around 60 per cent of existing woodland is coniferous, the rest comprising mostly deciduous trees such as chestnut, or evergreens, such as cork oaks and holm oaks. The majority of the forests are in the Var (340,00ha), with the Alpes-Maritime, Vaucluse and Hautes-Alpes all with less than half this amount of forest and the Bouches-du-Rhône with just 97,000ha.

Setting the forest alight The Provençal forests are particularly susceptible to fires due to summer droughts and strong winds. During the long, hot summer months the dried-up forest floor, littered with leaves, twigs and resinous pine needles, can easily catch fire. If there is any wind – or, worse still, a *mistral* – the flames can be quickly fanned into an inferno, creating a wall of fire up to 30m high that consumes all in its path.

Today the major causes of fire are carelessness on the part of walkers and picnickers – and the vandalistic acts of arsonists. The worst fires since records have been kept were in 1764 (when the whole of the Esterel burned down), 1864 (when 11,000ha of the Maures were destroyed), and in 1899 and 1964.

Devastation You don't have to drive far in Provence to witness blackened hillsides and stark slopes, littered with the charred skeletons of trees, where fire has passed. The unprotected slopes are prone to erosion and a new flora soon takes over, that of the *maquis*, a sparse, low-lying cover of thistles, gorse, stunted downy oaks, and hardy lavender, thyme and rosemary. Without help, the ancient forest cover seldom regenerates in this impoverished soil.

Prevention Since 1963 the various *départements* in Provence have co-ordinated their fire prevention and fire-fighting efforts, and this was strengthened in 1989 with the creation of the Fondation pour la Forêt Méditeranéene (Foundation for the Mediterranean Forests).

Through research, public education and experiments with fire-prevention techniques, they have had considerable success in reducing forest fires. New laws require undergrowth to be cleared around houses and along roads in high-risk areas, and a vast network of cisterns (over 700 in the Var alone) has been installed in the forests to give fire-fighters access to water.

Whole areas of forest are now closed off during the summer in periods of drought, and if you try and venture past the barriers you will soon find there is a forest patrol warning you away.

Aerial attack Sunning yourself on a Riviera beach during the summer, it is quite likely you will witness the extraordinary sight of a plane descending to the sea, skimming the surface as it scoops up millions of litres of water, before taking off again and heading inland. You have just seen a Canadair, one of the main weapons in the fight against fire. There is now a fleet of 11 of these *Bombardiers d'Eau* (water bombers), based at Marignane airport at Marseille. They are guided and assisted by 12 tracker aircraft that constantly patrol and monitor the hinterland. In 1986, the first helicopter water bombers (HBE) made their appearance, and 13 of these are also now on permanent stand-by during the summer.

Thanks to better co-ordination and more 'water bombers', in recent years 95 per cent of fires have been extinguished before they covered 5ha. In 1992, just 13,000ha in Provence were lost – a third of the previous annual average.

'Shoot the arsonists'
Arsonists are usually considered a latter-day phenomenon but this is not so, as evidenced by a letter from Napoléon to the Prefect of the Var, written on 21 August 1809: 'I have learnt that several fires have broken out in the Department which I have entrusted to you', he wrote, 'and I order you to shoot on the spot anyone convicted of the crime of having set them alight. If these fires break out again I shall be forced to replace you.'

165

ATTENTION AU FEU

High-risk areas are now closed off during the summer

Drive and country walk Ste-Baume

The Ste-Baume massif is only 12km long, but it shelters one of the most unusual forests in Provence and also a shrine sacred to Mary Magdalene. This drive encircles the whole of the massif, and includes two walks, a short one up to a beautiful abbey and a longer one up to the sacred grotto itself. Allow 4–5 hours from Gémenos.

Take the D2 out of Gémenos until you see the signs for the **Parc de St-**

Pons►► on the right. From the bridge, a delightful woodland path leads up through a valley shaded by beech and ash, with the waters of the Frauge constantly burbling over cascades and rocks. After 15 minutes, you will reach the **Abbaye de St-Pons►**, one of the best-preserved Cistercian convents in Provence. Established in 1205, it was a popular retreat for ladies of nobility. Just behind the abbey, the source itself gushes out of a small fissure in a rock-face.

Continue on up the D2, which curves around the rock circle of the

The summit of Ste-Baume

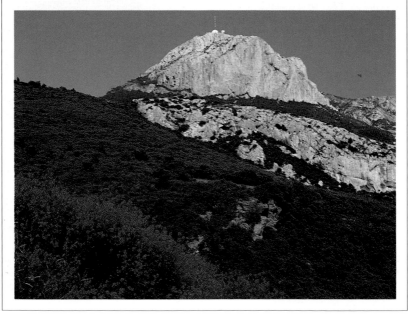

Pic de Bretagne before climbing up to the pass at the Col de l'Espigoulier. Here the view southwards suddenly opens out in front of you, with Marseille and the Chaîne de l'Etoile in the distance behind the Aubagne plain. Keep going through Plan d'Aups until you reach the Hôtellerie de la Ste-Baume. From here, follow the signboards for the Grotte de Ste-Baume. There are two paths up to the sanctuary. On the left is the Chemin des Rois (chosen by the kings of France – hence the name – who made pilgrimages here in the Middle Ages). The oratories were built in 1516 by Monseigneur Jean Ferrier, archbishop of Arles and Aix. The right-hand path, the Chemin des Canapés, follows broken-down, moss-covered stone steps. It is easier to take the former on the way up, and the latter back down.

Both paths meander through a forest of ash, beech, aspen, holly, maple and ancient yew trees. On the forest floor lichens, moss and wild mushrooms flourish. This fantastic forest, one of few locally where Northern European tree species grow, is the last remnant of the woodlands that once covered Provence in the tertiary era. Covering around 130ha, its survival is thanks to the shade created by the towering cliff faces above it. Always considered a sacred forest, it is now a Biological Reserve.

The two paths meet at the Carrefour de l'Oratoire (the oratory crossroads). Follow a flight of steps on the right up to the terrace where there is a good view.

Behind you is the **Grotte de Ste-Baume▶▶**, where Mary Magdalene is supposed to have spent the last years of her life. The cave is enormous, with stained-glass windows set in the rock, several statues of Mary Magdalene, and an altar with Bossan's *Rock of Penitence* behind it. Water drips constantly from the walls, and there is also a spring at the back of the sanctuary. Open every day, there are services at Whitsun, on 21 July (Mary Magdalene's saint day) and midnight mass on Christmas Eve.

Return to the oratory crossroads and, if you are feeling energetic,

take the GR9 zig-zagging up to the **Col de St-Pilon▶**, half an hour further on. From nearly 1,000m, the 360-degree view encompasses Mt Ventoux, the Massif des Maures and the Alpilles. The small chapel at the summit stands on the site of the column (hence 'St Pilon') that once stood here.

Back down at the car park, follow the D95 to Mazaugues, continuing on to la Roquebrussanne. Turn down the D5, bearing right at Méounes-lès-Montrieux (with several fountains) towards Signes, with more fountains and a 16th-century Gothic church.

Continue parallel to the southern slopes of Ste-Baume to reach the escarpment overlooking the Plan du Castellet and turn right on the N8 towards Gémenos.

In the lee of the cliffs, Ste-Baume's forest is now designated a biological reserve

An imposing town hall dominates the main square in Ollioules

▶ le Lavandou 148B1

At the start of the smarter part of the coast, yachts now outnumber fishing boats in le Lavandou's harbour, and the prices in the numerous restaurants, boutiques and cafés in the pedestrianised streets behind the port are beginning to tip towards those on the Riviera. Le Lavandou's main attraction is a good selection of beaches. The town's own wide, sandy beach curves around the bay towards the west, and there are several smaller and more secluded retreats hidden away nearby.

Around 3km to the east, **la Fossette** is a small horse-shoe-shaped beach with just one café-restaurant, whilst

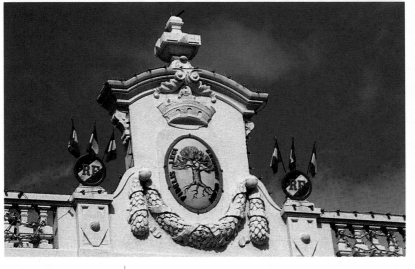

past here **Aiguebelle** has three beaches: the one on the sea front can be crowded, but half a kilometre further on a steep path leads down to a wonderful double bay, which is far less crowded. The east half is a nudist beach, as is the next beach along, the well-known **le Layet**, where *textiles* (i.e. people with clothes on, as French nudists call them) will be frowned upon. Finally, there is a superb beach at the pleasant little resort of **Cavalière▶** (not to be confused with the hideously built-up Cavalaire-sur-Mer further on). Le Lavandou is a good base for exploring the Massif des Maures, whose wooded slopes come almost down to the sea behind the coast road (the *Corniche des Maures*).

▶ les Lecques 148A1

The seaside suburb of the nearby town of St-Cyr, les Lecques is a popular family resort largely due to its safe, sandy, gently shelving beach. The family appeal is further enhanced by a massive water theme park, **Aqualand**, just outside St-Cyr.

Les Lecques claims to be the site of the ancient Greek settlement of *Tauroentum*, although only Roman remains have been found so far. These are on display in the **Musée Tauroentum** (*Open* daily except Tue in summer; weekend afternoons in winter. *Admission charge*), with mosaics, frescoes, vases and household utensils.

Coastal walk
At the eastern end of the Baie des Lecques is la Madrague, from where a coastal path leads around the headlands to Bandol. The *Sentier du Littoral* winds around the unspoiled coastline for some 9km, but it is an easy half-hour walk – scented with heathers, pine and sweet-smelling *salsepa-reille* (sarsaparilla)– out to the Pointe Grenier, where the Tour de Vigie (partially restored in 1993 under the auspices of APARE – see page 74) sits atop a head-land with lovely views back down the coast to la Ciotat and along the cliffs eastward.

▶▶▶ Maures, Massif des 148B1

Around 60km from end-to-end and 30km wide, the Massif des Maures stretches from Fréjus to Hyères, dipping down to the sea to form wide bays at Cavalière, Pampelonne (near St-Tropez) and Bormes. The glittering mica cliffs of the Îles d'Hyères are an extension of the chain out into the sea.

The hills of the Maures, up to 760m high, are thickly forested with chestnuts, cork oaks, and Aleppo and umbrella pines. The forest's shaded depths gave rise to its name, which comes from *mauram* – Provençal for 'dark'. In contrast to the wooded slopes, vineyards spread across sunlit valleys where there are signs of human habitation. Much of the forest is impenetrable – except by forest fires, which have taken their toll here as elsewhere.

In the Dark Ages the Maures was ruled by the Saracens, who built their strongholds (*fraxinets*) on the hilltops and plundered the surrounding countryside for more than 100 years before Count Guillaume drove them out in AD 972. There are still very few settlements in the heart of the Maures, the main ones being Collobrières (see page 155) and la Garde-Freinet (see page 161).

▶ Ollioules 148A1

The southern outskirts of Ollioules, with their ever-multiplying superstores, have become practically a suburb of Toulon, but, within the town itself, traffic-calming measures, re-cobbling of streets and facelifts for many buildings have created an entirely different atmosphere.

Behind the church, the picturesque streets lead up to the ruined 11th-century **château▶** (*Open* daily in summer), which was once a stronghold ruled over by the Seigneurs de Signe et d'Evenos. A lone window punctuates the sole remaining full-height wall of the castle; for several years, volunteers have been slowly restoring the remaining rooms and doorways.

Ollioules has an active crafts community, an arts exhibition centre, and a small amphitheatre with summer dance and drama.

Cork oak in the Massif des Maures

Drives and walks
One of the most rewarding tours through the Maures is the 71km *Routes des Crêtes*, which starts in la Garde-Freinet and circles around via Collobrières and the D14 to Grimaud. You can also make a slightly longer tour (around 110km) from le Lavandou, via Bormes-les-Mimosas, Collobrières, Grimaud and Cogolin.

For hikers, the GR9 from la Garde-Freinet skirts the highest points of the *massif* through the Forêt Domaniale des Mayons towards Pignans on the N97, whilst the GR51 takes a much longer, more southerly route from near Port Grimaud all the way to Pierrefeu-du-Var on the D12.

The neo-Byzantine Église-Notre-Dame de la Victoire rises up behind the Grand Casino in St-Raphaël

Bikini cover-up

Even in the summer heat-wave of 1993, the Mayor of St-Raphaël decided he had had enough of the bare flesh of tourists in the shops and streets of the resort. Dredging up an obscure municipal decree that forbids anyone to walk around the town in swimming costumes, he sent out the *gendarmes* to lay down the law, warning people wearing bikinis and swimsuits that they were not on the beach and had better cover up. The only other place where this might happen is Ste-Maxime, where there is a fine of 75 francs for any-one wearing less than a T-shirt.

▶▶   **Ramatuelle**   *148C1*

In the heart of the St-Tropez peninsula, Ramatuelle is a typical Provençal village with a typical influx of second-home owners. The vineyards surrounding Ramatuelle produce much sought-after Côtes-de-Provence wines, with the best place to sample them being the cellars of *Les Maîtres Vignerons de la Presqu'Île de St-Tropez* just outside Cogolin.

Nearby On the D89 heading out above Ramatuelle, three ancient windmills, **Les Moulins de Paillas▶**, are perched on a hillside with fabulous views across the Presqu'Île de St-Tropez and the Îles d'Hyères. There are also spectacular panoramas from the small village of **Gassin▶▶** further up the same road. Gassin was built as a look-out point during the time of the Saracen invasions, and several restaurants now enjoy the same views – although you may well feel plundered yourself when presented with the bill.

▶   **St-Raphaël**   *148C2*

St-Raphaël is a popular family resort with a big sandy beach curving around the bay between its marinas. It was popularised in the mid-19th century by the writer Alphonse Karr, who lured Maupassant, Alexander Dumas and Berlioz down for their winter holidays. Unfortunately all the grand hotels and *belle époque* villas were destroyed during World War II, although there are still remnants of the medieval village surrounding the Romanesque **Église St-Pierre** on the other side of the railway line that runs through the centre of town.

Just beside the church, the **Musée Archéologique▶** (*Closed* Tue in summer; Sun in winter. *Admission charge*) has some interesting displays on underwater archaeology (as well as local terrestrial finds), including an enormous number of amphorae dating from the 1st century BC onwards, discovered in wrecks off the coast.

The town plays host to a lively International New Orleans Jazz Competition during July, with outdoor performances along the promenade.

The Esterel Massif

■ **The heart of the Esterel is one of the most captivating areas on the whole of the Riviera coastline, as unexpected and as wild as the Massif des Maures, yet more beautiful, more precious, more astonishing for its proximity to the built-up areas and its serenity and total lack of habitation. ■**

The massif Like the neighbouring Massif des Maures, the Esterel is much older than the limestone that predominates in most of Provence, and presents a series of jagged profiles, rust-red canyons and dramatic rock formations. The vivid red porphyry (volcanic rock) has solidified in ridges and peaks that plunge into the sea, indented by small bays and inlets, creating a striking contrast with the deep blue of the Mediterranean. Elsewhere, the rocks have been mined for their blue tints, much favoured by the Romans for temple columns.

Flora and fauna The Esterel was originally heavily wooded with cork oaks and holm oaks, but forest fires have taken their toll: over 120 fires have ravaged the hills and valleys since 1828, four of which (in 1838, 1918, 1943 and 1964) have hit practically the whole of the *massif*.

The predominant vegetation is *maquis* (scrub), a dense covering of heathers, gorse, mimosas, lavender and other shrubs. Spring is one of the best times to be here, when wild flowers colour the landscape and scent the pure air.

The Esterel is home to wild boar, hares, partridge, pheasant, rabbit, and a huge variety of birds. Deer, introduced here in 1988, are so far doing well.

Protection and access Since 1984 the Esterel has been a protected area under the management of the National Forests Office, which maintains 114km of fire-roads through the *massif*. In addition, two special areas have been designated Biological Reserves: the Ravin du Mal-Infernet and the Ravin du Perthus. Both these gorges have cold, humid conditions that have produced an exceptional flora unknown elsewhere on the Mediterranean coast. They are both spectacular, and easily reached from the road.

Dying pines
Thousands of hectares of the Esterel were once covered in maritime pines, but since 1958 the pines have succumbed to a plague of toxic, parasitic insects (*Matsucoccus feytaudi*). Considerable reforestation has been taking place, but whether or not the new trees prove to be resistant to the insects or regenerate themselves has yet to be seen.

171

Rust-red rocks meet the sea on the Esterel's craggy coast

People-watching is the main pastime in 'St-Trop'

Pavement art in the old port

▶▶▶ **St-Tropez**   148C2

For many years a byword for all that was *chic* on the Riviera, St-Tropez is a summertime honeypot whose charms are not at all evident if you are stuck in a traffic jam trying to drive in, or being jostled in the streets by all the other tourists (around 100,000 every year) who have come here to find out what it's all about. Come by boat (from St-Raphaël or Ste-Maxime) or, better still, come in the spring or the autumn if you don't want to end up as red-faced and hot-tempered as St-Tropez's traffic police.

The huge reputation of this surprisingly small resort (which has only 6,000 inhabitants) started with Roger Vadim's film *Et Dieu créa la Femme* (*And Woman was Created*) in 1956, starring the then-unknown Brigitte Bardot. The bandwagon of celebrity fun, fashion and sex has rolled on since then, with every *poseur* with a yacht worthy of the name wanting to be seen dining in exhibitionist elegance, stern to the quay, for all to see.

The French have always known it as 'St Trop' ('St Too Much'), and as long as you are expecting just that (too much on the bills, too much posing, too much rubbish and pollution ...) then it can be fun for a day. The town boogies until the small hours and sleeps late. In the early morning hours, when no one else is around, the port is pretty as a picture, recalling the works of the Fauvist artists who were so inspired by St-Tropez at the beginning of the century.

St-Tropez was founded by the Greeks from Marseille, when it was known as Athenopolis. Later destroyed by the Saracens, it was rebuilt by settlers from Genoa in the 15th century who were granted indemnity from taxes by Good King René on condition that they defended the coastline from attack, which they did most notably when they fended off 22 Spanish galleons in 1637.

The first celebrity to breeze into St-Tropez was Guy de Maupassant, who arrived in the harbour in the 1880s on board his yacht. He set the scene to come for another century or so by his eccentric behaviour (in his case, it was due to pre-syphilitic insanity). A decade or so later, the Impressionist painter Paul Signac was forced into port by bad weather and liked St-Tropez so much he built a house here and invited all his friends down to take advantage of the wonderful southern light. Matisse was one of the first, followed by Dufy, Bonnard, Van Dongen, Vlaminck, Derain and others.

By the beginning of World War I, St-Tropez had already established itself as *the* artists' colony in Provence. Between the wars it received an influx of literary talent with the arrival of writers such as Colette and Anaïs Nin, and became a home-from-home for the in-crowd from St-Germain-des-Prés. Then, in the 1950s, it was the turn of film stars, starting with Vadim and Bardot.

What to see At the heart of St-Tropez is the *vieux port*, chock-a-block with sleek yachts, bad pavement artists, ostentatious fashion victims, and trendy bars such as *Café Sénéquier*. All is redeemed, however, by the superb **Musée de l'Annonciade►►** (*Closed* Tue and Nov. *Admission charge*) housed in the former chapel of the Annunciation on the south side of the port. The collection of paintings and sculptures features representative works by Paul Signac's circle and most of the other post-Impressionist and Fauvist artists who worked here at the turn of the century.

On the other side of the port, you can watch the boats coming back into harbour at dusk from the embankment of the Mole Jean Réveille. From behind the quai Jean-Jaurès the old streets lead up past the town hall, a massive tower (built by William I in AD 990) and the Italian-baroque church to the old **citadelle►**. There are views back over the rooftops of the town and across the Gulf from this 16th-century fortress, which also houses a small **naval museum** (*Closed* Tue and Nov. *Admission charge*) with maritime relics.

Apart from the port, St-Tropez's other main focal point is the enormous **place Carnot** (often called by its old name, place des Lices). Surrounded by cafés, there is nearly always a game of *pétanque* taking place here – except on Tuesday and Saturday, when the whole square is taken over by the local market. Between place Carnot and the port, endless designer-label shop windows display the latest items to tempt those with money to burn.

173

Still a fishing port, despite the razzmatazz

The St-Tropez bravades

Every year the residents of St-Tropez celebrate two *bravades* (literally, acts of bravado), the first of which coincides with the *fête* of their patron saint, St Tropez on 16 May. In this colourful, noisy 400-year-old tradition the townspeople parade in historical costumes, armed with breech-loaded muskets, through the streets to the town hall and the church. St Tropez is then paraded through the streets, with much noise and smoke from fusillades of muskets. The second *bravade* takes place on 15 June to commemorate the successful defence of the town against a Spanish fleet in 1637.

Beaches The beaches of St-Tropez are around the headland to the south of the port, and if you have not got your own speedboat then it is best to take the regular minibus from place Carnot, since parking charges are high.

In fact the 'beaches' are mostly private concessions (each with their own restaurants, bars, parasols and luxury beachchairs) along one huge, sandy beach in the Baie de Pampelonne. Some parts of the beach are free, but otherwise you will have to pay dearly for almost everything. In the summer months some 450 people work on these beaches, which generate an annual income of around 80 million francs – Pampelonne has come a long way since the first bamboo-and-thatch beach hut was built here in 1952.

That first beach bar was at **Tahiti-Plage**, at the start of the bay, and stars like Errol Flynn, Lana Turner and Clark Gable would come here to relax after visiting the Cannes film festival. Tahiti is still considered the 'movie stars' beach', although nowadays the neighbouring **Voile Rouge** attracts American celebrities such as De Niro, Eastwood, Stallone and Don Johnson. The Voile Rouge was also the first beach where women ever dared to go topless, doing for St-Tropez in the 1970s what one-piece bathing suits did for Juan-les-Pins in the 1930s.

Next to the Voile Rouge is **Moorea**, frequented by Alain Delon and best known for having launched the Gypsy Kings to stardom when they played in the bar. Following the South Pacific theme, other beaches on the northern section include **Bora Bora** (seafood a speciality) and **Pago Pago** (watersports and delicious chocolate profiteroles). Further down, **Club 55** is popular with Parisians, politicos and monarchs (Gorbachev, King Hussein and King Leopold of Belgium have all dropped by for lunch), whereas the **Aquaclub** is preferred by models (Linda Evangelista) and is a well-known gay rendezvous. **Tropezina** is more sporty, with a young crowd, whereas at **Le Blouch** or **Le Liberty** you won't even need to wear the minimum 'string' to go and have an ice-cream. Just your wallet will do.

Not as smart as St-Tropez, Ste-Maxime is just across the bay

Near by On the north shore of the Golfe de St-Tropez, **Ste-Maxime** has none of the glitz of its hyped-up neigh-

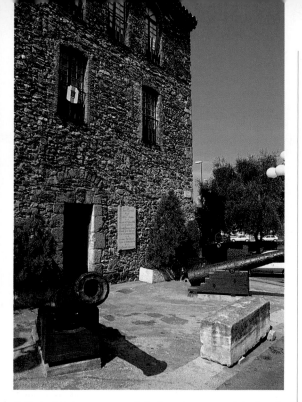

The Musée des Traditions Locales in Ste-Maxime

The headless saint
St-Tropez's name comes from the legend of a Roman soldier called Torpes who was beheaded by Nero for his Christian beliefs. His decapitated body was put in a boat, along with a cockerel and a dog, and set adrift in the Mediterranean. The animals were meant to eat the body but didn't, and the boat eventually drifted on to the shore here. A sanctuary was erected for the brave soldier, and in the 4th century the town adopted St Torpe's name.

175

Maritime trading in the 18th century is reflected in this statue of sea captain, Pierre André de Suffren de St-Tropez

bour and is happy enough in its role as a sedate family resort – with a casino thrown in for a bit of excitement. In front of the palm tree-lined promenade there is a big sandy beach with plenty of watersports (windsurfing, jet-skis and water skiing) and seductive beach-side bars.

Ste-Maxime has several colourful markets, including a daily food and flower market, crafts on Thursday and bric-a-brac on Friday. In the 16th-century **Tour Carrée►** on the sea front there is a small **Musée des Traditions Locales** (*Closed* Tue. *Admission charge*), which focuses on the history of the Golfe de St-Tropez. Far more compelling is the unusual **Musée du Phonographe et de la Musique Mecanique►** (*Open* Easter–mid-Oct, Wed– Sun 10–noon, 2–6. *Admission charge*), which is 10km north of town on the road to le Muy. Treasures in this collection include one of Edison's phonographs from 1878, the first ever recording machines, a language-teaching machine (the 'pathegraphe') from 1913, and an extraordinary assemblage of barrel organs, musical boxes, pianolas and the like.

A 17th-century representation of Pentecost in the Collégiale Ste-Pierre-aux-Liens

The Gothic-style nave of the Collégiale Ste-Pierre-aux-Liens adjoins a much older chapel

▶▶ **Sanary-sur-Mer** *148A1*

Sheltered from the *mistral* by wooded hills to the north, Sanary is a charming resort with a small harbour surrounded by palm trees and pastel-coloured buildings. Although fishing has never been of huge importance here, there is a small fleet (including several *pointus,* old-style boats with high curved prows) and every morning you can buy fresh fish, *oursin* (black spiny sea urchins), lobster and whatever else is in season from the quayside.

The discovery nearby of amphorae for exporting wine, as well as ovens dating from the 2nd century, proves the antiquity of the port. Like many Provençal towns, Sanary has gone through numerous name changes since antiquity: originally called St-Nazaire after its patron saint, during the Revolution it became Sanary, then St-Nazaire again from 1809 until 1890, then Sanary once more, finally settling on Sanary-sur-Mer in 1924.

Six-Fours-les-Plages *148A1*

The town of Six-Fours is a drab ribbon development stretching almost from la Seyne to Six-Fours-les-Plages across the neck of the Cap Sicié peninsula. Six-Fours itself is of limited interest but near by are two churches worth navigating your way around the suburban streets to find. The old village of Six-Fours once topped a small hill inland from the present-day town but was totally demolished to make way for the Fort (still in use, no visits).

Beneath the walls of the fort is the **Collégiale St-Pierre-aux-Liens**▶▶ (*Closed* Tue afternoon and Wed and Thu morning), which is unusual in that it has two naves, one (5th-century) from the original Romanesque chapel and another, larger Gothic-style nave added at right angles to the first in the 17th century.

The older chapel has one or two curious features, the most striking of which is a niche on the right-hand side of the massive stone altar that was known as the *reliquaire des morts*. Here, local people used to hang up coats, hats or the clothing of dead friends or relatives so that they could come and pray to them. This unique custom dates back to pagan times and, incredibly, was still being practised up to World War I (an old photo in the chapel shows the archway hung about with these reliquaries in 1909). Another niche inside the chapel contains beads and coins found during excavations of the 4th-century baptistry, fragments of a stained-glass window and a relic of Ste Philomene.

At the other end of the Romanesque chapel (or at the back of the Gothic nave, depending on which way you look at it) there is a polyptych by Louis Bréa which features popular local saints; look out also for the marble statue of the Virgin and the Assumption attributed to Puget which is in the Chapelle des Carmes on the right-hand side of the main church.

Also near Six-Fours is the **Chapelle Notre-Dame de Pépiole▶** (*Open* afternoons), which claims to be one of the oldest chapels in France, although little is known about it. It probably dates from the 3rd century (with a 10th-century nave added) and was restored from the 1950s onwards by a Belgian priest, M. Charlier. It contains two massive palaeo-Christian altar stones and 'stained-glass' windows that, as the *gardien* will explain, were made from old bottles because they had no money for the real thing. M. Charlier is buried outside the walls of this little old chapel to which he devoted his life.

The chapel can be hard to find: the easiest route is to take the D63 from Six-Fours towards la Seyne and turn left at the *Garage du Midi*, where there is a sign.

The sheltered little port at Sanary-sur-Mer

The Targo
A plaque opposite the Six-Fours fort commemorates the founding on 20 October 1880 of the *Escolo de Targo* (the Targo School), to promote the Provençal language – the school still functions today. The *targo* is an old Provençal game similar to jousting, with teams of eight using boats instead of horses. The aim is to knock your opponents off the prow of their boat with a long wooden 'lance'. The player who knocks three of his opponents off without getting a drenching himself wins a prize. *Targo* games are usually held in ports such as Toulon, Marseille, la Ciotat or Martigues.

The cloisters in the Abbaye du Thoronet, echoing the clarity of its pure Romanesque style

Imperial purple
On the western side of the port is the Roman district known as the Quartier de Castigneau, where excavations have revealed the remains of the dye works upon which Toulon's economy was once based. The port was renowned for the production of purple dye, which was used to colour silk and wool clothing worn by the Roman Emperor. It was obtained from the Murex molluscs that were once common along the coast; their glands were steeped in salt and boiled in leaden vats to obtain the distinctive, deep purple dye.

▶▶▶ **Thoronet, Abbaye du**   *148B2*
Open: daily. Admission charge
Hidden away in the forest of la Daboussière to the south of Entrecasteaux, the Abbaye du Thoronet is one of the most remarkable monasteries in Provence. It is the purest of the three great Cistercian monasteries (the other two are Sénanque and Silvacane) of the 12th century, and the first to be established. By the 14th century it had gone into decline; during the Wars of Religion the monks were chased out of the property; and it was finally abandoned in 1791. Restoration began in the 1850s.

The architecture of the complex (church, cloisters and chapterhouse) is in the purest Romanesque style, stripped of all decoration in accordance with the austere principles of the Cistercian order. The cloister is unusual in that it has been built on different levels and is one of very few to have a fountain-house in the middle, which fills the cloister with the gentle sound of running water. In the cellars there is a display documenting the restoration of the abbey over the last 150 years – and indeed, some of the outbuildings are still propped up with massive beams to counter the damage from subsidence caused by bauxite mining in the surrounding hills.

▶▶ **Toulon**   *148B1*
France's second-largest naval port, Toulon is often by-passed in favour of more glamorous locations further to the east – one guidebook dismisses it as 'a sprawling commercial and industrial city with many ugly buildings, dirty side streets, and much of the sordid underworld which grows up around a large port'. Grounds enough to keep going, you might think. However, given the port's enviable surroundings (a huge natural harbour, backed by a ring of high hills) and its lively character, Toulon is worth

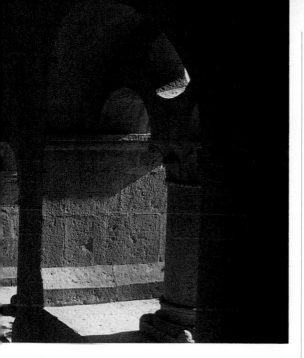

The siege of Toulon
Fiercely Royalist, Toulon accepted an offer of help from the English during the Revolution and welcomed their fleet into the bay in the summer of 1793. The British had built a seemingly impregnable fortress (on the site of the present Fort Napoléon), which they were so sure of they christened it 'little Gibraltar'. In the Siege of Toulon that followed, the Republicans set up a battery opposite the fort and it was here that the young Napoléon Bonaparte (then aged 24) distinguished himself as an artillery commander in the Republican forces.

a visit if you are near by. In fact for many years people driving along the coast have not had much choice about stopping here, since the streets of the town centre have been the only link between the A50 and A57 *autoroutes* on either side of Toulon. A tunnel is now being built which will take the *autoroute* beneath the town, but technical problems and cost overruns have delayed its completion.

Toulon's image as little more than a sleazy port is also fast disappearing as the city embarks on an imaginative transformation of the old parts of town. In what is possibly one of the largest architectural redevelopment programmes of its kind in Europe, over 20ha of the town centre have been smartened up and over 600 million francs has been invested in the restoration of old houses and shops and the creation of gardens, fountains and pedestrian areas.

Most of the current rebuilding has taken place in the lower town, which was Toulon's traditional red light district. The redevelopment has been boosted by the building of a huge new Law Faculty and an Electronics Institute as well as the gleaming Centre Mayol just near the port, with conference centres and a smart, two-storey shopping mall with over a hundred shops, boutiques and restaurants.

Toulon became a naval base soon after Provence became part of France in 1481, with Louis XII building the first fortifications here. Under Louis XIV, Toulon was elevated to the strategic centre for the Mediterranean fleet, a role that it still maintains today. The town was partially destroyed by Allied bombings in World War II and the Germans blew most of the rest up before surrendering on 26 August 1944. The story of the Allied victories in the South of France is recounted in a museum at the top of Mont Faron (see page 181).

One of sculptor Pierre Puget's famous Atlantes *propping up Toulon's old town hall doorway*

St-Exupéry's wreck
Antoine de St-Exupéry, author of *Le petit prince*, died in a plane crash whilst on a reconnaissance mission to survey German positions just before the Allied invasion of Provence in August 1944. Eyewitnesses reported seeing his Lightning P-38 go down in the Baie des Anges in Nice, but underwater soundings in 1992 found no wreckage. The search (led by those who discovered the *Titanic*) moved further west in 1993 after further witnesses reported seeing his plane crash off-shore from Toulon. What appears to be St-Exupéry's Lightning has now been found encased in sand in the Baie de Carquieranne.

Toulon in World War II
The French navy lost a large proportion of its fleet in Toulon harbour when Hitler made a surprise attack on the free French zone in November 1942; the fleet had insufficient time to escape and as a result 60 ships were scuttled in the approaches on 27 November. Four days after the start of the Allied landings to liberate Provence on 15 August 1944, French troops attacked the German defences around Toulon; after a week of fighting the city was liberated.

Toulon's town centre is a maze of pedestrian streets and well-shaded cafés

What to see In the post-war reconstruction of Toulon some fairly hideous buildings were put up, most notably the Soviet-style blocks of flats which now form a windswept wall along the back of the aptly named quai Stalingrad, the main waterfront promenade. However, beneath these monstrosities are the famous **Atlantes▶** by Pierre Puget on either side of the old town hall doorway; these powerful figures were one of Puget's first sculptures, their straining faces modelled on stevedores Puget had seen unloading ships in his native Marseille

The quai Stalingrad is the embarkation point for trips around Toulon's **harbour▶** and although modern catamarans have now replaced the old-style tourist boats, the boatmen's patter hasn't changed one whit: '*depart en quelques minutes*' still means they will leave when there are enough passengers, which could be anything up to an hour away. So – choose a boat and relax in a quayside café until it really does look like it is going to leave.

The majority of trips around the bay circle the inner roads (*la petite rade*) and the shipbuilding yards of neighbouring la Seyne. A lively commentary fills you in on the details of the warships, aircraft carriers and submarines of the Mediterranean fleet as well as any visiting warships that happen to be in port.

Toulon's maritime history is well documented in the **Musée de la Marine▶▶** (*Open* daily. *Admission charge*) near the entrance to the Arsenal. The excellent **Musée de Toulon▶▶** (*Open* daily) has an extensive collection of over 500 Provençal paintings from the 17th century onwards, as well as the second most important collection of French contemporary art in the country, starting from the 1960s. On the other side of the building is the **Musée d'Histoire Naturelle▶** (*Open* daily), which has an interesting room devoted to crystals and minerals and an embarrassingly large collection of stuffed animals.

Sandwiched between shopfronts on the cours Lafayette is the **Musée du Vieux Toulon** (*Open* afternoons; closed Sun) with various historic documents and memorabilia. The cours Lafayette itself is the setting every morning for Toulon's well-known market (*Open* daily except Mon in winter), a huge spread of the best and cheapest produce that Provence has to offer.

Within the network of pedestrian streets in the town centre, look out for the **Fontaine des Trois Dauphins**▶ in place Puget. Toulon has no less than 17 fountains (probably more than Aix, although they would not boast about it) but this is one of the best, with the three dolphins in the centre (sculpted in 1782) now completely obscured by a mini-jungle of fig trees, oleanders, ferns and ivy. Just near by is the **Opera**▶, which has a beautifully decorated interior inspired by Charles Garnier.

Toulon's tourist office (tel: 04 94 18 53 00) is in the charming place Raimu, named after the celebrated local actor Jules Raimu.

Near by The limestone *massif* of **Mont Faron**▶▶ rises 542m above the town and the bay of Toulon, with wonderful views from the top which are well worth the hair-raising, 9km drive to get there. A quicker way is via the *téléphérique* (funicular railway. *Closed* Mon and windy days. *Admission charge*), which whisks you up in about ten minutes from the terminus in blvd Amiral Vence.

181

Once at the top, a Sherman tank guards the entrance to the old Fort de la Tour Beaumont which is now the **Musée Memorial du Debarquement**▶ (*Open* daily. *Admission charge*), which commemorates the Allied landings of August 1944 in Provence. From the rooftop of the museum there is a panorama over the whole of the bay, with views that on a clear day reach as far down the coast as the Bec l'Aigle at la Ciotat. In the surrounding wooded park there are a couple of restaurants and a **Zoo** (*Open* daily in summer; variable hours in winter. *Admission charge*) that specialises in monkeys and big cats (it also breeds wolves and snow leopards).

Navigating or lost?
At the western end of the quai Stalingard is a statue by Daumas, 'the Genius of Navigation'. Local wags have it that the real story behind this is that the figure, naked except for a trailing loincloth, is in fact a drunken sailor emerging from the red light district (which he has his back to) in the early hours of the morning, having lost his all. His pointing finger has nothing to do with navigation at all – the poor sailor is in fact desperately pointing in the direction of his ship, which is departing over the horizon.

The 14th-century
Porte Saunerie leads
into rue Grande in
the heart of
Manosque, one of
the largest towns in
the Alpes de Haute-
Provence

▶▶▶▶▶ **REGION HIGHLIGHTS**

BARCELONNETTE *see page 186*
GRAND CAÑON DU VERDON
see page 190
MOUSTIERS-STE-MARIE *see
page 196*

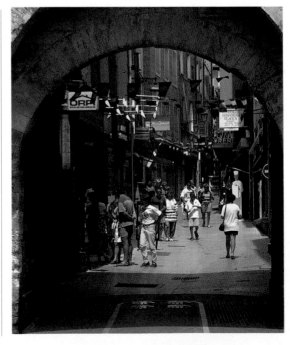

Introduction The northernmost *département* in Provence, the Alpes de Haute-Provence is a land of wild open spaces and clear skies, of captivating mountain peaks, deep ravines and rushing rivers, of tiny hamlets and twisting mountain roads. If you are looking for action in the discos, this is the wrong place – most of the action here is in the great outdoors, racing down rugged hillsides on a mountain bike, hang-gliding above deserted valleys, sailing on massive lakes, or simply walking peacefully amidst the Alpine landscapes.

Covering nearly 700,000sq km, the Alpes de Haute-Provence is the most sparsely populated region in Provence: its 130,000 inhabitants would fit into a city the size of Avignon with room to spare. It is also the least well-known area amongst tourists, with just 175,000 annual visitors (compared with over 2.5 million on the Côte d'Azur). Significantly, the average length of stay here is just as long as it is on the coast – those who have discovered the Alpes de Haute-Provence know a good thing when they see it and are prepared to take the time to unwind, to explore its hidden corners, and to relax in the pure mountain air.

Although temperatures can drop below zero in winter, the climate in summer is a serendipitous balance between Provençal sunshine and cool Alpine weather. It is the perfect antidote to the insufferable summer heatwaves which sometimes grip the rest of Provence.

Natural assets It is a region of great natural beauty, ranging from the superb Lac d'Allos (just one of 140 mountain lakes) to spectacular mountain passes (such as the Col d'Allos and the phenomenal Col de la Bonette) and the Grand Cañon du Verdon itself. This natural heritage is valued and protected, whether in the Réserve Géologique (the largest in Europe) around Digne, the Parc National du Mercantour (which is shared with the Alpes-Maritimes on the eastern boundaries of the *département*) or the innovative Conservatoire du Patrimoine Ethnologique de la Haute-Provence at the Prieuré de Notre-Dame Salagon near Mane.

It is a country where farmsteads hang out signs proclaiming *miel des mes ruches* ('honey from my hives') and where spring and autumn are eagerly awaited for their harvest of ceps, morels

The Fort de France guards the mountain passes above Colmars in the Haut Verdon Valley

Mountain cheeses
The Alpes de Haute-Provence is an important producer of goats' cheese, whose special flavour is attributed to the fact that the goats graze wild in the hills and *garrigue* (scrubland). Jean Giono evoked them in *Regain* where he wrote that: 'it seemed to him that he was kneading with his tongue a portion of the hill itself, with all its flowers'. At the beginning of winter, when the goats are brought down from the hills, cheese production stops. To preserve those already made, they are either wrapped in fresh chestnut leaves (this is the famous Banon method) or left to marinate in olive oil, garlic, herbs and bay leaves.

and other prize mushrooms, as well as truffles. This is the home of the delectable *agneau de Sisteron*, tender lamb cooked in herbs and garlic, in addition to the renowned goats' cheeses of Banon and honey-and-almond nougat for the sweet-toothed.

This is an area where picturesque mountain villages (such as Lurs or Simiane-la-Rotonde) have not yet been overrun with banal souvenirs – even though many are becoming increasingly popular as *residences secondaires* with city folk from Paris or Marseille.

This corner of the Alps has not always been so peaceful. The many wars which have been fought here have left a legacy of fortified towns and mountain strongholds that are visible everywhere from the 14th-century walls of Colmars to the 17th-century citadel of Entrevaux and the 20th-century pillboxes of the Maginot Line in the Vallée de l'Ubaye above Barcelonnette.

The Alpes de Haute-Provence is full of surprises: the unusual history of Barcelonnette, for instance, from where many impoverished inhabitants left for Mexico in the early 19th century and returned decades later to build themselves grand villas around the town, having made their fortunes. Another exotic connection is that of Alexandra David-Néel, who journeyed for decades in Tibet before settling in Digne, where her house is now a shrine to Buddhism and the spirit of adventure.

The great outdoors But above all it is a part of Provence where the rewards are to be found in the wilderness – in the air, there are five gliding centres and nine schools for hang-gliding, parascending and motorised ultra-lights (ULM). On the water, there are catamarans, windsurfing, rowing and sailing on half a dozen major lakes. On the rapids, you can raft, kayak, or white-water swim all the way down the Ubaye and the Verdon. On horseback, you can choose from 500km of bridlepaths and a dozen or more riding centres. On two wheels, there are over a hundred different mountain-biking routes some of which take several days to explore. On two feet, routes range from one to ten days (guided or on your own) along 5,000km of marked paths. And, of course, on two skis you can choose any one of 11 winter ski resorts.

The lie of the land The northwest of the Alpes de Haute-Provence is dominated by the Montagne de Lure whose peaks have traditionally marked the gateway to this part of Provence from the north. Wedged into a narrow gap protecting these approaches is the old town of Sisteron, whose citadel stands high above the Durance river as it flows southwards.

This turbulent river, once the scourge of low-lying villages, has been tamed by a complex system of dams and now irrigates fertile agricultural land in the valley. To the west of the Durance and the Marseille–Grenoble *autoroute* that runs alongside it is the Pays de Forcalquier, a rugged area of valleys and plateaux with a patchwork of forests and pasture lands.

To the east of the Durance the central section of the *département* starts to rise into the pre-Alps, with the dignified spa town of Digne-les-Bains at its heart. To the south, the Plateau de Valensole is one of the main lavender-growing areas in Provence, with the old lavender-distilling centre of Riez now starting to re-orientate itself towards tourism and reclaim its architectural heritage in the quiet backstreets.

Below Riez, the magnificent Grand Cañon du Verdon is the biggest tourist attraction in the *département*, and one that is best visited out of the peak season. At either end of the Cañon, Moustiers-Ste-Marie and Castellane are often swamped by traffic but provide numerous facilities for exploring Europe's longest and deepest limestone rift.

Following the Verdon back to its source brings you to the dramatic Alpine landscapes of the Parc National du Mercantour and, high up in the Vallée de l'Ubaye, the charming town of Barcelonnette, surrounded by towering peaks, which is the northernmost town in the whole of Provence.

Prehistory in the Alps
Although the dramatic Grand Cañon du Verdon is the most famous of the Verdon gorges, the western section (*les moyennes gorges*) is equally fascinating for different reasons. Here, on the edge of the Baume Bonne escarpment, a series of caves some 50m above the river has yielded a rich seam of archaeological finds that covers every stage of human development in Europe from paleolithic times to the Bronze Age. Over 80,000 artefacts from the site are to be displayed in the imaginative new Musée de Préhistoire des Gorges du Verdon, designed by the internationally renowned architect Sir Norman Foster, which is due to open in Quinson (28km south of Riez) in 1998.

Place Manuel, at the centre of Barcelonnette, a town with an unexpected past

Holiday chalets dot the countryside around Allos

► Allos
182C2

Where sheep once grazed on the pastures surrounding Allos, the slopes of the valley are now a patchwork of ski chalets and summer holiday homes in this remote spot in the Haute Vallée du Verdon (Haut Verdon Valley).

One of the main attractions in the vicinity is the dramatic **Lac d'Allos►►** (14km east along the D226), which is the largest high-altitude mountain lake in Europe. The road twists and turns as it climbs 800m above Allos, stopping around 1km short of the lake itself: a 30–40 minute walk brings you to an immense amphitheatre encircling the lake. Covering around 60ha, the Lac d'Allos is so cold that nothing grows in it. Its wonderful, pure colour reflects the surrounding peaks like a giant mirror.

The mountains around the lake are part of the Parc National du Mercantour (see page 236), and following the 3km-long path around the edge of the lake you are likely to see ibex, chamois and other wildlife high up on the scree, with birds of prey circling overhead. Just outside Allos there is a large leisure park and, to the north, the ski resort of la Foux d'Allos. From Foux d'Allos the D908 leads up to the spectacular **Col d'Allos►** (2,240m), with views towards the Vallée de l'Ubaye and Barcelonnette.

►►► Barcelonnette
182C3

High up in the Vallée de l'Ubaye in the most northerly corner of the Alpes de Haute-Provence, Barcelonnette is a graceful, welcoming town. In the summer it is a good base for exploring the Parc National du Mercantour, whose northernmost boundaries extend into the valley. The *Maison du Parc* (tel: 04 92 81 21 31) near the town centre has details on guided tours, walks and the park's wildlife. From the Col du Longet at the head of the valley the river Ubaye flows for 90km down to the Lac de Serre-

Ponçon, and downstream from Barcelonnette there are activity centres offering kayaking, canoeing and rafting. In the winter, when snow blankets the valley for up to five months, ski resorts (such as Pra-Loup, le Sauze/Super-Sauze and Ste-Anne-la-Condamine) come into their own.

Founded in 1231 by Count Raymond Berenger V, Barcelonnette ('little Barcelona') was named after the Catalan city where the count's family originated. But a more intriguing connection with the world outside the valley began in 1821 when three local men, the Arnaud brothers, emigrated to Mexico, via Amsterdam and New Orleans, to look for work. By the turn of the century, around 4,000–5,000 people from the region had emigrated and there may be around 40,000–50,000 of their descendants living in Mexico. The Arnaud brothers never returned, but many others came back to build sumptuous villas on the outskirts of town, mainly along the avenue des Trois Frères Arnaud and the avenue de la Libération.

The connection is presented in imaginative displays in the **Musée de la Vallée**▶▶ (*Open* daily 2–7. *Admission charge*) on avenue de la Libération; here too is an ethnographic section and a room devoted to the fantastic travels of writer Émile Chabrand, who went from Barcelonnette to Mexico via the Far East in the 1880s. There is also a **Maison du Mexique** (*Open* Jul–Aug,daily), which is more commercially oriented. At the heart of Barcelonnette is the **place Manuel**▶ where you can sip coffee and gaze at the snow-capped peaks.

TARIF NORMAL

Nº 034242

MUSÉE DE LA VALLÉE

LA SAPINIÈRE
04400 BARCELONNETTE
ALPES DE HAUTE-PROVENCE
TÉL. 92.81.27.15

MUSÉE MUNICIPAL CONTRÔLÉ
PAR L'ÉTAT

187

Alpine peaks rise up above the streets of Barcelonnette

The 'Mexicans' from Barcelonnette
In 1821, the three Arnaud brothers emigrated to Mexico (see text). In 1830 they were joined by two of their compatriots, Eugene Caire and Alphonse Jauffred. It was these two who opened the floodgates when they returned to Barcelonnette 15 years later with 250,000 francs apiece – a large fortune in those times – and precipitated a mass emigration which lasted for over a century as hundreds of people from the valley (and eventually the surrounding valleys as well) left to seek their fortunes. Some thrived in commerce; others simply managed to survive; and many ended their days in poverty.

Digne's geological reserve
Digne is at the centre of the largest geological reserve in Europe, the Réserve Géologique de Haute-Provence, which covers 150,000ha. Fossils and imprints from the Primary era some 200 million years ago are numerous, and include the skeleton of a large sea reptile. The Reserve is administered from the Centre de Géologie, 3km north of Digne along the D900A, which has a research centre, library and exhibitions (*Open* daily; closed Sat and Sun, Nov–Apr. *Admission charge*). The Centre provides leaflets detailing sites open to the public, and organises guided tours (tel: 04 92 31 51 31).

The modernised thermal baths in Digne offer all sorts of different cures

▶ **Castellane**   *182C1*

Advertising itself as the gateway to the Cañon du Verdon, Castellane is inevitably overrun during the summer season with foreign cars and overseas accents. Although it has no great attractions of its own, it is a useful place for stocking up on supplies (with plenty of camping and outdoor shops) or for arranging activities such as rafting, climbing, walking or mountain biking in the gorges. There are around a dozen hotels in town and no less than 14 campsites within a 3km radius.

The most striking aspect of the town is the sheer pinnacle rising up behind it that is topped off by the **Chapelle Notre-Dame du Roc**. If you are feeling energetic you can climb up to the chapel via a path to the left of the church (it takes around 30 minutes to reach the top).

▶▶ **Colmars**   *182C2*

Just down the Haut Verdon Valley from Allos (see page 186), Colmars is a lovely old fortified town in a picturesque position amidst the surrounding woodlands and peaks. It acquired its first defences in the late 14th century, and remained an important frontier town until 1713.

At the end of the 17th century two forts were added to protect the town from constant attacks by the Savoyards, each fort guarding a bridge at either end of the village. To the south is the **Fort de France**, with the much larger and more imposing **Fort de Savoie**▶ to the north. Inside the Fort de Savoie exhibitions are held in the summer in the *Centre Culturel de Colmars-les-Alpes*.

▶ **Digne-les-Bains**   *182B2*

Digne is a placid, genteel town that has built its reputation on the seven springs to the south of town which supply

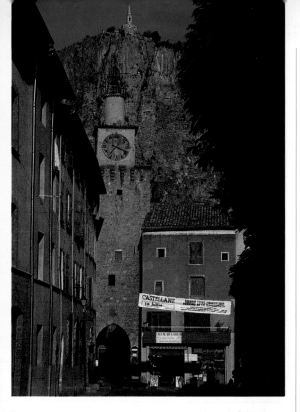

It is a steep climb up to the Chapelle Notre-Dame du Roc, which dominates the skyline above Castellane

Getting wet
Local tour operators in Castellane offer a mind-boggling number of adventurous methods for descending the Grand Cañon. These include rafting (in specially-adapted Zodiacs); white-water swimming (wetsuits, helmets and a special type of surfboard provided); 'hot dogging' (two-person inflatable canoes); canyoning (a combination of rappelling down into the canyon and white-water swimming); aquatic walks (*through* rather than on the water); 'flotting' (a Verdon speciality, floating feet-first with a specially designed inflatable back-pack); and kayaking. (Contact Aqua Verdon, tel: 04 92 83 72 75; Montagnes et Rivieres, tel: 04 92 83 73 57; Bureau des Guides, tel: 04 92 77 30 50.)

its renowned spa – where '*les cures anti-stress*' are now offered alongside the more traditional rheumatism treatments. It is also the main centre for lavender production in the mountains of Haute Provence, which it celebrates with the *Grande Foir Expo de la Lavande*, running for four days in early August.

The town centre is bisected by the boulevard Gassendi, at the eastern end of which is the place du Général-de-Gaulle where the Wednesday and Saturday markets are held (good value if you are looking for *miel de lavande* or other lavender products). On the south side of the boulevard is the old town with the crumbling **Cathédrale St-Jérôme**. Further up the boulevard is the **Musée Municipal▶** (*Open* daily in summer; afternoons in winter; closed Mon. *Admission charge*) with various archaeological finds and 19th-century Provençal paintings, as well as an extensive collection of 19th-century scientific instruments and a model for the first Channel tunnel, conceived by local engineer Alex du Breton in 1880. To the north the **Cathédrale Notre-Dame-du-Bourg▶** is a good – if neglected – example of the Provençal Romanesque.

Digne's star attraction is the **Fondation Alexandra David-Néel▶▶** (*Open* daily; guided tours only. *Admission* donation). In 1928 David-Néel (see panel) bought this house, which she called *Samten Dzong* ('the castle of meditation'), although then it was in the countryside and not next to a busy main road. It houses a fascinating collection of Buddhas, prayer-wheels, other Tibetan mementos and many of David-Néel's personal effects. The foundation (20 minutes' walk from the town centre, 27 avenue Maréchal Juin) also houses a meditation centre and a Tibetan shop.

An intrepid traveller
Born in Paris in 1868, Alexandra David-Néel studied Oriental languages at the Sorbonne and then spent many years in Tibet, travelling across the country on foot and living in the forbidden city of Lhasa in disguise. On her return she published several books, becoming one of the top Tibetan scholars in the West. At the age of 69, a decade after moving to Digne, she spent a further nine years in Central Asia. In 1968, aged over 100, she renewed her passport because she wanted to visit China. She died in Digne on 8 September 1969, having just started to write another four books.

▶▶ **Entrevaux** *182C1*

The first explorers

The first inhabitants of the Verdon gorges were the Ligurians; several centuries later, shepherds fleeing the Saracens converted caves near the Circque de l'Escales into farmhouses and haylofts. In the Middle Ages the gorges were reputed to be the home of 'wild men' and other assorted devils. The first scientific expedition was carried out in August 1905 by the speleologist E A Martel and several companions equipped with ropes, cameras, and collapsible canoes. It took them three and a half days to get from one end of the canyon to the other.

Approaching Entrevaux from either direction along the Var Valley it is easy to see why it was such an important town in the 17th century. The gorges here narrow to just a few hundred metres across – plug this, and you block a major route between France and Savoy.

On the west bank of the Var a jagged curtain of rock makes the hillside impassable. On the east bank, this natural barrier is reflected in the grand **fortifications**▶ (*Open* daily; closed Nov–Feb. *Admission charge*), built by Vauban, Louis XIV's military adviser, which zigzag up to the citadel perched 135m above the town.

The main access to the town is via a fortified **bridge**▶, another of Vauban's works. Entrevaux had drifted in the doldrums, but with a steady trickle of visitors drawn by Vauban's handiwork there are signs of life again in the old medieval streets. Some restoration is under way and there are concerts and festivals in the summer.

▶ **Forcalquier** *182A1*

From a simple village on the Domitian Way in Roman times, Forcalquier rose to become an independent state in the 12th century. The Counts of Forcalquier held sway over Sisteron, Apt and Gap from their citadel, and the town became the centre of cultural and commercial life in Haute Provence.

Only the ruins of one tower remain of the Counts' château on the **citadel** above the town. However, it is worth the walk for the view over the surrounding Pays de Forcalquier, and the 19th-century Chapelle **Notre-Dame-de-Provence**.

The spacious place du Bourguet is dominated by the austere, Gothic façade of the **Cathédrale Notre-Dame du Marché**. On Mondays, the *place* and the surrounding streets are transformed into a vast market, overflowing with local produce. South of the cathedral are the narrow streets of the **vieille ville**▶ (*Guided tours* start at the tourist office on Wed and Sat mornings at 10am), with many 13th- and 15th-century houses. You can skip the stuffy old **municipal museum**, but the **Couvent des Cordeliers**▶▶ (*Guided tours* several times daily in summer; closed Wed. *Admission charge*) is worth visiting. Founded in the 13th century, it is one of the oldest Franciscan monasteries in France.

Carving on the Chapelle Notre-Dame-de-Provence, Forcalquier

▶▶▶ **Grand Cañon du Verdon** *182B1*

Rising just above la Foux d'Allos in the Mont des Trois Evêchés, the Verdon river flows south before looping west just above Castellane to carve its way through the limestone plateau of Haute Provence on its journey towards the Durance.

Between Castellane and Moustiers-Ste-Mairie the river has hewn a deep crevice in the plateau – the spectacular, 21km-long Grand Cañon (or Canyon) du

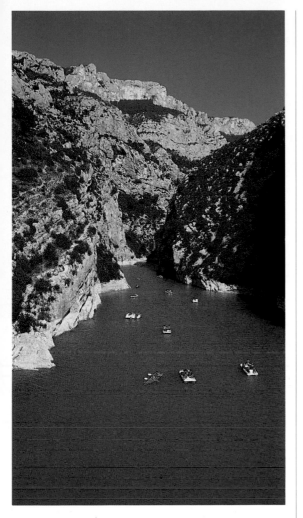

Taking to the water through the Grand Cañon

The Haute-Provence Observatory
After considerable research to find the location with the clearest atmosphere in Provence, the Observatoire de Haute-Provence was eventually built on a plateau just to the southwest of Forcalquier in 1936, near the village of St-Michel-l'Observatoire. Its 14 domes house a number of telescopes, but their usefulness has diminished in recent years due to increased pollution. Tours of the observatory take place on Wednesday afternoons and the first Sunday mornings of the month in summer (*Admission charge*), but since they take place in daytime they are not particularly enlightening.

Walking the canyon
The canyon is best appreciated on foot. On the right bank the *Sentier Martel* runs from Mayreste to Rougon following the GR4, but this takes about two days: a section of this route, from la Maline to Point Sublime, can be accomplished in about 7–8 hours. The *Sentier Imbut* follows the GR99 for part of the way on the left bank, crossing over at the Passerelle de l'Estellié to reach the refuge at la Maline (around 2.5 hours one way). Always take a torch, sweater, water and provisions, and beware of sudden changes in water-levels due to upstream power stations. A detailed colour booklet of the routes, *Canyon du Verdon*, is widely available (in several languages) in Moustiers or Castellane.

Verdon. From sheer cliffs some 700m above the rushing torrent there are panoramic views down the length of this corridor, with the emerald green waters of the river (which was named for its unusual colour) sparkling in the sunshine below.

The first survey of the canyon was not carried out until 1905, when the eminent speleologist E A Martel charted its course. His report that it was 'a marvel without parallel in Europe' prompted the Touring Club de France to build the first tracks and belvederes in 1928. In 1947 the first road (the *Corniche Sublime*) was built on the southern side of the canyon, and the northern half opened up in 1973 with the *Route des Crêtes*.

Since then traffic volumes have been inexorably increasing – in high season you are likely to find yourself in a slow-moving convoy of campervans and cars.

The Grand Cañon may soon become a *Parc Naturel Régional*, which will give greater protection to this unique area.

Drive Grand Cañon du Verdon

One of the classic tourist routes in Provence – and best undertaken outside the peak months of July and August. Allow at least the whole day for the entire circuit, departing from and returning to Moustiers.

From Moustiers take the D952 to the Belvédère de Galetas, the first of many viewpoints. Here, the view is of the impressive canyon mouth where the river pours out into the vast Lac de Ste-Croix.

From here, the road starts to climb upwards and shortly you arrive at the Mayreste Belvédère, which involves a 10-minute scramble over the rocks to the cliff edge from where there is the first overall view of the canyon upstream. After passing through the Col d'Ayen, the road temporarily leaves the gorge and descends to the plateau of La-Palud-sur-Verdon, now a major centre for mountain biking, climbing, trekking, canoeing and rafting.

Just after La Palud take a right turn down the D23, signposted *Route des Crêtes*. This loop returns after a nerve-racking 23km to La Palud. It passes by several dramatic viewpoints, most notably the

Trescaïre Belvédère, the Escales Belvédère (the view rendered even more dramatic by the climbers usually seen clinging to the cliff face – this is an internationally renowned rock-climbing site), the Baou Pass Belvédère (with a drop of 715m into the canyon), the Tilleul Belvédère (fabulous panorama back across the Plan de Canjuers) and the Imbut Belvédère.

Back in La Palud, continue on the D952 towards Castellane. After around 7km you will come to a large car parking area for the Point Sublime. Walk up to the viewpoint to see the meeting of the Verdon and the Baou rivers and the openings into the Couloir Samson and the Grand Cañon itself.

The route follows the Verdon through the Clue de Carejuan until it reaches the Pont-de-Soleils, the cross-over point between the right and left banks. Take the D955 on the other side of the bridge and then turn right into the village of Trigance. Turn right again onto the D71 and you soon reach the Balcons de la Mescla, a series of impressive belvederes almost directly opposite the *Route des Crêtes* on the north bank. Several hundred metres below, the Verdon meets the equally turbulent Artuby river in the middle of the bend.

From the Balcons de Mescla you cross the Artuby canyon on the impressive, single-span Pont de l'Artuby before arriving at the Tunnels de Fayet; between the tunnels, there are views of the Falaise des Cavaliers. The road follows these cliffs and then continues on the edge of the precipice past the Falaise de Baucher and the Imbut Pass before leaving the canyon and climbing up to the Cirque de Vaumale; from here, views extend over to the north bank and downstream to the opening into the lake.

At the Col d'Illoire the road finally leaves the gorges behind – stop at the belvedere for a last look back before continuing to the village of Aiguines. From here, a series of hair-pin bends downhill gives lovely views across the whole Valensole plateau and the Lac de Ste-Croix. Cross the Pont du Galetas (with a panorama of the lake on one side and the entrance to the gorges on the other) before joining the D952 into Moustiers.

The Grand Cañon is one of the natural wonders of Provence

Gréoux's spa baths
In the 2nd century the Romans built the first spa here. The baths then fell into disuse until being reopened in the 17th century. They became fashionable at the start of the 19th century when Napoléon's sister visited, but fell out of favour once again until being entirely rebuilt in 1962. Now popular with *curistes* from all over France., they pump out around three million litres a day at an average temperature of 36 °C.

► **Gréoux-les-Bains**   *182A1*

Dominated by the ruins of a 12th-century castle built by the Knights Templars, Gréoux has relied since antiquity on making a living from the warm, sulphurous springs that rise just to the south of this small town.

Gréoux's Grande Rue has plenty of excellent *traiteurs*, *boulangeries* and the like for stocking up on picnic supplies, as well as plenty of cafés, inviting restaurants, and bars. There are several craft galleries and exhibitions, amongst them the **Maison de Pauline** (near the tourist office; inquire for opening times), an old Provençal house furnished in traditional style. Further down the Grand Rue is the **Atelier Musée du Vitrail et de la Mosaique** (*Open* daily. *Admission charge*), which has extensive displays of stained glass and mosaics in several showrooms. Just outside town at 36, ave des Alpes is the **Crèche de Haute Provence** (*Open* daily, except Sun in winter. *Admission free*), a miniature village with Provençal *santons*.

A ruined Knights Templar castle stands guard over the town of Gréoux

►► **Lurs**   *182A1*

From its position high above the west bank of the Durance, Lurs commands a wonderful view across the surrounding countryside. The neatly kept streets and attractive houses amply justify the sobriquet of *village de caractère*, and the whole village is now classified as a historical site.

During the Middle Ages, Lurs thrived when the Bishops of Sisteron had their summer residence here, but the population fell to zero earlier this century when it was abandoned due to the lack of electricity and running water. The village was saved from oblivion by a group of graphic artists and printers (led by the typographer Maximilien Vox) who moved in after World War II.

Lurs now plays host every year to the prestigious *Rencontres Internationales de Lurs,* which brings together graphic artists, photographers, designers and printers during the last week in August.

Nearby The narrow D30 north of Lurs leads to the **Prieuré de Ganagobie**►► (*Open* 3–5pm; closed Mon. *Admission charge*), a Benedictine monastery founded in the 10th century. The 12th-century church has an unusual decorative doorway and an even more striking set of mosaics composed solely of white, black and red tiles: restored in the 1960s, the mosaics combine geometric motifs with wonderful representations of fantasy beasts and animals.

► **Mane** *182A1*

This small village 4km south of Forcalquier has a well-preserved old quarter, a château (private property) and a 16th-century church – but the chief attraction in the vicinity is the **Prieuré Notre-Dame de Salagon►►**, just outside Mane on the N100. Established at the end of the 11th century by Benedictine monks from Villeneuve-lès-Avignon, the priory complex includes a 12th-century Romanesque church, a small lodging house for the Abbot (added in the 15th century), and barns and farm buildings that date from the time the priory was deconsecrated after the Revolution.

Since 1981 Salagon has been home to the *Conservatoire du Patrimoine Ethnologique de la Haute Provence*, a conservation organisation actively involved in local heritage issues. As well as a museum dedicated to ethnography of the region there are also revolving exhibitions on traditional lifestyles. The centre (*Open daily in summer; Apr–Jun, 2–6pm; weekends in winter. Admission charge*) also has an excellent bookshop with titles on regional culture. Outside, there are two small gardens, a re-created medieval monastery garden and a medicinal herb garden.

Further down the same road you will find the 18th-century **Château de Sauvan►** (*Guided tours* daily 3.30 in summer; Sun in winter; closed Sat. *Admission charge*). The architecture of this classical mansion echoes that of the Petit Trianon and is all the more surprising for being found in Haute Provence, especially as it overlooks extensive lawns and a lake with geese. The interior style matches the palatial ambitions of the château's façade.

► **Manosque** *182A1*

'Certain towns can show you their proud cathedrals, their medieval ramparts, or the guts of martyrs but Manosque has only its beauty.' Thus wrote Jean Giono, who lived nearly all his life in Manosque and wrote evocative poems and stories about the surrounding countryside of Haute Provence and its inhabitants. His myopia can perhaps be forgiven but he certainly would not have appreciated the sprawling, ugly industrial suburbs that surround Manosque today, nor the Cadarache Nuclear Research Centre on the banks of the Durance.

Once you have penetrated the core of the old town via the 14th-century **Porte Saunerie**, Manosque takes on a more pleasing aspect. The pedestrianised **rue Grande** is the central axis of the old town, lined with shops (a plaque above a shoe shop at No 13 marks Giono's birthplace) and leading to the lively **place Hôtel-de-Ville**. Market days in the rue Grande are Monday, Wednesday, Friday and Saturday.

Manosque may not have a cathedral, but it has two churches: the **Église St-Sauveur** combines a Gothic doorway with a Romanesque nave and an intricate wrought-iron belfry from the 18th century; on place Hôtel-de-Ville, **Notre-Dame-de-Romigier** has a finely carved Renaissance doorway and a 12th-century blackwood Virgin.

The persistent Madonna
The black Madonna in Manosque's Église St-Sauveur is said to be the oldest in France. Found in a nearby pine wood in the 6th century, it was then mysteriously lost again for two centuries. Rediscovered, it was presented to the monks building the church, but they thought it too ugly and left it outside the door. The Madonna, so the story goes, made its own way to the altar. It was once more put outside, and again found its way back to the altar. The sceptical Manosquais finally decided it was a miracle, and the Madonna remained. Today, supplicants pray to her for rain in times of drought.

195

Flowers and plants to go, in the old town of Manosque

Modern-day faïences *for sale in Moustiers*

► ► ► **Moustiers-Ste-Marie**   *182B1*

The western gateway to the Grand Cañon du Verdon, Moustiers suffers badly in the summer months from traffic jams and overcrowding, and like the Grand Cañon itself, the village is best visited out of season. The old, tile-hung houses of the village cling precariously to the banks on either side of the Rioul, a torrent which descends from the craggy cliffs above Moustiers. Suspended across the gorge is a 220m-long chain with the famous star of Moustiers (see panel) hanging down in the middle.

As well as being one of the principal access points for the Grand Cañon, the village is famous for its glazed ceramics (*faïences*), examples of which can be seen in numerous museums throughout Provence. This centuries-old tradition (see panel) died out in the 1870s but was revived by Marcel Provence in 1927 and there are now around 15 studios in the village doing a thriving trade. However, do not expect any bargains (prices range from around 80 francs for the smallest butter dish up to around 8,000 francs for a large, decorative wall-plate) and there is a lot of overpriced rubbish on display.

If you want to see what the classic designs should look like you can visit the **Musée de la Faïence**►► (*Open*

Moustiers faïences
According to local tradition, it was an Italian monk who passed the secret of the glaze on to local potter Pierre Clérissy in 1668; his luminous blue designs on a brilliant white background became hugely popular during the reign of Louis XIV. Multicoloured designs were introduced around 1740, and by the end of the century there were a dozen or more workshops in the village. The potteries thrived until the Revolution but with many of their clients lost to the guillotine the industry declined, and the last kiln closed down in 1874.

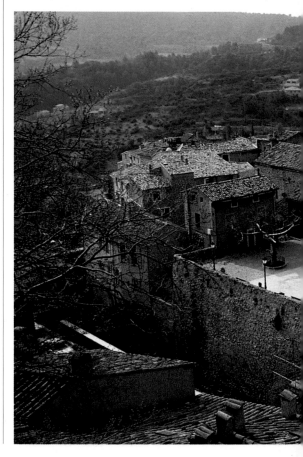

Apr–Oct, daily except Tue. *Admission charge*), which was founded by Marcel Provence in 1929. The museum has a superb collection of faïences by the master potters (such as Clérissy, Olérys, Laugier, Ferrat, and others) who made Moustiers' reputation in the 17th and 18th centuries.

In the town centre, the 12th-century **Église►** is dominated by a three-tiered Romanesque bell-tower; inside you can watch the rushing waters of the torrent beneath through a glass panel in the floor.

Moustiers was settled in AD 433 by monks from the Îles de Lérins, who moved into the caves high up in the rock face above the village and founded a monastery: in the 12th century the **Chapelle Notre-Dame De Beauvoir►** was built on this site. The 20-minute walk up to the chapel, via a winding path lined with oratories, is a popular way of escaping the pottery shops. The chapel was rebuilt in the 16th century and has an unusual Romanesque porch with carved wooden doors.

A pilgrimage to the chapel takes place on the first weekend after Easter, when villagers wearing 18th-century costumes climb the path for mass. There is also a procession to the chapel during the *Fête de la Nativité de la Vierge* on 8 September.

An ancient bell-tower looms above the tiled roofs of Moustiers

The chaine de l'Étoile
The chain with its five-pointed star which hangs high above Moustiers was originally placed here in the 12th century by a seigneur of the Blacas family: imprisoned during the Crusades, he vowed to make an offering to Notre-Dame de Beauvoir if he was released. The star on the chain was originally made from silver, but it was supposedly stolen during the Wars of Religion. It was replaced with a metal chain and star, although the chain is in such an exposed, windy position that it has frequently fallen down – the current one has been there since 1957.

The Rocher de la Baume, with its all but vertical strata, faces Sisteron's equally impressive citadel across the Durance

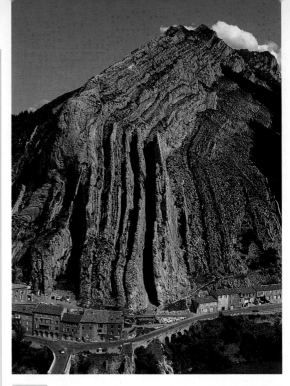

Roman Riez

Built at the confluence of two rivers (the Colostre and the Aivestre), Roman Riez was an important colony not least because it was on the borderline between Roman-occupied territory to the south and the unruly Alpine domain to the north. Despite Riez' significance, archaeological digs in the past have been piecemeal; recent excavations, however, have uncovered the ancient bed of the Colostre (to the south of the present river) and a monumental doorway, near the Corinthian columns, which indicates that this may have been the site of the Forum.

Music in the round

The circular tower in Simiane-la-Rotonde has very pure acoustics and concerts have been staged since 1986 under the patronage of the Simiane Festival. Recently the summer season has been renamed *Les Riches Heures Musicales de la Rotonde*, and although this tiny venue can seat only 150 people it has attracted musicians of considerable calibre. As befits the setting, the repertoire is mostly medieval music. Concerts take place from mid-July to mid-August (for details, tel: 04 92 75 90 14).

►   **Riez**   *182B1*

Riez is at the centre of the **Plateau de Valensole** which covers 800sq km to the northwest of the Lac de Ste-Croix and the Verdon. This huge plateau, bisected by the river Asse and punctuated by wooded ravines, is a patchwork of wheat fields and lavender – it is one of the largest lavender growing areas in Provence, and if you want to capture the endless rows of vivid plants on camera the time to come here is in July when they flower.

As well as being a centre for traditional lavender-distilling, Riez has a long history as a market town on the crossroads of the Roman route through Provence from Fréjus to Aix. From the Roman era – when it was known as Colonia Iulia Augusta Reiorum Apollinaris – all that remains are four Corinthian **columns►**, once part of a temple dedicated to Apollo which overlooked the road to Aix, which stand in splendid isolation in the middle of a field on the western edge of present-day Riez.

In the 5th century Riez became a bishopric and a **baptistry►** was erected over the ruins of the Roman baths (just near the Roman columns – ask at the tourist office for a key). It is one of only a handful from the Merovingian era still surviving in France, although the dome dates from a much later period. Inside, there is a small museum with bits of sculpture, inscriptions and other archaeological finds.

At the heart of the old town the **Grand Rue** has preserved several fine Renaissance houses and in the streets and alleyways off to either side are a number of craft workshops, *santonniers* and potteries. Local crafts also feature in exhibitions at the **Musée d'Histoire Naturelle en Provence** (*Open* daily except Mon. *Admission charge*) alongside the usual fossils and mounted birds.

Near by On the D953 towards Digne, just outside Riez, the intriguing **Maison de l'Abeille▶** (House of the Bee) presents displays on the old-fashioned production of honey, the life cycle of the bee and other aspects of apiculture. There is an insect museum (*Open* daily) and a shop.

▶▶   **Simiane-la-Rotonde**   *182A1*

Spiralling around a hillock on the edge of the plateau that marks the boundary between Haute Provence and the Vaucluse, Simiane-la-Rotonde is a charming *village de caractère* surrounded by farmland and lavender fields.

At the summit of the village is the **Rotonde▶▶** (*Open* daily in summer except Tue; closed Nov–May. *Admission charge*) from which it gets its name. Built in the 12th century, this curious, truncated structure is one of the few remaining examples of non-religious Romanesque architecture in Provence. The main feature of the Rotonde is the extraordinary domed ceiling with a series of finely detailed carved masks and figures on the columns supporting the cupola. Most of the buildings around the Rotonde have long since gone, except for part of the seigneurial manor linked to it on the south side.

▶▶   **Sisteron**   *182A2*

Strategically situated where the Durance valley narrows down to less than a kilometre wide, Sisteron guards the mountain gateway between Provence and Dauphiné.

This ancient fortified site is capped by a **citadel▶** (*Open* Mar–mid-Nov. *Admission charge*) standing 500m above the waters of the Durance, which has a 12th-century keep. The citadel was badly damaged (as was much of the town) during Allied bombing raids in August 1944.

At the centre of town is the place de la République, with three huge towers (remnants from the medieval ramparts) and the **Cathédrale Notre-Dame▶** to the east. Behind here is the **vieille ville▶▶**, a maze of steps and alleyways between tall houses linked by covered archways (known locally as *androne*). A signposted route leads past some fine houses in the old quarter, ending up in the place de l'Horloge on the north side, where a lively market is held on Wednesday and Saturday mornings.

Ramparts in Sisteron's old citadel

199

Close-up on the scant remains of Roman Riez

CÔTE D'AZUR AND ALPES-MARITIMES

CÔTE D'AZUR AND ALPES-MARITIMES

A year-round reminder of Cannes' international film festival

Introduction The most famous corner of Provence, the southeastern coastline known as the Côte d'Azur, often seems like part of another countryn giving rise to the idea of Provence as the California of Europe, a wealthy sunshine state where high-tech business parks will be the future motor for the economy.

But today, marinas rather than microchips still symbolise the real wealth here: in over 30 marinas from Menton to la Napoule, 15,000 yachts generate 1.5 billion francs in annual income. They seem to encapsulate the image of this glamorous playground: conspicuous riches, the jet-set lifestyle, and the joys of a sensual holiday next to the warm, blue Mediterranean.

The pleasures promised by the hyperbole surrounding the Riviera, as this 70km-long stretch of coastline is also called, can seem like a distant dream when you are stuck in a traffic jam along one of the corniches, contemplating a beach down below packed to overflowing, with the sea a mass of pedal boats, bobbing bodies, jet-skis and sailboards. And the glories of the *belle époque* hotels on the sea front have been eclipsed in many places by a contagious rash of houses and apartment blocks spreading up every available sea-facing hillside.

Inland peaks Fortunately, the real Provence is never far away with the mountains of the Alpes-Maritimes forming a splendid backdrop to the glittering coastline. Just an hour or so from the beach the *arrières-pays* (the backcountry) shelters dramatic hill villages, linked by twisting mountain roads where signs warn of multiple *lacets* (hairpin bends).

Some of the better known of these *villages perchés* (such as Èze or St-Paul-de-Vence) are horribly over-commercialised, but there are still plenty of others (such as Peille, Peillon, Coaraze or Gorbio) where the narrow streets retain more of an authentic flavour.

Behind Cannes the rolling hills culminate in the pre-Alps of Grasse. Behind Nice the narrow river valleys lead up to the wilderness of the Parc National du Mercantour. Further east, the remote Roya valley displays characteristic Italianate architecture and many fine works of art in the old border towns of Tende, Sospel, Saorge and Breil.

In the summer you can hike and mountain bike beneath the snow-clad peaks of the Alpes-Maritimes, whilst in winter the ski resorts come into their own. For the budget-conscious it can make sense to stay in the *arrière-pays*, where hotel prices are more reasonable, descending to the coast for a taste of the high life when the bright lights call.

The Riviera resorts Nice is the capital of the *département* of the Alpes-Maritimes and France's fifth largest city, with over 450,000 inhabitants. Around a third of all tourists who visit the Riviera come to Nice, drawn partly by its lovely setting on the big, blue *Baie des Anges* (the Bay of Angels). Nice has a well-preserved *vieille ville*, as has the charming port of Antibes, which houses the remarkable Picasso museum – just one of an extraordinary number of first-class modern art museums along the coast, a legacy of the contemporary artists who settled here from the end of the 19th century onwards. The beaches at Antibes are mostly shingle and those on the neighbouring Cap d'Antibes largely private, but neighbouring Juan-les-Pins has a fine sandy beach.

Cannes is perhaps the most snobby of the Riviera resorts, a place to see-and-be-seen – but avoid it during the Film Festival! It is, though, the jumping-off point for the lovely, unspoiled Îles de Lérins – the only islands on this part of the coast.

East of Nice, the picturesque port of Villefranche and the old resort of Menton, with its sedate charms, both have their devotees. In between is the independent principality of Monaco, where the harbour with its massive yachts moored below the famous Monte-Carlo casino has to be seen at least once.

The 'perched village' of Gourdon, with its bird's-eye view into the gorge of the river Loup

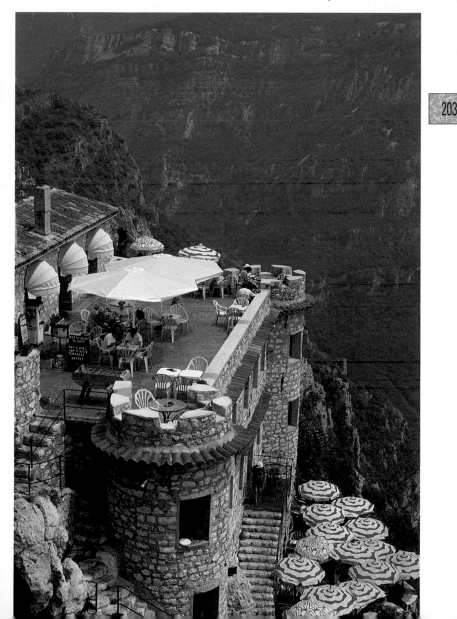

►► Antibes
200C1

For Riviera regulars, Antibes holds a special place – not
just because of its setting but for the *ambiance* of a lively
town that does not rely solely on tourism for a living.

Across the Baie des Anges from Nice, the old town of
Antibes is protected from the sea by stout ramparts.
Inside the ramparts the narrow, bustling streets evoke
another world – but step through an old gateway and you
are immediately on a quay alongside the multi-million-
dollar yachts of movie moguls and megastars. Antibes
has its share of ugly modern flats on the outskirts, in one
of which Graham Greene lived until his death in 1991.

Antibes is the largest horticultural centre in the Alpes-
Maritimes *département* and is well known for its roses
(which are exported worldwide), tulips and carnations.

Flowers brighten the produce market (*Open* daily
except Mon) in the cobbled **cours Masséna►**, the main
street of the old town. Barrels of herb-flavoured olives,
little roundels of goat's cheese, melons, asparagus, figs
and Provençal *primeurs* (early vegetables) offer a treat for
the eyes and nose.

Wander southwards from the cours Masséna between
the tall 17th- and 18th-century houses ('climbing on top of
each other for a view of the sea', as one writer put it) until
you come to the **Château Grimaldi►** at a strategic point
overlooking the ramparts. Converted into a museum of
local history in the 1920s, the château was in a fairly run-
down state in the 1940s when the curator offered Picasso
(then living in a cramped flat in Juan-les-Pins) the use of it
as a studio. When Picasso moved to Vallauris, in thanks
he left behind the majority of the work that he had done
on permanent loan. This *oeuvre* now forms the core of
the **Musée Picasso►►►** (*Open* daily; closed Mon and
Nov. *Admission charge*).

Alongside the astonishing Picasso collection are works
by Nicolas de Staël, Léger, Modigliani, Max Ernst and
many others, as well as photographs of Picasso by Bill
Brandt and Man Ray.

*Porte de l'Olivette, a
small bay on the Cap
d'Antibes*

Interior of the Chapelle Notre-Dame-du-Bon Port

205

Housed in the Bastion St-André to the south of the Grimaldi château, the **Musée d'Histoire et d'Archéologie** (*Open* daily; closed Mon and noon–2 in winter. *Admission charge*) draws together Etruscan, Greek, Roman and medieval finds from the vicinity, as well as *objets trouvés* from shipwrecks. Just next to the château the old cathedral, the **Église de l'Immaculée Conception**, is worth a look inside for the 16th-century altarpiece, the *retable du Rosaire*, attributed to Louis Bréa.

To the east of the huge marina are boat-building yards and a stadium, behind which stands the massive **Fort Carré▶** (*Open* in Jul and Aug). This impressive, geometric structure was started in the 16th century and finished by Vauban.

Children will enjoy **Marineland** and **Aquasplash** on the road towards Biot.

▶   **Antibes, Cap d'**   *200C1*

Between Antibes and Juan-les-Pins the **Cap d'Antibes** is dotted with sumptuous villas and private beaches; on the eastern side of the peninsula there is a huge sandy public beach, la Salis, and further round the Plage de la Garoupe and the Plage Joseph are also both free. From Plage Joseph a coastal path meanders for 3km around the shoreline to Cap Gros.

Most of the Cap d'Antibes is cordoned off into millionaires' private estates and you can but glimpse some of the palatial houses behind their massive gates and high electric fences. However, you can visit the **Chapelle Notre-Dame-du-Bon Port** at the top of the Garoupe plateau, where there is an extensive collection of sailors' *ex-votos.*

Just beneath the Garoupe plateau, the **Jardin Thuret▶** (*Open* daily except weekends) covers 4ha with collections of rare exotic and tropical plants. Plant-lovers can also visit the world-famous **Roseraies Meilland** on blvd Cap d'Antibes.

At the westernmost point of Cap d'Antibes there is the **Musée Naval et Napoléonien** (*Open* daily; closed Nov–mid-Dec and Tue. *Admission charge*). As well as model ships and cannons there are all sorts of items relating to Napoléon's return from exile in Elba and his connections with Antibes.

The macabre dance

The *Danse Macabre* is a mysterious 15th-century tableau, which some say is an invocation against the plague, whilst others claim it is a sort of collective exorcism. The most likely explanation is that it illustrates the legend of the Count of Bar, who insisted on throwing a grand ball in his château during Lent: several of the 'sinners' who took part died as a result, and the painting shows the dancing couples being struck by Death's arrows and dragged off down to hell.

The old dungeon of le Bar-sur-Loup's château, now a tourist information centre

► le Bar-sur-Loup   200B2

High above the river, le Bar-sur-Loup has been a military encampment under the Celts, the Gauloise, the Ligurians and the Romans. From the Roman period the only traces that remain are two tombstones (one set in the base of the church clock tower) and, from medieval times, the château's cylindrical towers in the town centre. In the main square is the château's dungeon, once seven storeys tall, reduced to just a single storey during the Revolution.

The **Église St-Jacques►** has a fine Renaissance doorway with carved wooden panels, but the strangest sight in the village is the curious painting of the *Danse Macabre* (see panel) at the back of the church.

► Beaulieu-sur-Mer   201D2

Like nearby Menton, Beaulieu has an exceptionally mild climate (they claim a mere four nights of frost per year, and even bananas are grown here) and was a fashionable retreat during the late 19th century. The town's name is due to a visit made here by Napoléon, who, not at his most eloquent, exclaimed in Corsican *'O qual bel luogo!'* ('Oh what a lovely place!').

In contrast to the sedate, palm-fringed sea front on the Baie des Fourmis, fantasy takes over completely in the extraordinary **Villa Kerylos►►** (*Open* daily; closed Nov. *Admission charge*), past the casino on the northern headland. Designed in 1908 by archaeologist Theodore Reinach, it is a faithful reproduction of an Athenian villa and was built using lavish amounts of Carrara marble, alabaster and rare woods. Decorated with reproduction frescoes, furniture, vases and bronze statues, the only concessions that Reinach made to the 20th century were modern plumbing, glass windows and a hidden piano. For the last 20 years of his life Reinach lived here in emulation of Greek society, exercising and bathing with his male friends – women were banished to separate suites. The villa is now a museum (*Open* daily; closed Nov. *Admission charge*).

A glass-blower at work in one of the many glass workshops in Biot

▶▶ **Biot** *200C1*

As you approach Biot there is little doubt as to the village's main industry, with signboards at every corner of the road announcing *verrerie* – glassware. Biot started out in Roman times producing huge clay storage jars but this trade ended in the 19th century. Biot's conversion to glass and ceramics is largely due to the brief sojourn here of artist and sculptor Fernand Léger, who bought a plot of land to build a ceramics museum in 1955. Sadly he died soon afterwards, but his inspiration led to the opening of the Biot Glassworks, and in 1960 the **Musée Fernand Léger**▶▶ (*Closed* Tue. *Admission charge*).

The museum was later expanded to include nearly 400 of his works including ceramics, tapestries, stained glass and mosaics. On the façade is a monumental mosaic designed for the entrance of the Olympic stadium in Hanover, whilst the galleries trace Léger's artistic development through Cubism (he was a fellow pioneer alongside Picasso) to his obsession with machinery to the bright, geometric tableaux that became his trademark.

On the outskirts of the village the **Verrerie de Biot**▶▶ (*Open* daily. *Admission free*) has grown into a mini-commercial centre with several galleries, shops, the glass works itself (where you can watch the local speciality of *verres à bulles* being blown), a museum (now fashionably relabelled as the *Eco-Musée du Verre*) and an exhibition centre with extraordinary and imaginative glass art exhibits.

Biot itself is a delight, especially the unusual **place des Arcades**▶ at the heart of the village. At the south end of place des Arcades is the tiny place l'Église, where a doorway in a crumbling bell tower leads into a surprisingly capacious **church** hidden away behind the houses. On the left as you enter is a red-and-gold altarpiece, the 16th-century *Retable de Rosaire*, from the Bréa school; on the right, *Christ aux Plaies*, also 16th-century, attributed to Canavesio.

In the **Musée d'Histoire Locale**▶ (*Open* afternoons; closed Mon and Tue. *Admission charge*) are photographs, documents and *objets trouvés* from Biot's past.

Fernand Léger's mosaics embellish the exterior of a museum in Biot devoted to his works

La Brigue's situation, well off the beaten track, belies its remarkable artistic heritage

Kayaking on the Roya
By the time it reaches Breil the Roya has broadened out enough after its sinuous passage through the gorges to justify a hydro-electric station and to provide enough open water for kayaking. This can be arranged (as can trekking and mountain biking in the surrounding hills) through a small agency in the village, Roya Evasion (tel: 04 93 04 91 46).

▶▶ **Breil-sur-Roya**   *201E3*

The first major town you meet when travelling up the Roya valley from the border with Italy, Breil straddles the Roya river with the old quarter on the eastern bank. At the centre of the narrow streets in the *vieille ville* is the 18th-century church of **Sancta-Maria-in-Albis**, with an altarpiece by Bréa hidden away somewhere inside its gloomy baroque interior. Far more cheerful are the two bell towers with their jolly caps of colourful Niçois tiles. Next door, the pastel-coloured, Renaissance **Chapelle Ste-Catherine** is literally falling apart.

Just outside Breil, the quaint **Ecomusée du Haut Pays** (*Open* daily except Tue Jun–Sep; weekends only Oct–May) has been set up inside three old railway carriages in the station sidings. On display are the flora and fauna, agricultural activities and history of the valley.

▶▶ **la Brigue**   *201E4*

La Brigue is an attractive and welcoming village set amidst the lovely landscapes of the Levenza valley, 6km southeast of Tende. The Levenza burbles past the main square in the village, from where the snow-capped peak of Mont Bégo is visible to the west. The old houses of the village are built from the local grey-green schist, as is the Romanesque **Église St-Martin▶▶**, which contains an astonishing collection of primitive paintings by Louis Bréa and his followers from the Niçois school of the late 15th and early 16th century. There is a notable contrast between the nobility of Bréa's wonderful nativity altarpiece and his gruesome painting of St Elmo having his intestines pulled out with a rope, which shows a degree of cruel realism unusual for Bréa.

But the most macabre paintings are the truly remarkable frescoes in the **Chapelle Notre-Dame des Fontaines▶▶**, 4km up the valley to the east. Any hotel or bar in the village will give you a key to the chapel (in exchange for your passport), which is reached via a winding road that passes a pretty zigzag bridge, the Pont du Coq, which dates back to the 15th century. Perched above a mountain stream in the middle of a woodland valley, the chapel is all the more extraordinary for being in such a remote location. The compelling 15th-century frescoes, painted by Giovanni Baleison and Giovanni Canavesio, depict the life of Christ in a series of 38 episodes culminating in a grisly Last Judgement on the back wall, where the tortures of the damned are shown in gory, violent detail.

▶▶ **Cagnes-sur-Mer** 200C2

The seaside section of Cagnes (known as Cros-de-Cagnes) is the sort of place you want to leave as quickly as possible, but there are two compelling reasons to slow down and turn inland. The first of these, in Cagnes-Ville, is the **Musée Renoir**▶▶ (*Closed* Tue and mid-Oct–mid-Nov. *Admission charge*) in the Domaine des Collettes. The museum and gardens contain several works by Renoir (including bronzes and sculptures in the gardens) as well as portraits and sketches by friends and visitors such as Bonnard, Dufy and Albert André.

The medieval streets of **Haut-de-Cagnes**▶▶, with their vaulted passageways and steep steps, are crowned by a crenellated castle built by Rainier Grimaldi in 1309 and which now houses the **Château-Musée**▶ (*Open* daily; closed mid-Oct–mid-Nov. *Admission charge*). Spanning several centuries of culture, the château not only houses an olive museum on the ground floor but also a display of over 40 paintings of the cabaret star Suzy Solidor by well-known names such as Dufy, Cocteau, Van Dongen, Otto Friesz and others. In one section is the **Musée d'Art Méditerranéen Moderne** which embraces a wide assortment of painters including Chagall, Matisse, Brayer and many more who have worked on the coast. In the summer, the château hosts the prestigious *Festival Internationale de la Peinture*.

The Genoese who worked on the château also created the frescoes in the **Chapelle Notre-Dame-de-Protection** (*Open* afternoons; closed Tue and Fri. *Admission charge*) just behind the château.

A mural in la Brigue

Renoir in Cagnes
Renoir moved to Cagnes in 1908 in the hopes that the warm weather would alleviate his arthritis. He built the Domaine des Collettes amidst luxuriant gardens which also included a grove of 100-year-old olive trees. His talent flourished in this setting, despite the crippling disease that forced him to strap paintbrushes to his fingers in order to work. His north-facing studio has been preserved just the way Renoir left it, with his palette, easel and wheelchair in place. He died here in 1919.

The **vieille ville** *of la Brigue*

■ The Côte d'Azur has always been one of the glitziest holiday destinations in Europe, and curiosity about the lifestyles of the rich and famous has no doubt contributed considerably to its popularity in the past. Today, however, superstars and the ultra-rich are more likely to be ensconced behind the security fences of private villas than spotted speeding along the *corniche* in an open-top roadster. ■

Above: The Monte Carlo Story

Bardot's woes
Once the icon of St-Tropez, Brigitte Bardot is never long out of the headlines, however hard she tries. Having turned her back on the limelight and sold all her jewels to set up an animal sanctuary, she caused a furore by marrying right-wing politician Bernard d'Ormale in 1992, celebrating the wedding on the yacht of Front National leader Jean-Marie Le Pen. Since then she has criticised Muslim ritual slaughter and been accused of being a fascist – millions of francs in donations have been withheld from her animal foundation. 'I would have been better off falling in love with a shoe salesman,' said Bardot.

Bardot burst upon the scene in 1957

Early decadence In the early days of tourism the Côte d'Azur was principally a sedate winter resort for the English and Russian nobility, but the pace changed in the late 1800s when the first casino was opened in Monte-Carlo, and the Riviera first acquired its racy image. Stories of the *fin-de-siècle* decadence that followed abound: a Russian princess, for instance, was celebrating a big casino win in a hired villa one night, but when the owners decided that the revelry had gone on too long, she simply bought the house rather than stop the party.

The first yachts had already begun to frequent the coastal ports, with the writer Guy de Maupassant putting in to St-Tropez in the 1880s, followed by the painter Paul Signac in 1892, who stepped ashore and liked the place so much he bought a house and started the first wave of contemporary artists to settle there.

The American influx After World War I the Riviera got back into the swing again with a new wave of clients, mostly wealthy Americans and stage and opera stars. Jazz clubs sprang up everywhere and Zelda and F Scott Fitzgerald arrived to document the shenanigans (Gertrude Stein and Cole Porter were amongst the guests who stayed at the Antibes villa of rich Bostonians Sara and Gerald Murphy – a couple who served as role models for Dick and Nicole Driver in Fitzgerald's novel, *Tender is the Night*).

Noel Coward, Ernest Hemingway, Katherine Mansfield (who adored Menton, and now has a street named after her there) and Colette (who preferred St-Tropez) were amongst those descending for the season – which had now become a summer rather than a winter phenomenon, prompted by Coco Chanel who made suntans fashionable in the late 1920s. The American dancer Isadora Duncan came to a tragic end in Cannes in 1927 when her scarf caught in a wheel of her Bugatti and strangled her.

The American influx came to an abrupt end with the stock market crash of 1929, although royalty (the Prince of Wales and King Faisal of Saudi Arabia) and the rich (such as the Aga Khan) remained faithful to the Riviera up until World War II.

Star turns The first Cannes Film Festival was planned for 1939, although it did not take off properly until 1947 (which was also the year that Picasso moved into his studio in Antibes). The Festival soon became a compulsory stop on the itinerary of international movie stars, and by the 1950s the likes of Clarke Gable, Errol Flynn, Lana Turner and Kirk Douglas were to be seen taking a post-Festival break on the beaches of St-Tropez. It was at the Cannes Festival in 1955 that Prince Rainier fell in love with the American movie star Grace Kelly, whom he later married.

In 1957 the Riviera took on a whole new dimension when Roger Vadim filmed Brigitte Bardot in St-Tropez in the film *Et Dieu créa la Femme* (*And God Created Woman*, also known as *And Woman Was Created*). The coast again became a byword for all that was chic and sexy. More recently, celebrities such as Mick Jagger and Elton John, plus the Onassis family and the composer Herbert von Karajan, have all owned houses in St-Tropez.

The beaches of St-Tropez continue to attract megastars (see page 174) and although you might see the occasional television celebrity shopping in Monaco or lunching in Mougins, today's beautiful people are keeping a much lower profile – and not necessarily staying on the coast.

Where are they now?
St-Rémy-de-Provence in the Bouches-du-Rhône is one of the latest haunts of the rich and famous – Princess Caroline of Monaco moved there in 1990 to recover from the loss of her husband, Stefano Casiraghi. She set the tone for a more discreet lifestyle, renting an old *mas* (farmhouse) and sending her children to the local school.

Now the Parisian *beau monde* and wealthy American and English families have followed, happy with the quiet, rural life.

Luxury yachts line the Riviera's many marinas

Franco Zeffirelli is one of many show-biz talents to have left his mark on la Croisette at Cannes

The Film Festival
It will come as no surprise to discover that Cannes is twinned with Beverly Hills, and even if the outrageous cost of hotel rooms does not give you a clue then the snobbery and hype associated with the International Film Festival certainly will. Over 12,000 movie moguls, directors and celebrities, a press contingent of around 3,000 journalists, hundreds of films screened around the clock, wheeler-dealers wining and dining with fat cheque-books at the ready, aspiring starlets posing on the beach for the photographers – yes, the best place to be in May is … somewhere else.

Golden aspirations – or just too many movies?

▶ **Cannes**   *200C1*

'Closed for the summer' – a signboard on Cannes' casino long ago, when winter holidays on the Riviera were all the rage – would not be tolerated today during the high season, with visitors arriving in their thousands to catch a glimpse of the glitter and glamour for which Cannes is now famous. That glitzy reputation is, of course, largely due to the International Film Festival (see panel) held in May each year, when thousands of agents, producers, distributors and stars descend for a two-week expense-account binge of celluloid consumption.

It was in December 1834 that the Lord Chancellor of England, Lord Brougham, arrived here by accident – *en route* to Italy, but prevented from going further due to an outbreak of cholera. Cannes then was a sleepy fishing village of some 4,000 souls. Brougham slept so well in the one and only auberge that he decided to stay, and built a house – the Château Eleonore behind avenue du Docteur Picaud – where he spent the next 34 winters up until his death. Many of the mansions built by the English (and the Russian nobility) have been demolished, but you can seek out those that still stand with the help of a booklet, *Ces Belles Demeures qui on fait Cannes* ('These lovely homes which made Cannes'), available free from the tourist office.

The sea front promenade, **la Croisette**▶, is bordered by elegant hotels with big reputations, such as the Carlton, the Martinez and the Majestic. The beach itself is divided up into the colour-coded concessions where you will not have to budge from your sun-lounger for a cocktail or a snack. The only free section is in front of the hideous, orange-coloured **Palais des Festivals** where all the real work goes on during the film festival: known as 'The Bunker' to regulars, its basement screenings represent the real *marché du film*, where options change hands at astronomical prices. Beside the Palais is the **allée des stars**, where you can look for your favourite film star's handprints.

Behind la Croisette the streets around rue d'Antibes have window displays that look like colour spreads for glossy magazines, but for mere mortals the shops in rue Meynadier two blocks further back might be more useful, with excellent *charcuteries*, pasta shops, *patisseries* and cheese shops. At the western end of rue Meynadier there is a great food market in the Forville covered market (*Open* daily except Mon).

On a small hill above the port is Cannes' oldest quarter, le Suquet. In the 11th century it belonged to the monks from the Îles de Lérins (see below), who fled here after Saracen raids on their island retreat. The monks built a watch-tower to warn of coastal raids, and fortifications, remnants of which are behind the Gothic **Notre-Dame de l'Espérance** on the hilltop. The monks' fortified priory now houses the **Musée de la Castre►** (*Open* daily. *Admission charge*), which has an eclectic archaeological and ethnographic collection covering five continents. Admission to the museum includes the **Tour du Suquet**, the monks' watch-tower – the platform at the top has views down the coast and out to the Îles de Lérins.

As an antidote to the traffic and crowds in Cannes there can be no better place than the **Îles de Lérins►►**, just 15 minutes away on a ferry from the *gare maritime* in the port (up to a dozen departures daily in summer, five daily in winter).

The smaller of the two, **St-Honorat►►**, is completely unspoiled and has been the property of monks since the 4th century when Honoratus first landed here. Today it is Cistercian monks who cultivate the vineyards, olive groves and lavender fields around the abbey, which was rebuilt in the 19th century. Apart from visiting the remains of a fortified 11th-century abbey on the cliff tops, there is little to do except wander amongst the eucalyptus and pine trees and enjoy the peaceful atmosphere of this little haven.

Ste-Marguerite►► is nearly twice as big (although it still only takes two hours to walk around), has some good beaches on the southern shores and walking trails through the woods. The **Fort Royal** (*Open* daily) was built by Richelieu and reinforced by Vauban; the Man in the Iron Mask (see panel) is supposed to have been held prisoner here. On the ground floor is the **Musée de la Mer** (*Open* daily), with archaeology exhibits and finds from shipwrecks.

'The Man in the Iron Mask'
In 1687, a prisoner was brought to one of the cells in the Fort Royal on Ste-Marguerite who was later immortalised by Alexander Dumas as 'The Man in the Iron Mask'. He was held here for over ten years, but the question of his identity has never been fully resolved. Was he the illegitimate brother (or the twin) of Louis XIV? Or a loose-mouthed relative of the doctor who performed an autopsy on Louis XIII? That autopsy showed that the King was incapable of fathering children – and when the doctor's son-in-law inherited his papers, he couldn't keep this secret to himself.

213

The monks' watch-tower rises high above Cannes harbour

► ► **Clues de Haute-Provence**   *200B3*

As the Var river changes course in Haute-Provence and heads down towards the sea it encircles a sparsely populated region cut through with rifts known as *clues*. Forged by torrential streams, the valleys traverse limestone mountains where small, isolated villages hang onto a precarious existence. In the middle of this region is the 1,777m-high Montagne du Cheiron, to which skiers from the Riviera resorts flock in the winter months.

At the centre of the *clues* on the northern slopes of the mountain is **Roquestéron**, a fortified village that is separated in two by the Esteron river (prior to 1860 this river formed the frontier between France and Savoy, so each half of the village was in a different country). Leaving the village westwards on the D17 the **Clue du Riolan**► opens up on your right; further past here on the D10 is the **Clue d'Aiglun**►, which is perhaps the most spectacular of these narrow gorges, with a vertical torrent pouring down from the mountains above. Further west, the village of St-Auban perches on a hillside at the opening to the **Clue de St-Auban**►, where the steep sides are riddled with grottos and caves.

Sunny ceramics
The sunshine theme in Coaraze – the *village du Soleil* – inspired a clutch of artists to create a series of massive and colourful ceramic sundials through-out the village in the 1960s: those by Henri Goetz and Ponce de Léon are in the place Félix Giordan in front of the church, whilst others by Cocteau, Mona-Christie, Douking and Valentin are less happily placed on the pink façade of the town hall/post office building.

► ► **Coaraze**   *201D3*

This little circular village perched atop a peak in the hills behind Nice has a sunny reputation – signboards proclaiming *Village du Soleil* mark the entrances to Coaraze – although why it should get more solar rays than anywhere else is not easily explained.

The village has its fair share of cobbled stairways and vaulted passageways, as well as a handful of *artisans d'art* and second homes for Niçois trendies.

On the outskirts of the village, the **Chapelle Notre-Dame des Sept Douleurs**► (Our Lady of the Seven Sorrows) took on a much more cheerful character and a new name, the Blue Chapel, when Ponce de Léon redecorated the interior in 1965 with bright murals and a vivid green stained-glass window. To reach the chapel, take the small road beside the *Bar Tabac Les Arts* either by car or on foot (20 minutes return).

A curious fountain in the village square, Èze

Contes   *201D2*

This old town is full of legends, which may possibly account for its name, *conte* meaning story. The most famous fable is that of the caterpillar plague (see panel), and there are several others revolving around appearances by the devil, who has his tail glued down by villagers and is forced to shed it and flee. Contes' myths are far more colourful than the village itself, which is now surrounded in the Paillon valley by numerous suburbs, factories and a huge cement works.

► ► **Èze**   *201D2*

Half-way along the *Moyenne Corniche* between Nice and Monte-Carlo, the dramatic location of Èze – 430m above the sea, making it the highest perched

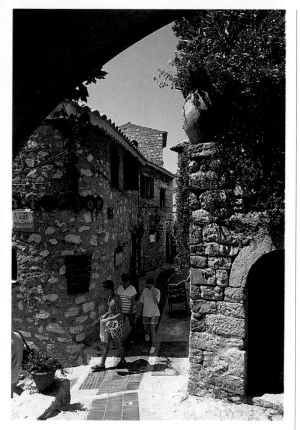

A quiet day in picturesque Èze

Nietzsche's path
An old mule path which wends its way down to the seaside at Èze-sur-Mer from just outside the village of Èze is now known as the Sentier Frédéric-Nietzsche. This is in recognition of the fact that Nietzsche is supposed to have conceived the third part of *Thus Spake Zarathustra* whilst walking through the countryside here.

village you will find anywhere in Provence – has contributed to its popularity, with amateur snappers keen to capture the extraordinary sight of this settlement clinging to a cone of rock.

Entering the village through a crenellated 14th-century gateway, you find yourself in a maze of narrow streets and stepped alleys, a labyrinth designed to be easily defended. The *bijou* flower-filled passageways are now chock-a-block with boutiques, antique dealers and artisans; in the summer, the crowds can be insufferable.

Some respite can be gained in either the **Chapelle des-Pénitents Blancs** (which has an unusual 13th-century Catalan crucifix with Christ smiling down from the cross) or in the **Jardin Exotique** (*Open* daily. *Admission charge*) surrounding the ruins of the château at the top of the village; the château itself was dismantled in 1706 on the orders of Louis XIV.

Golfe-Juan   *200C1*

This rather bland resort does at least have the merit of a long sandy beach, sheltered by the headlands of Cap d'Antibes and the Pointe de la Croisette on either side. Unless you are stopping for a swim, though, it has little else to detain you except for a glance at the mosaic on the **quai du Port** marking the spot where Napoléon stepped ashore on 1 March 1815 after escaping from Elba.

Plagues of caterpillars
In 1508 Contes was inundated by hordes of large caterpillars, nasty little beasties that defoliated the woods by munching their way through massive amounts of pine needles, secreting a poison that causes painful rashes and allergies in humans. The villagers were so desperate they called in the Bishop of Nice, who performed an exorcism to banish the creatures. Faced with a similar dilemma in 1993, the municipality of Villefranche – evidently with more faith in germ warfare than prayer – brought in helicopters to spray the district with a bacteria which, when eaten by the caterpillars, causes their intestines to burst.

► **Gorbio** *201D2*

An attractive *village perché* 10km northwest of Menton, remarkable for being practically a souvenir-free zone, Gorbio is often swept by clouds and mists, which has led to the locals being nicknamed *les nebuleux* ('the cloudy ones'). Although it has at least half a dozen chapels and churches in or near the village, the most arresting spectacle in Gorbio is the annual *Procession dai limaca* (see panel), which takes place during the *Fête Dieu* (Corpus Christi) in mid-June.

►► **Gourdon** *200B2*

Situated in a remarkable position some 500m above the river Loup, Gourdon merits the description *nid d'aigles* (eagles' nest) with its stunning views embracing 80km of the coastline on a clear day. A fort was built on this dizzying site in the 9th century to watch out for Saracen invaders; the vast rectangular **château►►**, which stands at the heart of the village today, dates from between 1607 and 1654, when it was entirely rebuilt by the Lombard family.

This immaculately preserved building contains a pair of museums, the better of which is the **Musée Historique►►►** (*Open* daily in summer; afternoons except Wed in winter. *Admission charge* includes guided tour). A veritable treasure house on the ground floor of the château, the museum houses a large collection of antique armaments and suits of armour, 16th- and 17th-century furnishings (including Marie-Antoinette's writing desk and an Aubusson tapestry), and religious works of art in the chapel (including a rare sculpture of St Sebastian by Greco).

On the first floor, the **Musée de Peinture Naïve** (same hours as above) is less compelling, although amongst the 150 works on display there is a self-portrait by Douanier-Rousseau. Outside the château the curved stone balconies of the lovely Le Notre-designed gardens jut out over the hillside, where you can admire the view while waiting for the next guided tour.

Apart from the château, Gourdon has several fountains and the usual clutch of shops with Provençal souvenirs such as olive-wood carvings, honey, nougat and scented soap.

Magical procession
The *Procession dai limaca* is a pagan ritual giving thanks for the previous winter's olive harvest and exorcising any demons that might damage the next crop. The whole village of Gorbio is illuminated by little flickering lamps made from snail shells (*limaca* in Provençal; snails are also a pagan symbol of renewal) set in beds of sand and filled with olive oil. Dabs of plaster fix the shells on walls, doorways, windowsills and on the pavements; a night-time procession makes its way from the church through the magically lit streets for the blessing.

Santons – *Provençal dolls* – *on sale in Gourdon*

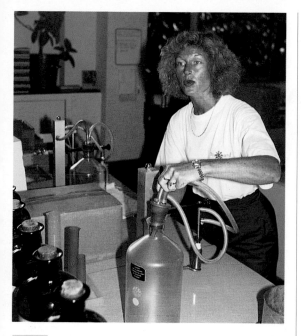

Demonstrating the art of perfumery in Grasse

The salt seat
One of the curiosities in the château at Gourdon is a small *fauteuil à sel*, which dates from the time when there were heavy taxes on salt: the family's salt supplies were hidden under the seat and granny promptly sat down on top when the taxmen called – a crafty solution, since it was also forbidden to force old people to stand up!

217

Heady blooms
In the valleys surrounding Grasse lavender, jasmine, mimosa, roses and other sweet-scented plants are cultivated before being harvested (always at dawn, when the dew is still upon them) to undergo the alchemical process of extracting their essences. It takes 900,000 rose buds or eight million jasmine blooms to render just one kilo of the heady elixir which is the essence of the flower.

►►► Grasse   *200B2*

On a still day the scent on the air as you enter Grasse is probably a lot more appealing than first impressions of the town itself, which sprawls unattractively across the lower slopes of the Provençal Alps and down across the valley. But apart from the famous *parfumeries*, which are the main lure for tourists, Grasse has a quaint old quarter and several sights worth seeking out once you have done the obligatory tour of the perfume factories.

Grasse started out in the Middle Ages by specialising in the less-than-fragrant industry of tanning sheep skins from Alpine pastures and hides imported from Spain and Sicily. In the middle of the 17th century many of the tanneries abruptly switched over to glove-making to meet demand from Parisian society for perfumed gloves, which had become a hot fashion item since being adopted by Italian aristocracy during the Renaissance. The Grassois became *gantiers parfumeurs* until gloves ceased to be a status symbol after the Revolution, at which point they became simple *parfumeurs*.

With the rise of the big perfume companies in Paris at the beginning of the 19th century, the Grassois abandoned making the finished product and decided to specialise instead on what they did best, the distillation of raw materials into concentrated fragrances for perfume-making. The ancient techniques of *enfleurage* (whereby flowers are placed in trays of fat, which are then washed in ethyl alcohol to extract the scent) and *maceration* (whereby hot fat is saturated with blooms) and subsequent distillation will all be explained if you take a factory tour at one of the *parfumeries*.

Up to 300 different essences may go into a single fragrance

The main *parfumeries* in the centre of town are Galimard (73 route de Cannes), Molinard (60 blvd Victor Hugo) or Fragonard (20 blvd Fragonard). Tours in English and French are free, and naturally enough end up in the factory shop (although there is no pressure to buy).

The Fragonard *parfumerie* also has an enchanting **musée►►** (*Open* daily) in the same building, which covers over 5,000 years of perfume making and has a beautiful collection of over 3,000 rare perfumery objects, with many exquisite antique *flacons* from Egypt, the Orient, Rome and Greece. Unfortunately the **Musée International de la Parfumerie** (*Open* daily; closed Nov and Mon and Tue in winter. *Admission charge*) just near by – which also deals with the history and manufacture of perfume – cannot compete with the Fragonard collection and is a bit of a disappointment.

Grasse's *vieille ville* was at the core of the city when it declared itself an independent republic in the Middle Ages, allying itself with Pisa and Genoa, and the influence of Grasse's trading partners is evident in the Italianate architecture of the old town (Stendhal, visiting in the 19th century, declared it to be 'completely Genoese in character'). The old quarter has the friendly atmosphere of a working community.

At the centre of the old town is the **place aux Aires►►**, which is best seen in the early mornings when there is a colourful fruit and vegetable market; by late morning, the square has been taken over by tables from the cafés and restaurants underneath the surrounding arcades. Above the arcades are the old mansions of the 18th-century tanning magnates, including in one corner the grand Hotel Isnard with a typical Provençal balcony with wrought-iron work.

On the south side of the old quarter is the **Cathédrale ` Notre-Dame-du-Puy►**, whose spartan, 12th-century interior contains several interesting works including three early paintings by Rubens, a rare religious painting by Fragonard, and an altarpiece from the Bréa school. Note also the splendid 18th-century carved wooden doors at the entrance.

Finally, there is the **Villa-Musée Fragonard** (*Open* daily. *Admission charge*) which has works by this famous rococo painter, scion of a local family, and the **Musée d'Art et d'Histoire de Provence►** (*Open* daily. *Admission charge*) in an 18th-century Italianate mansion which once belonged to Count Mirabeau's sister. Along with a good cross-section of Provençal decorative arts and furniture, the collection includes Mirabeau's death-mask.

The smell of success
There are currently around 30 *parfumeries* surrounding Grasse, each of which employs a head perfumer known as *le nez* (the nose). He has his own laboratory where he performs a sort of olfactory orchestration to select and blend different essences to create a fragrance. He has around 3,000 different essences to choose from, and may include anything up to 300 of these in a single fragrance. There are only 300 'noses' worldwide with a good enough olfactory memory of the raw materials to be able to do this, 150 of whom work in France, and 50 of whom work in Grasse.

𝒟rive Gorges du Loup

The River Loup, on its short journey from its source on Montagne de l'Audibergue down to the sea, cuts a spectacular path through the mountains. Allow 3–4 hours for this round trip from Grasse.

Take the N85 northwest out of Grasse, which climbs up to the Col du Pilon. In St-Vallier-de-Thiey (see pages 240–1) turn right along the scenic D5, which soon climbs up to the Col de Ferrier at 1,041m. Beyond the Col de la Sine, follow the road down into the valley and across the Pont-du-Loup.
  At the les 4 Chemins crossroads, turn right towards Gréolières, crossing the Plan-du-Peyron, bordered by pine forests and pastureland. The road starts to descend down the Clue de Gréolières, and, as the rift opens out, there is a series of tunnels through the rock face and a belvedere for a view of the river a dizzying 400m below you.
  After crossing a small stone bridge outside Gréolières, the road divides: the eastern, left-hand fork, the D2, ends up in Vence (see page 247); the western side of the gorge is just as spectacular, ending up in Gourdon (see page 216). Continue through Gourdon to return to Grasse.

PERFUMERY MUSEUM

CÔTE D'AZUR AND ALPES-MARITIMES

The Côte de Swing
In Juan-les-Pins during the inter-war 'Années Folles' (Mad Years), Scott and Zelda Fitzgerald painted the town red, Rudolph Valentino lived in the Château de Juan and Gloria Swanson became engaged to the Marquis de Falaise. Cole Porter made Douglas Fairbanks, Mary Pickford, Maurice Chevalier and the King of Montenegro dance, and at night everybody drank and caroused the clubs and casinos. After World War II, the American Sixth Fleet, stationed in the Mediter-ranean, came to Juan to party. Sidney Bechet married here in 1951, amidst wild celebrations and Dixieland bands playing in the streets. He returned annually, bringing other jazz musicians with him, and by his death in 1959 Juan-les-Pins was established as the jazz capital of Europe.

Enjoying the sun, sea and silvery sands on the beach at Juan-les-Pins

▶ Guillaumes   200B4

Dominated by the ruins of a château and perched some 800m above the confluence of the Var and the Tuébi, Guillaumes is one of the largest villages in the Upper Var valley. At its entrance is the chapel of **Notre-Dame-du-Buyei▶**, which houses a remarkable painting showing the village in flames during the terrible fire of 1682.

From Guillaumes the D2202 leads southwards through the spectacular **Gorges de Daluis▶▶** (named after the village of Daluis), which cut through the red schist down towards Entrevaux. Dramatic views of the Var below can be had from the serpentine road on the west bank.

▶ Isola 2000   200C5

A popular ski resort due to its proximity to Nice (1½hrs away), Isola 2000 was purpose-built in the 1970s. Its unimaginative name derives from the altitude (at 2,000m it is the highest ski resort in the Sud-Alpes) and the old village of **Isola**, 17km away back down the valley.

▶▶ Juan-les-Pins   200C1

Protected by the headland of Cap d'Antibes on one side and la Croisette on the other, Juan-les-Pins has a fine sandy beach in front of what used to be a magnificent pine forest.

Although a resort had been established amidst the pines as early as 1881 (by the Duke of Albany, Queen Victoria's son, who coined its name), it did not really take off until the 1920s when a restaurateur from Nice, M Baudoin, bought up the old wooden casino and opened a cabaret restaurant. On honeymoon near by with his third wife, American railroad heir Frank Jay Gould (who already owned two hotels on the coast) decided to go into partnership with Baudoin, and together they launched the

Place de la République in Levens, at the mouth of the Gorges de la Vésubie

Jazz Nights
The first jazz festival took place in 1960, attracting 250 musicians from 15 countries. Over the following years all the great artists (such as Count Basie, Charlie Mingus, Louis Armstrong, Ella Fitzgerald, Duke Ellington, Sarah Vaughan and Charlie Parker) came to Juan. In later years they were followed by contemporary jazz musicians such as Chick Corea, Stan Getz, Sonny Rollins and Al Jarreau. Jazz à Juan is still going strong, with outdoor performances taking place in the pine grove of Gould against the romantic backdrop of the Esterel and the Mediterranean. It runs for ten days in the middle of July. (For information, tel: 04 92 90 53 00.)

first summer season on the Riviera – at the time, it was still only a winter holiday destination.

By the 1930s Juan-les-Pins had become a huge success, helped along by scandalised publicity – here was the first beach in France where young women dared to bathe in one-piece swimming suits.

Outside the jazz festival (see panel), Juan-les-Pins' reputation for nightlife remains undiminished, with live bands competing on decibel levels in cafés, bars and discos. Not a place to stay, unless you have a pair of earplugs, but tons of fun to visit late at night and people-watch over an exotic cocktail in a plush, street-side bar.

▶ **Lantosque**   *201D3*

There can be few other villages in Provence that have suffered quite so many landslides and earthquakes as Lantosque, with almost the entire village having been sent hurtling down into the ravine below numerous times during the 15th, 16th and 17th centuries. It was rebuilt so many times because Lantosque was an important staging post on the *route du sel* (the salt route), which was followed by caravans of pack animals carrying this precious commodity from the *salines* of Hyères up to the Sud-Alpes and beyond into Piedmont.

Lantosque still looks like it is about to slide down the hillside from its perch on a rocky spur overlooking the Vésubie valley, but beyond here the valley itself opens out into richer greener pastures. When covered in snow, these slopes are much appreciated by skiers from the coast who flock here in winter to the small but trendy ski resort of **la Bollène-Vésubie**, northeast of Lantosque along the D70.

▶ **Levens**   *200C3*

This large village (unusual because it once had two rows of encircling medieval ramparts) dominates the plains at the mouth of the **Gorges de la Vésubie**▶▶ leading back up into the Vésubie valley. From Levens, the D19 on the east bank and the D2565 on the west bank snake round the scenic gorges before meeting up at **St-Jean-la-Rivière**. A hair-raising, 6km detour from here leads up to one of the most isolated sanctuaries in the mountains, the **Madone d'Utelle**▶▶. The panorama down towards the sea from the peak just past the chapel is outstanding; the chapel itself is still an active pilgrimage centre, with processions on Easter Monday, Whit Monday, 15 August and 8 September.

The all-seeing village
The village of Utelle, just below the sanctuary of the Madone d'Utelle, has long benefited from its strategic viewpoint, and until the 15th century it was known as Uels ('eye' in Provençal). Its role as a sentinel outpost led to the granting of a strange privilege: the royal decree decreed that the citizens could carry at their belts 'a knife of any length they wish', and need not be limited as other subjects were to a knife the length of 'un pain et demi' (literally, 'a bread-and-a-half', although evidently this didn't refer to *baguettes*!)

►►► Menton   *201E2*

Hemmed in by a chain of mountains behind the bay which protect it from the cold north winds, Menton is known for its unusually warm climate. No doubt this is what prompted the first ever visitors to the Riviera to settle here: the 30,000-year-old skull of 'Menton man', discovered near by in 1884, is one of the oldest palaeolithic relics in France.

The name Menton was first mentioned in the 13th century, and the town was acquired by Charles Grimaldi of Monaco in 1346. In 1793 it became part of France, then reverted to the Grimaldi family in 1814 under the Treaty of Paris. In 1848 Menton revolted against the high taxes demanded by Monaco and opted for independence under the protection of Sardinia. In 1860 the town decided to rejoin France, when Napoléon III bought Menton and its neighbour, Roquebrune, from Charles III of Monaco for 4 million gold francs.

Today Menton is a charming resort which tries hard to counter its image as a retirement haven with a lively programme of arts, culture and festivals. The most celebrated event is the 60-year-old Fête du Citron (Menton has been famous for its lemons for more than 500 years), which lasts for ten days from Shrove Tuesday onwards. Now equally as well known is the Chamber Music Festival in August, which is held in the attractive setting of the **Parvis St-Michel** overlooking the harbour. There is also a biennial Art Exhibition.

The most important museum in Menton is the excellent **Musée Cocteau►►** (*Closed* Tue. *Admission free*) housed in a quaint truncated watch-tower on the sea front. The museum contains mosaics and tapestries and his portrayal of love affairs in the *Inamorati* series as well as photographs, poems and ceramics. Another must is the Cocteau-decorated **Salle des Mariages►** (*Open* daily except Sat and Sun) on the right-hand side of the town hall in the main square. The skull of 'Menton man' can be found in the **Musée Municipal de Préhistoire Régionale** (*Closed* Tue), which also houses rock carvings from the Vallée des Merveilles (see page 246) and thousands of prehistoric exhibits.

Dying for a holiday
As early as 1861, Menton was put on the map of international tourism thanks to a book written by an English doctor, J Henry Bennett, which lauded the virtues of its climate for invalids. By 1870 Menton had become a *chic* seaside resort with sumptuous villas and luxury hotels financed by aristocratic English, German and Russian tourists. Many more people came in the hopes that Menton's warmth and sunshine would alleviate the symptoms of consumption (tuberculosis): among the better known, whose graves can be found in the hilltop cemetery, were Katherine Mansfield, Aubrey Beardsley and the Spanish writer Blasco Ibáñez.

Menton, a resort which enjoys a particularly favourable climate

■ **Rare is the Provençal market without at least one stall groaning under the weight of colourful vats or baskets of olives, with as many different herb flavourings as there are days in the month.** ■

Top: olive trees are planted with enough space between them for a mechanical harvester to operate
Left: a scene typical of any Provençal market

All thanks to the Greeks Wild olive trees grow naturally in Provence but their fruit is sour and produces very little oil. The cultivation of more productive varieties (and the art of grafting) was introduced by the Greeks some time around 600 BC.

Olives grow equally well in limestone or sandy soil and, provided their roots do not get too wet, they can live for hundreds of years. What *will* kill them is a late, hard frost – such as the one in 1956 that destroyed hundreds of olive groves.

A young tree starts to bear fruit in its fifth or sixth year and attains its full yield when around 25 to 30 years old. Wild trees can reach heights of 15 to 20m, but modern varieties are pruned, making them easier to harvest.

The harvest Olives are usually harvested from the beginning of November through to January. At first the olives are green, but they ripen on the tree, turning brown and then black.

Harvesting is traditionally a family affair, with friends and neighbours joining in. The old method was for someone to climb up the tree and shake the fruit loose on to mats spread on the ground beneath, although green olives have to be picked by hand because they do not dislodge so easily. Nowadays mechanical harvesters do the work; grasping the tree trunk and shaking it until the olives tumble down.

Olive oil A mature tree can produce up to 30 kilos of olives, yielding between 5 and 6 litres of oil. Even if you only have one or two trees in your garden, the nearest *moulin à huile* (olive mill) will process your olives to give the appropriate amount of oil.

The first pressing produces the best olive oil, sold as *premier pression à froide vierge extra*, or simply *vierge extra* (extra virgin). The residue (the *grignon*, or pulp) is pressed again with more cold water added, and labelled *fine* or *extra fine*. The third pressing, with warm water, produces an oil which is used commercially.

Cracked olives
Raw olives are inedible unless properly cured, and one of the most popular ways of doing this at home is to make *olives cassées*, or cracked olives. The recipe is simple: the olives are broken with a mallet and then mixed with water and equal amounts of wood ash (preferably olive or vine wood). This mixture is left for two days (with frequent stirrings) and the olives are then rinsed in cold water and left to soak for another week. Finally, they are covered in brine flavoured with coriander, fennel and orange peel, and put into storage jars.

Scourtins
Before the advent of modern hydraulic presses, the olive paste was spread on flat, densely woven mats called *scourtins* before the oil was squeezed out in a hand mill. The first *scourtins* were made from straw, but later sisal or coconut fibre was used instead. *Scourtins* are still produced in Provence, and you can sometimes find them in souvenir shops.

Casino de Monte-Carlo
Musée de Poupées
et Automates

Musée
d'Anthropologie
Préhistorique

St-Martin

Grotte de
l'Observatoire

Jardin
Exotique

Gare

Port de Monaco

La
Condamine

PLACE
D'ARMES

RUE GRIMALDI

R PRINCESSE CAROLINE

BOULEVARD RAINIER III

BOULEVARD CHARLES III

AVE DU PORT

BOULEVARD ALBERT 1er

Stade

Zoo

Palais du
Prince

QUAI ANTOINE 1er

AVE DU PRINCE HÉRÉDITAIRE ALBERT

Musée
Historial des
Princes de Monaco

PORTE NEUVE

Yacht
Club

Fort
Antoine

FONTVIEILLE

PLACE DU
PALAIS

Musée du
Vieux
Monaco

Chapelle de
la Miséricorde

Port de
Fontvieille

RUE ÉMILE

PL DE LA
VISITATION

AVE
DES PINS

Stade
Louis II

Palais
de Justice

DE LOTH

Cathédrale

St-Nicolas

AVENUE SAINT - MARTIN

Jardins St-Martin

Musée
Océanographique

0   100   200 m

0   100   200 yards

Safe on the streets

Monaco likes to portray an image of stability and safety, and is said to have more remote-controlled cameras and police on the streets than practically anywhere else in Europe (yes, you can walk around wearing jewellery at night). Crime (apart from the white-collar variety) and delinquency are virtually non-existent: it is said that if it were not for a steady stream of divorce cases, the Law Courts could have shut up shop long ago.

The view from old Monaco down to a new marina

►►► Monaco and Monte-Carlo   *201D2*

Monaco conjures up images of glamour and wealth, of high-rollers winning or losing fortunes in the casino, high-octane Formula One racing cars screeching through the streets during the annual Grand Prix, high society cavorting in nightclubs until dawn. Yet Monaco is a surprisingly sedate place: in the lobby of the Hôtel de Paris you are more likely to see bored-looking businessmen hammering out deals. In the gaming room built on the side of the Café de Paris, gambling has been reduced to the unglamorous level of ranks of one-armed bandits. The sanitised streets of the old town hold about as much allure as a tawdry souvenir shop – of which it also has plenty.

But Monaco is still worth visiting for the day, if only to gaze at the wonderful *belle époque* casino and the lavish hotel lobbies – and to marvel at the justly famed Musée Océanographique, probably one of the best in Europe, which alone justifies the trip.

The principality of Monaco covers a mere 195ha (just under 2sq km, much of which has been reclaimed from the sea), making it Europe's second smallest independent state after the Vatican.

After they had seized Monaco, the Grimaldis (see panel) continued to expand along the coast, eventually taking control of Menton, Roquebrune, Antibes and Grimaud. In 1848 Menton and Roquebrune declared themselves independent republics, fed up with the high taxes imposed by the Grimaldis on their lemons and olives. Facing bankruptcy, Charles III decided to take advantage of his independence from France and open a casino, since gambling was still illegal in France at the time. But the venture failed, and it was not until 1863 when he called in François Blanc, director of the hugely successful casino in Bad Homburg, that it began to take off. The royal coffers were so flush that Charles decided to abolish all taxes, a situation that still holds today.

His successor Albert I lavished money on the arts and sciences and commissioned Charles Garnier (architect of the Paris Opéra) to rebuild the Casino, incorporating an opera house, which became the home of Diaghilev's Ballet Russe. He initiated the first Monte-Carlo rally in 1911, but spent most of his vast inherited wealth roaming the oceans on a series of fabulous yachts collecting scientific data for his beloved Oceanographic Institute.

These halcyon days came to an abrupt end in 1933 when France legitimised gambling, and by the time Rainier III came to the throne in 1949 Monaco was relatively down on its luck. However, this tax-free zone still attracted offshore finance and Rainier has tried to build on this as well as encourage business tourism, conferences (a brand-new convention centre was recently opened) and diversification into light industry. Even though Monte-Carlo now has four casinos, gambling today only brings in 4 per cent of revenues – compared to 95 per cent in the golden days at the turn of the century.

The principality continues to attract numerous anonymous tax exiles, not to mention more well-known faces such as Boris Becker, Claudia Schiffer, Karl Lagerfeld and (until his death in 1993) the writer Anthony Burgess.

Guarding the Grimaldi home, the Palais du Prince, in Old Monaco

225

François the Spiteful
In the 12th century Monaco became the property of the Genoese, who were split between the Guelfs (allied to the Pope) and the Ghibellines (allied to the German emperor). Legend has it that in 1297 the chief of the Guelf faction, a Grimaldi known as François the Spiteful, disguised himself and his men as monks and knocked on the door of the Ghibelline garrison in Monaco asking for help. Having been admitted, they pulled out their swords and massacred the garrison. This is the origin of the two monks brandishing swords on the crest of the Grimaldi family, who have (apart from a couple of hiccups) ruled Monaco ever since.

The Jardin Exotique,
overlooking the sea

Monaco-ville►► On the northwest corner of the rock on which the old town was built is the **Palais du Prince**► (*Guided tours* Jun–Sep, daily. *Admission charge*), with its Court of Honour, Hercules Gallery (with 17th-century frescoes), Throne Room and various plushly decorated state apartments. The ornate façade of the palace overlooks the **place du Palais**►, where the rows of cannons (a donation from Louis XIV) are complemented by neatly stacked piles of cannon balls: the Toytown impression is further reinforced by the changing of the guard, which takes place at 11.55am sharp every day.

The **old town** stretches south from the palace; it is immaculately kept but about as stimulating as the endless Prince Rainier mugs, tea towels and ashtrays on sale. The **Musée Historial des Princes de Monaco** (*Open* daily. *Admission charge*), which promises 40 'bigger than life' waxworks tracing the history of the Grimaldi family, is equally dull. The **Musée Nationale** (*Open* daily. *Admission charge*) has over 400 dolls, miniature dolls' houses and working automata from the 18th and 19th centuries.

At the heart of the old town is the **cathédrale**, a neo-Romanesque structure inside which is one of Louis Bréa's masterpieces, the **retable de St-Nicolas**, as well as his *Pietà de curé Teste*. Here too are the tombs of all the Grimaldi including that of Princess Grace, which is often smothered in bouquets from admirers.

The highlight of the old town is undoubtedly the splendid **Musée Océanographique**►►► (*Open* daily. *Admission charge*) on the headland. Founded in 1910 by Prince Albert I, this huge edifice was built into the cliff face to hold the specimens he collected on his many voyages and to house marine research laboratories (under the direction of Jacques Cousteau 1957–88). The excellent aquarium features the weirdest and most wonderful fish from the world's oceans, including the spectacular giant groupers and jacks, piranha, and black-tipped sharks swarming over a small, sunken boat. There are also beautifully lit displays of living corals. Don't come on a Sunday (particularly a wet one) when the crowds will be three or four deep around every tank.

The first floor has a bit of everything, from natural history to displays on the atmosphere and deep sea trenches. It also has the world's first submarine (powered by pedals, it was built in 1774 and used against English ships during the American War of Independence) and models of all the magnificent ships which Albert had built for his voyages.

If the museum prompts your curiosity about the underwater world you can take a ride on the **Seabus** (tel: 93 30 64 15) which does a one-hour tour departing from the quai des États-Unis in the port.

Fontvieille Just off the **Moyenne Corniche** above Fontvieille is the **Jardin Exotique▶** (*Open* daily. *Admission charge*), which has an extensive collection of some 7,000 succulents and cacti. Guided tours of the **Grotte de l'Observatoire**, an ancient cave, once inhabited, are included in the ticket.

Monte-Carlo▶▶▶ No visit here is complete without a look (let alone a flutter) inside the **Casino de Monte-Carlo▶▶**, for many years the chief income-earner of the principality and still its main showpiece. You have to be over 21 (with passport as proof) to enter the American Room, where slot machines line the walls around the crap, roulette and black-jack tables – and the gilded rococo ceilings have to be seen. The stakes get higher and the decor more extravagant once you reach the European rooms, which you will have to pay to enter.

227

'The Man Who Broke The Bank'
When Garnier's casino first opened in 1878 the clientèle were almost entirely wealthy, visiting several times a week from the other resorts for a bit of fun. But the passion for gambling spread and people began to believe they could make their fortunes – partly inspired by Charles Deville Wells, who turned $400 into $40,000 in a three-day gambling spree in 1891, later immortalised in the song *The Man Who Broke The Bank At Monte Carlo*. Other gamblers were not so lucky, and the growing number of suicides was covered up by the casino for fear of bad publicity.

Founded in 1910, the Musée Océanographique is one of France's most popular museums

Flanking the casino on either side are the **Café de Paris** and the **Hôtel de Paris**, both worth a look-in: the Café de Paris for the clientele and the Hôtel de Paris for its sumptuous lobby.

On the other side of Monte-Carlo are the artifical beaches and Olympic-size pools of the Larvotto beaches (*Admission charge*).

You will also have to pay for pavement space during the annual Monte-Carlo Grand Prix (May). Tickets can be hard to obtain (they are often sold out months in advance), but you may be able to purchase one for standing space in the old town, from where there is a bird's eye view of the circuit. The Monte-Carlo rally takes place in January. The best time to visit the old town is during the annual carnival and fireworks display (September) – there is also an International Fireworks Festival in July and August.

Faites vos jeux –
Monaco's famous
Casino

Sky-high gastronomy
Although there are 'only' half a dozen restaurants in the village, Mougins' gastronomic reputation has extended far and wide largely due to the presence of Roger Vergé, one of France's most celebrated and charismatic chefs, who owns two of the restaurants and also runs an expensive gourmet food shop. Critics say that the exorbitant prices (up to 800 francs per person in some restaurants) are not matched by the quality of the food and that it is all just hype: nonetheless, Mougins continues to be popular, although anyone on a tight budget will have a hard time finding an affordable meal.

►► Mougins   200C1

It makes a change to find a *village perché* behind the coast that has not been overrun with souvenir shops – but then such down-market commercialism probably would not be allowed to spoil the tasteful medieval streets of Mougins, where the much more serious art of gastronomy holds sway (see panel).

If you are not here to eat, Mougins is still worth a visit, if only to wander around the immaculate streets with their carefully restored houses. There is also an interesting **Musée de la Photographie►** (*Open* Jul–Aug, daily 2–7pm; Sep–Jun, Wed and Sun 2–5pm. *Admission charge*) just next to the Porte Sarrasine. Art exhibitions are also held in the old wash house, **la Lavoir**, on the picturesque place de le Mairie.

Just outside Mougins (2km southeast on the D3) is the charming **Chapelle de Notre-Dame de Vie►►** on a hilltop flanked by ancient cypress trees. This 12th-century retreat was largely rebuilt in 1646 and used to be a popular place of pilgrimage: stillborn babies were brought here and it was believed that they came back to life during Mass just long enough to be baptised. Picasso spent the last years of his life in a villa hidden away behind the trees just opposite the chapel.

Back down towards Cannes at the *Aire des Breguieres* turn-off from the A8 *autoroute* is the huge **Musée de l'Automobiliste►►** (*Open* daily except mid-Nov–mid-Dec. *Admission charge*), which has a vast collection of vehicles, from vintage Bugattis to racing cars and armoured cars.

► la Napoule   200B1

At the western end of the Golfe de Napoule opposite Cannes, la Napoule marks the start of the Riviera. On the road above the marina is the extraordinary **château►**, a folly rebuilt on the site of a medieval castle in 1918 by the American sculptor and millionaire Henry Clews. The gateway is ornamented with a series of mythical beasts, grotesque monkeys, toads, serpents and fish, a theme which is carried through in the interior (*Guided tours* May–Oct, 3pm, 4pm; Jul–Aug, 3pm, 4pm, 5pm; closed Tue and Nov–Apr. *Admission charge*). The château also houses the Napoule Art Foundation.

■ As Provençal as *pastis*, the outdoor game of *boules* is a familiar sight in every town and village during daylight hours – sometimes even at night too, if there is a floodlit *boules* court. ■

The game *Boules* looks like a fairly easy game; certainly anyone can take part and enjoy it from the first throw. However, for serious players there is a great deal of gamesmanship involved – not to mention plenty of noisy Gallic exclamations and dramatic gesticulation.

The game starts with a small wooden ball, the *cochonnet*, being thrown some distance up the court, which is usually a reasonably flat, hard area of gravel or sand – or even a tarmac car park or road. Each player has three steel balls (they were once made from wood, studded with tacks), usually etched with different patterns or colours for identification. The winner is the person who throws their ball closest to the *cochonnet*.

Tactics Although it sounds straightforward enough, the skill (and the fun) of *boules* is in choosing the right tactic to get your ball next to the marker. For instance, you can simply roll your ball along the ground until it gently comes to rest (you hope) next to the *cochonnet*. But your opponent (who becomes the *tireur*) can 'fire' his ball at yours, knocking it out of the way. Or he can 'fire' at the *cochonnet*, knocking it towards his other balls on the court – a tactic called *faire le carreau*. At the conclusion of the round, there will be much careful scrutiny of the positioning of the balls to see who has won, often involving a tape measure to check distances to the millimetre.

Pétanque The original game of *boules* was known as *la longue* – that is, over a long distance (usually 16–20m) – in which players would take a running start and make three short hops from a marker before throwing their balls. Nowadays, *la longue* has been overtaken in popularity by *pétanque*, a variation which originated in la Ciotat. The game starts off *pieds tanqués* ('feet together') and the balls are thrown over a shorter distance, usually 6–10m.

Social boules
Glance at the window of any rural café and you often see a handwritten notice announcing '*Boules Tournament – Vendredi 6pm*'. For many little villages this is the social event of the week, with much discussion as to who is going to be on which team, and plenty of *pastis* to lubricate play. Championships are often held between different villages, with prizes for the winners. Competitions are usually between teams of three (*triplettes*) or four (*quadrettes*), with points awarded for each of the team's balls closest to the *cochonnet*.

229

Boules *is part of the fabric of life in Provence*

CÔTE D'AZUR AND ALPES-MARITIMES

Up and down the hill
Around 1000 BC the Ligurians built two forts here, one near the mouth of the Paillon river and the other further up the valley. The Phocaeans set up a small trading post, Nikaia, from the 6th century BC. Plagued by Ligurian pirates, they asked the Romans for help, who arrived in 200 BC, founding a town near the old *oppidum*, which they named *Cemenelum* (now the district of Cimiez). Cemenelum became the capital of the Roman Alpes-Maritime, with 20,000 inhabitants by the 3rd century AD. It was destroyed during the barbarian invasions, and the inhabitants moved down to the more easily defended site of Nikaia in the bay.

▶▶▶ **Nice** 201D2

Like the bubbling fountains in the place Masséna, Nice sparkles by day and night, confident of its position as Queen of the Riviera. It might not attract celebrities in the way Monaco or St-Tropez do, but it is far more interesting for that – a lively, energetic city with an independent character which is not at all swayed by tourism.

After the fall of the Roman town of *Cemenelum,* the port of Nikaia was the main medieval settlement. The city prospered under the Counts of Provence but in the 14th century it passed into the hands of the Counts of Savoy, and mostly remained under Italian control for the next 400 years. In 1860 Napoléon III signed a secret treaty with the House of Savoy in which Nice would revert to France in return for helping Vittoria Emanuele II of Savoy drive the Austrians out of northern Italy.

By this time the first tourists had begun to arrive, and in 1864 the building of the railway station sealed Nice's future as a Riviera resort. By 1827 around 600 visitors were descending on Nice for the winter season, and by the end of the century this had risen to 20,000. Construction began of the many *belle époque* mansions and follies so beloved of the aristocracy. Queen Victoria and other titled heads of state added to the allure of the resort, and by the start of World War I there were 150,000 visitors per year. With the advent of the 'summer holiday' in the 1920s, Nice switched seasons. Now the emphasis is on year-round tourism, with the development of such facilities as the Acropolis convention centre.

The Riviera corniches
The three famous corniches ('cliff roads') of the Riviera run between Menton and Nice along a dizzying stretch of coastline overlooking the resorts and beaches. The most spectacular views are from the Grande Corniche (D2564), built by Napoléon along the route of the old Via Julia Augustus; the route passes through la Turbie (see page 243) and some of the most sweeping panoramas are found above Èze. The Moyenne Corniche (N7) also has good views and is the only way to reach Èze itself (see page 214) by car. The lowest of the three is the Corniche Inférieure (N98), which gives access to all the coastal resorts and is the most prone to traffic jams during summer. The top two corniches are notoriously accident-prone, so if you are in a hurry it is better to take the A8 autoroute, which carves its way through the mountains behind the three coast roads from Nice as far as the Italian border.

Sea front and town centre►► The Promenade des Anglais►► (see panel, page 234) has been widened many times since the 1820s and has since been extended right out to the Nice–Côte d'Azur airport, becoming fairly traffic-clogged as a result. About midway along the promenade the **Hôtel Negresco** still stands facing the Mediterranean in all its domed splendour. Behind the Negresco is the **Musée d'Art et d'Histoire** (*Open* daily; closed Mon and Nov); it does contain a couple of fine 15th-century paintings by Jacques Durandi and a Bréa polyptych but the rest is all-too-predictable Napoléonic souvenirs and dusty First Empire mementoes.

West of the Musée Masséna is the **Musée des Beaux-Arts** (*Open* daily; closed Mon), with 17th-century Italian works right through to the Impressionists and contemporary works, with all sorts of oddities such as Kess Van Dongen's entertaining paintings of bejewelled and/or completely naked *belles dames* of the roaring twenties.

It is worth the trek north up boulevard Gambetta to the **Cathédrale Orthodoxe Russe►►** (*Open* daily except Sun morning. *Admission charge*) beyond the flyover and railway tracks. This colourful, elaborate cathedral (which is still in use) was financed by Tsar Nicolas I in memory of his son Nicolas, who died of consumption in Nice.

At its eastern end, the Promenade des Anglais stops at the Jardin Albert 1er, where there is a small *Théâtre de Verdure* (it offers a programme of concerts in the summer months). Behind here is the **place Masséna►** with its gardens, fountains and *belle époque* façades, such as that of the Hôtel Plaza Concorde.

From the place Masséna a broad concourse runs northeast, following the course of the river Paillon, now buried underground. This boulevard was the site chosen for Jacques Médecin's grand civic projects such as the enormous **Musée d'Art Moderne et d'Art Contemporain**►► (*Open* daily 11–6, until 10 on Fri; closed Tue), known as MAMAC; four octagonal marble towers linked by glassed-in walkways. The museum concentrates on the Second Nice School, with Pop Art and New Realist works, as well as other influential figures from the 1960s and 1970s such as Lichtenstein, Warhol and Niki de St-Phalle. Most of the displays were conceived as a send-up of not just consumer society but the whole art world. Next to it is a huge conference centre: cunningly disguised as a gigantic air-conditioning vent, the **Acropolis** could not be more inappropriately named.

West of the Paillon is the central district of Nice, bisected by the main high street, the avenue Jean Médecin, busy with cafés, cinemas, banks, department stores and the large Nice–Etoile shopping centre.

Cimiez►►► Beyond the railway line to the north the streets start to climb up to the smart district of Cimiez, at the beginning of which is the intriguing **Musée National Message Biblique Marc Chagall**►►► (*Open* daily; closed Tue. *Admission charge*), dedicated to Chagall's canvasses on Old Testament themes. Chagall also contributed the stained-glass windows.

Further up the hill is the **Musée Matisse**►►► (*Open* daily except Tue), recently reopened after a major refit. Matisse came to live in Nice in 1917, and the museum contains a good cross-section of his works from the early experiments with Fauvism through to the cut-out compositions done just before he died here in 1954, aged 85. The museum holds the world's largest collection of his drawings (238), etchings (218) and nearly all the bronze sculptures he ever made.

Crowds enjoying the Mardi Gras in Nice

Niçois traditions
Nice even has its own language, 'Nissart' (derived from the ancient Occitan dialect), which is still spoken and kept very much alive through language courses, theatre productions and traditional songs. The latter are often performed at fêtes, when girls wear the traditional costumes of a *bouquetière* (red-and-white striped cotton skirt, blouse, and black velvet waistcoat) and boys don fisherman's costume (red-and-white striped corsaire trousers, a broad belt of red wool, and white cotton shirt).

Next to the museum is the **Musée Archéologique de Cimiez►** (*Open* daily; closed Mon and public holidays. *Admission charge*), which stands on the site of the Roman town of *Cemenelum*.

Vieille ville►►► The *vieille ville* is beneath the Colline du Château at the eastern end of the Baie des Anges. You might once have risked losing your wallet in these alleyways, but since the 1980s massive redevelopment has turned it into one of the trendiest areas in the city – an admirable mix of bistros and boutiques alongside shops serving residents' needs and no-nonsense cafés.

In the backstreets you will come across the 17th-century **Cathédrale de Ste-Réparate►**, a baroque extravaganza topped by a roof of colourful Niçois tiles. One block north is the Genoese-style **Palais Lascaris►** (*Open* daily; closed Mon and Nov), which houses a museum with sumptuous 17th- and 18th-century paintings, furnishings and tapestries. On one corner of the **cours Saleya►►**, site of the daily market, is the **Chapelle de la Miséricorde►**, with a distinctive baroque façade. Next to it is the tiny **Galerie de Malacologie** (*Open* daily; closed Sun, Mon and Nov) with a collection of 1,500 shells from around the world.

On the south side of the cours Saleya a double row of low buildings, known as les Ponchettes, houses a number of seafood restaurants, whilst on the seaward side there are a pair of quirky museums: the **Galerie-Musée Mossa►** (*Closed* Sun mornings and Mon) houses the Symbolist works of Gustav-Adolf Mossa, whose morbid water-colours revolve around the themes of love, sex and death. A few doors along the **Musée Raoul Dufy►** (same hours as Galerie-Musée Mossa) shows a revolving selection of much more light-hearted fare from the extensive collection of Dufy's works held by the Musée des Beaux-Arts.

233

One of many processions during the famous Nice Carnival

The Promenade

One of the first celebrities to visit Nice was the English writer Tobias Smollett, who lived here for ten months in 1763. He was soon followed by a bevy of English milords and ladies attracted by the climate and the casino. In the 1820s they clubbed together to build a promenade (later named the Promenade des Anglais) so they could stroll along the shoreline: and also supposedly for the altruistic motive of helping the local unemployed through the harsh winters of 1820 and 1821, but in reality because they were fed up with being bothered by beggars on the streets.

234

Parks and gardens

The city's oldest garden is the Jardin Albert 1er, which leads into the Espace Massena and the Promenade de Paillon in the town centre. The Jardin des Arènes de Cimiez in the northern districts (near to the Musée Matisse) is a lovely old olive grove often used for traditional festivities, and in the nearby Jardin du Monastère de Cimiez, masses of roses climb over pergolas; in neighbouring St-Maurice, the Parc Chambrun features a delightful 'temple of love' at its summit. Out to the west the Jardin Botanique, 78 ave de la Corniche Fleurie (*Closed* Mon. *Admission free*), displays a classic collection of Mediterranean flora. Near the airport the spectacular Parc Flora Phoenix, 408 Promenade des Anglais (*Open* daily. *Admission charge*) features a vast conservatory with tropical plants, palms and orchids as well as fish, birds and butterflies.

A wedding ceremony in Nice's cathedral

Eastern hills and the port► Above the *vieille ville* is the **Colline du Château►**, where from the belvedere an artificial cascade draws the eye down to the rooftops of Vieux Nice. On the other side of the hill is the **port►►**. Nice's first 'port' was simply an anchorage on the other side of the Colline du Château; the present harbour, excavated in the late 18th century and named Port Lympnia, was enlarged a hundred years later.

At the back of the port is the **Musée de Terra Amata►** (*Closed* Mon), which occupies the ground floor of a block of flats. The explanation for this rather bizarre location is that when excavations were started to build the flats they discovered traces of the very first settlements in the area, dating back 400,000 years: these now form the core of the museum.

The road continues beyond the port up to the wooded slopes of **Mont Boron►**. The 60ha Mount Boron forest was planted in the 1860s and now has about 11km of walking trails around the hilltop. The best of the several forts around the hill is **Fort Alban►**, a rare example of French military architecture of the 16th century. Its four turrets, adorned with glazed Niçois tiles, give it a sort of Toytown look, but as a watch-tower its position is superb.

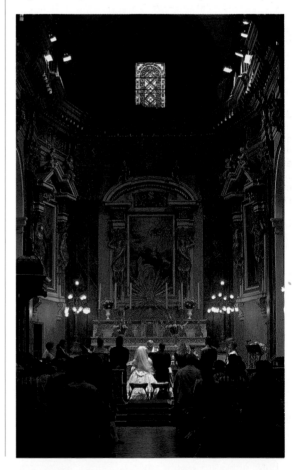

■ **Ever since *The French Connection* hit cinema screens, Marseille's reputation as an international drug-trafficking centre has been well known, and the local papers are never short of copy on shoot-outs between members of the local mafia (known as the *milieu*) or arrests of leading gang members involved in vice rings and protection rackets. But that's Marseille, and the Riviera is a different matter...or is it?** ■

Grahame Greene's bête noir Nice likes to portray an image of the *grand dame* of the Riviera but beneath the surface the murky currents of civic corruption run deep. As long ago as 1982 the late Graham Greene published a booklet entitled *J'Accuse: The Dark Side of Nice*, which pilloried the city's mayor, Jacques Médecin, for his links with the *milieu* and for siphoning off public money for his private use. The Médecin dynasty had been in power in Nice since 1928: Jacques, who took over the post from his father in 1966, vehemently denied Greene's accusations. However, the author's prophecies proved correct when Jacques fled to Uruguay in 1990 after the Justice Department uncovered a swindle involving funds for the Nice Opéra being siphoned off into his personal bank account. He was arrested by Interpol in 1993 and now faces charges involving the misuse of millions of francs of public money.

Jewel-heists and bombs Outside of Nice the *milieu* continues to operate with impunity. Kickbacks on big projects are a way of life (see panel). A popular and successful nightclub in Hyères was recently destroyed by a bomb – attributed to Mafia rivals. The Mafia were also suspected when Hollywood mogul Marvin Davis's gold Cadillac was hijacked in 1993 and he was robbed of $10 million worth of jewels at Cap d'Antibes. But worse was to come...

Death of a 'saint' In February 1994 Yann Piat, dubbed 'Yann d'Arc' by the French press for her relentless campaign against Mafia corruption, was murdered near her home in Hyères. Two masked gunmen shot Mme Piat from a motorcycle as she was being driven home – the murder bore all the hallmarks of a classic contract killing and shocked the nation not just for its brutality but because the assassination of a prominent member of the National Assembly was seen as a direct challenge to the French state. Just prior to her death, Mme Piat claimed to have uncovered evidence of Mafia money being laundered through Hyères's casino and various real estate projects.

Unanswered allegations Three months after Yann Piat's death an employee of the right-wing PACA administration was found dead just before he was due to hand over to a magistrate documents naming politicians involved in corruption along the coast. Fernand Saincène, who claimed trade tax exemptions were being traded for political favours, had apparently 'committed suicide'.

Mafia-sur-Mer
The dockyards of La Seyne near Toulon have been derelict since 1985, but a recent attempt to revitalise 30ha of docks has been scuppered by greedy local *milieu* bosses. A British consortium had spent three years planning an innovative maritime and business complex, the World Sea Centre, but the £120 million Franco–British deal was called off in 1994 after demands for £1 million in bribes were turned down by the project's backers. Now the dockyards will remain empty in La Seyne, which has been dubbed Mafia-sur-Mer by the French media.

235

Gene Hackman in French Connection II

Park rules
Picking flowers is forbidden in the park, as are camping, fires and dogs. There are park information centres at Allos, Barcelonnette, Entraunes, St-Dalmas-de-Tende, St-Étienne-de-Tinée, St-Martin-Vésubie and St-Sauveur-sur-Tinée. Any of these bureaux can provide information on walking and ATB (All Terrain Bike) trails, as well as guided tours.

The Parc National du Mercantour is a region of unspoiled wilderness and imposing peaks

▶▶▶ Parc National du Mercantour   *200C4*

Covering the highest peaks and the most dramatic scenery of the Alpes-Maritimes, the Parc National du Mercantour stretches for over 128km along the Italian border. Established in 1979, it is the most recently designated national park in France.

Covering over 68,000ha, the park lies mostly in the *département* of the Alpes-Maritimes (53,000ha), with the rest in the Alpes de Haute-Provence (15,000ha). It is divided between a central protected zone (a core strip of the most inaccessible areas, including the Vallée des Merveilles, see page 246) and the peripheral access zone surrounding it.

The landscapes of the Mercantour are highly varied, ranging from pastureland and alpine forests to glacial lakes, canyons and picturesque peaks. The park starts at an altitude of 490m, and as you climb upwards the pines and larches of the lower slopes give way to beautiful Alpine meadows and rock-strewn scree, before reaching permanent snow on peaks around 3,000m high.

Above these wild landscapes circle birds of prey such as golden eagles, kestrels and falcons – and the rare lammergeyer vulture, successfully reintroduced after becoming extinct here. Other feathered fauna include the ptarmigan, which changes its summer plumage of mottled brown for a winter plumage of pure white, the great spotted woodpecker, hoopoe, citril finches, ortolan and rock buntings.

The small Alpine marmot can be seen sitting on its haunches in meadowlands – until it spots a predator, and disappears in a flash down its burrow. Mouflons (wild mountain sheep) were reintroduced from Italy in the 1950s, and the chamois, ibex and boar populations are all now increasing. There are also foxes, stoats and hares – including the mountain hare which, like the ptarmigan, changes colour to white in winter.

The flora of the park is equally remarkable, with around 2,000 of the 4,200 species found in France represented, including 40 which are endemic to the region. In springtime the meadows are ablaze with bellflowers and blue gentians. There is also the elusive edelweiss, and, rarest of all, the big, spiky saxifrage (*Saxifraga florulenta*) which has become the symbol of the park.

▶▶ Peille 201D2

An unspoiled *village perché* with a great deal of character; there are several lovely old buildings in the cobbled alleys and passageways. Inside the Église Ste-Mairie▶ (ask at the hospice for the key) is an interesting painting of the village in medieval times, with its castle (now in ruins) which once belonged to the Counts of Provence, and a fine 16th-century *Polyptych of the Rosary* by Honoré Bertone of the Niçois school.

▶ Peillon 201D2

Peille's twin and neighbour, Peillon enjoys a spectacular setting high above the Paillon valley. The vaulted alleys and steep steps which climb up through the village are lined by carefully restored houses, many looking older than their 16th-century origins. The **Chapelle des Pénitents Blancs▶** is decorated with dramatic frescoes depicting *The Passion of Christ*, painted in 1485 by Giovanni Canavesio.

▶ Puget-Théniers 200B3

This attractive old town straddles the confluence of the Var and the Roudoule rivers and is dominated by the ruins of the Château des Trainières, which belonged to the Grimaldis until it was pulled down in 1691.

On the west bank of the Roudoule the old town, centred around the place A-Conil, was once the Templars' quarter and features many fine old doorways with carved shields on the lintels. On the other side of the river the parish church of **Notre-Dame-de-l'Assumption▶** contains a couple of remarkable 16th-century altarpieces, the *Polyptyque de Notre-Dame-de-Secours* by Antoine Ronzen, and the carvings of the *Passion* by Mathieu d'Anvers.

Near by A short detour from Puget-Théniers (5.5km along the D116) brings you to the small village of Puget-Rostang whose main attraction is the excellent **Écomusée du Pays de la Roudoule▶▶**. Unlike many 'ecomuseums' that have simply jumped on the bandwagon by adding the éco tag to their names, this écomusée plays an active role in the surrounding area and runs guided tours based on themes such as architecture, geology and botany (tel: 04 93 05 07 38 for details). In the *Maison de l'Écomusée* (Open Easter–Sep, daily; winter on demand) itself there are a series of exhibitions on local heritage topics.

A typical medieval street in the village perché *of Peille*

Auguste Blanqui
A monument in the town square of Puget-Théniers (*L'Action enchaînée* by Aristide Maillol) commemorates the town's most famous son, Auguste Blanqui. Born in 1805, Blanqui was one of the leaders of the Paris Commune of 1871.

Cap Ferrat, crowned by the Italianate Villa Ephrussi de Rothschild

A celebrated procession
Roquebrune's château is the only surviving example in France of a Carolingian castle, the forerunner of feudal citadels. Built in the 10th century by the Count of Vertimiglia, it later belonged for several hundred years to the Grimaldis. The village stages a celebrated procession on 5 August, as it has done for over 500 years since being delivered from the plague – after nine days of prayer – in 1467. Over 150 villagers (in roles handed down through families over the generations) play out the principal scenes of the Passion, moving between the Église Ste-Marguerite in the village and the Chapelle de la Pausa (Peace) 1km away.

▶ **Roquebrune-Cap-Martin**   *201D2*

Sandwiched between Menton and Monte-Carlo, **Cap Martin** and the village of **Roquebrune** seem to have merged into one big suburb of Menton. The medieval village of Roquebrune is a maze of steps and passageways, covered by arches and vaults, culminating at the **château** (*Open* daily; closed Fri and Nov. *Admission charge*).

Cap Martin, an exclusive enclave of fenced-off villas amongst the cypresses, pines and mimosa, had its heyday towards the end of the last century when aristocrats fluttered like moths around the socialites Empress Eugenie and Elizabeth, Empress of Austria. W B Yeats died here in 1939, and Le Corbusier also met his maker whilst swimming off the cape in 1965. The superb coastal path amongst the rocks and battered pine trees has since been named in his honour.

▶▶ **St-Jean-Cap-Ferrat**   *201D2*

Like the Cap d'Antibes and Cap Martin, Cap Ferrat was long ago taken over by luxurious mansions and villas hidden away behind tall gates and impenetrable hedges. The peninsula's past residents have included Leopold II of Belgium, Otto Preminger, Somerset Maugham and David Niven. It is, however, a little more welcoming than some of the other privacy-obsessed capes, with a tourist office of its own which is happy to point you in the direction of the **Zoo** (*Open* daily. *Admission charge*), the little harbour area at **St-Jean-Cap-Ferrat** itself, or the marked walking trails around its 14km coastline.

The highlight of Cap Ferrat is the amazing **Villa Ephrussi de Rothschild**▶▶▶ (*Open* daily in summer; weekends in winter. *Admission charge*). An avid art collector, Beatrice de Rothschild built this Italianate-style villa after marrying the banker Baron Ephrussi – the choice of site was because he liked to gamble at nearby Monte-Carlo.

The villa was built over a period of seven years, with around 40 different architects having worked on it (some did not last more than a few hours, thanks to the Baroness' capriciousness), and contains something in the region of 5,000 art treasures. Critics say that the Baroness had more money than taste but this is not borne out by either her background or the many exquisite pieces she assembled here, ranging from Beauvais tapestries to Sèvres porcelain, Renaissance furniture, rare Chinese chests and vases, frescoes, paintings…the list goes on and on. Don't miss the lovely tearoom, with its huge bay windows framing the Bay of Villefranche. The villa was bequeathed to the Académie des Beaux-Arts on the death of the Baroness in 1934.

Visits to the villa are by guided tour only, but you are free to wander around the extraordinary gardens (see page 245) on your own.

▶▶ St-Martin-Vésubie   201D4

This cool mountain retreat at the head of the Vésubie valley, the only substantial town in the area, is a popular base for excursions into the Parc National du Mercantour (see page 236). From the Mercantour, the streams of le Boréon and la Madone de Fenestre descend and meet at St-Martin to form the Vésubie itself.

Swiss-style houses overhang the main street of rue Dr-Cagnoli, where another torrent is channelled through a conduit between the cobbles creating a lovely effect – not the original intention, since the channel once carried the village sewage.

Descending rue Dr-Cagnoli from place Félix-Faure, the main square, you pass the **Chapelle des Pénitents-Blancs** with its bulb-shaped bell-tower, the **Église** (which has an altarpiece from the Bréa school) and a massive Gothic mansion, the **Maison des Contes de Gubernatis**.

The polychrome wooden statue of the Madonna only stays in the parish church for part of the year: at the beginning of July it is carried in procession up to the **Sanctuaire de la Madone de Fenestre▶**, 12km northeast of St-Martin, and brought back again in September. The procession and the monthly summer pilgrimages are good reasons to make the steep trip. An ancient refuge, the chapel gets its name from a natural window in the rocks above it through which you can see the sky.

Nearby walks Following the Boréon 8km upstream from St-Martin-Vésubie leads you to the charming resort village of **le Boréon**, whose speciality is fresh trout pulled from the mountain streams in the vicinity (the season is from mid-March to early September). Some of the wild and beautiful landscapes of the Mercantour Park can be explored on a four-hour circular walking tour of the Haut-Boréon area above the village, skirting the isolated Lac de Trecoulpes.

Massacre of the Templiers
The origins of the Madone de Fenestre are obscure, but it is thought to have been brought to St-Martin-Vésubie in the 12th century by the Templiers (Knights Templar) when they acquired this territory. In the 14th century, the sanctuary (then half ruined) was pillaged by brigands, who slit the throats of the Templiers; their bodies remained slumped under the snow in the ruined eaves, and when the chapel was later restored, 15 skeletons were found. Their ghosts are said to haunt the sanctuary, walking ceaselessly in procession around it on dark nights, howling and wailing like the glacial winds that sweep down the mountain.

St-Martin-Vésubie is a popular base for exploring the neighbouring mountains

Sculpture is just one of the strengths of the Fondation Maecht. Above: a Giacometti piece

► St-Paul-de-Vence 200C2

Probably the only medieval village in the country with compulsory underground car parking, St-Paul-de-Vence is another of those tourist honeypots that have become so overrun with boutiques that their identity has been totally swamped. Proudly proclaiming 18 ateliers, 15 art galleries, 17 artisans, seven antique and gift shops and 12 restaurants and hotels, it is a wonder that St-Paul does not come to a complete standstill with shoppers clogging the narrow streets in the summer months.

There is a small but interesting **Musée►** (*Open* daily. *Admission charge*) housed in a 12th-century keep next to the town hall. At the exit, hundreds of photographs record the numerous celebrities who have visited or lived in this overblown village.

Unmissable is the **Fondation Maecht►►►** (See panel on opposite page. *Open* daily. *Admission charge*) set on a wooded hill just outside St-Paul-de-Vence. Incorporated into the grounds and the outside of the building are mosaics by Braque and Chagall, a moving tubular fountain by Pol Bury, a stick-like cat by Giacometti and a Calder mobile. Also within the grounds is the small Chapelle St-Bernard, with stained glass windows by Braque. The vast permanent collection includes major works by the most important artists of the last 50 years, as well as temporary exhibitions of young artists and retrospectives.

Also here are a huge arts library, a bookshop, workshops and studios, and a cinema screening films (at 3pm daily) on the lives of artists represented here.

► St-Vallier-de-Thiey 200B2

This small town set in wooded hills 12km above Grasse has few attractions of its own, but near by are three of the best cave systems in Provence (see map, page 219).

The **Grotte de Baume Obscure►►** (*Open* daily from Easter–Sep. *Admission charge*), is signposted off the D5 west of town. Inside a 700m-long path climbs and winds up and down through vast galleries and caverns draped

The Colombe d'Or

St-Paul-de-Vence was no doubt a much more peaceful place in the 1920s when a clutch of artists settled here after World War I and ended up paying their bills at the famous *La Colombe d'Or* restaurant with paintings that are now priceless: the walls are hung with works by Picasso, Matisse, Vlaminck, Léger, Dufy, Bonnard, Derain and Modigliani – but you will have to stump up a small fortune for a meal to be able to eat in these rarified surroundings.

The baroque interior of the Église-St-Sauveur in Saorge

with stalagmites and stalactites; the caves descend to around 60m and are beautifully lit, with fluorescence fed into some of the cascades for added effect.

Continue on down the same road and turn left onto the D613 for the **Grottes de St-Cézaire**▶ (*Open* daily; closed Nov–mid-Feb. *Admission charge*). The circuit here is only 200m long, but is known for the unusual red colouring of its iron-rich stalactites and stalagmites.

Finally, there is the **Grotte des Audides**▶ (*Open* daily. *Admission charge*). The cave descends almost vertically (with 279 steps!) to a depth of 60m, and has some unusual and very beautiful formations. There is also a jolly **Parc Prehistorique** in the woodland setting around the cave mouth, with life-size mock-ups of the prehistoric settlements which existed here.

Modern art at the Fondation Maecht

▶▶ **Saorge** 201E3

The next village up the Roya valley after Breil-sur-Roya (see page 208), Saorge is set on a steep slope high above the river: seen from below it seems amazing that this jumble of houses clinging to the rock does not just slide gracefully down the hillside. The tortuous drive up to the village is well worth it to see how this peculiar place has been built, with houses piled one on top of the other and connected by obscure stairways and alleys where daylight never penetrates.

In this semi-troglodytic world, the inhabitants of Saorge have retained some of their own, ancient dialect, which contains elements of Provençal and Ligurian Italian. The site was an important defensive post in the Middle Ages, guarding the approach to the Col de Tende, but the fort was destroyed by Napoléon.

At the centre of the village the **Église St-Sauveur** contains *trompe l'oeil* frescoes and an organ built in Genoa and brought here by pack-mules. From the village a track leads across the terraces to a 17th-century **Franciscan convent** and the adjoining 11th-century chapel of **la Madone del Poggio**▶, containing some fine 15th-century works.

Playful rhythms
The Maecht foundation was established by collectors Aime and Marguerite Maecht, who commissioned the building from Spanish architect Jose-Luis Sert (a protégé of Le Corbusier) in the 1960s, with numerous contemporary artists contributing to the ornamentation: the result is an extraordinary temple to modern art where the structure itself is 'a play between the rhythms of the interior and exterior spaces', as Sert himself put it.

241

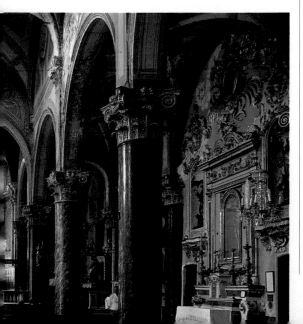

Sophia-Antipolis   200C1

Dubbed 'France's answer to Silicon Valley', Sophia-Antipolis was the nation's first Science Park and now covers a huge area – 5,000ha, and another 2,400ha are to be added soon – behind Vallauris and Antibes on the Plateau de Valbonne. Created in the 1970s, this futuristic complex amidst rolling hills has attracted around 830 businesses, employing around 15,000 people working in information technology, life sciences, pharmaceuticals, robotics, and other high-tech areas.

►► Sospel   201D3

A charming Alpine-Italianate town on the banks of the river Bévéra, Sospel thrived from the Middle Ages to the 18th century when it was an important crossroads on the trade routes between Haute Provence, the coast, and Piedmont via the Col de Tende.

The tollgate through which travellers then had to pass sits in the middle of an 11th-century **bridge►►** connecting the two halves of the town. Damaged during the war, it was restored in 1947 and now houses a small tourist office. From the road bridge downstream, there is a fabulous view of the medieval/Italianate houses on the right bank of the river, with the tollgate bridge and the mountains behind.

In the western half of the town, the narrow streets unexpectedly open up into the **place St-Michel►►**, a large square surrounded by magnificent, colourful baroque façades. The main building is the vast Église St-Michel, built in the 17th century and incorporating, somewhat incongruously, the Romanesque bell-tower of the 12th-century church which it replaced. Inside, there is a magnificent Bréa altarpiece, the *Annunciation*.

To the left of St-Michel are the chapels of the Pénitents Gris and Pénitents Rouges (helpfully colour-coded grey and red respectively) and, to the right, the Palais Ricci with *trompe l'oeil* windows.

Tende   201D4

Once the capital of the Upper Roya, Tende is the last town before the Col de Tende and once played an

Underground fort
Just outside of Sospel on the D2204 there is an old Maginot Line fortress, the *Fort St-Roch*. Built in 1932 against the threat of an Italian invasion, it was put to effective use towards the end of the war and has over 1km of underground tunnels. It now houses the Musée de la Résistance (*Open* Jul–Aug Tue–Sun. *Admission charge*).

The lovely old medieval bridge and tollgate spanning the Bévéra river at Sospel

important role guarding the route across to Piedmont. Tende's tall, gaunt houses and bell-towers cling to the side of the valley, with a terraced, slightly depressing cemetery high above the town.

Many of the houses are roofed with stone slabs (*lauzes*) in the local green schist, with door lintels dating back to the 15th century which bear coats of arms and the symbols of old trades. The **Collégiale Ste-Marie des Bois** has a handsome Renaissance doorway and a 17th-century organ.

The tourist office here (tel: 04 93 04 73 71) can provide information and bookings for tours to the *Vallée des Merveilles* (see page 246). An easier option is to visit the new **Musée des Merveilles▶** (*Open* daily except Tue. *Admission charge*), which has dioramas and models on the history of the valley and the rock engravings.

▶▶   la Turbie
201D2

The chunky silhouette of the monument for which this village is famous, the **Trophée des Alpes▶▶▶**, is an unmistakable landmark. Situated at the loftiest point of the main Roman highway (the *Via Julia*) between Cimiez and Italy 480m above sea level, the trophy was built in the 6th century BC to commemorate Augustus' triumphs over the Alpine tribes. Originally topped off with a statue of Augustus, it stood 50m high and 38m wide: despite being vandalised, turned into a fortress in the Middle Ages, partly dismantled on the orders of Louis XIV in 1705, and then finally quarried to build the neighbouring church in the last century, enough of it survived to make partial restoration feasible – even though it is now 'only' 35m high. The long inscription on its base, listing all 44 tribes conquered by Augustus, has also been restored.

In the gardens (*Open* daily. *Admission charge*) surrounding the trophy there is a small museum documenting its restoration, financed by an American, Edward Tuck, and from the terrace behind there is a wonderful panorama of Monaco and the coastline from Italy to the Esterel.

Next to the trophy, the baroque **Église St-Michel-Archange** contains works attributed to or from the schools of Veronese, Raphael, Bréa, Ribera and Murillo.

Intricate paintwork on Sospel's riverside houses

The Roman monument that put la Turbie on the map, the Trophée des Alpes

■ **Water gardens, stone gardens, secret gardens, kitchen gardens – there is almost no end to the different types of garden you can find in Provence. Here is a selection of just a few, all of which can be visited.** ■

A perfumed garden
One of the most charming books ever written about Provençal gardens is the classic *Perfume from Provence* by Lady Winifred Fortescue, first published in 1935. Lady Fortescue and her husband, Sir John, settled in a small stone house outside Grasse between the wars and set about trying to tame the terraced landscape of vines, roses, lavender and wild flowers that surrounded them. The book's patronising attitude to Provençals now seems very dated, but this warm-hearted account (it was an instant best-seller) conveys the magic of Provençal gardens very convincingly.

Cacti (below and right) flourish in the hot, dry climate

244

Châteaux gardens The castles of Provence have not always had a great deal of space surrounding them in which to plant gardens. The garden was often an afterthought, squeezed on to a terrace between the castle and the village streets surrounding it.

Such is the case with the Château de Sabran at Ansouis, where the stone-walled terraces were filled in during the 17th century (the castle itself dates back to the 10th century): on the west side of the château, hemmed in by the adjoining chapel, the Paradise garden displays an elegant pattern of clipped box hedges in the northern French style.

At Entrecasteaux, the castle sits on a small knoll with its garden (with magnolias, box hedges and eucalyptus surrounding a small pool) some way beneath. The garden was designed by Le Notre, who created the gardens of Versailles; he also designed the gardens at the château of Gourdon (spectacularly perched on the edge of the hillside) and those at the **Château de la Barben**► (*Open* daily 10–12, 2–6 in summer; closed Tue in winter and during Jan. *Admission charge*) outside Salon. Rebuilt many times over the centuries, the château is remarkable for its elegant 18th-century ceilings; also on display is the bedroom which belonged to Pauline Borghese, Napoléon's sister, who once lived here. The formality of the flower borders, statues and basins is emphasised by the untamed woodland which surrounds them. In the grounds there is a large zoo and a children's playground.

Herb gardens Although herbs are a vital part of Provençal cuisine and folk medicine, herb gardens are rare for the good reason that most herbs grow wild. But there are two exceptions: the first is at the Ethnological Conservatory of Haute Provence (Conservatoire du Patrimoine Ethnologique de la Haute Provence) in the old Prieuré de Salagon near Mane, where they have planted a medicinal herb garden with over 100 of the most commonly used species; there is also a medieval monastery garden with ornamental, edible and herbal plants.

The second is the *Harmas* of the entomologist J-H Fabre at Sérignan-du-Comtat, a little wilderness which

Provençal gardens

Fabre allowed to grow untended simply so that he could study the insect inhabitants. This untamed botanic park contains over 800 plant species.

Exotic gardens In the 18th century the first botanic gardens were opened in Aix and Salon to nurture exotic plants brought back from Africa and the Orient. Palm trees arrived in Hyères in 1867, and palms – along with a multitude of other exotic species – form an important part of the huge Jardin Olbius Riquier on the outskirts of Hyères. In contrast, thousands of species of cacti are the main feature of the Jardin Exotique in Monaco, and papyrus, ferns and pineapple plants are interspersed with thousands of orchids in Provence Orchidées just outside Barbentane. The Parc Naturel de Mugel at la Ciotat is predominantly Mediterranean, with *garrigue* species and wild flowers, but it also contains cacti and thickets of wild bamboo.

City gardens Framed by monumental ruins or grand buildings, city gardens often have a dramatic setting. The Rocher des Doms in Avignon, for example, is perched above the Rhône with the Palais des Papes rising up beside it. Its leafy paths, rock gardens, lawns and splashing fountains offer a respite from the hurly-burly below. In Nîmes, the best-loved public park is the Jardin de la Fontaine which incorporates not only the Temple of Diana but also the old Roman baths and the spring itself, landscaped into a series of balustrades and monumental steps beneath the shade of chestnuts and hackberries. Aix has its French-style gardens in the Pavillon de Vendome and Arles its charming Jardin d'Été on the boulevard des Lices with enormous cedars backing on to the Théâtre.

Unusual gardens One of the most extraordinary gardens is that of the Villa Ephrussi de Rothschild on St-Jean-Cap-Ferrat, created by Baroness Ephrussi de Rothschild from 1905 onwards. The Île de France garden in the centre, created in the form of a boat, is flanked on either side by a series of smaller gardens designed in Japanese, Spanish, Florentine, Oriental and Provençal styles: an instant tour of the world's gardens, completely mad and great fun.

Colette in Nîmes
Writing of her 'Elysian refuge, the Gardens of the Fountain' in Nîmes, Colette says, 'the baths of Diana, over which I lean, still, as always, reflect Judas trees, the terebinths, the pines, the paulownias with their mauve flowers and the double purple thorns. A whole garden of reflections is spread out there below me, turning, as it decomposes in the aquamarine water, dark blue, the violet of a bruised peach, and the maroon of dried blood. Oh beautiful garden and beautiful silence, where the only sound is the muted splashing of the green, imperious water, transparent and dark, blue and brilliant as a bright dragon.'

Pottery is one of the mainstays of Vallauris

Mysterious markings
Little is known about the purpose of the carvings of the Vallée des Merveilles, which represent human figures, animals and tools, and include many mysterious symbols, but they are thought to date from between 1500 and 1800 BC. It is possible that the valley was an ancient sacred site, and that the symbols were made by pilgrims. However, the tools which were used to carve them have never been found and it has even been whispered that they may be fake. The first systematic investigation of the site was carried out earlier this century by an Englishman, Clarence Bicknell.

► **Vallauris**   *200C1*

Vallauris is a fairly hideous town – the modern part, at least – which is stuffed to the gunwales with pottery and ceramic shops of variable quality that owe their popularity (if not their style) to Picasso's stay here in the 1940s and 1950s. He got hooked on a new passion when he started working with clay in the Poterie Madoura (giving fresh impetus to an industry that has existed here since Roman times). Pottery-making thrived here during the Middle Ages, was knocked out by the plague, and was then re-invigorated by the arrival of Genoese potters in the 16th century. After World War II it suffered at the expense of the aluminium industry, only to take off again thanks to Picasso's ten-year stay here.

Picasso-inspired designs can be purchased at the Poterie Madoura (off rue 19 Mars 1962); many of his originals are in the **Musée Municipal►** (*Closed* Tue. *Admission charge*), housed in a Renaissance château on place de la Libération. The same ticket allows you entry to the **Musée National Picasso►►**, which is in fact a small, deconsecrated chapel that Picasso decorated in 1952 with his seminal paintings *La Guerre et La Paix*.

►►► **Vallée des Merveilles**   *201D4*

Part of the Mercantour National Park (see page 236), the Vallée des Merveilles contains one of the richest collections of open-air petroglyphs (rock carvings) in Europe. Lying on the western flank of Mont Bégo between Lac du Basto and Lac Long, the valley covers over 30sq km and contains an estimated 30,000 carvings.

The carvings may be the work of pilgrims (see panel) but since latter-day visitors with less reverential attitudes have also left their mark, the two most important areas are now protected and you must stick to the marked paths unless accompanied by an official guide.

Although there are thousands of symbols they are not easily visible to the untrained eye, which is another good reason for visiting with a guide. *Destination Merveilles* (tel: 04 93 89 88 98) organises regular guided visits from

June through to October, with the main access point being St-Dalmas-de-Tende south of Tende (see page 243).

▶▶▶ Vence *200C2*

Although only 10km from the coast, this lively town has more in common with its counterparts in inland Provence than with the frenetic resorts of the Riviera. Vence was popular with artists and the intelligentsia during the 1920s (including the likes of Dufy, André Gide, Paul Valéry and D H Lawrence – the latter dying here of tuberculosis in 1930). Matisse moved here in 1941 to escape the bombings on the coast but fell dangerously ill; he was nursed back to health by the Dominican sisters and in thanks to them he started work in 1946 on his famous **Chapelle du Rosaire▶▶▶** (*Open* Tue and Thu).

'I think it is my masterpiece' declared Matisse after five years of work. The white tiled walls of the chapel are covered in black line drawings of the Stations of the Cross, the Virgin and Child, the Crucifixion and St Dominic – the only colour to intrude on the simple, stark interior comes from the stained glass windows which throw patterns of yellow, green and blue across these surprising murals.

The *vieille ville* of Vence is an enjoyable place to wander – starting off at the **place du Peyra**, where there is an obligatory stop to taste the mineral-rich waters from the urn-shaped fountain. From here, head down the lively **rue du Marché**, which is crammed with mouth-watering food shops – little *patisseries*, fish shops with sacks of *moules* and mounds of fresh-cooked *crevettes*, charcuteries, cheese shops and *poulet grillé à la flame* wafting tempting aromas down the narrow street.

The rue du Marché leads to the central place Clemenceau, where you can see Roman tombstones incorporated into the walls of the **cathédrale▶**. As well as a mosaic by Chagall (in the baptistry at the back) there are all sorts of odds and ends inside including finely carved Gothic choirstalls, the sarcophagus of St Veran, and stone reliefs from the 5th-century church that it replaced.

Above: detail on a church in Vence's vieille ville

A Picasso ceramic (1953) from his Vallauris period

Villefranche harbour and fishing boats

The harbour
Protected by the Cap Ferrat peninsula, Villefranche harbour has a long history. Its deep waters (over 60m in places) sheltered galleys in Roman times, when it was known as *Olivula*. In the 14th century the Comte de Provence, Charles II of Anjou, declared it a duty-free port, *Villam-Francam* – hence its name today. In the 16th century Charles V moored his imperial galley here: one tale has it that when his sister (then Queen of France) came to visit, the entire entourage – dukes, Queen and all – was plunged into the sea when his gangplank collapsed.

Cocteau's chapel

►►► **Villefranche-sur-Mer** *201D2*

Just around the Boron headland east of Nice, Villefranche is a small 'fishing village' that the Niçois visit at the slightest opportunity for a meal out in one of the harbour-side restaurants. It is indeed one of the most delightful spots on the Riviera to spend a summer's evening dining on the quayside, with fishing boats and yachts bobbing about in the harbour.

Villefranche has been a military port for many centuries and although warships sometimes still put in to the deep, sheltered harbour, it was the small fishing community that inspired Villefranche's most famous resident, Jean Cocteau, when he lived here.

In homage to them he decorated the **Chapelle St-Pierre►►►** (*Open* daily in summer; closed Mon and mid-Nov–mid-Dec. *Admission charge*) just near the waterfront; depicting the fisherwomen of Villefranche, gypsies and the life of St Peter, these extraordinary, luminous frescoes are suffused with Cocteau-esque symbolism. Above the chapel the **Galerie Jean-Cocteau** (*Open* daily) is one of the few outlets for his original drawings, lithographs and ceramics. Changing exhibitions also feature his work.

Within the massive walls of the **Citadelle St-Elme►►** above the port is the *mairie* (town hall) and, tucked away in various corners, an open-air theatre and two museums. The **Fondation-Musée Volti►** (*Open* daily except Sun morning and Tue. *Admission free*) is dedicated to the provocative sculptures of local artist Volti. The **Musée Goetz-Boumeester** (same hours as Fondation-Musée Volti) contains two works by Picasso and one by Miró as well as various displays of ceramics.

At the entrance to the citadel there is a display of maritime archaeological finds from the wreck of a Genoese trading ship which went down in the harbour in a violent storm in 1516.

Behind the port is the **rue Obscure►**, a vaulted passageway which has altered little since the 13th century; this dark, cavernous alleyway has sheltered the inhabitants of the port from bombardments throughout history, including during World War II.

Visitors to Provence have a choice of international airports

By air Nice and Marseille are Provence's two main international gateways. Nice is the second busiest airport in France after Paris, with around 6 million passengers annually. Over 41 airlines have scheduled flights into Nice, with 90 direct flights to 33 countries. During the summer months, the best deals are on charter flights from London and elsewhere. If you are heading primarily for the Vaucluse, the Bouches-du-Rhône or the Var it is more convenient to fly into Marseille–Provence airport (previously Marseille–Marignane). With around 4.5 million annual passengers, Marseille caters mostly for business traffic and is France's third busiest airport.

By sea The classiest way to arrive on the coast is on your own yacht, and with over 125 marinas and ports and 57,000 berths there is no shortage of mooring space. An average of between 120,000 and 130,000 annual passengers arrive on cruise ships, with the principal ports of call being Cannes, Marseille, Nice, Toulon, St-Tropez and Villefranche. Regular ferry services operate between Marseille and Tunisia and Algeria.

By train French National Railways (SNCF) operates an efficient and comfortable service from Paris right the way down the coast.

The fastest option is the high-speed TGV (Train à Grand Vitesse), which plunges southwards at 270kph and reaches Avignon in just under 4hrs and Marseille in 4hrs 40mins. The dedicated TGV track at present only reaches Valence, after which the train runs at normal speeds, but SNCF is planning the TGV Mediterranéen which will push the high-speed track further south (due for completion after 2000). TGV tickets are slightly more expensive than normal tickets, and you will need to reserve a seat in advance or before boarding the train. If you are travelling to northeast Provence you can take the TGV to Grenoble or Valence and change to local trains from there.

Another option is an overnight sleeper train from Paris, which is one of the most relaxing and evocative ways to arrive as the Provençal landscapes unfold outside your window in the early morning hours.

If you are taking your own car or motorbike, the Motorail service operates from Channel ports to Avignon, Fréjus/St-Raphaël and Nice, and from Paris to the same stations plus Marseille and Toulon. Again, these are overnight trains with couchettes (berths) for sleeping, and although ticket prices are fairly exorbitant it is safer and more relaxing than driving all the way there.

For further information and bookings, contact the overseas branches of SNCF in European capitals or major US or Canadian cities. Discounts on rail tickets are available for students and senior citizens and with rail passes (see **Getting around** page 255).

Coach Regular long-distance coach services connect Provence with European cities such as London, Paris, Brussels, Madrid, Geneva, and elsewhere.

Car Travelling down from Paris the quickest route is on the *Autoroute du Soleil* (the A6 from Paris, then the A7

❏ Although the *autoroute* is fast it is not cheap: toll charges from Calais to Nice add up to around 450 francs. An alternative is to take the N7 south from Paris to Lyon. Both should be avoided in July and August. ❏

❏ Duty-free allowances
Allowances are for bringing into France goods bought duty-free or from outside the EU:

Cigarettes	200
or Cigars	50
or Tobacco	250g
Table wine	2 litres
Alcohol over 22 proof	1 litre
or	
Alcohol under 22 proof	2 litres
or Additional table wine	2 litres
Perfume	60ml
Toilet water	250ml
	❏

from Lyon), which goes to Marseille. However, if you are continuing down the coast you will need to branch off at Aix along the *Autoroute la Provençale* (A8), which runs all the way to the Italian border. If you are coming from the UK the quickest route is via the A26 to Reims and Troyes, followed by the A5 and A31 to Dijon, after which you join up again with the *Autoroute du Soleil*. This completely avoids the nightmare of the *Boulevard Périphérique* around Paris.

Customs There are no limits on the import or export of tax-paid goods between EU countries (provided they are for personal use). For duty-free goods, see table.

Insurance Travel insurance should cover medical expenses, loss of luggage or money, cancellation of your holiday or flight, delayed departure and delayed baggage. If you are taking your own car, breakdown and accident insurance is recommended (third party insurance is compulsory).

Visas A valid passport only is required for citizens of the EU. Visa requirements for other nationalities vary: check with a travel agent or the French Government Tourist Office.

Departing There is an airport departure tax of 22 francs for international flights, and 15 francs for internal flights.

Made in Provence

Climate and when to go Although renowned for its temperate weather and sunshine, Provence is a land of climatic extremes – veering between blistering hot summers and freezing winters during which the *mistral* can blow for several days. What's more, normal weather patterns are no longer as predictable as they once were, with extensive flooding of some coastal areas in 1993 and 1994.

Spring A delightful time to be in Provence, with wild flowers in profusion and mimosa and almonds blossoming on the coast from March onwards. In April and May it is warm enough to sit out in the sunshine in restaurants and cafés, although the sea is still a bit chilly for swimming.

Summer Peak season throughout Provence, hot and dry with minimal rainfall and temperatures which rarely drop below 20°C between June and September (summer heatwaves can push temperatures even higher). The sea is warm enough for swimming from June onwards, and the crowds not yet unbearable.

Avoid the coast in July and August. It is at its worst then, with overcrowding, traffic jams, over-inflated prices

MARSEILLE

September–December

mm   May–September   °C

and short-tempered service. Festivals, however, are in full swing.

If you are planning on walking (particularly on any of the long-distance paths), wooded areas and sometimes entire hill ranges are closed off from 1 July through to 12 September if they are in a high-risk Red Fire Zone. Summer is the ideal time to be in the Alpes de Haute-Provence, where cooler temperatures favour outdoor activities.

Autumn September and October can be extremely pleasant – you can still sunbathe although there are occasional rainstorms. The vineyards and forests take on their mantle of

Dining al fresco

Harvesting grapes in the late summer

autumn colours and, after early September, resorts start to empty when the French school holidays end.

Winter In November colder weather settles in and most museums (and many hotels and restaurants) close. Snow starts to settle on the Alps from late November onwards, with the skiing season in the high altitude resorts lasting through to March/April.

A predominate feature of the winter months is the dreaded *mistral*, which whips down the Rhône valley and can make life unpleasant for days on end. However, it can be avoided by moving further east down to the Côte d'Azur.

National holidays (*jours fériés*)
1 January, Easter Sunday, Easter Monday, 1 May (Labour Day), 8 May (VE Day), Ascension Day (40 days after Easter), Pentecost (7th Sunday after Easter) and the following Monday, 14 July (Bastille Day), 15 August (Assumption Day), 1 November (All Saints' Day), 11 November (Armistice Day) and Christmas Day.
Banks, businesses and most shops and museums are closed.

Time differences France operates according to Central European Time, which is one hour ahead of Greenwich Mean Time from 26 September to 28 March, and two hours ahead for the rest of the year.

Money matters The unit of currency is the French franc (denoted as F or FF), which is divided into 100 centimes. There are banknote of 20, 50, 100, 200 and 500 francs; coins of 1, 2, 5, 10, 20 francs and 5, 10 and 20 centimes.

Unlimited currency can be imported, but you must declare amounts over 50,000F being re-exported.

On January 1, 1999, the euro became the official currency of France, and the franc became a denomination of the euro. French notes and coins continue to be legal tender during a transitional period. The introduction of euro bank notes and coins is likely to start by January 1, 2002.

Travellers' cheques are a safe way of carrying holiday money. Foreign currency, travellers' cheques and Eurocheques can be changed at banks and bureaux de change. You can also change currency in hotels and some tourist offices, and Eurocheques can be cashed in post offices.

Banks generally open 9–12, 1.30–4, close Sundays, public holidays and often Saturdays or Mondays. Bureaux de change (in main railway stations and town centres) open longer hours and sometimes on holidays. Buy some French francs before leaving home, in case there is nowhere open.

Exchange rates fluctuate widely, as do commissions on changing travellers' cheques (hotels and bureaux de change usually have the worst rates). If changing large amounts, shop around.

Credit cards such as Visa/Barclaycard (Carte Bleu in France), Access/Mastercard (Eurocard), American Express and Diners Club are widely accepted. In remote places or small restaurants cards may not be accepted.

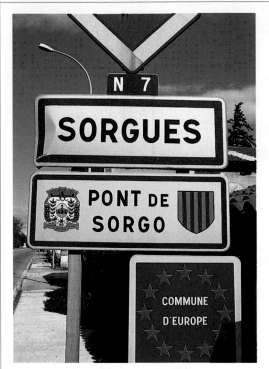

You will need a car if you wish to seek out the best of Provence

Driving Provence lends itself to gentle exploration by car, with many unexpected sights and delightful corners of the countryside which are accessible only with your own transport. Unfortunately the public transport network is just not extensive enough to cater to the needs of most visitors unless you are planning on staying put in a coastal resort with just the occasional excursion to major tourist sights. Over 70 per cent of overseas visitors (and nearly 80 per cent of French tourists) travel around by car.

Driving documents If you are taking a car to France, it is compulsory to carry a full driving licence, current insurance certificate and the original vehicle registration document (plus a letter of authorisation from the owner of the vehicle if it is not registered in your name). You should also display a nationality sticker and your headlights must be adjusted with beam deflectors: as long as your lights are properly adjusted, tinting them yellow is not required. A spare set of headlight bulbs is a good idea, since driving with faulty lights is illegal. A red warning triangle is advisable, although not compulsory if your car is fitted with hazard warning lights.

Car hire There are plenty of car hire agencies but the major drawback is price, with costs that exceed most other European countries. Hiring a car locally is the most expensive option. Usually the best deals are fly-drive packages arranged by a travel agent or tour operator in your home country, or train/car hire arrangements with SNCF. Sometimes competitive rates can be obtained by booking in advance through major car hire companies (such as Hertz, Avis, Budget or Europcar, all of whom are represented in Provence).

The minimum age to hire a car is 18 years old, although many international firms have now raised this to 20 or even 23 years old (with the national licence having been held for at least a year). A valid licence and credit card are required for local bookings.

Car breakdown A warning triangle must be placed 50m behind the car in case of breakdown. On *autoroutes* emergency telephones are located every 2km, with breakdown services provided by nearby garages 24 hours a day, seven days a week (including holidays). Tow and repair rates are fixed by the government, and carry a 25 per cent surcharge at night and on Saturdays, Sundays and holidays. These rates are shown on the emergency telephones, and start at around 345 francs (430 francs with surcharge).

Public transport Air Air Inter, the French domestic airline, has frequent flights connecting Paris with local air-

❑ SNCF discount rail passes include:

Eurodomino: coupons for 3, 5 or 10 days' travel within one month, must be bought outside France.

Carrissimo: For under-26-year-olds.

Carte Couple: Half-price for second person on some trains.

Carte Vermeil: For over-60-year-olds, half-price on some trains.

Carte Kiwi: Family card, gives discount for parents and other children. ❑

ports such as Cannes, Toulon, Fréjus and Nîmes, as well as Nice and Marseille. Information from Air France or travel agents.

Rail The main SNCF line links towns in the Rhône valley with Marseille and coastal resorts. Trains are clean, efficient, reliable and an excellent way of avoiding summer traffic along the coast (the Metrazur service links Riviera resorts with trains at half-hourly intervals in peak season). All tickets must be date stamped in the orange machines on station platforms, and you will face a surcharge if you forget to *compostez votre billet*.

Information from tourist offices or SNCF stations (tel: Nice 04 93 87 50

Parking can be a problem in the coastal resorts

50; Marseille and Avignon 04 36 35 35 35 (premium rate)).

There is a wonderful narrow-gauge railway which winds up through 151km of mountain scenery from Nice to Digne, operated by the Chemins de Fer de la Provence (tel: 04 93 82 10 17).

Bus The bus network is not brilliant. Where they exist at all, buses in rural areas are geared to school runs and market days. Between towns and cities, they tend to duplicate the rail services and are not necessarily cheaper or faster. In addition, timetables are not co-ordinated because services are run by so many different private companies. Most large towns have a *gare routière* (coach station), usually near the railway station. SNCF also operates buses to various places on the rail routes where trains no longer stop.

❑ The most efficient bus network in Provence is in Nice, where computerised signboards at every bus-stop let you know the exact time of arrival of your service. ❑

Keep to the right (*serrez à droite*). The most common cause of confusion (and accidents) is the rule of giving priority to traffic coming from the right (*priorité à droite*) at any intersection unless indicated otherwise. It does not matter how small the side-turning is, you must give way. In any town, treat junctions with the utmost caution. On main roads outside towns main roads usually have priority – which is indicated by roadsigns with a yellow diamond or marked *passage protégé*. Beware a yellow diamond crossed-out, which signals that you do not have right of way. On roundabouts traffic already on the roundabout has priority.

In rural areas driving behaviour is normally fairly sedate; the main hazard in small villages is locals suddenly stopping their cars in the middle of the road to lean out of the window and talk to friends in cars coming the other way. On the Côte d'Azur different standards apply, with tempers and the blare of car horns reaching a crescendo in July and August, which probably equals Parisian driving conditions (possibly because many of them are Parisians).

In villages and small towns many streets are now closed off to cars *sauf riverains* (except for residents). Although these restrictions can usually be disregarded out of season, in peak season only foolish drivers would ignore them. Pay attention to signs in village centres indicating market days – you will not be popular if you leave your car overnight and block stallholders setting up in the early hours.

Parking Finding somewhere to park can be a headache in peak months although most large towns have sufficient underground car parking (follow the blue 'P' signs). If you lose your car park ticket be warned that you will need to produce your vehicle registration document to exit (they will reluctantly let foreigners off the hook if you do not have it with you) as well as having to pay the full day price. If you can find a space, on-street parking is cheaper for short periods in *stationement paymant* zones (you will need change for the ticket machines).

Petrol stations These are plentiful, and most sell unleaded petrol (*sans plomb*). However, be careful on weekends (many are closed on Sundays) and in mountainous areas, where there are far fewer of them.

Rules and regulations Speed limits are 130kph (80mph) on the *autoroutes*, 110kph (68mph) on dual carriage-

Old-style road markers even give the altitude

ways, 90kph (56mph) on other roads and 50kph (31mph) in urban areas. These limits are lower in poor weather conditions. Signs saying *Rappel* (reminder) mean that the speed restriction has not ended.

Fines for speeding or other violations are levied on the spot, with only cash or a cheque drawn on a French bank account accepted: the minimum fine for speeding is 900 francs and for exceeding the drink/drive limit 900 to 39000 francs.

Accidents If you are involved in an accident take the registration number of the other car and exchange insurance details with the other driver: try and take the names and addresses of witnesses. Once you have contacted the police, you will be required to fill in a statement (a *constant aimable*), but if your written French is not good enough to do this you will have to find someone to translate.

Autoroutes The *autoroutes à péage* generally offer safe, hassle-free driving (at a price, except for limited stretches near urban areas which are free) and service stations are plentiful – and are obliged to provide free tyre checks, oil checks and windscreen washes in the interests of motorway safety. Most have small

❑ To tell whether you should be honking someone or politely waiting, local car registration codes are:
Vaucluse: 84
Bouches-du-Rhône: 13
Var: 83
Alpes de Haute-Provence: 04
Alpes-Maritimes: 06 ❑

supermarkets (where you can buy everything from snacks to souvenirs) and usually also a café/restaurant; some provide free showers (ask for the key at the cash desk), which is a great way of freshening up during a long drive. Payments at motorway toll booths can be made using credit cards; if you are planning multiple trips you can apply for the *Carte Voie Libre*, which can only be used on *autoroutes*.

To avoid holiday weekends and regular traffic jams a leaflet obtainable from *autoroute* offices lists all the seasonal blockages, or you can call the Centre d'Information Routière (tel: 04 91 78 78 78 for Provence, open 24 hours).

Tollbooths (péages) *on an autoroute*

257

258

Media Local papers include *La Marseillaise*, *Le Provençal*, *Le Méridional*, *Var-Matin* and *Nice-Matin*. All these carry details on local events and entertainment. Hotels usually carry copies of freesheets such as the monthly *Farandole* or the weekly *Semaine des Spectacles,* which cover exhibitions and events. The *Riviera Reporter* serves the expatriate community on the coast, but one of the best magazines is the quarterly *Vivre en Provence,* which has colour features on a wide range of regional topics. The *International Herald Tribune* is widely available, as are London newspapers and other foreign publications, in most big towns and holiday resorts.

French television relies heavily on game shows and foreign films. There is a wide selection of radio stations including France Inter (1829 long wave), which has English-language news bulletins twice daily in summer. At the eastern end of the coast Radio Riviera (104FM) broadcasts in English. BBC World Service and Voice of America can be picked up.

Post Offices Known as the *PTT* (*Poste et Telecommunications*), *Bureau de Poste* or simply *la Poste,* post offices (which deal with both telephone and mail services) are

The post is usually efficient

usually open 8am–7pm weekdays, 8am–noon Saturdays in large towns; in villages they may have shorter hours and close for lunch. The range of services includes selling stamps and phonecards, *poste restante,* and in some cases fax-sending and

cheque-cashing facilities. Stamps (*timbres de poste*) can also be bought in tobacconists' kiosks (*tabacs*).

Telephone and fax In 1996 all telephone numbers in France changed to ten digits. There are now five telephone regions in the country. All numbers in Paris and the Île de France begin with 01; all the areas covered in this book (apart from Monaco) start with 04. Monaco has its own international code 00 377, but its numbers have not otherwise been changed. Most public phone booths (*cabines*) are now card-operated, and phonecards (*telecartes*) can be bought in post offices, *tabacs*, and newsagents in denominations of 40.60 (50 units) or 97.50 (120 units).

Some post offices and major hotels offer fax facilities, but it is cheaper to use a newsagent or other fax bureaux.

Language guide
English is spoken by many people involved in tourism (at campsites, hotels, etc.) and in the smarter shops and restaurants. In rural areas this is less often the case, and your attempts at French will be appreciated – even if you master only '*Bonjour*', '*monsieur*', '*madame*' and '*s'il vous plaît*'.

Basic vocabulary

yes	oui
no	non
hello/good morning	bonjour
good evening	bonsoir
goodbye	au revoir
please	s'il vous plaît
how are you?	comment allez-vous?
thank you (very much)	merci (beaucoup)
sorry	pardon/excusez moi
I understand	je comprends
I do not understand	je ne comprends pas
I don't know	je ne sais pas
please help me	aidez-moi, s'il vous plaît
help!	au secours!
toilets	les toilettes
no smoking	défense de fumer
entrance	entrée
exit	sortie
at what time?	à quelle heure?
today	aujourd'hui
tomorrow	demain

yesterday	hier	behind	derrière
the morning	le matin	in front of	devant
the afternoon	l'après midi	opposite	en face de
the evening	le soir	before	avant
the night	le nuit	after	après
now	maintenant		
later	plus tard	**Numbers**	
closed	fermé	one	un/une
open	ouvert	two	deux
prohibited	interdit	three	trois
when?	quand?	four	quatre
why?	pourquoi?	five	cinq
with	avec	six	six
without	sans	seven	sept
big	grand	eight	huit
small	petit	nine	neuf
good	bon	ten	dix
bad	mauvais	eleven	onze
hot	chaud	twelve	douze
cold	froid	twenty	vingt
cheap	bon marché	fifty	cinquante
expensive	cher	one hundred	cent
		one thousand	mille

259

Shopping

shops	les magasins
market	le marché
bakery	la boulangerie
chemist	la pharmacie
food shop	l'alimentation
butcher	la boucherie
newsagents/stationers	la libraire
supermarket	le supermarché
I would like	je voudrais…
this one	ceci
that one	cela
that's enough	ça suffit
how much…?	combien…?

Days of the week

Monday	lundi
Tuesday	mardi
Wednesday	mercredi
Thursday	jeudi
Friday	vendredi
Saturday	samedi
Sunday	dimanche

Eating and drinking

to eat	manger
to drink	boire
breakfast	le petit déjeuner
lunch	le déjeuner
dinner	le diner
coffee/tea	café/thé
beer (draught)	une bière (pression)
wine (white/red)	le vin (rouge/blanc)
wine list	la carte des vins
the bill, please	l'addition, s'il vous plaît

A public cardphone box

Directions

where is…?	où se trouve…?
left	à gauche
right	à droite
near/not far	près/pas loin
far	loin
straight on	tout droit
there	là

Provence offers an enormous variety of things to buy, ranging from local produce such as olives and garlic to handicrafts or brightly printed clothes. Provençal markets are not to be missed (local tourist offices can provide lists of nearby market days) and often feature crafts alongside traditional products such as honey, cheeses and olive oil.

Clothes Block-print fabrics were first produced in Provence in the 17th century after the import of cheap Indian prints was banned: Provençals responded by producing their own cotton prints, still known today as *indiennes*. These colourful prints can either be bought by the length or ready-made into skirts, tops, scarves or furnishing items. The two most famous retail chains for traditional prints are Souleiado and Les Olivades, both of which have numerous outlets throughout Provence.

Superb traditional costumes, flamboyant waistcoats, *gardians*' jackets and hats and other items can be found at Les Indiennes de Nîmes/Mistral (4 rue Collège du Roure, Avignon) and Bandido (12 rue Pasteur, Aigues-Mortes). Provençal

and Camarguais clothes and fabrics can also be found at L'Arlesienne (12 rue du Président Wilson, Arles).

Haute couture boutiques are thick on the ground in Monte-Carlo and Cannes, with a fair smattering in Nice and St-Tropez. Many of the Riviera hill villages also have designer boutiques hidden away down their narrow streets.

Clothes are not cheap in France, but if you need something essential then large markets (such as in Toulon, Avignon and elsewhere) are the best place to look.

Crafts The small figurines known as *santons* are one of the most typical traditional crafts. Local tourist offices can provide addresses of *santonniers*; well-known workshops include those of Sylvette Amy (Aubagne), Atelier Fouque (Aix), Santons Reboulins (l'Isle-sur-la-Sorgue), Elizabeth Ferriol (Arles) and the Atelier Carbonel (Marseille).

Olive-wood carvings can be found in most souvenir shops and basketry, cork bowls and hand-woven woollen garments are also popular. Hundreds of different kinds of pipes are sold in Cogolin, and traditional handmade paper products in Fontaine-de-Vaucluse.

Souvenirs of Provence

Herbs, scents and soaps Small sachets of herbs de Provence and pot-pourri are ubiquitous, although a much wider selection of dried and fresh herbs and herbal products is available at L'Herbier de Provence (34 blvd Victor Hugo, St-Rémy-de-Provence), La Parfumerie Artisanale de St-Rémy-de-Provence (34 blvd Mirabeau, St-Rémy), Le Musée des Aromes et du Parfum (near Graveson) and the Maison de la Lavande (58 blvd Gassendi, Digne). All the perfume factories in Grasse have retail outlets.

Marseille soap was once exported worldwide, with the industry reaching its peak in the 17th century. With the advent of washing powders manufacturing declined, but it is now enjoying a revival thanks to the pure, biodegradable properties of the soaps (which are often scented with mountain herbs). Beautifully packaged Marseille soaps (as well as bath oils, perfumes and herbal essences) are available at the Éco-Musée du Savon (9km from Mane at Les Fours à Chaux, Volx, in the Alpes de Haute-Provence). Another traditional manufacturer is Rampal-Patou (71 rue Félix-Pyat, Salon; visits by appointment, tel: 04 90 56 07 28).

Pottery, ceramics and glassware Practically every *village perché* has its share of pottery shops, with the quality varying widely and prices

Local produce

which are in many cases unjustified. However, you can often find original pieces that are well worth the investment. Handcrafted enamelled tiles can be found at the Établissements Vernin (Les Carreaux d'Apt, le Pont Julien, Bonnieux); good-value rustic cookware is available at the Poterie Provençale (avenue des Goms, Aubagne).

Moustiers-Ste-Marie is the Provençal capital for faïences (fine, glazed ceramics) and among the more reputable establishments are Michèle Blanc, Bondil à Moustiers, Lallier à Moustiers, le Grillon and Ségriès (all within the village centre).

Finally, an extensive range of hand-blown glassware is on sale at the Verrerie de Biot (chemin des Combes, Biot).

❏ Provence is a great place for the sweet toothed, with candied fruits in Apt, *calissons* (almond biscuits) in Aix, nougat in Vence, *berlingots* (mint-flavoured caramels) in Carpentras, and *marrons glacés* (glazed chestnuts) in Collobrières. The best jam in Provence is the sensational Les Merveilles range, which includes bilberry, black fig, apricot and plum. ❏

Provence has a well-developed infrastructure providing first-rate facilities for outdoor activities and sports. As well as sports listed here, you can also find locations for hang-gliding, gliding, water skiing, scuba-diving and, of course, skiing.

Canoeing and kayaking There are numerous locations for canoeing and kayaking, the two most spectacular of which are the Grand Cañon du Verdon and the Ubaye valley in the

Alpes de Haute-Provence, where they also organise 'hydrospeed' (white-water swimming with wet suit and floats). Canoeing is also possible on the Durance and the Sorgue.

Note that many rivers in Provence are harnessed to hydroelectric power schemes and therefore subject to sudden changes in water level as barrages are opened or closed: always seek local advice before setting off on your own.

Climbing The top climbing regions are the Grand Cañon du Verdon, the Calanques of Cassis, and the

Bicycles can be hired in many areas

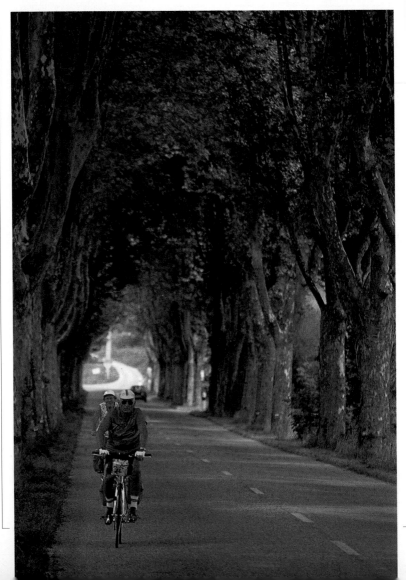

Dentelles of Montmirail and the cliffs at Buoux in the Vaucluse. Contact either the Club Alpine Français or the Fédération Française de la Montagne et de l'Escalade, both at 14 avenue Mirabeau, 06000 Nice (tel: 04 93 62 59 99).

Cycling The French have always been keen cyclists and they have taken to mountain bikes (called VTT – *Vehicules Tout Terrain*) like ducks to water. Daily or weekly rentals are available in coastal resorts as well as the more spectacular (and demanding) mountain areas. Many of the long-distance hiking paths (see below) have now been waymarked with a VTT logo indicating permitted routes (in some forestry areas and fragile environments VTT is prohibited).

One of the most stunning areas near the coast is the Esterel *massif*, which has 90km of VTT tracks; some of the most extensive trails are in the Alpes de Haute-Provence, and a colour brochure in English detailing biking tours of several days' duration, plus guides and hire shops, is available from the Comité Départemental du Tourisme, 19 rue du Dr Honnorat, 04000 Digne-les-Bains (tel: 04 92 31 57 29).

Golf Golfers are spoilt for choice in Provence with dozens of courses to play on – particularly on the coast. Some of the best are the Golf de Fregate near Bandol, the Golf d'Esterel near Fréjus (designed by Robert Trent Jones), Golf de Ste-Maxime (a challenging new course), the Golf de Fuveau in the Bouches-du-Rhône (one of the biggest courses in Europe), and the prestigious Pont Royal at Mallemort in the Lubéron.

Other good courses include those at Cannes, Mandelieu, Ste-Baume and Barbaroux.

Full details are obtainable from the Ligue de Golf de Provence-Alpes-Côte d'Azur, Domaine de Riquetti, 13290 les Milles (tel: 04 42 39 86 83).

Hiking There is a comprehensive network of hiking trails throughout Provence, starting with the long-distance footpaths, the *sentiers de grande randonnée* (known as GRs for short), which criss-cross the mountains and coastal hinterland. Each GR is described in a detailed *Topoguide*, which is published by the Comité National des Sentiers de Grande Randonnée (8 ave Marceau, Paris) and is available in local bookshops.

National and regional parks also have their own signposted trails, and guides can usually be hired if required (details from local tourist offices).

Horse-riding Particularly popular in the Camargue, although there are many short- and long-distance trails throughout Provence and numerous *centres équestres* where you can hire horses (as well as *gîtes* and *relais équestres* which provide board and lodging as well). Association Camarguaise du Tourisme Équestre, Centre de Gines, Pont de Gau, Stes-Maries (tel: 04 90 97 86 32).

Sailing With 125 ports and marinas along 833km of coastline, Provence offers plenty of opportunities for the nautically inclined. Most ports and marinas have sailing schools and boats for hire. For a complete list of marina facilities write to: Office Régional de la Mer, CMCI, 2 rue Henri-Barbusse, 13001 Marseille.

Sailing (as well as water skiing and windsurfing) is also popular on the big mountain lakes of the Alpes de Haute-Provence such as Lac de Quinson, Lac du Castillon and Lac de Serre-Ponçon. For details contact the Comité Departmental de Voile des Alpes de Haute-Provence, 322 les Aliziers, 04100 Manosque (tel: 04 92 77 15 25).

Windsurfing With the benefit of the *mistral*, which gusts at over 100km an hour, it is perhaps not surprising that world windsurfing records have been broken here; but beginners will also find plenty of gentler spots along the coast. Two world-class locations are les Stes-Maries-de-la-Mer and l'Almanarre near Hyères, both of which have staged championship events. Boards can be hired in many resorts, with week-long courses costing around 500 francs.

Crime and police Although crime gangs (the *milieu*) operate in Marseille and on the Côte d'Azur, you are unlikely to be affected unless you are in the seriously rich category and a target for a jewel-heist. The most common causes of theft from unfortunate tourists are pickpockets and car break-ins.

Always leave valuables locked up or in the hotel safe, and be particularly careful when parking at remote tourist spots where car break-ins are common – never leave cameras or valuables in your car. Burglars tend to

insurance, carry traveller's cheques rather than cash, and keep a separate record of credit card numbers, cheque numbers and emergency phone numbers for cancelling credit cards and travellers' cheques.

If you are the victim of a theft report it to the nearest *gendarmerie* and keep a copy of the statement if you intend to claim on your insurance.

Police In cities and towns police duties are the responsibility of the Police Municipale whilst the Gendarmes (part of the national

Pharmacists will give first aid

target rented villas: always secure the house at night or if going out, and do not leave anything on the terrace overnight – thieves often terrace-hop between villas to see what they can quickly pick up.

In the big cities, thefts from cars waiting at traffic lights are becoming common (the thieves escape at high speed on their motorbikes): don't leave valuables on the back seat, and keep doors locked.

Make sure you have adequate travel

police force) cover smaller places and the countryside. You are unlikely to encounter the fearsome CRS (*Compagnies Républicains de Securité*), a flying squad who deal with riots and civil unrest, although strangely they also look after security on public beaches. The *Garde Mobile* or *Police de la Route* look after highway security.

Embassies and consulates
Embassies in Paris
UK: 16 rue d'Anjou, 75008 (tel: 01 42 66 91 42).

US: 2 rue St-Florentin, 75001 (tel: 01 42 96 14 88).
Canada: 35 ave Montaigne, 75008 (tel: 01 47 23 01 01).

Consulates in Provence
UK: 24 ave du Prado, 13006 Marseille (tel: 04 91 15 72 10).
US: 31 rue Maréchal Joffre, 06000 Nice (tel: 04 93 88 89 55).

Emergency telephone numbers
Police: 17
Fire (*sapeurs pompiers*): 18
Ambulance: 15

❏ The French passion for wild mushrooms means that inevitably dozens of people fall ill or die every year eating poisonous varieties: during the autumn, pharmacists' windows display mushroom identification data to help prevent this, and anyone can take in a mushroom so that the pharmacist can check if it is an edible variety. ❏

Lost property
Serious losses should be reported to the police (keep a copy of the statement for your insurance). Lost passports should be reported to the

nearest embassy or consulate (see left), who will be able to issue emergency documents. Report loss of credit cards and travellers' cheques to the relevant company immediately.

Health and pharmacies
France does not require any vaccinations, and health care standards are high. Water is safe everywhere except for taps marked *eau non potable*.

All EU citizens are entitled to reciprocal health care (British citizens should bring with them form E111, which allows you to claim back expenses: apply at main post offices in Britain).

If you need a doctor urgently, contact SOS Médecins (telephone numbers are in the directory under *Urgences* or call directory enquiries, tel: 12). Otherwise, pharmacies can provide addresses.

Pharmacists (marked by a green cross) are trained to administer first aid and can also dispense advice on minor ailments. On weekends or holidays, pharmacies operate on a rota basis (addresses are posted in the window or in local papers) or you can call the *gendarmerie* for the nearest *pharmacie de garde* (duty chemist).

A local resident finds time for a pause in the sunshine

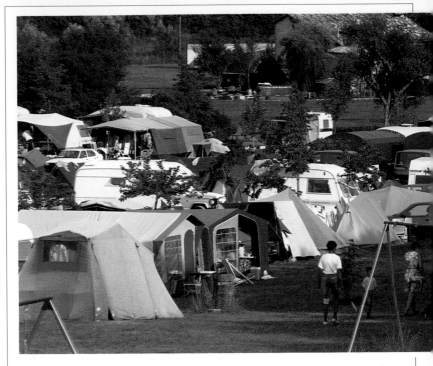

Campsites in popular areas can be crowded

Camping Camping is extremely popular in Provence, particularly amongst the French themselves. Campsites are well organised and graded from one to four stars depending on the facilities provided. The best have swimming pools, sports facilities, supermarkets or shops, and a restaurant/bar.

Camping municipals are the most basic, run by local authorities and found in nearly every town; other possibilities include *camping à la ferme*, where you can pitch your tent on farmland, although generally there will be no facilities. Camping outside recognised sites (*camping sauvage*) is sometimes possible but often forbidden (*interdit*) by local authorities (always check with the town hall first). Never camp in the forests in summer because of the fire risk.

In July and August campsites on the Côte d'Azur are notoriously over-crowded (and can be insanitary). Always phone ahead to check space availability.

Lists of campsites are available from local tourist offices or French Government Tourist Offices (in the UK, send a £1 stamp and a self-addressed envelope to: FGTO, 178 Piccadilly, London W1V 0AL, tel: (0891) 244123)).

Pre-booked camping packages are an increasingly popular option for budget holidays. UK holiday firms include: Eurocamp Travel, tel: (01565) 626262; Eurosites, tel: (01706) 830888; Canvas Holidays, tel: (01383) 621000; Keycamp Holidays, tel: (0181) 395 4000.

Self-catering There are numerous options for self-catering in Provence, ranging from isolated *mas* (farm-houses) to beach apartments and grand villas on the Côte d'Azur. Good value self-catering in or near small country villages is offered by the Gîtes de France organisation, with properties ranging from village houses to converted farm outbuildings or country cottages. Membership will provide you with a full list of properties and discount offers on ferry crossings (in the UK, contact Gîtes de France Ltd, 178 Piccadilly, London W1V 0AV, tel:

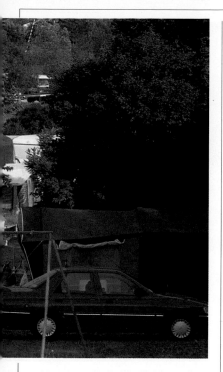

❑ There are approximately 780 campsites in Provence, providing a total of around 86,000 individual sites with room for 260,000 people. The majority are in the Var (321), followed by Alpes-Maritimes (120), Alpes de Haute-Provence (157), Bouches-du-Rhône (83) and Vaucluse (100). In France as a whole there are over 9,000 campsites. ❑

Jeunesse (27 rue Pajol, 75018 Paris, tel: 01 44 89 87 27). Some places also have more comfortable accommodation in *Foyers des Jeunes Travelleurs/euses,* which usually provide individual rooms.

For discounts on museum admissions, entertainments and public transport anyone under 26 can apply for a special youth card (*Carte Jeune*); details at tourist offices or post offices.

Visitors with disabilities France is no better or worse than other EU countries in providing access facilities for travellers with disabilities, although the situation is gradually improving and ramps and other forms of access are now provided at many museums and tourist sites (nearly all new museums and public buildings are wheelchair-friendly). There are accessible hotels in most major towns and resorts. Public transport is difficult; Hertz is the only car hire company to offer rental cars with hand controls.

Information on accommodation, transport and other topics is covered in a booklet, *Touristes quand même*, available from the bigger tourist offices or from the Comité National Française de Liaison pour la Réadaption des Handicapés, 28 boulevard Raspail, 75007 Paris (tel: 01 45 48 90 13). The red *Guide Michelin* lists hotels with facilities for the handicapped.

In the UK, information on all aspects of disabled travel is available from RADAR (The Royal Association for Disability and Rehabilitation), Unit 12, City Forum, 250 City Road, London

(0171) 408 1343; membership £3).

Discounts on flights or ferries can sometimes also be arranged through specialised accommodation agencies such as the following:

Allez France, 27/29 West Street, Storrington, West Sussex RH20 4DZ (tel: 01903 742345).
French Life Holidays, 26 Church Road, Hosforth, Leeds LS18 5LG (tel: 01132 390077).
The Villa Centre, 175 Selsdon Park Road, South Croydon CR2 8JJ (tel: 0181 651 1231).
Holiday France, 3 Lower Camden Place, Bath BA1 5JJ (tel: 01449 737678).
Vacances en Campagne, Bignor, Pulborough, West Sussex RH20 1QD (tel: 01798 869433).

Student and youth accommodation Budget accommodation is available in dormitory rooms in youth hostels (*Auberges de Jeunesse*) in most towns; contact your home branch of the International Youth Hostel Federation (IYHF) or the Fédération Unie des Auberges de

Nice Airport is one of the busiest in France

EC1V 8AF (tel: 0171 250 3222) or Holiday Care Service, Imperial Buildings, Victoria Road, Horley, Surrey RH6 7PZ (tel: 01293 774535).

Opening times Lunch is a serious business in Provence – almost every-thing closes for two hours at mid-day. Normal working hours are 8am–noon, 2–6pm. Food shops are usually open at 7.30am, closing at lunchtime and not reopening in some cases until 3 or 4pm but they then stay open until 7.30 or 8pm. Shops and supermarkets in large towns and resorts often don't close in the lunch hour, but may not open until 10am. Sunday and Monday (or sometimes Tuesday) are the standard closing days, although food shops are usually open on Sunday mornings until noon. Food markets (weekly in small villages, daily in the cities) operate mornings only.

Museums and monuments are normally open from 9 or 10am to noon, then 2 or 3pm to 5 or 6pm depending on the season. The longer hours are during the summer (mid-May or early June until September), when some also remain open over lunchtime. Closing days are usually Monday (for municipal museums) or Tuesday (national museums and monuments), sometimes both. Many tourist sights close altogether during

November, with some of the smaller ones staying closed throughout the winter.

Churches and cathedrals are usually open for tourists all day except during services, although a handful spurn tourists altogether and are only open during Mass (sometimes you can request the key from the priest's house, the *presbytère*, near by).

On national holidays (see page 253) shops, banks and businesses are closed; some museums stay open (apart from Christmas Day and New Year's Day) and you can be sure that restaurants will usually be open.

Places of worship Nearly every town or village has a Catholic church, with the times of Mass usually pinned on the door. Anglican churches with English-language services are found in Nice, St-Raphaël and Menton. There are synagogues in Avignon, Carpentras, Nice and Cavaillon, and Greek and Russian Orthodox churches in Nice.

Toilets There is no such thing as a free pee in France, since you either have to pay to use one of the coin-operated, self-cleansing public toilets found on the streets or buy a coffee or drink to use the facilities in a bar or café – you are not obliged to, but signs indicating that the WC is *strictement réserve pour la clientèle* indicate that it's frowned on not to do so. Most of the horrors of French hygiene (or lack of it) have disappeared, but you do still come across old-fashioned type toilets with footrests where you have to squat. Public toilets (other than the automatic ones) usually have a dish for small change. Women's are labelled *Dames*, men's *Hommes* or *Messieurs*. If you have to ask, request the WC (pronounced ve-se).

Electricity Usually 220V, with double, round-pin wall sockets; adaptors are necessary for foreign appliances. In some remote areas the supply is still 110V.

Women travellers Women travellers should take all the normal precautions if travelling alone and hitchhiking is not recommended. You will probably find the French courteous and charming and it is quite normal to be offered a drink without the expectation that it will lead any further than a pleasant chat. It may sound like a cliché but it's none the less true that practically the only time male French drivers stop at pedestrian crossings is so that they can watch a woman cross. Topless bathing is perfectly acceptable and doesn't provoke harassment.

Tourist offices
Overseas Overseas branches of the French Government Tourist Office can provide reams of information on every aspect of travelling in France. However, getting through by telephone (particularly in London) is often a nightmare.

● Australia: Maison de la France, BNP Building, 12th Floor, 12 Castlereagh Street, Sydney, NSW 2000 (tel: 02 9231 5244).

● Canada: Maison de la France, 1981 Avenue McGill College, Suite 490, Montreal, Quebec H3A 2W9 (tel: 514 288 4264).

● Ireland: Maison de la France, 35 Lower Abbey Street, Dublin 1 (tel: 01 703 40 46).

● UK: Maison de la France, 178 Piccadilly, London W1V 0AL (tel: (0891) 244123 (premium rate service).

CONVERSION CHARTS

FROM	TO	MULTIPLY BY
Inches	Centimetres	2.54
Centimetres	Inches	0.3937
Feet	Metres	0.3048
Metres	Feet	3.2810
Yards	Metres	0.9144
Metres	Yards	1.0940
Miles	Kilometres	1.6090
Kilometres	Miles	0.6214
Acres	Hectares	0.4047
Hectares	Acres	2.4710
Gallons	Litres	4.5460
Litres	Gallons	0.2200
Ounces	Grams	28.35
Grams	Ounces	0.0353
Pounds	Grams	453.6
Grams	Pounds	0.0022
Pounds	Kilograms	0.4536
Kilograms	Pounds	2.205
Tons	Tonnes	1.0160
Tonnes	Tons	0.9842

MEN'S SUITS

UK	36	38	40	42	44	46	48
Rest of Europe	46	48	50	52	54	56	58
US	36	38	40	42	44	46	48

DRESS SIZES

UK	8	10	12	14	16	18
France	36	38	40	42	44	46
Italy	38	40	42	44	46	48
Rest of Europe	34	36	38	40	42	44
US	6	8	10	12	14	16

MEN'S SHIRTS

UK	14	14.5	15	15.5	16	16.5	17
Rest of Europe	36	37	38	39/40	41	42	43
US	14	14.5	15	15.5	16	16.5	17

MEN'S SHOES

UK	7	7.5	8.5	9.5	10.5	11
Rest of Europe	41	42	43	44	45	46
US	8	8.5	9.5	10.5	11.5	12

WOMEN'S SHOES

UK	4.5	5	5.5	6	6.5	7
Rest of Europe	38	38	39	39	40	41
US	6	6.5	7	7.5	8	8.5

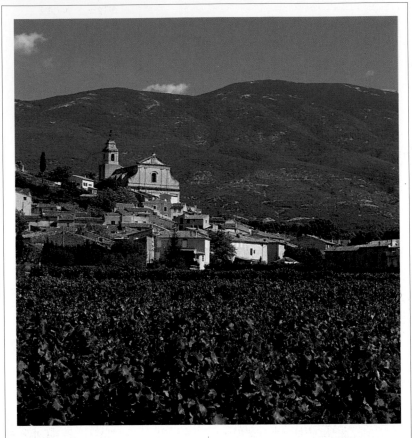

● USA: Maison de la France, 444 Madison Avenue, New York NY 10022 (tel: 212 838 7800).

In Provence Tourist offices are called either *Offices du Tourisme* or *Syndicats d'Initiatives* (which are smaller and may not open every day). Larger towns have tourist offices called *Accueil de France* (which can also make hotel bookings for personal callers on the same day or up to eight days in advance). The quality of information available varies widely from office to office, and nearly all of them have the annoying habit of keeping some brochures under the counter instead of on open display (so if you are not aware of the existence of something before you go in, you are unlikely to leave with the relevant material).

The main tourist offices in Provence are:

A Provençal view, with Mont Ventoux in the background

Aix-en-Provence: 2 place Général de Gaulle (tel: 04 42 16 11 61; fax: 04 42 16 11 62)
Arles: 35 place de la République (tel: 04 90 18 41 20; fax: 04 90 93 17 17)
Avignon: 41 cours Jean-Jaurès (tel: 04 90 82 65 11; fax: 04 90 82 95 03)
Cannes: Palais des Festivals (tel: 04 93 39 24 53; fax: 04 92 99 84 23)
Digne-les-Bains: le Rond-Pont (tel: 04 92 31 42 73; fax: 04 92 32 27 24)
Fréjus: 325 rue Jean-Jaurès (tel: 04 94 17 19 19; fax: 04 94 53 87 83)
Marseille: 4 la Canabière (tel: 04 91 13 89 00; fax: 04 91 13 89 20)
Nice: Acropolis, Esplanade Kennedy (tel: 04 93 87 07 07; fax: 04 93 92 82 98)
Nîmes: 6 rue Auguste (tel: 04 66 67 29 11; fax: 04 66 21 81 04)
Toulon: place Raimu (tel: 04 94 18 53 00; fax: 04 94 18 53 09).

HOTELS AND RESTAURANTS

ACCOMMODATION

The following hotels have been divided into three price categories:

- **budget (£)**
- **moderate (££)**
- **expensive (£££)**

VAUCLUSE

Ansouis

Le Jardin d'Ansouis (£) rue du Petit Portail, 84240 (tel: 04 90 09 89 27). Small, friendly *chambre d'hôte* with rooms overlooking the garden, where lunch and tea (including tempting home-made *pâtisseries* and ice-creams) are served.

Apt

Auberge du Lubéron (££–£££) 17 quai Léon Sagy, 84400 (tel: 04 90 74 12 50). Conveniently located on the river bank – the best hotel in Apt.

Avignon

Hôtel de l'Angeleterre (£–££) 29 boulevard Raspail, 84000 (tel: 04 90 86 34 31). Good-sized rooms, good value in a quiet location.
Hôtel d'Europe (£££) 12 place Crillon, 84000 (tel: 04 90 82 66 92). Royalty and celebrities by the dozen have all enjoyed the first-class service and antique-furnished rooms in Avignon's smartest hotel.
Hôtel Mignon (££) 12 rue Joseph Vernet, 84000 (tel: 04 90 82 17 30). As the name (Hotel Dainty) implies, cutely decorated rooms; reasonable prices.
Hôtel de Mons (££) 5 rue de Mons, 84000 (tel: 04 90 82 57 16). Converted from a 13th-century chapel; comfortable and central.
Hôtel du Palais des Papes (££–£££) 1 rue Gérard Philippe, 84000 (tel: 04 90 86 04 13). Traditional furnishings but with all mod cons, a popular restaurant and a great view of the Palais des Papes.
Hôtel Provençal (££) 13 rue Joseph Vernet, 84000 (tel: 04 90 85 25 24). Centrally located.

Carpentras

Hôtel le Coq Hardi (££) 36 place de la Marotte, 84200 (tel: 04 90 63 00 35). Modern hotel but well-situated in the centre of town, with a pleasant terrace.
Hôtel Le Fiacre (££) 153 rue Vigne, 84200 (tel: 04 90 63 03 15). Housed in an elegant 18th-century mansion with an attractive courtyard. Good value.
Hôtel du Théâtre (£) 7 boulevard Albin Durand, 84200 (tel: 04 90 63 02 90). Unpretentious and friendly; budget prices for the town centre.

Cavaillon

Hôtel du Parc (££–£££) 40 place Francois Tourel, 84300 (tel: 04 90 71 57 78). Opposite the *arc de triomphe*; old-fashioned but comfortable.

Fontaine-de-Vaucluse

Hôtel le Château (££) quartier Petit Place, 84800 (tel: 04 90 20 31 54). Lovely situation on the riverbank, with reasonable rates and a dining terrace over the river.
Hôtel du Parc (££) les Bourgades, 84800 (tel: 04 90 20 31 57). Also within earshot of the river; reasonable prices for the location.

Gordes

Auberge de Carcarille (££–£££) les Gervais, 84220 (tel: 04 90 72 02 63). Old restored *mas* just outside of town in a peaceful location. Two pools.
Hôtel la Mayanelle (£££) rue de la Combe, 84220 (tel: 04 90 72 00 48). Stylish, comfortable rooms; fabulous views from the terrace.

L'Isle-sur-la-Sorgue

Hôtel Araxe (£££) route d'Apt, 84800 (tel: 04 90 38 40 00). Smart and well-run hotel complex, in extensive grounds leading down to the river. Two pools.
Le Bassin (££) avenue du Général de Gaulle, 84800 (tel: 04 90 38 03 16). Reasonable value in the centre of town – request a room with a view over the river.
Hôtel Restaurant Le Pescador (££) le Partage des Eaux, 84800 (tel: 04 90 38 09 69). Good location next to the weir where the Sorgue divides. Eight rooms (booking essential).

Malaucène

Hôtel Origan (££) Cours des Isnards, 84340 (tel: 04 90 65 27 08). Clean and friendly hotel right on the main street.

Orange

Hôtel Arcôtel (£) 8 place aux Herbes, 84100 (tel: 04 90 34 09 23). Centrally situated; cheap.
Hôtel Arène (£££) place de Langes, 84100 (tel: 04 90 34 10 95). Overlooking a small, quiet square in the heart of town, with a long-standing reputation as Orange's finest hotel.
Hôtel Cigaloun (££) 4 rue Caristie, 84100 (tel: 04 90 34 10 07). Recently renovated, straight-forward rooms, in the heart of town.
Hôtel de la Gare (£) 60 avenue Frédéric Mistral, 84100 (tel: 04 90 34 00 23). Ten minutes' walk from the centre, but reasonable prices.
Hôtel Louvre et Terminus (£) 89 avenue Frédéric Mistral, 84100 (tel: 04 90 34 10 08). Opposite the above; also reasonable.

Vaison-la-Romaine

Hostellerie Le Beffroi (£££) rue de l'Évêché, 84110 (tel: 04 90 36 04 71). Housed in a lovely old 16th-century building in the narrow streets of the *haute ville*; not cheap, but well worth it for the atmosphere.
Hôtel Burrhus (££) place Montfort, 84110 (tel: 04 90 36 00 11). Comfortably furnished rooms right in the heart of town.
Hôtel Restaurant du Théâtre Romain (£–££) avenue Général de Gaulle, 84110 (tel: 04 90 28 71 98). Simply furnished rooms; a good budget choice.

BOUCHES-DU-RHÔNE

Aix

Hôtel des Augustins (£££) 3 rue de la Masse, 13100 (tel: 04 42 27 28 59). Recently renovated to a very high standard, the hotel is housed inside the 15th-century Convent of Grand Augustins right in the heart of town. The spacious and tastefully decorated rooms all have their own jacuzzis.

Hôtel de France (£–££) 63 rue Espariat, 13100 (tel: 04 42 27 90 15). In a busy part of Vieil Aix, this old-fashioned hotel is reasonable value.

Hôtel Le Manoir (£££) 8 rue d'Entrecasteaux, 13100 (tel: 04 42 26 27 20). Housed inside a 14th-century monastery, the hotel is furnished in period style but with all modern comforts. The cloister itself has been turned into an atmospheric outdoor dining area.

Grand Hôtel Nègre Coste (££–£££) 33 cours Mirabeau, 13100 (tel: 04 42 27 74 22). An old hotel with a long history and plenty of character, although rooms are on the small side.

Hôtel St Christophe (££) 2 avenue Victor Hugo, 13100 (tel: 04 42 26 01 24). Basic, no-frills hotel just off the cours Mirabeau. Good value for Aix.

Le Moulin (££) 1 avenue Robert Schuman, 13090 (tel: 04 42 59 41 68). A modern building, but quiet and not overpriced.

Le Pigonnet (£££) 5 avenue du Pigonnet, 13090 (tel: 04 42 59 02 90). Set in a wooded park five minutes' walk to the southwest of the city centre, this old Provençal farmhouse (where Cézanne once painted in the grounds) has been lovingly converted into a luxury hotel. Pool.

Aigues-Mortes

Les Mas des Sables (££–£££) On the CD979, 30220 (tel: 04 66 53 79 73). Just outside Aigues-Mortes, with rooms furnished in Provençal style opening out onto lovely gardens. Pool.

St Louis (£££) 10 rue Amiral Courbet 30220 (tel: 04 66 53 72 68). Comfortable rooms in a wonderful old building right in the heart of Aigues-Mortes.

Arles

Grand Hôtel Nord-Pinus (£££) place du Forum, 13200 (tel: 04 90 93 44 44). Full of character and very attractively decorated throughout.

Hôtel D'Arlatan (£££) 26 rue du Sauvage, 13200 (tel: 04 90 93 56 66). Delightful hotel in a converted 15th-century mansion with a patio and walled garden just off the place du Forum. Rooms are all individually furnished, with many distinctive features (four-poster beds, beamed ceilings, etc.). Parts of the old Roman baths are visible through a glass floor in the reception area.

Hôtel du Forum (££–£££) 10 place du Forum, 13200 (tel: 04 90 93 48 95). Modern hotel in a restored mansion, in need of refurbishment but rooms in the lower price range are reasonable value for the location.

Hôtel Gauguin (£) 5 place Voltaire, 13200 (tel: 04 90 96 14 35). Simple and friendly hotel with basic rooms at budget prices.

Hôtel Jules César (£££) 5 boulevard des Lices, 13200 (tel: 04 90 93 43 20). Gracious and elegant hotel, top of the range for Arles, with spacious reception areas and very comfortable rooms.

Hôtel du Musée (£–££) 11 rue du Grand Prieuré, 13200 (tel: 04 90 93 88 88). Pleasant traditional-style hotel opposite the Musée Reattu; good value for Arles centre.

Hôtel St-Trophime (£–££) 16 rue de la Calade, 13200 (tel: 04 90 96 88 38). Reasonable value.

les Baux-de-Provence

La Benvengudo (£££) Vallon de L'Arcoule, 13520 les Baux (tel: 04 90 54 32 54). Traditional-style converted farmhouse in a delightful setting. Pool.

La Cabro d'Or (£££) Val d'Enfer, 13520 les Baux (tel: 04 90 54 33 21). Sister hotel to L'Oustau de Baumanière; slightly less luxurious but also set in lovely gardens (with pool).

Le Mas d'Aigret (£££) 13520 les Baux (tel: 04 90 54 33 54). Set just below the village, a delightful old converted farmhouse with 3ha of gardens, a dining room carved out of the rocks, and a pool. Most rooms have their own private terrace, balcony or garden.

L'Oùstau de Baumanière (£££) Val d'Enfer, 13520 les Baux (tel: 04 90 54 33 07). Luxury and refinement are the hallmarks of this famous hotel, which features immaculate gardens, pool, flowered terraces and elegant guest rooms.

Cassis

Les Jardins du Campanile (£££) rue Favier, 13260 (tel: 04 42 01 84 85). Stylish hotel in an old Provençal farmhouse, with a pool and garden.

Les Roches Blanches (£££) route des Calanques, 13260 (tel: 04 42 01 09 30). Set on a promontory 1km west of Cassis, this converted villa has fine views of the sea and Cap Canaille. Pool and private beach.

la Ciotat

Ciotel Le Cap (£££) corniche du Liouquet, 13600 (tel: 04 42 83 90 30). 6km east of town in a parkland setting, with two pools, tennis, private beach.

Provence Plage (£££) 3 avenue de Provence, 13600 (tel: 04 42 83 09 61). 150m from the beach, shaded terrace. Reasonable rates.

La Rotonde (££) 44 boulevard République, 13600 (tel: 04 42 08 67 50). Modern but pleasant hotel that stands above the old town. Very reasonable.

Marseille

New Hôtel-Vieux Port (£££) 3b rue Reine-Elisabeth, 13001 (tel: 04 91 90 51 42). In the pedestrian zone, a few minutes' walk from the old port. Attractive rooms.

HOTELS AND RESTAURANTS

Hôtel Caravelle (£) 5 rue Guy-Moquet, 13001 (tel: 04 91 48 44 99). Centrally located, family-run hotel with a friendly atmosphere and basic rooms at budget prices.

Hôtel Estérel (££) 124–125 rue Paradis, 13006 (tel: 04 91 37 13 90). Recently renovated with pleasant, modern rooms.

Hôtel Le Corbusier (££) 280 boulevard Michelet, 13008 (tel: 04 91 16 78 00). Incorporated into Le Corbusier's famous *Unité d'Habitation*; good value for money (reservations advisable).

Hôtel Montgrand (£) 50 rue Montgrand, 13006 (tel: 04 91 33 33 81). Behind the Opéra in a quiet street; clean, comfortable and very popular – reservations are necessary.

New Hôtel Bompard (£££) 2 rue des Flots Bleus, 13007 (tel: 04 91 52 10 93). Set in its own grounds 2km east of the city, New Hôtel Bompard makes for a peaceful retreat.

New Hôtel Select (£££) 4 allées Gambetta, 13001 (tel: 04 91 50 65 50). Modern hotel with good prices for its central location.

Pullman Beauvau (£££) 4 rue Beauvau, 13001 (tel: 04 91 54 91 00). Overlooking the Vieux Port with comfortable, sound-proofed rooms.

Nîmes

Le Cheval Blanc (£££) 1 place des Arènes, 30000 (tel: 04 66 76 32 32).Opposite the arena, ultra-chic hotel with individually designed furniture in comfortable, modern rooms.

Hôtel Imperator Concorde (£££) quai de la Fontaine, 30900 (tel: 04 66 21 90 30). Right in the heart of Nîmes opposite the Jardin de la Fontaine, with its own enclosed terrace and garden. De luxe rooms that are top of the range in Nîmes.

Hôtel Le Louvre (££) 2 square de la Couronne, 30000 (tel: 04 66 67 22 75). Centrally located, a lovely 17th-century mansion with a courtyard/garden.

Hôtel de la Mairie (££) 11 rue des Greffes, 30000 (tel: 04 66 67 65 91). Basic rooms at reasonable prices, standing right in the town centre.

Hôtel Plazza (£–££) 10 rue Roussy, 30000 (tel: 04 66 76 16 20). Characterful hotel that has been recently renovated, with small but tastefully furnished rooms.

Le Lisita (£) 2 boulevard des Arènes, 30000 (tel: 04 66 67 66 20). Bullfighting décor and personalised rooms; good value.

St-Rémy-de-Provence

Auberge de la Reine Jeanne (££) 12 boulevard Mirabeau, 13210 (tel: 04 90 92 15 33). Just 10 rooms set above the restaurant in this charming little hotel, which is reasonably priced.

Le Castelet des Alpilles (££) 6 place Mireille, 13210 (tel: 04 90 92 07 21). Reasonable value for the levels of comfort provided in this old mansion with an enclosed garden.

Grand Hôtel de Provence (£) 36 boulevard Victor Hugo, 13210 (tel: 04 90 92 06 27). Huge old building right on the main boulevard, old-fashioned and charming with a rambling garden out the back. Bargain prices in a town not known for them.

Hôtel du Cheval Blanc (££) 6 avenue Fauconnet, 13210 (tel: 04 90 92 09 28). Smart rooms in the heart of St-Rémy; modest prices.

Villa Glanum (££) 46 avenue Vincent van Gogh, 13210 (tel: 04 90 92 03 59). Just next to the Roman ruins, a welcoming hotel with a pool and gardens.

Saintes-Maries-de-la-Mer

Chez Kiki (£) route de Cacharel, 13460 (tel: 04 90 97 83 27). Modern and functional, with reasonably priced rooms.

L'Etrier Carmarguais (££) chemin Bas-des-Launes, 13460 (tel: 04 90 97 81 14). Popular hostelry outside town; large rooms in bungalows in the grounds. Pool, tennis, riding.

Le Galoubet (£££) route de Cacharel, 13460 (tel: 04 90 97 82 17). Modern hotel with rustic touches, close to the beach and the old port.

Mas des Rièges (£££) route de Cacharel, 13460 (tel: 04 90 97 85 07). Just outside town in a quiet location, small but attractively furnished rooms. Small garden and pool.

Salon-de-Provence

Abbaye de Ste-Croix (£££) Val de Cuech, 13300 (tel: 04 90 56 24 55). Set in a woodland park 5km north east of Salon, this converted abbey is one of the region's top hotels. Sweeping views from the terrace. Pool, horse-riding. The rooms (former monks' cells) are small but tastefully furnished; the apartments have private gardens.

Hôtel Angeleterre (£–££) 98 cours Carnot, 13300 (tel: 04 90 56 01 10). Recently renovated and good value. Town centre.

Hôtel du Midi (£–££) 518 allées Craponne, 13300 (tel: 04 90 53 34 67). On the southern outskirts of town; good-sized, modern rooms at decent prices.

Tarascon

Provence (££) 7 boulevard Victor-Hugo, 13150 (tel: 04 90 91 06 43). Huge rooms (with equally large bathrooms), most with balconies. Quiet and tasteful; good value for the facilities provided.

Le St-Jean (£–££) 24 boulevard Victor-Hugo, 13150 (tel: 04 90 91 13 87). Large, comfortable rooms at reasonable prices.

VAR
Bandol

Master Kermocotte (£££) 103 rue Raimu, 83150 (tel: 04 94 29 46 53). Lovely old house with a Provençal garden and a private beach.

L'Oasis (££–£££) 15 rue des Écoles, 83150 (tel: 04 94 29 41 69). Small, friendly hotel half-way between the port and the beach. Large shady garden, terrace.

La Réserve (£££) route de Sanary, 83150 (tel: 04 94 29 30 00). Directly on the beach; popular for its restaurant.

Splendid Hôtel (££) plage de Renécros, 83150 (tel: 04 94 29 41 61). Quiet, peaceful hotel right on Bandol's best beach.

Brignoles
Le Caramy (£) 11 place Caramy, 83170 (tel: 04 94 69 11 08). Budget prices in the centre of town.
Château de Brignoles (££) avenue Dréo, 83170 (tel: 04 94 69 06 88). On the outskirts of town, comfortable and quiet. Pool, tennis.
Hôtel Ibis (££) chemin du Val, 83170 (tel: 04 94 69 19 29). Part of the Ibis chain; moderately priced. Pool.

la Cadière
Hostellerie Bérard (£££) rue Gabriel-Peri, 83740 (tel: 04 94 90 11 43). Right in the heart of the village, this converted monastery has comfortable rooms at reasonable prices.

le Castellet
Le Castel Lumière (££–£££) rue Portail, 83330 (tel: 04 94 32 62 20). There are just six rooms above this well-known restaurant next to the gateway into the village. Good value.

Draguignan
Hôtel le Dracenois (£–££) 14 rue du Cros, 83300 (tel: 04 94 68 14 57). Just off the market square, this small, friendly hotel has decent rooms at budget prices.
Hôtel du Parc (££) 21 boulevard de la Liberté, 83300 (tel: 04 94 68 53 84). The quietest and best rooms overlook a courtyard at the back.

Fréjus
Auberge du Vieux Four (£–££) 49 rue Grisolle, 83600 (tel: 04 94 51 56 38). Budget-priced rooms above an excellent restaurant; homely atmosphere.
Hôtel il etait un fois (££) 254 rue Frédéric Mistral, 83600 (04 94 17 19 69). The 'once upon a time' hotel is 500m from the beach with its own flourishing gardens around a charming Provençal farmhouse. Good value.
Hôtel La Riviera (£) 90 rue Grisolle, 83600 (tel: 04 94 51 31 46). Budget choice in the heart of the old town.
Residence du Colombier (£££) route de Bagnols, 83600 (tel: 04 94 51 45 92). A good choice for families, with individual bungalows spread out in a woodland setting. Pool, tennis.

Grimaud
Hostellerie du Côteau Fleurie (£££) place des Pénitents, 83360 (tel: 04 94 43 20 17). Pleasant Provençal auberge on the village outskirts, with views over the Massif des Maures.

Hyères
Hôtel-Pension de la Poste (£) 7 avenue Lyautey, 83400 (tel: 04 94 65 02 00). A popular budget option; small and friendly.
Hôtel du Soleil (££) 2 rue Rampart, 83400 (tel: 04 94 65 16 26). In a quiet location just near the Parc St-Bernard; reasonable value.

La Reine Jane (£–££) le port de l'Augade, 83400 (tel: 04 94 66 32 64). Excellent value down by the seaside.
Relais Bon Accueil (££) Presqu-île des Giens, 83400 (tel: 04 94 58 20 48). A member of the *Relais du Silence* group, set in a large garden out on the peninsula past Hyères. Pool, tennis, riding.

le Lavandou
L'Escapade (£–££) 1 chemin du Vannier, 83980 (tel: 04 94 71 11 52). Small hotel in a peaceful location; good value.
Hôtel Belle-Vue (££) St Clair, 83980 (tel: 04 94 71 01 06). Peaceful hotel overlooking the Corniche des Maures; lovely gardens, reasonable prices.
Les Roches (£££) Aiguebelle, 83980 (tel: 04 94 71 05 07). Top-notch hotel on the beach in neighbouring Aiguebelle; superb rooms. Pool, tennis.
Les Tamaris (££) plage de St-Clair, 83980, (tel: 04 94 71 79 19). A few steps from the beach, unpretentious yet classy food at the right prices.

St-Raphaël

Hôtel Golf de Valescure (£££) avenue Pierre Lermite, 83700 (tel: 04 94 82 40 31). 5km from town, set in woodlands with easy access to the golf course. Pool, tennis.
Hôtel La Potiniere (££–£££) 169 avenue de Boulouris, 83700 (tel: 04 94 95 21 43). Very peaceful location 5km from St-Raphaël, 300m from the sea, this *Relais du Silence* is set in pine woods and has a pool, tennis court, sauna, etc.
Le Provençal (££) 197 rue de la Garonne, 83700 (tel: 04 94 95 01 92). Not far from the port; standard rooms at budget prices.
Hôtel des Pyramides (£–££) 77 avenue Paul Doumer, 83700 (tel: 04 94 95 05 95). Cheap and cheerful hotel in the town centre.

St-Tropez
Le Byblos (£££) avenue Paul Signac, 83990 (tel: 04 94 56 68 00). Chic hotel with luxuriously decorated rooms and a fabulous pool.
Les Chimères (££–£££) quartier du Pilon, 83990 (tel: 04 94 97 02 90). Ten minutes' walk from the port, very reasonable for St-Tropez. Request a room overlooking the garden.
La Ferme d'Augustin (£££) plage de Tahiti, 83350 (tel: 04 94 97 23 83). Quiet location just a few metres from Tahiti beach; de luxe rooms in traditional style.
Lou Cagnard (££–£££) rue Paul Roussel, 83990 (tel: 04 94 97 04 24). Not far from the town centre; reasonable prices considering the location.
La Ponche (£££) place du Révelin, 83990 (tel: 04 94 97 02 53). Just off the port, this small, romantic hotel converted from a row of fishermen's cottages is popular with celebrities.
Hôtel Souleias (£££) Plage de Gigaro, 83420 (tel: 04 94 79 61 91). This well-run property has a fantastic position overlooking the Baie

HOTELS AND RESTAURANTS

de Cavalaire (on the other side of the peninsula from St-Tropez), with a pool set amidst pine trees high above the sea. The de luxe rooms are superbly appointed.

Ste-Maxime
Hostellerie de la Belle Aurore (£££) 4 boulevard Jean Moulin, 83120 (tel: 04 94 96 02 45). Ste-Maxime's most prestigious hotel, on the edge of the sea with views of the St-Tropez Gulf. Pool.
Hôtel de la Poste (££–£££) 7 boulevard Frédéric Mistral, 83120 (tel: 04 94 96 18 33). Modern hotel with a pool and gardens; reasonably priced rooms.

Toulon
La Corniche (£££) 17 littoral Frédéric Mistral, 83000 (tel: 04 94 41 35 12). A modern hotel near the beach with views over the bay. Fairly pricey.
Hôtel St Nicolas (££) 49 rue Jean Jaurès, 83000 (tel: 04 94 91 02 28). Centrally located, sound-proofed rooms at reasonable rates.
Le Jaurès (£) 11 rue Jean Jaurès, 83000 (tel: 04 94 92 83 04). Right in the town centre, budget rooms all with bathrooms.

ALPES DE HAUTE-PROVENCE
Allos
Hôtel Pascal (£) centre village, 04260 (tel: 04 92 83 00 04). Small, friendly hotel with clean and very reasonably priced rooms.

Annot
Hôtel du Parc (£) place du Germe, 04240 (tel: 04 92 83 20 03). An old hotel with a large garden; reasonable value.
Hôtel Restaurant de l'Avenue (££) avenue de la Gare, 04240 (tel: 04 92 83 22 07). Small but comfortable rooms at the right price.

Barcelonnette
Choucas Bar-Hôtel (£) 4 place Manuel, 04400 (tel: 04 92 81 15 20). On the central square, basic rooms at budget prices.
Le Grand Hôtel (££) 6 place Manuel, 04400 (tel: 04 92 81 03 14). On the central square, old-fashioned but good value.
Hôtel Azteca (££–£££) 3 rue François Arnaud, 04400 (tel: 04 92 81 64 36). Decorated in Mexican style, with every available comfort.
Hôtel du Cheval Blanc (£) 12 rue Grenette, 04400 (tel: 04 92 81 00 19). Welcoming hotel; the auberge has a good value restaurant.
Hôtel La Grand Epervière (£££) 18 rue des 3 Frères Arnaud, 04400 (tel: 04 92 81 00 70). Peaceful location, with mountain views from all the rooms.

Castellane
Nouvel Hôtel du Commerce (££–£££) place de l'Église, 04120 (tel: 04 92 83 61 00). Not much atmosphere but comfortable rooms.
Ma Petite Auberge (££–£££) 8 boulevard de la République, 04120 (tel: 04 92 83 62 06). Just 16 rooms in this welcoming inn.

Château-Arnoux
La Bonne Étape (£££) chemin du Lac, 04160 (tel: 04 92 64 00 09). Lovely rooms. Garden and pool.
Hôtel Restaurant du Lac (££–£££) 12/14 allées des Érables, 04160 (tel: 04 92 64 04 32). Pleasant rooms and good value. It is worth paying extra for a room that overlooks the lake.
La Taverne Jarlandine (£) montée de l'Oratoire, 04160 (tel: 04 92 64 04 49). Very reasonable prices. Stands right in the centre of the village.

Digne-les-Bains
Hôtel Central (££) 26 boulevard Gassendi, 04000 (tel: 04 92 31 31 91). Stylish and comfortable hotel in the mid-price range.
Hôtel L'Origan (£) 6 rue du Pied de Ville, 04000 (tel: 04 92 31 62 13). Friendly budget hotel.
Hôtel Restaurant de Grand Paris (££–£££) 19 boulevard Thiers, 04000 (tel: 04 92 31 11 15). Luxurious hotel housed in a former convent. Garden, garage parking.
Hôtel Restaurant du Petit St-Jean (£) 14 cours des Arès, 04000 (tel: 04 92 31 30 04). An old hotel with very attractive rooms at budget prices.

Forcalquier
Le Grand Hôtel (£–££) 10 boulevard Latourette, 04300 (tel: 04 92 75 00 35). Large rooms at reasonable rates. Garden with panoramic views.
Hostellerie des Deux Lions (££–£££) 11 place du Bourguet, 04300 (tel: 04 92 75 25 30). Top choice in town, this ancient hotel has been welcoming travellers since the 18th century. Extremely comfortable and atmospheric rooms. Excellent value.

Gréoux-les-Bains
La Crémaillère (££–£££) route de Riez, 04800 (tel: 04 92 74 22 29). Modern but comfortable rooms. Gardens, pool.
Hôtel Restaurant Villa Borghese (££–£££) avenue des Thermes, 04800 (tel: 04 92 78 00 91). Charming hotel with flower-filled balconies and delightful rooms. Pool, tennis, spa, gardens.

Manosque
Le François-1er (£–££) 18 rue Guilhempierre, 04100 (tel: 04 92 72 07 99). Central and reasonably priced.
Hôtel Peyrache (£) 37 rue Jean-Jacques-Rousseau, 04100 (tel: 04 92 72 07 43). Simple, clean rooms at budget prices.
Le Provence (££) route de la Durance, 04100 (tel: 04 92 72 39 38). Modern rooms but comfortable and good value. Pool.

Moustiers-Ste-Marie
La Bastide des Moustiers (£££) la Grisolière, 04360 (tel: 04 92 74 62 40). Charming hotel in a restored 17th-century farmhouse; heated pool. The superb restaurant is presided over by Michelin-rated chef Alain Ducasse.

Bonne Auberge (£–££) route du Castellane, 04360 (tel: 04 92 74 66 18). Adequately comfortable and not too expensive.

La Palud-sur-Verdon
Hôtel des Gorges du Verdon (££) 04120 La Palud-sur-Verdon (tel: 04 92 77 38 26). A welcoming Logis de France just outside La Palud, with superb views; an ideal spot to break a journey through the gorges. Rooms are modern, the restaurant excellent.

Riez
Hôtel Carina (££) rue Hilarion Bourret, 04500 (tel: 04 92 77 85 43). Smart new hotel; comfortable if lacking in atmosphere.
Hôtel Restaurant des Alpes (££) 2 avenue de Verdon, 04500 (tel: 04 92 77 80 03). Old-fashioned but reasonable value.

Sisteron
Grand Hôtel du Cours (££–£££) place de l'Église, 04200 (tel: 04 92 61 04 51). Centrally located and very comfortable.
Hostellerie Provençale (£) 2 avenue Jean Moulin, 04200 (tel: 04 92 61 02 42). Central and cheap.
Hôtel Restaurant de la Citadelle (££) 126 rue Saunerie, 04200 (tel: 04 92 61 13 52). Well-run hotel where some rooms have excellent views over the river valley.
Hôtel Restaurant Tivoli (££) place de Tivoli, 04200 (tel: 04 92 61 15 16). Spacious rooms; good value.

CÔTE D'AZUR/ALPES MARITIMES
Antibes
L'Auberge Provençale (££–£££) 61 place Nationale, 06600 (tel: 04 93 34 13 24). Popular small hotel (it only has five rooms) on a shady square in the heart of the old town. Booking essential.
Mas Djoliba (££–£££) 29 avenue de Provence, 06600 (tel: 04 93 34 02 48). Lovely old Provençal farmhouse set in 3ha of grounds within walking distance of the town and the beach. Pool. *Demi-pension* obligatory in season; booking essential.
La Méditerranée (££) 6 avenue du Maréchal-Reille, 06600 (tel: 04 93 34 14 84). Agreeable mid-price range hotel with some rooms overlooking a delightful small garden.
Modern Hôtel (£–££) 1 rue Fourmillière, 06600 (tel: 04 93 34 03 05). Clean and economic hotel, although some rooms can be noisy.

Beaulieu-sur-Mer
Le Havre Bleu (££) 29 boulevard de Maréchal-Joffre, 06310 (tel: 04 93 01 01 40). Lovely old hotel with attractive rooms.
Hôtel Select (£) 1 montée des Myrtes, place Général de Gaulle, 06310 (tel: 04 93 01 05 42). Clean, simple rooms at bargain prices.
Metropole (£££) boulevard Maréchal-Leclerc, 06310 (tel: 04 93 01 00 08). Splendid *belle époque* hotel with bright and cheerful rooms.

Terrace, pool and gardens overlooking the sea and private beach.
Réserve de Beaulieu (£££) boulevard Maréchal-Leclerc, 06310 (tel: 04 93 01 00 01). Fabulous old hotel on the sea front, pool, private beach; very expensive but worth it.

Breil-sur-Roya
Le Castel du Roy (££–£££) route de Tende, 06540 (tel: 04 93 04 43 66). Modern but extremely comfortable hotel, impeccable rooms, heated pool.

la Brigue
Auberge St-Martin (££–£££) place St-Martin, 06430 (tel: 04 93 04 62 17). Charming family-run hotel in the village centre.

Cannes
Carlton Inter-Continental (£££) 58 la Croisette, 06400 (tel: 04 93 68 91 68). The magnificent façade of this grand old hotel is a familiar Riviera landmark. Inside, the keynote is luxury on a palatial scale – and you will need a princely sum to stay here.
Le Chanteclair (£–££) 12 rue Fortville, 06400 (tel: 04 93 39 68 88). In a quiet location just back from the sea front.
Hôtel de Provence (££) 9 rue Molière, 06400 (tel: 04 93 38 44 35). Small, comfortable hotel with reasonably priced rooms.
Majestic (£££) 14 la Croisette, 06400 (tel: 04 92 98 77 00). Another classic hotel. Extremely comfortable, heated pool, private beach.
Martinez (£££) 73 la Croisette, 06400 (tel: 04 92 98 73 00). Flamboyant *belle époque* hotel; rooms have all mod cons. Heated pool and tennis court.

277

Èze
Château de la Chèvre d'Or (£££) rue Barri, 06360 (tel: 04 93 41 12 12). A converted castle with 15 rooms and eight suites, all with fabulous sea views. Pool and terrace.

Grasse
Hôtel Panorama (££–£££) 2 place du Cours, 06130 (tel: 04 93 36 80 80). Centrally located, modern hotel with rooms at reasonable rates.
Hôtel du Patti (££–£££) place du Patti, 06310 (tel: 04 93 36 01 00). Extremely comfortable and central.
Pension Michèle (£) 6 rue du Palais-du-Justice, 06130 (tel: 04 93 36 06 37). In the heart of town, welcoming and well-kept little establishment with a small garden. *Demi-pension* compulsory.

Juan-les-Pins
La Marjolaine (££) 15 avenue du Docteur-Fabre, 06160 (tel: 04 93 61 06 60). Large old house standing in a quiet street; smart but reasonably priced.
Pré-Catalan (£££) 22 avenue des Lauriers, 06160 (tel: 04 93 61 05 11). Small, comfortable hotel behind the casino. *Demi-pension* compulsory in season.

HOTELS AND RESTAURANTS

Menton
Hôtel Pension Beauregard (££) 10 rue Albert 1er, 06500 (tel: 04 93 35 74 08). Superb little hotel surrounded by gardens; good value.

Monaco
Hôtel Cosmopolite (££) 4 rue de la Turbie, MC 98000 (tel: 93 30 16 95). One of the few 'budget' hotels in Monaco; basic but pleasant rooms.

Hôtel de France (££) 6 rue de la Turbie, MC 98000 (tel: 93 30 24 64). Pleasant hotel; good value for Monaco.

Hôtel Hermitage (£££) square Beaumarchais, MC 98000 (tel: 92 16 40 00). Perched up above the town with splendid views, the Hermitage is another magnificent *belle époque* hotel, one that many consider to be at least the equal of the Hôtel de Paris.

Hôtel de Paris (£££) place du Casino, MC 98000 (tel: 92 16 30 00). The most prestigious hotel in Monte-Carlo, frequented by gamblers and aristocrats for over a hundred years. Superb rooms, many with views over the harbour and the old town.

Nice
La Belle Meunière (£–££) 21 avenue Durant, 06000 (tel: 04 93 88 66 15). Close to the station, comfortable and very hospitable hotel with a shady garden.

Hôtel Central (£) 10 rue de Suisse, 06000 (tel: 04 93 88 85 08). Small, simple rooms at budget prices.

Mercure Marché aux Fleurs (££–£££) quai des États-Unis, 06000 (tel: 04 93 85 74 19). Despite the forbidding façade, the hotel's rooms are attractive and sound-proofed, with sea views.

Hôtel Windsor (££–£££) 11 rue Dalpozzo, 06000 (tel: 04 93 88 59 35). Characterful hotel, with rooms decorated in different styles, just near the beach. Pool and garden.

Negresco (£££) 37 promenade des Anglais, 06000 (tel: 04 93 88 39 51). Nice's flagship hotel, one of the great landmarks of the Riviera. Impeccable service and luxurious rooms decorated with original art works.

Relais de Rimiez (££) 128 avenue de Rimiez, 06000 (tel: 04 93 81 18 65). Peaceful hotel 10 minutes from the city centre, with views of Nice and the sea.

St-Paul-de-Vence
La Colombe d'Or (£££) place des Ormeaux, 06570 (tel: 04 93 32 80 02). This famous hostelry needs to be booked months in advance, despite the exorbitant cost of the rooms.

Les Orangers (££–£££) route de la Colle, 06570 (tel: 04 93 32 80 95). Tranquil location with a view over the village.

Sospel
Hôtel des Etrangers (££–£££) 7 boulevard de Verdun, 06380 (tel: 04 93 04 00 09). Comfortable rooms overlooking the river. Terrace and pool.

Vence
la Closerie des Genets (£–££) 4 impasse Maurel, 06140 (tel: 04 93 58 33 25). Small hotel in a peaceful location right in the town centre; nine rooms at surprisingly reasonable prices.

La Rosaraie (££–£££) 14 avenue Henri Giraud, 06140 (tel: 04 93 58 02 20). Small hotel on the edge of town with a pretty terrace and pool.

Villefranche-sur-Mer
Hôtel Provencal (££) avenue Maréchal Joffre, 06230 (tel: 04 93 01 71 42). Family-run hotel with attractive rooms (ask for a sea view) at reasonable prices.

Hôtel Welcome (£££) 1 quai Amiral Courbet, 06230 (tel: 04 93 76 76 93). Famous hotel on the sea front that can count many artists and writers among its past guests. Well-furnished, air-conditioned rooms.

RESTAURANTS

The following restaurants have been divided into three price categories:

- budget (£)
- moderate (££)
- expensive (£££)

VAUCLUSE
Avignon
Christian Étienne (£££) 10 rue Mons, 84000 (tel: 04 90 86 12 50). Housed in an old building overlooking the Palais des Papes, sophisticated restaurant with a long-standing reputation. Imaginative vegetarian menu available.

Hiély (£££) 5 rue République, 84000 (tel: 04 90 86 17 07). With its long-standing gourmet reputation, Hiély never fails to please with dishes such as *feuillete de légumes aux truffes, pistou d'homard* and *cassoulet des moules aux épinards*.

Le Pain Bis (£) 6 rue Armand de Pontmartin 84000. Vegetarian meals served with considerable flair in this popular little bistro.

Le Petit Bedon (££) 70 rue Joseph Vernet, 84000 (tel: 04 90 82 33 98). Generous portions of Provençal cuisine with innovative touches; good-value lunchtime menu.

Tache d'Encre (£) 22 rue des Teinturiers, 84000 (tel: 04 90 85 46 03). Friendly café-theatre (live music Friday and Saturday nights) with excellent-value set meals such as cod *aioli*.

Le Venaissin (££) place de l'Horloge, 84000 (tel: 04 90 86 20 99). The best-value restaurant on the central square, with good quality food that is not compromised by their very reasonable prices. Neighbouring restaurants live by the trade that is turned away from this busy restaurant, but standards elsewhere are low by comparison. Arrive early to be sure of a table.

Le Vernet (££) 58 rue Joseph Vernet, 84000 (tel: 04 90 86 64 53). The perfect setting on a summer's evening, with tables set under the trees in the walled back garden of this ancient townhouse. Specialities include fish dishes and vegetarian meals.

Bonnieux

Hostellerie du Prieuré (££–£££) rue J B Aurard, 84480 (tel: 04 90 75 80 78). 18th-century building at the bottom of the ramparts. Meals are eaten in front of open fire or in the garden.

Carpentras

Le Marijo (£) 73 rue Raspail, 84200 (tel: 04 90 60 42 65). Cheerful, intimate restaurant handy for the town centre. Regional menu includes *crevettes* and *salade niçoise* followed by *filet de dorade Mistral*. Excellent value evening menu.

La Vert Galant (££) 12 rue Clapiès, 84200 (tel: 04 90 67 15 50). Imaginative cuisine, with local seafood a speciality.

Cavaillon

La Fin de Siècle (££) 46 place de Clos, 84300 (tel: 04 90 71 12 27). Café-restaurant embellished with brass and glass in *fin de siècle* style, serving tempting dishes at very reasonable prices.

Restaurant Pantagruel (£–££) 5 place Philippe-de-Cabassole, 84300 (tel: 04 90 76 11 30). Atmospheric and lively restaurant, with an attractive terrace for warm days. Specialities include char-grilled *gigôt d'agneau*. Inexpensive, with plentiful portions.

Fontaine-de-Vaucluse

Hostellerie le Château (££) quartier Petit Place, 84800 (tel: 04 90 20 31 54). Restaurant on a shady terrace on the river's edge; specialities include trout, *lotte moutarde à l'ancienne* and *canard avec cèpes*.

Restaurant Philip (££) 'au pied des cascades', 84800 (tel: 04 90 20 31 81). On a prime site opposite the soothing cascades on the footpath up to the source. Seafood and grills plus snacks and sandwiches in the bar.

Gigondas

Les Florets (££) route des Dentelles, 84190 (tel: 04 90 65 85 01). 1.5km outside Gigondas in the middle of a pine forest, this popular local restaurant is excellent value for money. Specialities include *noisettes d'agneau à la crème d'ail*.

Gordes

Chez Tante Yvonne (£–££) place Genty-Panataly, 84220 (tel: 04 90 72 02 54). Cosy restaurant, with an original menu featuring specialities such as *terrine d'épinards au thon* or *tarte au roquefort*.

La Mayanelle (££) 6 rue de la Colombe, 84220 (tel: 04 90 72 00 28). Classic Provençal cooking, with lovely views of the Lubéron from the outside terrace.

L'Isle-sur-la-Sorgue

La Guinguette (££) le Partage des Eaux, 84800 (tel: 04 90 38 10 61). Outside of town, in a tranquil setting next to the 'parting of the waters' where the Sorgue divides; food is reasonable value, with fresh fish and seafood (such as *filet de perche au beurre blanc* and *croustade de moules*) providing the mainstay.

Le Pescador (££) le Partage des Eaux, 84800 (tel: 04 90 38 09 69). Smarter and slightly more expensive than its neighbour La Guinguette, and not so well positioned, but with a long-standing reputation for good fish dishes.

La Saladelle (£) 33 rue Carnot, 84800 (tel: 04 90 20 68 59). Simple menus at very reasonable prices.

Malaucène

Hostellerie La Chevalerie (£) centre ville, 84340 (tel: 04 90 65 11 19). In a charming location with a garden below the medieval ramparts, good value and very popular with locals.

L'Origan (£–££) centre ville, 84340 (tel: 04 90 65 27 08). Well-presented Provençal cooking at prices that will not hurt your wallet.

279

Ménerbes

Clémentine (£–££) place Albert Roux, 84560 (tel: 04 90 72 32 81). Fabulous panoramic views from the terrace; menus featuring *soupe de poissons*, *daube Provençale* and other classics.

Orange

Le Français (£–££) 34 rue des Lilas, 84100 (tel: 04 90 34 18 30). Traditional brasserie food, such as *couscous* and *bouillabaisse*, as well as pizzas; there are also occasional floor shows.

Le Parvis (££–£££) 3 cours Pourtoules, 84100 (tel: 04 90 34 82 00). Elegant restaurant, Provençal cooking with innovative touches. Specialities include *escalope de loup au fenouil*.

Le Pigraillet (££) colline St-Eutrope, 84100 (tel: 04 90 34 44 25). Set in a wooded park at the top of the St-Eutrope hill above Orange; a delightful setting, and you can use the large swimming pool to work up an appetite before lunch. The menu includes grills, fish, salads and dessert.

Le Yaca (£) 24 place Sylvian, 84100 (tel: 04 90 34 70 03). Near the theatre, this restaurant in an old vaulted chamber is cheerful and good value.

Roussillon

La Gourmandine (£) place de l'Abbé-Avon, 84220 (tel: 04 90 05 68 86). Lovely panoramic terrace; good value crêperie.

Restaurant David (££) place de la Poste, 84220 (tel: 04 90 05 60 13). Provençal cooking, tables outdoors in the summer, popular with locals. Specialities include *cassolette de moules* and *pintade aux cerises*.

HOTELS AND RESTAURANTS

Séguret

Domaine de Cabasse (££–£££) route de Sablet, 84110 (tel: 04 90 46 91 12). Just outside of the village, this renowned gastronomic restaurant is extravagant but well worth it.

Vaison-la-Romaine

Le Bataleur (££) place Theo Aubanel, 84110 (tel: 04 90 36 28 04). Small and cosy restaurant just near the bridge, with a one-price menu that has a choice of eight starters and ten main courses. Speciality of *carré d'agneau frisée aux amandes*.

La Pomme Crêperie (£) Haute-ville, 84110 (tel: 04 90 36 38 80). Inexpensive savoury and sweet *crêpes*, salads, ice-creams. Breezy terrace with views over the river.

Restaurant du Vieux Vaison (£–££) Haute-ville, 84110 (tel: 04 90 36 19 45). Terrace with panoramic views down from the old town; *pizza au feu du bois* and reasonably priced menus.

BOUCHES-DU-RHÔNE

Aigues-Mortes

Restaurant Chez Laurette (£) 9 rue Alsace-Lorraine, 30220 (tel: 04 66 53 62 67). Small, cosy restaurant serving traditional Camarguais specialities such as *taureau à la gardienne* and seafood at exceptionally reasonable prices.

Aix

Le Bistro Latin (££) 18 rue de la Couronne, 13100 (tel: 04 42 38 22 88). Well-prepared food at reasonable prices.

La Brocherie (££) 5 rue Fernand Dol, 13100 (tel: 04 42 38 33 21). Rustic atmosphere, with game roasted on a spit in the large chimney. Fish also a speciality.

Le Grillon (£–££) 49 Cours Mirabeau, 13100 (tel: 04 42 25 58 81). Good but simple food in café setting, frequented by locals. Efficient service.

Clos de la Violette (££–£££) 10 avenue Violette, 13100 (tel: 04 42 23 30 71). One of Aix's best restaurants, therefore essential to book. Specialities include *petits farcis Provençaux* and *rougets de roche et caillettes d'herbes*.

Les Deux Garcons (££) 53 cours Mirabeau, 13100 (tel: 04 42 26 00 51). Wonderful *fin de siècle* atmosphere, at least worth visiting for a morning *cafe crème* and *croissants*. Otherwise, the brasserie-style dishes (which include seafood) tend to be expensive.

L'Hacienda (£) 7 rue Merindol, 13100 (tel: 04 42 27 00 35). Very good value Spanish restaurant.

Keops (£) 28 rue de la Verrèrie, 13100 (tel: 04 42 96 59 05). Aix has a number of ethnic restaurants, and this Egyptian eaterie is one of the best, serving traditional cuisine (*falafel*, etc.) at reasonable prices.

Arles

Hostellerie des Arènes (£) 62 rue du Réfuge, 13200 (tel: 04 90 96 13 05). Home-style cooking presented with panache; good value.

Hôtel-Restaurant d'Arlatan (£) 7 rue de la Cavaleire, 13200 (tel: 04 90 96 24 85). The hotel's restaurant serves a basic, well-priced three-course menu; booking advisable.

Lou Marques (££) Hôtel Jules César, boulevard des Lices, 13200 (tel: 04 90 93 43 20). Traditional gourmet food in Arles' top hotel; monkfish soup and *carré d'agneau* with artichokes are two notable specialities.

Le Tourne-Broche (£) 6 rue Balze, 13200 (tel: 04 90 96 16 03). Pasta and seafood at affordable prices.

Le Vaccarès (££) place du Forum, 13200 (tel: 04 90 96 06 17). Inventive variations on traditional Provençal dishes, making use of seasonal produce.

Vitamine (£) 16 rue du Docteur-Fanton, 13200 (tel: 04 90 93 77 36). Inexpensive restaurant with 50 different salads plus 15 varieties of pasta.

les Baux

Le Mas d'Aigret (££–£££) 13520 les Baux (tel: 04 90 54 33 54). This charming hotel also has a very good restaurant, with imaginatively prepared food.

L'Oustau de Baumanière (£££) Val d'Enfer, 13520 les Baux (tel: 04 90 54 33 07). This renowned restaurant is expensive, but with its two Michelin rosettes you may feel it is worth the extravagance. Specialities include *ravioli de truffes* and *filets de rougets au basilic*.

Cassis

César (£) 21 quai des Baux, 13260 (tel: 04 42 01 75 47). Cassis' sea-front restaurants are not renowned for their budget prices, but this is one of the very few where you can enjoy the port's famous fresh seafood without overspending.

Chez Gilbert (££) 19 quai des Baux, 13260 (tel: 04 42 01 71 36). *Bouillabaisse* (which must be ordered in advance) is a speciality of this reliable restaurant on the sea front.

El Sol (£) 23 quai des Baux, 13260 (tel: 04 42 01 76 10). Similarly priced to César's. Deservedly popular – book a table or get there early.

la Ciotat

Ciotel Le Cap (££) corniche du Liouquet, 13600 (tel: 04 42 83 90 30). The gourmet restaurant in this hotel serves classic dishes with regional touches – *bourride de chapon* is a speciality.

Restaurant Les Flots (£) 3 rue Gueymard, 13600 (tel: 04 42 08 24 61). La Ciotat has a good selection of inexpensive restaurants and this is one of the better ones.

Marseille

Les Arcenaulx (££) 25 cours d'Estienne d'Orves, 13001 (tel: 04 91 54 77 06). Housed inside an ancient arsenal, with massive stone walls and lined with books, this atmospheric restaurant serves regional food with *nouvelle cuisine* overtones (such as *compote d'agneau aux amandes, gigot aux artichauts*, etc.). Lunch-time menus are budget priced and good value.

Le Chaudron Provençal (££) 48 rue Caisserie, 13002 (tel: 04 91 91 02 37). *Bouillabaisse* and other fish dishes are the mainstay of this reputable restaurant; fairly expensive but worth it.

Chez Angèle (£–££) 50 rue Caisserie, 13002 (tel: 04 91 90 63 35). Inexpensive, small and lively bistro near the old port., with good-sized portions of Provençal dishes and friendly service.

Michel-Brasserie des Catalans (£££) 6 rue des Catalans, 13007 (tel: 04 91 52 30 63). Traditional *bouillabaisse* restaurant.

Le Petit Nice (£££) corniche Kennedy, Anse de Maldorme, 13007 (tel: 04 91 59 25 92). Beautifully decorated villa overlooking the sea. Marseille's top restaurant, with a very inventive menu.

Le Rascasse-Dauphin (£) 6 quai de Rive-Neuve, 13000 (tel: 04 91 33 17 25). One of the most reasonable seafood restaurants on the old harbour, with interesting menus.

Martigues
Chez Marraine (££) 6 rue des Cordonniers, 13500 (tel: 04 42 49 37 48). Delicious fresh fish and superb *bouillabaisse* made in the traditional way (for the latter, you must phone to order in advance).

Restaurant Pascal (£) 3 quai Lucien Toulmond, 13500 (tel: 04 42 42 16 89). Martigues is Provence's premier fishing port, so you can always be sure that the fish in this inexpensive restaurant is absolutely fresh.

Maussane
Ou Ravi Provencau (££) avenue Vallée des Baux, 13520 (tel: 04 90 54 31 11). Small restaurant that comes with a big reputation: recommended.

Nîmes
La Belle Respire (£) 12 rue de l'Étoile, 30000 (tel: 04 66 21 27 21). Good value in the heart of the old town.

Le Cheval Blanc (£££) place Arènes, 30000 (tel: 04 66 76 32 32). Elegant, top of the range restaurant right opposite the arena.

L'Enclos de la Fontaine (£££) Hôtel Imperator Concorde, quai de la Fontaine, 30900 (tel: 04 66 21 90 30). Reckoned by many to be the best restaurant in Nîmes', serving imaginative dishes and classic cuisine while overlooking the delightful courtyard garden.

Lou Mas (£) 5 rue du Sauve, 30900 (tel: 04 66 23 24 71). Pleasant rustic-looking restaurant serving a selection of Catalan-style dishes at reasonable prices.

St-Rémy-de-Provence
Café des Arts (£) 30 boulevard Victor-Hugo, 13210 (tel: 04 90 92 08 50). Fashionable watering-hole with a wide selection of bistro-type food.

La Gousse d'Ail (££) 25 rue Carnot, 13210 (tel: 04 90 92 16 87). Intimate restaurant, good value for money with some interesting dishes such as *noix d'entrecôte à la crème d'ail* and *escargots à la Provençale*.

Lou Grillado (£) impasse Jaume Conte, 13210 (tel: 04 90 92 21 04). Hidden away down a side street, a busy and welcoming pizzeria.

Le Marceau (££) 13 boulevard Marceau, 13210 (tel: 04 90 92 37 11). Refined décor; excellent food for the price.

Salon-de-Provence
Abbaye de Ste-Croix (£££) val de Cuech, 13300 (tel: 04 90 56 24 55). The hotel has a superb restaurant featuring classic Provençal cuisine with innovative touches.

Le Mas du Soleil (££) 38 Chemin St-Côrne, 13300 (tel: 04 90 56 06 53). This restaurant has a long-standing reputation and is not outrageously expensive for the excellent dishes on the menu.

Tarascon
Le St-Jean (£) 24 boulevard Victor-Hugo, 13150 (tel: 04 90 91 13 87). Simple, regional cooking at affordable prices, with an interesting atmosphere.

VAR
Bandol
Auberge du Port (££) 9 allées Jean-Moulin, 83150 (tel: 04 94 29 42 63). Seafood restaurant on the port with a long-standing reputation, featuring *langoustines*, *rouget*, *rascasse* and *loup* among the many fish dishes available on the extensive menu.

Au Fin Gourmet (££) 16, rue de la République, 83150 (tel: 04 94 29 41 80). Popular restaurant with a choice of three reasonably priced menus.

le Beausset
La Grange (£–££) 34 boulevard Chanzy, 83330 (tel: 04 94 90 40 22). Busy local restaurant, with an open-spit fire; good value.

Bormes-les-Mimosas
La Bellevue (£–££) opposite the hotel La Terrasse, place Gambetta, 83230 (tel: 04 94 71 15 15). Good regional cooking at budget prices, with views of the coast.

La Tonnelle des Délices (££) place Gambetta, 83230 (tel: 04 94 71 34 84). Delightful setting, with tables beneath hanging vines. Even more delightful *nouvelle cuisine*, using the freshest of local ingredients, at prices that are a pleasant surprise.

la Cadière
Hostellerie Bérard (£££) rue Gabriel-Peri, 83740 (tel: 04 94 90 11 43). Extensive menu with regional specialities, on a panoramic terrace overlooking the valley.

le Castellet
Le Castel Lumière (££–£££) rue Portail, 83330 (tel: 04 94 32 62 20). A gastronomic

281

treat, the Castel Lumière features *suprême du loup aux truffes* and *l'agneau au basilic* among the many other mouth-watering dishes on offer.

Fréjus

Cadet Rousselle (£) 25 place Agricola, 83600 (tel: 04 94 53 36 92). Popular crêperie in the heart of town.

Lou Grillado (£) 80 place Agricola, 83600 (tel: 04 94 53 48 27). Copious pizzas and lasagne, as well as a well-priced *plat du jour*.

Les Potiers (£–££) 135 rue des Potiers, 83600 (tel: 04 94 51 33 74). In the heart of the old town, very popular and atmospheric restaurant featuring standard dishes with a touch of *nouvelle cuisine*.

Grimaud

Restaurant du Café de France (££) place Neuve, 83310 (tel: 04 94 43 20 05). Large outdoor terrace for eating in the summer; very reasonable menu (featuring steak or *lapin au moutarde*).

Hyères

La Bergerie (£) 16 rue de Limans, 83400 (tel: 04 94 65 57 97). Inexpensive and tasty salads and pizzas in a friendly atmosphere.

La Reine Jane (£) le port de l'Aygade, 83400 (tel: 04 94 66 32 64). Good cooking at good prices.

le Lavandou

Auberge Provençale (£–££) 11 rue du Patron-Ravello, 83980 (tel: 04 94 71 00 44). Busy Provençal-style restaurant with well-thought-out menus.

Les Lavandou La Bouée (£) 2 rue Charles Cazin, 83980 (tel: 04 94 71 11 88). Good value and friendly. Lobster a speciality.

St-Tropez

La Cascade (£) 5 rue de l'Église, 83990 (tel: 04 94 54 83 46). Lively restaurant with food oriented towards the Caribbean as well as *soupe de poissons* and other local staples. Good value.

L'Échalote (££) 35 rue Allard, 83990 (tel: 04 94 54 83 26). Attractive little restaurant with a pretty garden for eating on warm nights. *Boeuf grillé à l'échalote* is a speciality; very reasonably priced menus.

Les Oliviers (££) rue des Carles, 83990 (tel: 04 94 97 58 16). In a lovely garden just outside the town centre, with a menu that is terrific value for the area.

Lou Revelen (££) 4 rue des Ramparts, 83990 (tel: 04 94 97 06 34). Just behind the port (in an area where there are more rip-offs than starlets) this restaurant offers honest, well-presented dishes, plus an exceptional, well-priced seafood menu. Bookings are essential in summer.

Toulon

Le Cellier (£) 52 rue Jean-Jaurès, 83000 (tel: 04 94 92 64 35). Friendly and welcoming bistro.

La Corniche (£££) 17 littoral Frédéric Mistral, 83000 (tel: 04 94 41 35 12). On the outskirts of Toulon, gastronomic cooking with prices to match but well worth it.

Le Galion (££) 10 rue Jean-Jaurès, 83000 (tel: 04 94 93 02 52). Pleasant atmosphere and an extensive menu at reasonable prices.

Madeleine (££) 7 rue des Tombades, 83000 (tel: 04 94 92 67 85). Homely restaurant with good, solid country cooking. Very popular; booking advisable.

ALPES-DE-HAUTE-PROVENCE

Annot

Hôtel de l'Avenue (£–££) avenue de la Gare, 04240 (tel: 04 92 83 22 07). Family-run restaurant with a three-course menu and a 'gourmet' menu. Generous portions and honest cooking.

Barcelonnette

La Mangeoire (££) place Quatre-Vents, 04400 (tel: 04 92 81 01 61). Atmospheric restaurant in an old sheep barn; lovingly prepared food at a reasonable cost.

Château-Arnoux

La Bonne Étape (£££) chemin du Lac, 04160 (tel: 04 92 64 00 09). One of the top restaurants in Provence, inside this château-hotel. Exceptionally high quality – and high prices, but it is worth it. Fresh, local ingredients prepared with imagination and flair are the hallmarks of chef Pierre Gleize's cooking.

La Taverne Jarlandine (£) montée de l'Oratoire, 04160 (tel: 04 92 64 04 49). The rustic-style restaurant in this budget hotel serves generous meals with a reasonably priced menu. Recommended.

Digne-les-Bains

Le Grand Paris (££–£££) 19 boulevard Thiers, 04000 (tel: 04 92 31 11 15). A distinguished restaurant with imaginative and well-presented menus.

Restaurant Mistre (££) 63 boulevard Gassendi, 04000 (tel: 04 92 31 00 16). One of Digne's longest-established and best-loved restaurants, serving regional specialities at reasonable prices.

Forcalquier

Hostellerie des Deux Lions (££–£££) 11 place du Bourguet, 04300 (tel: 04 92 75 25 30). The restaurant in this renowned hotel is noted for its excellent cooking, particularly game and fish. Booking essential.

Manosque

Chez André (£) 21 bis place des Terraux, 04100 (tel: 04 92 72 03 09). Basic menus at budget prices.

Riez

Les Abeilles (£) allées Louis-Gardiol, 04500 (tel: 04 92 77 89 29). Pleasant little café serving local staples (such as *aïoli*) as well as original dishes at highly affordable prices.

Sisteron
Hôtel Restaurant de la Citadelle (££) 126 rue Saunerie, 04200 (tel: 04 92 61 13 52). Wonderful views from the terrace restaurant of this hotel, with a choice of two reasonably priced menus.

CÔTE D'AZUR/ALPES MARITIMES
Antibes
Le Caméo (£) 5 place Nationale, 06600 (tel: 04 93 34 24 17) in the old town. Unpretentious restaurant with a terrace; specialities include *sardines fraîches à l'espagnole* and grilled *daurade*.
La Clafoutis (££) 18 rue Thuret, 06600 (tel: 04 93 34 66 70). Popular restaurant with a menu featuring *terrine de crustaces* and *filet de canard* followed by *fromage blanc* and *clafoutis aux kiwis*.
La Marmite (£) 20 rue James Close, 06600 (tel: 04 93 34 56 79). Attractive little restaurant with good-value menus.

Biot
Bistro du Jarrier (££–£££) 'au village', 06410 (tel: 04 93 65 53 48). Excellent restaurant inside an old converted jar factory, with a superb terrace. Classic cooking with a regional slant; particularly good value is the four-course *menu du marché Provençale*.

Cannes
Au Bec Fin (£) 12 rue du 24-Août, 06400 (tel: 04 93 38 35 86). The décor might not be inspiring but almost every dish is appetising and well presented. Generous portions and interesting *plats du jour*.
Lou Souleou (££) 16 boulevard Jean-Hibert, 06400 (tel: 04 93 39 85 55). This restaurant with a nautical theme overlooks the sea and the Esterel *massif* and serves consistently good food at cheerful prices.
La Palme d'Or (£££) Hôtel Martinez, 73 boulevard de la Croisette, 06400 (tel: 04 92 98 74 14). Rating two Michelin rosettes, this renowned restaurant is well worth considering for a one-off treat, despite the cost. Chef Jacques Chibois' specialities include *pigeonneau de ferme en crépinette de laitue, crème de févettes à la sarriette*.

Èze
Le Troubadour (££) 'au village', 06360 (tel: 04 93 41 19 03). Pleasant, welcoming restaurant with a menu featuring *saumon fumé artisanal, magret de canard à la compôte d'oignons*, goat's cheese and desserts.

Grasse
Maître Boscq (£–££) 13 rue de la Fontette, 06130 (tel: 04 93 36 45 76). Provençal and local specialities (such as Grassois stuffed cabbage, *sous fassoun*) of a consistently high standard.

Juan-les-Pins
Auberge de l'Esterel (££) 21 rue des Îles, 06160 (tel: 04 93 61 86 55). Excellent menu; attractive outdoor terrace for summer eating. Booking essential.
Lou Capitole (£) 26 avenue Amiral-Courbet, 06160 (tel: 04 93 61 22 44). Good value.

Menton
L'Oursin (££–£££) 3 rue Trenca, 06500 (tel: 04 93 28 33 62). Seafood of every conceivable variety is the speciality of this popular restaurant, just near the covered market.

Monaco
Bar-restaurant Bacchus (£) 13 rue de la Turbie, 98000 (tel: 93 30 19 35). Family-run café near the station; generous helpings of basic, decent cooking.
Le Louis XV (£££) Hôtel de Paris, place du Casino, 98000 (tel: 92 16 30 01). Three Michelin rosettes indicate that the food here is as sumptuous and ornate as the gilded restaurant itself. Expensive, but worth it.
Polpetta (£) 6 avenue Roqueville, 98000 (tel: 93 50 67 84). Rustic Italian-style restaurant with a good selection of reasonably priced pasta dishes.

Nice
Acchiardo (£) 38 rue Droite, 06300 (tel: 04 93 85 51 16). Popular and busy little restaurant with red oilcloth table coverings, serving a variety of excellent regional dishes at incredibly reasonable prices. Recommended.
Atmosphère (££) 36 cours Saleya, 06000 (tel: 04 93 80 52 50). Long-established seafood restaurant, with a delightful ambience and classic cooking at affordable prices. One of the few decent restaurants on the cours Saleya.
Chez Les Pêcheurs (££) 18 quai des Docks, 06300 (tel: 04 93 89 59 61). Famous for its wonderful *bouillabaisse* and *bourride*.
Nissa-Socca (£) 7 rue de Ste-Réparate, 06000 (tel: 04 93 80 18 35). In the old town, enormously popular for Niçois specialities such as *socca* (a savoury cake made from chickpea flour), *ravioli* and *beignet d'aubergines*.
La Toque Blanche (£££) 40 rue Buffa, 06000 (tel: 04 93 88 38 18). This small restaurant has a growing reputation for carefully prepared fish dishes. Due to its size, booking is advisable.

Vence
La Farigoule (££) 15 rue Henri-Isnard, 06140 (tel: 04 93 58 01 27). Genuine Provençal country cooking of a consistently high standard, with a shaded patio-garden at the back.

Villefranche-sur-Mer
La Mère Germaine (£££) quai Courbet, 06230 (tel: 04 93 01 71 39). One of the largest and most popular waterfront seafood restaurants, with *bouillabaisse* and a reasonably priced set menu based on the day's catch.
Le Nautic (££) 1 quai Courbet, 06230 (tel: 04 93 01 94 45). Good value for seafood, overlooking the port.

INDEX

PICTURE CREDITS/CONTRIBUTORS

Picture credits

The Automobile Association would like to thank the following photographers, libraries and associations for their assistance in the preparation of this book.

COURTAULD GALLERIES 107 Cézanne 'Still Life with apples, bottle and chairback', 112b Vincent Van Gogh 'Self Portrait with Bandaged Ear'
DIGITAL WISDOM PUBLISHING LTD top map on back cover
MARY EVANS PICTURE LIBRARY 28 Greek heptareme, 32 Troubadour, 36/7 Louis XIV, 37 Bishop of Marseille, 39a Execution of Robespierre, 40 Somerset Maugham
FOOTPRINTS COLOUR PICTURE LIBRARY 13b Cassis, 14/5, 15 Farmhouse, 116 Gardian's cabane, Camargue, 117a Trees, Camargue, 124 Walkers (N Hanna)
RONALD GRANT ARCHIVES 210/1 The Monte Carlo Story, 210b And Woman was Created, 235 French Connection II
PICASSO MUSEUM 'Nature Morte' (A Ramie)
PICTURES COLOUR LIBRARY LTD Front cover c, 17 Lavender, 18/9 Gypsy festival, 117 Horses
BARRIE SMITH 133 Bullfight
SPECTRUM COLOUR LIBRARY 19 Procession of Gardians, 20/1 St-Raphaël, 132 Bullfight, 170 St-Raphaël
TONY STONE Front cover a, b, spine
THE MANSELL COLLECTION 35 Pope Benedict XII, 38/9 Ships of war, 60/1 Mistral and his wife, 61 Mistral

The remaining photographs are held in the Automobile Association's own library (AA PHOTO LIBRARY). Adrian Baker took all the pictures except pages 112a (P Kenward), 157 (E Meacher), 23, 182, 184, 185, 186, 187, 195, 207a, 207b, 208, 209b, 234, 236, 239, 240/1, 242, 243a, 246, 258, 259, 264, 266 (R Moss), 49a, 93, 220 (T Oliver), 211, 232, 232/3 (N Ray), 12/13, 42/3, 133, 146/7, 160, 196/7, 213, 256 (B Smith), back flap, 4b, 5b, 6/7, 10/1, 10, 11, 13a, 16/7, 27, 28/9, 30/1, 30b, 33, 34/5, 40/1, 41, 44, 45, 46, 47, 49b, 73a, 74a, 78, 80/1, 81, 92a, 95, 96, 97, 98/9, 104a, 104b, 105, 106, 107, 114/5, 115, 119, 120/1, 121, 122, 123, 132b, 138, 140, 149, 151, 153, 156, 158b, 164, 168, 169, 172a, 172b, 175b, 183, 201, 202, 212a, 212b, 222, 223a, 225, 229b, 238, 243b, 247a, 248a, 248b, 250, 253, 261, 265, (R Strange).

Contributors

Original copy editor: Lynn Bresler
Revision verifier: Nick Hanna
Indexer: Marie Lorimer